BORDERLANDS

GOVERNANCE SERIES

Governance is the process of effective coordination whereby an organization or a system guides itself when resources, power, and information are widely distributed. Studying governance means probing the pattern of rights and obligations that underpins organizations and social systems; understanding how they coordinate their parallel activities and maintain their coherence; exploring the sources of dysfunction; and suggesting ways to redesign organizations whose governance is in need of repair.

The Series welcomes a range of contributions—from conceptual and theoretical reflections, ethnographic and case studies, and proceedings of conferences and symposia, to works of a very practical nature—that deal with problems or issues on the governance front. The Series publishes works both in French and in English.

The Governance Series is part of the publications division of the Program on Governance and Public Management at the School of Political Studies. Nine volumes have previously been published within this series. The Program on Governance and Public Management also publishes electronic journals: the quarterly www.optimumonline.ca and the biannual www.revuegouvernance.ca

BORDERLANDS

Comparing Border Security *in* North America *and* Europe

Edited by
EMMANUEL BRUNET-JAILLY

University of Ottawa Press

NATIONAL LIBRARY OF CANADA CATALOGUING IN PUBLICATION

Borderlands : comparing border security in North America and Europe / edited by Emmanuel Brunet-Jailly.

(Governance series, 1487-3052)
Includes bibliographical references and index.
ISBN 978-0-7766-0651-4

1. Boundaries. 2. Border security – North America. 3. Border security – Europe. 4. National security – North America. 5. National security – Europe. 6. Globalization. I. Brunet-Jailly, Emmanuel, 1961- II. Series: Governance series (Ottawa, Ont.)

JC323.B6666 2007 320.1′2 C2007-901923-4

Published by the University of Ottawa Press, 2007
542 King Edward Avenue
Ottawa, Ontario K2P 0Z3
www.uopress.uottawa.ca

The University of Ottawa Press acknowledges with gratitude the support extended to its publishing list by Heritage Canada through its Book Publishing Industry Development Program, by the Canada Council for the Arts, by the Social Sciences and Humanities Research Council, and by the University of Ottawa. We also gratefully acknowledge the Centre for Public Sector Studies at the University of Victoria whose financial support has contributed to the publication of this book.

CONTENTS

Preface...ix

Acknowledgements xi

Introduction: Borders, Borderlands, and Porosity
Emmanuel Brunet-Jailly with Bruno Dupeyron 1

Chapter 1. The Maritime Borders of Europe: Upstream Migratory Controls
Olivier Clochard and Bruno Dupeyron 19

Chapter 2. Whose Security? Dilemmas of US Border Security in the Arizona–Sonora Borderlands
Julie A. Murphy Erfani...41

Chapter 3. Border Acrobatics between the European Union and Africa: The Management of Sealed-off Permeability on the Borders of Ceuta and Melilla
Xavier Ferrer Gallardo 75

Chapter 4. Fayuca Hormiga: The Cross-border Trade of Used Clothing between the United States and Mexico
Mélissa Gauthier 95

Chapter 5. A New Northern Security Agenda
Lassi Heininen and Heather N. Nicol...117

Chapter 6. From Iron Curtain to Paper Wall: The Influence of Border Regimes on Local and Regional Economies—The Life, Death, and Resurrection of Bazaars in the Łódź Region
Martin van der Velde and Szymon Marcińczak...................................165

Chapter 7. The Economic Cost of Border Security: The Case of the Texas-Mexico Border and the US VISIT Program
J. Michael Patrick 197

Chapter 8. The Costs of Homeland Security
Tony Payan and Amanda Vásquez 231

Chapter 9. Managing US–Mexico Transborder Cooperation on Local Security Issues and the Canadian Relationship
José M. Ramos 259

Chapter 10. Anti-terrorism in North America: Is There Convergence or Divergence in Canadian and US Legislative Responses to 9/11 and the US–Canada Border?
Patrick J. Smith 277

Chapter 11. The Southern Border of Mexico in the Age of Globalization
Daniel Villafuerte Solís 311

Chapter 12. Conclusion: Borders, Borderlands, and Security: European and North American Lessons and Public Policy Suggestions
Emmanuel Brunet-Jailly 351

List of Contributors 359

Index 361

PREFACE

The Westphalian state system developed from the establishment of sovereign powers within the confines of borderlines recognized by international agreements. During the construction of the modern state, the nationalist period resulted in the development of center–periphery economies and polities. Today, however, globalization appears to make borders irrelevant in many ways—as exemplified by our increasing awareness that trade, migration, environmental, and health issues cross over the borders of many states—and to include large regions of the world, while, on the contrary, security and terrorism seem to reassert the importance of the borders of each states. Monitoring borders raises important questions of governance for scholars and policy-makers, which call for profound institutional changes and a reconceptualization of our basic understanding of the symbolic and functional role of borders, borderlands, and boundaries in the international order.

The twelve chapters of this edited volume focus on eleven case studies of border security policies and borderland environments in seven different states in North America and the European Union. A key point is the difficulty and complexity of filtering and monitoring increasingly porous borders. The authors and editor of this book conclude that, in light of the complicated and often countervailing economic, social, cultural, and institutional forces that shape borders, governments have to broaden their traditional focus on the boundary line to include the governance of borderlands as the territory central to security policy. What arises as the new challenge to government policy in security matters is their aptitude to cooperate, collaborate, and co-produce policy, sharing goals and policy objectives.

Gordon Smith and Rodney Dobell
Centre for Global Studies
University of Victoria

ACKNOWLEDGEMENTS

This project was undertaken between the meeting of the Border Region in Transition network (BRIT), held in Jerusalem, Israel, in January 2005, and the annual meeting of the Association of Borderland Studies (ABS) in Albuquerque, New Mexico, in April 2005. Having participated at a number of conference panels on border theory and border security, I became aware of the rapidly growing number of scholars working on the various underpinnings of border security theory and policy. I contacted members of both BRIT and the ABS to put together a group of scholars dedicated to the idea that research work focusing on border security policies and border theory would lead to important policy recommendations.

This book would not have been possible without the support of the BRIT network and the ABS, which, through their respective executive secretariats, helped circulate the call for proposals and recommended scholars.

The financial contributions of the consulate general of France in Vancouver, British Columbia, the European Commission, the European Studies Program, and the Centre for Public Sector Studies of the University of Victoria, as well as the particularly generous support of the Social Science and Humanities Research Council of Canada, made it possible to organize a workshop at the Local Government Institute, School of Public Administration, University of Victoria, in December 2005. At the time twenty-six scholars from seven different countries in North America and Europe met for two days to present and compare their work on border and borderland security. These papers are now presented in the twelve chapters of this volume.

This work suggests that the nature of borders is to be porous, which is a serious issue for those who make security policy. It argues that dense economic, cultural, or political human activities crossing over a border and straddling a borderland result in increasing porosity, which governments on both sides of the border can better control when they increase cooperation, collaboration, and the co-production of security policy goals.

I am grateful to academic colleagues for advice and comments on earlier drafts of some of these chapters, particularly Stuart Farson, David Good, Helga Hallgrimsdottir, Antoine Pecoud, Gordon Smith, and Amy Verdun. Special thanks go to Rodney Dobell for reading and providing extensive comments on earlier versions of the introduction and the conclusion. The theoretical discussion presented in both the introduction and the conclusion were summarized at the Linea Terranum conference, held at the University of Texas, El Paso, in March 2006, and at the BRIT conference in Lublin, Poland, in September 2006. These resulted in rich comments and questions that also helped me clarify my thoughts on this model of border security study.

Emmanuel Brunet-Jailly
Local Government Institute
School of Public Administration
University of Victoria

INTRODUCTION

BORDERS, BORDERLANDS, AND POROSITY

Emmanuel Brunet-Jailly with Bruno Dupeyron

Border security has been high on public-policy agendas in Europe and North America since the September 11, 2001, attacks on the World Trade Center in New York City and on the headquarters of the US military in Washington, DC. Governments are now confronted with managing secure borders, a policy objective that, in this era of increased free trade and globalization, must compete with intense cross-border flows of people and goods. Border-security policies must enable security personnel to identify and filter out dangerous individuals and substances from among the millions of travellers and tons of goods that cross borders daily, particularly in large cross-border urban regions. For scholars the events of 9/11 triggered a greater interest in border studies. Currently, scholarship on borders, borderlands, and security is scarce, and the complexities and influence of borderlands on border-security policies are misunderstood.

This book is a first attempt to address this gap between security needs and an understanding of borders and borderlands. Specifically, the chapters in this volume ask policy-makers to recognize that two fundamental elements define borders and borderlands: first, *human activities* (the agency and agent power of individual ties and forces spanning a border); and second, the *broader social processes* that frame individual action, such as market forces, government activities (law, regulations, and policies), and the regional culture and politics of a borderland.

In other words, borders emerge as the historically and geographically variable expressions of human ties (agent power or agency), exercised within social structures of varying force and influence. It is the interplay and interdependence between individuals' incentives to act and the surrounding structures (constructed social processes that contain and constrain individual action, such as market forces, government activities, the culture and politics of a place) that determine the effectiveness of formal border policy, and particularly of security policies. In short, in the face of increasing border security priorities, policy-makers have to recognize that the porosity of borders depends on the relative degree and form taken by human interaction across borders (Brunet-Jailly 2005).

This book argues that the nature of borders is to be porous, which is a problem for the makers of security policy. It shows that when, for economic, cultural, or political reasons, human activities increase across a border and borderland, then governments need to increase their cooperation, collaboration, and co-production of security policies, if only to avoid implementing mismatched security policies.

Acceptance of the concept of borders has contributed to the emergence of the modern political order, in which states recognize each other's sovereign boundaries and their legitimate power over a demarcated territory. Since the First World War, however, the international recognition of boundaries has not always been enough. In effect, the legacy of Woodrow Wilson—that national self-determination is an essential principle of political legitimacy—modified the founding principles of numerous states and concurrently suggested that boundaries, borders, and borderlands may be more fluid than was generally assumed.

The scholarship on borders and borderlands is enlightening in this matter because, during the last part of the twentieth century, scholars argued that borders were human creations. Originally, scholars focused on the nature and purpose of borders, while presenting a great diversity of views. Semple (as cited in Minghi 1963), for instance, suggested that ideal borders were natural geographic frontiers known for their scarcity of human settlements. Similarly, Holdich (1916) and Lyde (1915) suggested that there were good or bad borders. Holdich suggested that good borders were those that balanced economic tensions or lessened political difficulties between states. Spykman (1942) argued that it was not borders but borderlands that were central to geographic balances of power, while both Peattie (1944) and Jones (1959) suggested that borderlands or international organizations could reduce tensions.

This literature emphasized the role of borders as buffer zones: borders were borderlands at the convergence of complex human interactions of an economic, political, and cultural nature. Borders and borderlands included temporal and geographic elements, a "desert" being probably the best answer to tensions between human communities. This explains why, during the first part of the twentieth century, armies rehearsed for combat in borderland regions. However, the influence of this literature progressively vanished during the second half of the twentieth century, when changes in boundary functions, such as military or policing, were also recognized as important reasons for possible tensions across borderlands (Jones 1959). Clearly, the activities of states were viewed as having an impact on the nature of borders and borderlands.

What remained, however, from those early analyses of borders and borderlands was the concept that borders were central to the national agenda of states, that they were established by international agreements, and that they were challenged by individual activities (human agency and agent power). In the end their nature was the centre of attention, and from this emerged the belief that borders as institutions were results of complex interactions between multiple government policies, which were often back to back, not integrated, and, in most cases, had mismatched goals and priorities. Clearly, mismatched policies occur when two central governments struggle to see their policy goals and decisions, first, implemented within intergovernmental networks by lower government levels (province or state, county and local governments), and, second, accepted by their contiguous neighbours.

More recent scholarly analyses of borders and borderlands point to four strands of research. Some scholars see borders as institutional constructs; others see them as challenged by national communities, with or without political clout, or by market forces. The multiple activities of governments, the role of borderland cultures, the political clout of borderland communities, and the impact of market forces are thus the four strands that are now prominent in the social science literature that organizes debates among scholars on the nature of borders and borderlands (Brunet-Jailly 2005; Chen 2005).

Whether those strands of research address structural (broad social construct) or agency (individual action) questions is not always clear, however. Each strand of research may suggest an analytical dimension of borders and borderlands that should be understood not as exclusively structural (broad) or exclusively agent-oriented (focusing on individual action, agency), but rather as providing a historically *variable expression of agent power*. Concurrently, each research strand suggests that either culture, local political clout, market forces, or the multiple activities of governments may be *variably structuring*, where structure is understood as those social processes that contain individual action across borderland regions. In other words, there is a "tug of war" between culture, local political clout, market forces, and the multiple activities of governments, as they may be variably structuring a borderland. The following section details the literatures of those four strands of research.

That states have a great responsibility for the structural nature of borders and borderlands is clear. Some argue that borders result exclusively from the multiple activities of governments, where the domestic setting of two countries is central. Hataley (2006), for instance, argues that for the United States the border institution is about security, inclusion, and exclusion, and that security frames all border issues, whereas for Canada border issues primarily belong to the economic-policy arena; thus, for the two countries the structuring policies vary widely, despite certain parallelisms. The contemporary analysis of complex government activities includes references to policy networks, policy communities, and multi-level governance spanning borderlands (Brunet-Jailly 2004a; Hataley 2006). Marks (1993) and Marks and Hooghe (2001) originally argued that multi-level governance was not only both vertical and horizontal but also of two types: (1) general-purpose and (2) task-specific. Their analysis of the traditional intergovernmental relations of the European Union (EU) is the best illustration of vertical governance as a process in which multiple levels of government interact to co-produce and co-implement policies. This view is relevant when scholars study, for instance, the EU's legal system or its border-security policies (Andreas and Snyder 2000; Brunet-Jailly 2004b; Eriksen 2001; Kohler-Koch 1998; Marks and Hooghe 2001; Mayntz 1998; Ziller 2003). Such governance processes lead diverse actors to either co-produce and co-implement policy regulations or co-deliver specific services; a good example would be security policy in Europe or North America (Brunet-Jailly 2004b, 2006). Such policies result from complex, intermeshed networks of government policies and functions that interact to form international boundaries delineating sovereign spaces, as well as networks of security agencies straddling the boundary to co-produce border security. However, as shown by Villafuerte Solis in this volume, not all borders and borderlands experience the implementation of such security mechanisms. Thus, the multiple activities of governments should not be assumed to be systematically structuring and should be analyzed in context—in time and space—and in relation to borderland culture, market forces, and local politics.

For instance, the complex and multiple roles and activities of governments do not account for the increasingly relevant role of market forces and flows of goods across international borders and borderlands. This second strand of research makes the case that market forces have been credited for the emergence of a borderless world and the rise of economic regions, but this is not without controversy. Although the specific exigencies of flows of individuals, goods, or currencies are not yet fully understood, they clearly have significant implications for borders and borderlands. Some economists argue that boundaries have a cost, while others argue, convincingly, that they are withering away due to increased amounts of global trade.

For specialists of location or transportation, such as August Loesch (1954) or Engel and Rogers (1996), borders have a cost because they are barriers to trade and free trade (the free flow of goods, labour, or skills). Loesch equated borders with distances, that is, the marginal transportation cost necessary to cross the border, as do Engel and Rogers. John Helliwell (1998, 2002) underlines that borders matter because they run deep in the social and cultural underpinnings of social interactions. In other words, because Canadians are culturally Canadians they primarily interact with Canadians. Contrary to those views is the argument that globalization—not only the increase in global trade and transaction of goods and labour or capital but also economic integration in Europe and North America—challenges states. Ohmae (1996, 11–12) and Chen (2005) have found that trade is the main driver behind the emergence of economic regions, some of which are cross-border regions. Ohmae explains that an economic region emerges out of a culturally homogeneous borderland region, where both culture and trade are structuring the borderland.

These arguments suggest that flows of goods, capital, and migrants not only limit the influence of central governments but also modify local cultures and political identities. Clearly, what is central to this debate is the acknowledgement that global market forces and economic integration are reshaping the relationship between markets and politics in borderland regions. This, in turn, is important for border-security matters because the assumption that free trade and globalization are systematically structuring borders and borderlands is true only relative to other structuring forces, such as government policy objectives. This book's chapters on the borders between Guatemala and Mexico, the United States and Mexico, and Poland, Ukraine, and Belarus suggest that market forces may be as structuring as security policies.

The third strand of research on borders and borderlands concerns the cultures of borderlands and emphasizes the important role that communities play in bridging or dividing borders. This literature suggests that certain communities actually enhance the border effect because they have no interaction with one another. Clearly, when culture differentiates, it enhances the border effect. In contrast, when culture bridges a borderland region, it challenges the border as a filtering or dividing device and weakens the border effect. Culture and cultural communities are therefore able to challenge or even undermine an international border when their cultures cross over, that is, when their language, ethnicity, or socioeconomic status and their place of belonging bridge the border (Reitel et al. 2002). Indeed, the literature on nations has shown that national borderland communities present an important challenge to borders in both Europe and North America. Other works are strong reminders that multinational communities are historically recent and that multiculturalism is a relatively new phenomenon (Taylor 1983).

That culture is important to our understanding of borders and borderlands is not contentious. There is a vast literature by historians, geographers, anthropologists, and economists that points to borderland communities as cultural communities and organized polities (Brown 2001; DePalma 2001; Dobell and Neufield 1994; Meinhof 2004; Pavlakovich-Kochi, Morehouse, and Wastl-Walter 2004). However, the relative influence of their claims and the relative sense of belonging to a larger state are still debatable (Newman and Paasi 1998; Paasi 1999). Although international borders divide stateless nations, borderland communities may remain unified by culture (ethnicity, language, and/or religion) or by the nature of local political institutions. For example, three international borders divide the Kurds, two divide the Flemish, and one each divides the Basques, the Catalans, and the Irish, yet scholars generally agree that these borderland communities also bridge their borders (Hansen 1984; Keating 1996, 2001; Keating and McGarry 2001; Mitrani 1975; O'Dowd and Corrigan 1995; Tannam 1999).

The current debate illustrates that the unifying and symbolic, yet dividing and exclusionary role of borders as a founding principle of sovereign states is under pressure (Balme 1998; Fry 1998; Risse-Kappen 1995; Smith, Chatfield, and Pagnucco 1997). A large scholarship describes how local actors and local communities are crossing borders and weakening the sovereign integrity of states, due either to economic need or to an ethnic, social, or religious sense of belonging. There is also a wealth of scholarly characterizations of how non-central-state actors, plurinational communities, and stateless nations perforate borders or undermine the integrity of state borders because of ethnic, religious, social, or economic identities (Castells 1998, 2000; Duchacek, Stevenson, and Latouche 1998; Keating 2001; O'Dowd and Corrigan 1995; Ohmae 1990, 1996; Papademetriou and Waller-Meyers 2001). It may be that culture is structuring borders and borderlands more effectively than market forces or the multiple activities of governments. In this volume, Tony Payan and Amanda Vasquez, as well as Melissa Gauthier, suggest that both market forces and shared culture are defeating the border-security policies of the United States and Mexico.

Thus, local culture is another important strand for our understanding of borders and borderlands. The cultural influence of borderland communities, however, seems to depend on a central characteristic, namely, their political clout, which is understood as local political activism and organizational capacity. Underpinning this political clout is the existence of either tensions or strong linkages straddling the border. The literature documents two broad categories of case studies of cross-border communities that demonstrate either cooperation or tension. Some of these thrive while developing linkages and others either ignore each other or deal with ongoing tensions. There are few examples of borderland communities that have developed institutions spanning an international border (Brunet-Jailly 2004a), but there are many instances of contiguous borderland communities that have established linkages.

Border cities serve as good examples of cities that experience tension with the central state (Ehlers 2001; Ehlers, Buursink, and Boekema 2001). In such cases the literature documents local tensions with the central-state level (Hansen 1984; Lunden and Zalamans 2001); local divergence of views across the border, despite the influence of higher-level governments (Mattiesen and Burkner 2001); local multicultural tensions and wide binational differences, despite shared infrastructures

(Bucken-Knapp 2001); and local tensions or an absence of sociopolitical relations, despite strong economic linkages (Brunet-Jailly 2004a; Sparrow 2001).

In some cases, however, linkages have developed across an international border. Susan Clarkes (2000) has demonstrated the existence of policy networks and large interest-focused communities (such as scientific and policy-focused communities in the environmental policy arena) across the Canada–US border linking Vancouver, British Columbia, and Seattle, Washington. Brunet-Jailly (2004a) and Perkman (2005) have described institutions spanning the border in Enshede and Gronau (a large and well-institutionalized borderland community with its own parliament and bureaucracy, serving about 149 municipalities and districts) in the EU. In this case, local political clout may be structuring the borderland more effectively than market forces or the multiple activities of governments. In this volume, the ethnographic work of Julie Murphy Erfani on the Arizona–Sonora border and the Guatemalan case discussed by Daniel Villafuerte Solis corroborate the structuring influence of local political clout in border-security matters.

In the end, the variably structuring nature of borderlands as analyzed in all four strands of border scholarship underlines the contemporary analytical complexity of borders and borderlands. Indeed, borders and borderlands are at the junctures of human cultural, political, and economic activities, and emulate the tremendous security challenges currently facing central governments and agencies. Thus it should come as no surprise that most of the research on border security concludes that border-security policies are mostly unsuccessful (Andreas 2000; Andreas and Biersteker 2003; Andreas and Snyder 2000). Peter Andreas (2003) argues that we may be witnessing a policy paradigm shift from military to economic to border policing, each linked to a specific historical path, first of demilitarization, then economic liberalization, and now criminalization of border policies. Furthermore, in the current era of increased security the "borderless world" argument—the underpinning issue of globalization and economic integration—does not seem to be called into question (Ohmae 1990, 1996; Survey of Migration 2002). Clearly, the study of borders and borderlands requires more than the partial explanations currently available to explain the relative porosity of borders.

This book is a partial contribution to this incomplete account in the literature. It assumes that the human agency aspect of borderlands sets up a critically important environment for border-security policies.

First, its aim is to illustrate the border porosity that results when governments overlook such critical factors as market forces, local culture, and the political clout of borderland communities. It also aims to illustrate that, in most instances, central-government agencies and their intergovernmental partners are poorly informed about a critical factor, namely, the policies and policy goals of the multitude of governments that actively enforce border security, hence contributing to a porous mismatch of security policies.

Today two large international scholarly networks focus on border studies in Europe and North America: Border Region in Transition (BRIT), a primarily European network of researchers; and the Association of Borderland Studies (ABS), which originated in the United States with scholars interested in the southwestern region of North America but has since grown to include a large number of scholars in other countries. This book brings together the work of several border scholars, in both Europe and North America, who are currently researching the impact of border-security policies on borders and borderlands.

The chapters in this book are based on research presented at a workshop organized by the Centre for Public Sector Studies at the University of Victoria in December 2005. At the workshop, about twenty scholars discussed the current implications of the new security measures on borders and borderlands. Specifically, the gathering allowed for a systematic discussion and comparison of border-security policies on the EU's external borders and on the three borders of Canada, the United States, and Mexico, the member states of the North American Free Trade Agreement (NAFTA).

The general conceptual underpinning of their work, as summarized above, is the border model derived from Brunet-Jailly (2005), which suggests that local border culture and political clout, market forces, and the multitude of government activities play concurrent and essential roles in the agency and structure of borders and borderlands (see Figure 1).

Using this model as a reference, the authors have assumed that as national border-security policies attempt to enable security personnel to recognize dangerous individuals and substances, they must compete not only with the increasingly large market-driven flows of goods and people crossing borders and borderlands but also with the local culture and political clout of borderlands, and the border-security policies implemented by other government levels and agencies. In other words,

Figure 1: Theory of Borderland Studies

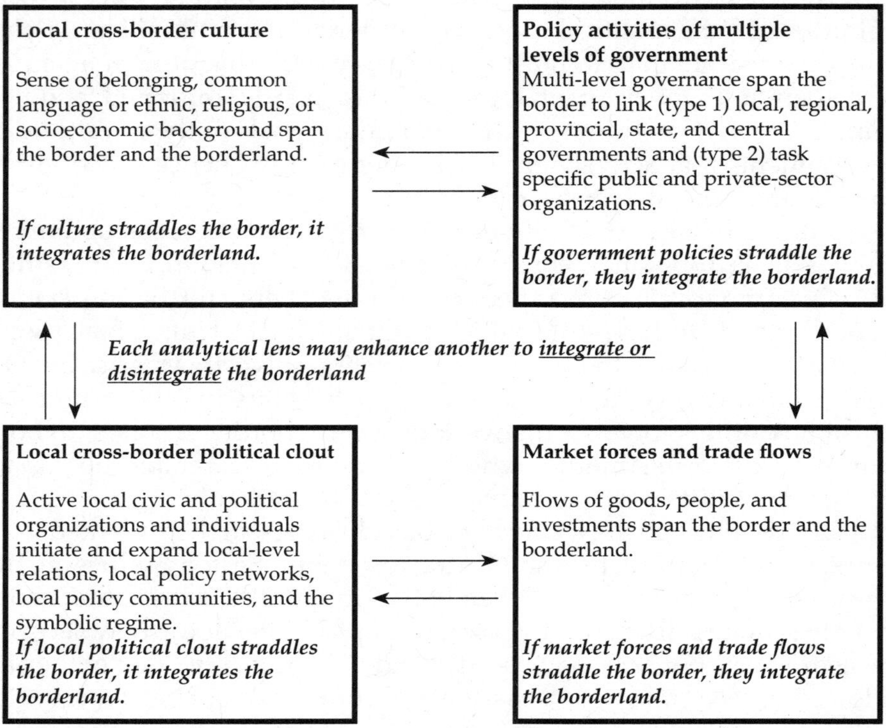

from a conceptual perspective, there is an agency-structure dilemma in the analysis of borders and borderlands, and the success of security depends primarily on the appropriate assessment of human agency across borders and borderland regions.

The authors of this volume shared two overall goals: to document the impact of new security measures on the borderland regions of EU and NAFTA member states and to generate knowledge regarding the specific and common traits of the Canada–US border, the US–Mexico border, and the Mexico–Guatemala border, as well as the external border of the EU, with a focus on its northern border (the Arctic), its eastern border (Poland), and its southern border (the Mediterranean). A comparative analysis of the impact of security policies on the borders and borderlands of these two continental regimes is presented in the book's conclusion.

Olivier Clochard and Bruno Dupeyron, in "The Maritime Borders of Europe: Upstream Migratory Controls," document the policy instruments used by EU member states to reduce and control immigration flows. Consular agents administer a discerning visa policy, which multiplies requirements abroad in an attempt to filter "bad" immigrants from "good" immigrants. The European Commission calls upon the transportation sector to meet high-compliance requirements. Similarly, peripheral states cooperate in order to limit immigration flows, signing twinning agreements that include hosting of "transit processing centres" outside the EU. Clochard and Dupeyron argue that these policies exemplify the increasing exportation of EU border policing to adjacent countries and suggests that, in the face of massive immigration flow, the structural success of border-security policies requires the collaboration of neighbouring governments.

In "Whose Security? Dilemmas of US Border Security in the Arizona–Sonora Borderlands," Julie Murphy Erfani presents political ethnographic research that demonstrates the pernicious effects of competition between private and public security actors concerned with controlling cross-border flows of legal and illegal people and goods in the Arizona–Sonora borderlands. The author has discovered that, while increased central-government controls galvanize social networks, anti-migrant activists have effectively blocked the emergence of an integrated cross-border security policy. Murphy Erfani concludes that local culture and local political clout have significantly reduced the effectiveness of a border-security policy, and that there are strong and integrating local market forces.

Xavier Ferrer suggests in "Border Acrobatics between the European Union and Africa: The Management of Sealed-off Permeability on the Borders of Ceuta and Melilla" that the implementation of EU border-security policies leads to an "acrobatic" policy exercise in which border security focuses primarily on illegal aliens rather than on the large flow of goods that are indispensable to the survival of the economies of both cities. The author suggests that the relative structuring effect of this border-security policy is key to understanding the negotiated fortification of each of these border towns.

Melissa Gauthier, in "*Fayuca Hormiga*: The Cross-border Trade of Used Clothing between the United States and Mexico," describes the illegal flow of used clothing and argues that its effective border crossing confirms the integrative force of human ties. Gauthier details the tug of war between such illicit networks, which are culturally and socioeconomically part of the borderland economy, and increased border-security policies. This competition underlines the structuring precedence of the borderland culture, which increased security does not sway. Because those market flows are rooted in the local borderland culture and local political clout of El Paso, Texas, and Ciudad Juarez, Chihuahua, their permanence remains the most convincing evidence that the border-security policies are unsuccessful.

Lassi Heininen and Heather Nicol, in "A New Northern Security Agenda," document important changes in security agendas concerned with the Arctic region. The authors have found that Arctic security agencies, which have traditionally focused on issues of military geopolitical security, now also deal with human and environmental security. They argue that these changes are conducive to new policy goals, which reflect the cooperative nature of the peoples of the Arctic region and which include greater circumpolar cooperation with indigenous peoples, and with local governments and organizations. Heininen and Nicol conclude that, in debates regarding Arctic borderlands, borderland cultures and political clout are increasingly structuring.

In "From Iron Curtain to Paper Wall: The Influence of Border Regimes on Local and Regional Economies," Martin van der Velde and Szymon Marcińczak address the imposition of the EU's security policy, that is, the implementation of the Schengen Agreement, on the eastern Polish border, its longest territorial border. They focused on the effects of this agreement on the regional economy of Łódź, Poland, and discovered that different local and regional responses to structural trends emerged as they followed the various actors' interests and resources. Overall, despite increased security, economic agents have successfully adapted to those structural trends by reorganizing trade flows, and the economic vitality of the Łódź market has remained undisturbed.

The chapter by J. Michael Patrick is entitled "The Potential Economic Cost of Border Security: The Case of the Texas–Mexico Border and the US VISIT Program." Patrick argues that the US VISIT program may have a serious economic impact on the Texas–Mexico borderland region, in terms of reductions in economic activity, job creation, and cross-border shopping. He also argues that only increased consultation with borderland communities can increase security. In other words, although the structuring effect of US government policy is relative to the influence of border agency, border security also depends upon the active participation of a multitude of levels of government, which requires the participation of local communities.

Tony Payan and Amanda Vasquez, in "The Costs of Homeland Security," assess the total cost and cost-effectiveness of the new border-security environment that has been imposed on the Mexico–US border region. They draw a parallel between the cost efficiency of the security policy and the scholarly debate regarding agency and structure in order to argue that imposing border security is both highly ineffective and extremely costly, and that, in the end, illegal agents, including those that traffic in illegal migrants or drugs, adapt to new government policies. The chapter also suggest that the borderland "Chicano" culture and political clout, as well as market forces, are structuring the borderland, which remains unchallenged by centrally designed US security policies.

In "Managing US–Mexico Transborder Cooperation on Local Security Issues and the Canadian Relationship," José Ramos suggests that deeply rooted institutional dependency leads to a conflict between US and Mexican border and border-security policies, which are profoundly mismatched. Indeed, border-security policies come into direct conflict on the US–Mexico border because they oppose the US security priority with the Mexican migratory priority. Ramos suggests that the Canada–US border experiment is an example of better collaboration. He also suggests that a tug-of-war is taking place between (winning) market forces and (unsuccessful) policy activities of multiple levels of government on the US–Mexico border.

In contrast to Ramos, Patrick Smith, in "Anti-terrorism in North America: Policy Convergence or Divergence in Canadian and US Legislative Responses to 9/11 and the US–Canada Border?" notes the increasing legislative and policy convergence occurring between Canada and the United States in the areas of security, particularly border security. He emphasizes that, despite a growing opposition among some Canadians, the Canadian government has enacted legislation, such as the Smart Border Agreement, in accordance with US expectations. Smith proposes that such negotiated convergence may be perceived as the emergence of new forms of continental governance. Thus the Canada–US model of border security cooperation may not only strengthen the structuring effect of government policy in the borderland but also be more secure because it results from increasing convergence and a common security goal.

An original perspective on the Mexico–Guatemala border is provided by Daniel Villafuerte Solis in "The Southern Border of Mexico in the Age of Globalization." This "third" border of the United States faces important challenges due to the increased market and migration flows as a result of NAFTA. Since the signature of NAFTA the southern Mexican borderland has been progressively transformed into a buffer zone that no government can control effectively. In the southern regions the Mexican military deals with political uprisings in the province of Chiapas, as well as unmanageable flows of migrants now linked to networks of criminal organizations that feed off poverty and social exclusion. Villafuerte Solis argues that policy-makers should implement economic development policies in these borderland regions that will reduce the labour flows linking the southern and northern Americas. The current situation suggests that market forces and local culture and local political clout are structural and clearly undermine the policy activities of government.

Finally, in "Borders, Borderlands, and Security: European and North American Lessons, and Public Policy Suggestions," Emmanuel Brunet-Jailly compares and contrasts the research findings presented in these chapters, and suggests a model for the implementation of border-security policies. This concluding chapter argues that to control porosity in densely populated borderlands, where culture, local political clout, and market forces cross over, central governments and their intergovernmental agencies have to work harder at creating networks of cooperation and policy goals common to the borderland.

LITERATURE CITED

Andreas, Peter. 2000. *Border Games: Policing the U.S.-Mexico Divide*. Ithaca, NY: Cornell University Press.

———. 2003. "Redrawing the Line: Borders and Security in the Twenty-first Century." *International Security* 28:2, 78–111.

———, and Thomas Biersteker. 2003. *The Rebordering of North America*. New York: Routledge.

———, and Timothy Snyder. 2000. *The Wall Around the West*. Boulder, CO: Rowman & Littlefield.

Balme, Richard. 1998. *Les Politiques du Neo-Regionalism*. Paris, France: Economica.

Brown, Chris. 2001. "Border and Identity in International Political Theory," *Identities, Borders, Orders: Rethinking International Relations Theory,* eds.

Michael Albert, David Jacobson, and Yosef Lapid. Minneapolis: University of Minnesota Press, 117–137.

Brunet-Jailly, E. 2004a. "Comparing Local Cross-border Relations under EU and NAFTA." *Canadian American Public Policy* 58, 1–59.

———. 2004b. "NAFTA, Economic Integration and the Canadian-American Security Regime in the Post-September 11, 2001, Era: Multi-level Governance and Transparent Border?" *Journal of Borderland Studies* 19:1, 71–93.

———. 2005. "Theorizing Borders: An Interdisciplinary Perspective." *Geopolitics* 10:4, 463–69.

———. 2006. "Security and Border Security Policies: Perimeter and Smart Border." *Journal of Borderland Studies* 21:2, 3–22.

Bucken-Knapp, Gregg. 2001. "Just a Train-ride Away, But Still a World Apart: Prospects for the Oresund Region as a Binational City." *GeoJournal* 54, 51–60.

Castells, Manuel. 1998. *End of Millennium*. Oxford, UK: Blackwell.

———. 2000. *The Rise of the Network Society*. Oxford, UK: Blackwell.

Chen, Xiangming. 2005. *As Borders Bend: Transnational Spaces on the Pacific Rim*. New York: Rowman & Littlefield.

Churchill Semple, Ellen. 1911. *Influences of Geographic Environment*. New York: Holt.

Clarke, Susan 2000. "Regional and Transnational Discourse: The Politics of Ideas and Economic Development in Cascadia." *International Journal of Economic Development* 2:3, 360–78.

DePalma, Anthony 2001. *Here: A Biography of the New American Continent*. Reading, MA: Perseus.

Dobell, Rod, and Michael Neufield, eds. 1994. *Trans-border Citizens*. Vancouver, BC: Oolichan Books.

Duchacek, Ivo, Garth Stevenson, and Daniel Latouche, eds. 1988. *Perforated Sovereignties and International Relations: Trans-Sovereign Contact of Subnational Governments*. New York: Greenwood Press.

Ehlers, Nicole. 2001. "The Utopia of the Binational City." *GeoJournal* 54, 21–32.

———, Jan Buursink, and Frans Boekema. 2001. "Introduction: Binational Cities and Their Regions: From Diverging Cases to a Common Research Agenda." *GeoJournal* 54, 1–5.

Engel, Charles, and John Rogers. 1996. "How Wide is the Border?" *American Economic Review* 86:5, 1112–25.

Eriksen, E. O. 2001. *Governance and Democracy? The White Paper on European Governance*. Oslo: Arena.

Fry, Earl. 1998. *The Expanding Role of State and Local Governments in US Foreign Affairs*. New York: Council on Foreign Relations.

Hansen, Neil. 1984. "Regional Transboundary Cooperation Efforts in Centralist States: Conflicts and Responses in France and Mexico." *Publius* 14, 137–52.

Hataley, Todd. 2006. "Exporting American Border Control: An Institutional Analysis of the Canada–United States Border." Ph.D. dissertation, Queen's University, Kingston, Ontario.

Helliwell, John. 1998. *How Much Do National Borders Matter?* Washington, DC: Brookings Institution.

———. 2002. *Globalization and Well Being*. Vancouver: University of British Columbia Press.

Holdich, Thomas H. 1916. *Political Frontiers and Boundary Making*. London, UK: Macmillan.

Jones, Stephen B. 1959. "Boundary Concepts in the Setting of Place and Time." *Annals of the Association of American Geographers* 49, 241–55.

Keating, Michael. 1996. *Nations Against the State*. London, UK: St. Martin's Press.

———. 2001. *Plurinational Democracy: Stateless Nations in a Post-Sovereignty Era*. Oxford, UK: Oxford University Press.

Keating, Michael, and John McGarry, eds. 2001. *Minority Nationalism in the Changing State Order*. Oxford, UK: Oxford University Press.

Kohler-Koch, B. 1999. "The Evolution and Transformation of European Governance." *The Transformation of Governance in the European Union*. London and New York: Routledge, 14–35.

Loesch, August. 1954. *The Economics of Location*. New Haven, CT: Yale University Press.

Lunden, Thomas, and Dennis Zalamans. 2001. "Local Cooperation, Ethnic Diversity and State Territoriality: The Case of Haparanda and Tornio on the Sweden-Finland Border." *GeoJournal* 54, 33–42.

Lyde, Lionel William. 1915. *Some Frontiers of Tomorrow: An Aspiration for Europe*. London, UK: A. & C. Black.

Marks, Gary. 1993. "Structural Policy and Multilevel Governance." *The State of the European Community*, eds. Alan Cafruny and Glenda Rosenthal. Harlow, UK: Longman, 126–45.

Marks, Gary, and Liesbet Hooghe. 2001. *Multi-Level Governance and European Integration*. Boulder, CO: Rowman & Littlefield.

Matthiesen, Ulf, and Hans-Joachim Burkner. 2001. "Antagonistic Structures in Border Areas: Local Milieux and Local Politics in the Polish-German Twin City Gubin/Guben." *GeoJournal* 54, 43–50.

Mayntz, R. 1998. "New Challenges to Governance Theory." *Jean Monnet Chair Papers* (EUI/RSCAS), 50.

Meinhof, Ulrike, ed. 2004. *Living (with) Border: Identity Discourses on East-West Borders in Europe*. Aldershot, UK: Ashgate.

Minghi, Julian. 1963. "Review Article: Boundary Studies in Political Geography." *Annals of the Association of American Geographers* 53:3, 407–28.

Mitrani, David. 1975. *The Functional Theory of Politics*. London, UK: Martin Robertson.

Newman, David, and Anssi Paasi. 1998. "Fences and Neighbours in the Post-modern World: Boundary Narratives in Political Geography." *Progress in Human Geography* 22:2, 186–207.
O'Dowd, Liam, and James Corrigan. 1995. "Buffer Zone or Bridge: Local Responses to Cross-border Economic Cooperation in the Irish Border Region." *Administration 42*, 335–51.
Ohmae, Kenichi. 1990. *The Borderless World*. New York: HarperCollins.
———. 1996. *The End of the Nation State*. New York: Free Press.
Paasi, Anssi. 1999. "Boundaries as Social Practice and Discourse: The Finnish-Russian Border." *Regional Studies* 33:7, 669–80.
Papademetriou, Demetrios G., and Deborah Waller-Meyers, eds. 2001. *Caught in the Middle: Border Communities in an Era of Globalization*. Washington, DC: Carnegie Endowment for International Peace, Migration Policy Institute Publications.
Pavlakovich-Kochi, Vera, Barbara Morehouse, and Doris Wastl-Walter. 2004. *Challenged Borderlands: Transcending Political and Cultural Boundaries*. Aldershot, UK: Ashgate.
Peattie, Roderick. 1944. *Look to the Frontiers: A Geography of the Peace Table*. New York: Harper.
Perkmann, Markus. 2005 "The Construction of New Scales: A Framework and Case Study of the EUREGIO Cross-border Region." University of Loughborough [UK], Faculty of Engineering, Woflson School of Mechanical and Manufacturing Engineering Working Paper [online]. hdl.handle.net/2134/714.
Reitel, André, et al. 2002. *Villes et Frontieres*. Paris: Economica.
Risse-Kappen, Thomas. 1995. *Bringing Transnational Relations Back In: Non-State Actors, Domestic Structures, and International Relations*. Cambridge, UK: Cambridge Studies in International Relations.
Smith, Jackie, Charles Chatfield, and Ron Pagnucco, eds. 1997. *Transnational Social Movements and Global Politics: Solidarity Beyond the State*. Syracuse, NY: Syracuse Studies in Peace Conflict and University of Syracuse Press.
Sparrow, Glen. 2001. "San Diego–Tijuana: Not Quite a Binational City or Region." *GeoJournal* 54, 73–83.
Spykman, Nicholas John. 1942. "Frontiers, Security and International Organization." *Geographical Review* 32, 430–45.
Survey of Migration. 2002. *The Economist* (November 2–8) 50.
Tannam, Etain. 1999. *Cross-border Cooperation in the Republic of Ireland and Northern Ireland*. London, UK: St. Martin's and Macmillan Press.
Taylor, Paul. 1983. *The Limits of European Integration*. London: Croom Helm.
Ziller, Jacques. 2003. *The Europeanization of Constitutional Law*. Paris: L'Harmattan.

CHAPTER 1

THE MARITIME BORDERS OF EUROPE: UPSTREAM MIGRATORY CONTROLS

Olivier Clochard and Bruno Dupeyron

Beginning in the 1990s, the member states of the European Union (EU) began to restrict the entrance of third-country migrants and, as a result, a greater number of asylum applicants began to resort to clandestine methods of immigration to enter the EU. The Mediterranean Sea, the maritime border of Europe, was a place of particular concern, and the monitoring of the EU's external borders did not slow down these migratory flows. Within this Mediterranean space and on various scales, this chapter explores the migration-monitoring devices that were set up in the 1990s.

In order to stop these migratory flows from reaching the EU's external borders, member states first sought to promote increased cooperation in (and with) the migrants' countries of origin and countries of transit. A common visa policy and interstate information networks were developed, while conveyance companies (such as airlines and shipping firms) were financially penalized if they did not work as "auxiliary" border police to monitor the movement of illegal migrants. In the Mediterranean, military means were employed to stem the migratory flows from the south.

This chapter documents how the EU has imposed cooperation on peripheral states in order to limit immigration overflows. The case is made that the structural success of the EU's border-security policy in the face of massive immigration largely depends on the collaboration of the governments of neighbouring states that are not members of the EU.

THE VISA: THE FIRST INSTRUMENT OF CONTROL

Since the mid-1980s the member states of the EU have increasingly resorted to using the Schengen visa, a component of the Schengen Agreement of 1985, as a way to control flows of illegal migrants. This visa is rarely mentioned in debates on illegal immigration, although in France the important research carried out under the direction of Elspeth Guild and Didier Bigo (2003) and the work by the GISTI (an association that helps migrants) has underlined the difficulties encountered by migrants when they go to the consulate of a member state of the EU. If a consulate denies them a Schengen visa, foreigners can file a formal protest at the consulate or, within two months, can file a protest at the secretariat in Nantes, France.

The Schengen visa is thus an important tool for migratory control, used either in the migrants' country of origin or on the external borders of the EU. The first border of Schengen space that third-country nationals encounter is often located within the consulate of an EU member state; the decision to grant a visa that will make it possible for them to travel in EU space is made within such a consular establishment. Various cooperative agreements initiated between EU foreign ministries have established generally restrictive practices for consular agents to follow in the granting of visas. Since 2001 there has been a common list of countries whose nationals are subject to visa requirements, but the European Commission has been unable to ensure the consistent use of this list and, consequently, the rules for third-country nationals wishing to enter an EU member state remain diverse.

Schengen-space Borders

Consular agents, authorized by their ministries of foreign affairs, are the first controllers of Schengen-space borders. Border police and customs agents or immigration officers at airports comprise the next levels of control. These portals through which foreigners must pass are similar to real borders because people can be stopped from entering Schengen space before they even depart. The perception of these ports of entry as borders of Schengen space becomes even more of a reality when a visa is not granted. Many countries base their decisions to deny visas on purely technical aspects of their visa policy, in order to avoid having to explain why some foreigners are not granted visas and, as Guild and Bigo (2003) have asserted, "to remain in the shade of the debates on the borders." The individual granting of visas, the complex procedures involved, and the delocalization of controls all serve to conceal the authorities' deep suspicion of the applicants.

Much more than simply one instrument of control, the visa gives Schengen authorities the power to decide the fate of those who will profit from EU protection or want quite simply to travel to the EU. The Schengen visa policy makes it "possible to reduce the material and visible presence of the delimitation without decreasing its effectiveness, . . . so much it seems that the violence of the power is unacceptable only when one sees it acting" (Razac 2000, 102). As well, as Guild and Bigo (2003) noted, "The concept of border is detached from the territory in the sense that it is not the terminal, the limit, the envelope." The Schengen visa fits into the list of instruments of control that Didier Bigo (1998) calls "policing from a distance" or a "round of applause optics." In the consulates, these strategies are aimed at determining which foreign candidates will not be granted visas, apart from what occurs at the external borders.

The Schengen visa policy harmonization that occurred in 2001 has led to increasingly distinct regional policy sets. On the southernmost edge of the EU all the countries of the southern and eastern Mediterranean, except for Israel and Croatia, have become part of the visa policy process. The difficulty of obtaining a visa leaves applicants in these countries feeling imprisoned. In Tangier, Morocco, for example, the passports of people on standby are sometimes stamped "*Hakou Tanja*," which means that their passports have no validity beyond Tangier (Daoud 2002). Thus, for many, this administrative dead end leaves them little choice but to resort to illegal methods of immigration, which can cause them severe suffering.

What is the relationship between this distrust of western European countries for people from third countries and the number of people who must mortgage their lives to go to Europe? The question is very complicated, but it is important to note that, in many cases, visa regulations are contradictory. This is illustrated, for example, by comparing the goals set out in the Declaration of Barcelona (November 27–28, 1995) with the current obstacles that nationals of the countries of the southern and eastern Mediterranean must overcome in order to be legally admitted to Schengen space. The aim of the Declaration of Barcelona was to reinforce the Euro-Mediterranean partnership. Signatories committed to

> acting in accordance with the Charter of the United Nations and with the Universal Declaration of Human Rights, as with other obligations resulting from the international law, in particular those which rise from the regional and international instruments to which they are a party.

Moreover, the declaration noted that

> the parties will abstain from developing a military capacity which goes beyond their legitimate needs for defence, while reaffirming their determination to arrive at the same level of security and found mutual confidence with the least possible quantity of troops and armaments.

In many capitals of developing countries, access to embassies of member states of the EU is characterized by long queues in the streets. For example, in the cities of Tangier (Morocco), Ouagadougou (Burkina Faso), or Algiers (Algeria), the lines of people start before dawn, the only visible sign of the process they will have to undergo. In the district of Hydra in Algiers "hundreds of Algerians, come from almost all the areas of the country, wait, sometimes all day, to penetrate in[to] what resembles a fortress" (Maschino 2003). The consular agents' strict interpretation of the rules can have a devastating effect on applicants, particularly those in line who do not speak the language of the consulate and thus do not understand the process. As well, the forms are not always translated into the local language.

Criteria for Granting Visas

Third-country nationals wishing to travel within the EU must meet a set of demanding standards in order to be granted a Schengen visa. Among the principal criteria taken into account is the "migratory risk." Those applying for a visa, and especially those from developing countries, are automatically suspected of wanting to remain beyond the period that may be granted to them. The Common Consular Instruction published in the *Official Journal of the European Communities* (C313) on December 16, 2002, and addressed to the diplomatic and consular representations of the member states, specified the various types of Schengen visas, the documents that must accompany a request for visa, the checks to be carried out by the diplomatic representation on each applicant, the conditions for the delivery of visas, and so forth. The Instruction clearly specifies that

> the consular cooperation . . . will relate to the evaluation of the migratory risks. Its particular aim will be the determination of mutual criteria on the instruction of the files, the exchange of information on the use of false documents, on the possible clandestine immigration networks and on the refusal of a visa in the case of obviously nonfounded or fraudulent requests. [Finally] it is appropriate for this purpose to exert a particular vigilance on the "populations at risk": unemployed, people stripped of stable resources . . .

Thus the criteria for applicants can vary according to a person's nationality, situation, profession, and so on.

The important analysis carried out under the direction of Elspeth Guild and Didier Bigo (2003) in *The Setting Apart of the Foreigners: The Logic of the Schengen Visa,* as well as various academic articles (see, for example, Maschino 2003), has revealed the difficult process that foreigners must undertake in their country in order to obtain a Schengen visa. These works also revealed the secret arbitrary practices that take place within the consulates of member states of the EU. Although applicants face a great diversity of obstacles, the most crucial is the linguistic barrier. The country in which the visa candidate is located is the next most crucial element, as it is generally easier to apply for a Schengen visa from one's country of origin. This is not as important for those who have a good social and professional situation, such as company managers or highly qualified professionals, but it is an additional barrier for those who are refugees in another country and wish, for various reasons, to live in an EU member state.

Applicants must give many guarantees. In addition to the usual documents required for a visa request, such as the completed form and a passport, each Schengen consulate may require other documentation, the inevitable result of the adoption of certain arbitrary criteria by some member states' consulates. These may include a letter from the applicant's employer authorizing the person to take leave, a certificate from the airline on which the applicant will travel, the applicant's latest payroll statement, and a statement from the applicant's bank for the previous six months. Some member states' consulates in Lebanon, for example, require candidates to provide not only their completed application form and passport but also photocopies of their old Schengen visas; if necessary, a certificate of medical insurance that will be valid in the EU for the duration of their stay; bank statements; a certificate from their employer, specifying the date they were recruited, the wage they receive, and the duration of their vacation; their social security card; their airline reservation and ticket at the time the visa is issued; a certificate of accommodation from their host, certified by the proper authorities; a copy of the host's identity card or the residency permit of a relative in the EU; and a certificate of marital status. Completing all these elements is a long and tiresome process, particularly since an incomplete form often results in the applicant having to return to the consulate. Moreover, if an applicant's completed document arouses suspicion, it is often denied and the applicant is not told on what grounds this decision has been made. Thus obtaining the invaluable stamp of approval often comes at considerable cost to the applicant.

In the end, applicants may never hear back from the consulate. (Maschino 2003 gives several examples of Algerians who never received an answer to their request.) If, after two months, applicants have not received an answer, they can assume they have been rejected and their request will no longer be considered. They receive no explanation for why they have been rejected, which for many evokes feelings of incomprehension, injustice, and arbitrariness: it is as though they have been part of a lottery they could never win (Guild and Bigo 2003). Although there are no statistics, the obstacles generated by some EU countries for certain visa applicants are very real.

The Schengen Visa and the Control of Illegal Immigration

The governments of the member states of the EU have also used the Schengen visa to force peripheral third countries to control the number of their nationals who are allowed to migrate to or travel within Schengen space. These governments increase the number of visas awarded to third-country nationals provided that their state of origin improves its border controls and readmits people in unusual situations who have transited through its territory. These visa negotiations take place within various diplomatic frameworks, and in certain countries of origin it becomes clear that some of these practices violate the immigration-offences section of the Universal Declaration of Human Rights. This new type of infringement violates the rights of those who have illegally crossed the borders of their own state or of Schengen space, or who have remained in an EU member state beyond the authorized period. As Salvatore Palidda noted in March 2003 at the ELISE Declaration meeting sponsored by the Centre for European Policy Studies (CEP), "Tunisia is taking this route and several African countries would be under pressure from the States of the [European] Union to create this type of offence" (cited in Bigo and Guild 2003). In 2003, in return for agreeing to cooperate closely with the Italian police to supervise the Strait of Sicily, Tunisia obtained 60,000 visas for its nationals who wished to profit from seasonal work in Italy. These types of debates are increasingly on the agenda of meetings between member states of the EU and third countries. One of the principal objectives of the French minister of the interior's visits to Senegal and Mali in 2003 concerned this issue. The minister, on behalf of the French state, proposed to increase the number of French visas for Senegalese nationals in exchange for a substantial increase in the number of consular passes necessary to escort Senegalese without residency permits out of France and back to Senegal. In 2002 foreign nationals of Senegalese origin or those who had crossed through Dakar into France could not be deported without such passes; of the 632 consular passes that were requested by French border police from the Senegalese consulate, only 26 percent of the requests were granted (Zappi 2003).

Fifteen years after the signing of the Schengen Agreement, the member states' ministries responsible for the management of migratory flows were delighted that the Schengen consular network guaranteed "preliminary controls of the borders, that there is a dense fabric of relations between the consulates making it possible to filter the *bona fide* from the *mala fide* and that dissuasion regarding those who want to come on the Schengen territory is effective" (European Commission 2001). However, the current monitoring of illegal immigration that is carried out within the representations of the various member states is not sufficient. Between the consulates and the ports of departure, illegal migrants have considerable room to manoeuvre, either bypassing border controls without being stopped or resorting to using intermediate agents (frontier runners, customs officers, obliging people, and so forth).

In this climate of distrust, since 1992 EU legislators have constrained peripheral third countries by forcing them to assume and share responsibilities that previously were the domain of border police. The legislators' subsequent development of a network of liaison officers who are posted to third countries for the purpose of increasing migratory controls within them has further constrained the third-country governments.

THE INCREASING DELOCALIZATION OF MIGRATORY CONTROLS

During the 1990s,the member states of the EU became increasingly worried about the inadequate border controls in visa applicants' countries of origin or transit. Consequently, they first reinforced their legislation concerning the responsibility of applicants' countries of origin or those who allowed the transit of foreigners who did not have the required documentation. They then developed methods to control the flow of illegal migrants into countries vulnerable to this problem. Liaison officers from member states were put in place to anticipate the levels of external frontier checks necessary to the EU, and these officers have increasingly functioned as part of a network. Indeed, this collaboration was recognized officially by authorities of the EU in 2004.

The Systematization of Financial Sanctions

Transport companies play a large role in the control of migratory flows. With the implementation of the Schengen Agreements of 1990, the member states of the EU were given the authority to force all conveyors to collaborate in the control of migratory flows (until this time, only air-transport companies were required to do so). In order to avoid financial penalties, companies implemented controls that were equal to, and as effective as, those of the border police. In this field the policy followed by France is often a precursor to those followed by the EU as a whole. For example, the French directive passed in June 2001 considerably reinforced the sanctions against conveyance companies. Conveyors carrying illegal foreigners would now face financial sanctions of up to XEU 500,000. In 2003 the French agency known as CIVIPOL carried out a study of the feasibility of maritime frontier checks for the European Commission. Its report affirmed that "the reporting and the recovery of the fines planned for the conveyors in accordance with the directive . . . should be more systematic and a part of the product could be mutualized to ensure the technical operations of improvements of controls" (CIVIPOL 2003, 53).

In the present context of increased competition and in order to avoid state sanctions, legal conveyors inevitably refuse to transport people who wish to leave their country to seek asylum. Although it is impossible to estimate the number of times this occurs, the multiple examples revealed by the work of Kristenn Le Bourhis (2001) indicate that the policies of these new controllers of immigration lead to discriminatory practices.

Finally, it is important to recall that during the European Council of Seville in June 2002 the prime ministers of Spain (José María Aznar), Italy (Silvio Berlusconi), and the United Kingdom (Tony Blair), whose countries were all confronted with the problem of illegal immigration, called for financial sanctions against these migrants' states of origin or transit outside the EU. This idea was rejected immediately by the European Council, but it did stimulate the European Commission to develop ways to "integrate the problem of migration in the foreign relations of the European Union" (European Commission 2003).

EU Police Activity in Countries of Departure

According to Regulation (EC) 377/2004 of the European Council of February 19, 2004, relating to the creation of a network of "immigration" liaison officers, such an officer is

> a representative of a member State detached abroad by the immigration department or other proper authorities . . . to establish and maintain the contacts with the authorities (of one or more country) in order to contribute to the prevention of illegal immigration and the fight against this phenomenon, the return of the illegal immigrants and the management of legal immigration.

Since the end of the 1990s each member state of the EU has increased the number of liaison officers it stations in third countries. Their principal functions are to supervise migratory flows and to facilitate cooperation between third countries and member states. The liaison officers thus try to negotiate their ability to operate in third countries and an agreement for the readmittance of migrants turned away from EU borders in exchange for a more flexible visa policy. Until 2004 the authorities in Morocco, for example, refused to allow the French liaison officer to operate in Tangier, so his action was limited to Rabat Airport.

The functions of these officers have been increasingly harmonized within the member states to achieve greater effectiveness. For instance, French liaison officers call upon their EU colleagues in countries where their physical presence is not ensured anymore, and vice versa. Within the framework agreement for investigating the enormous number of illegal immigrants arriving on the southernmost coasts of the EU, member states make a concerted effort to pressure the authorities of the third country from which the boat departed. The liaison officers stationed in that third country work to have all those involved in the transit of illegal migrants arrested and to slow down this type of migration. Although these types of arrivals always have an important media impact, their numbers are small. According to CIVIPOL (2003), this type of arrival accounts for only 2 to 3 percent of clandestine arrivals. However, typically, these events cause member states to take action.

The example of the *East Sea,* a ship that left Latakieh in Syria and was wrecked in 2001 on the beaches near Fréjus in France, is interesting. Various letters of request from member states for the names of those responsible were addressed to Lebanon and Syria, leading in 2003 to the arrest of one of the organization's covert partners. The organizer, a Syrian national supposedly responsible for the transport of 900 Kurds to Europe, was arrested and imprisoned in Lebanon. The divisional commission agent of the Police International Technical Cooperation Service (SCTIP) in Beirut, Lebanon, noted, however, "that the pressure of the European countries was not enough, because officially the sleeping partner was released on a decision of the Lebanese court" (Clochard and Doraï 2005).

Many Kurds pass through Lebanon. The political institutions of countries of transit such as Lebanon tolerate the organization of these migratory networks insofar as it is a lucrative trade. According to various sources, the price of crossing the Mediterranean on board the *East Sea* was about US$ 3,000 per person, a total cost of almost US$ 3 million for a shipload of migrants. The trade also enables countries of transit to deport foreigners whom they do not wish to have in their country (Clochard and Doraï 2005).

In an attempt to prevent further problems, a system for the control of sea transport was set up in the eastern part of the Mediterranean, although until 2005 there was no legal basis for stopping suspect ships on the open sea. For example, the ship *Le Monica,* while transporting several hundred Syrian Kurds to Lebanon in March 2002, was stopped by the French navy, but because the navy was not authorized to intervene the ship was able to continue on to Catane, Sicily.

In order to support aircraft or warships belonging to maritime patrols, the navies of other member states of the EU now "directly or through the antiterrorist mission of Euromarfor" (CIVIPOL 2003, 34) monitor suspect ships. Their goal is to keep departing boats close to the coast of the country of departure in order to enable countries such as Greece, whose coastguard patrols the Aegean Sea, to intercept suspect vessels. Within sight of the Italian coast the Italian navy has, on several occasions, caused suspect boats to deviate from their sea route, going beyond the twenty-four-mile limit, sometimes with dramatic consequences. For example, on March 31, 1997, the Italian navy collided with a boat while trying to intercept it in the Strait of Otranto. The boat capsized and eighty-seven Albanian nationals drowned. The CIVIPOL (2003) report, which has become a tool for the establishment of the EU's maritime borders, indicated that such maritime operations "fall under a strategy of containment" (CIVIPOL 2003, 37). However, at sea, international law (notably Article 98 of the UN Convention on the Law of the Sea, December 10, 1982) requires all human beings to lend assistance to those in distress.

The illegal transit through third countries, the increasing number of illegal migrants arriving by boat, and the analysis of the CIVIPOL report led the French government to introduce Law 2005–371 of April 22, 2005, which modified certain arrangements relating to the method used by France's maritime police to combat illegal migration by sea. Until that time the French state could not in theory fulfill any operation aimed at preventing an infringement of its immigration laws beyond its contiguous zone (the maritime zone in which migratory controls can be carried out). By legalizing this type of control, France can now use its navy throughout its entire maritime space to fight illegal immigration. Whereas, before 2005, monitoring of illegal immigrants was mainly carried out by border police at ports of entry, French territorial waters are now monitored by the French navy, which has the legal authority to stop any ship not raising a flag or without a nationality.

In the case of suspect ships flying the flag of another state, French navy ships can intervene provided they are authorized to do so by the other state. In the same way, monitoring can be carried out in territorial waters of a foreign state provided that the foreign state has delegated this power to the proper French authorities. In the current context, it is assumed that in the near future the European Commission will develop a general directive based on the French initiative. A new function of French liaison officers is to negotiate with authorities of third countries to extend the monitoring privileges of the member states of the EU.

The Euro-Mediterranean Partnership (MEDA) Program

In January 1998 the High Level Asylum and Immigration Group, a group of experts set up by the EU, developed an action plan to control irregular immigration and to decrease the number of requests for asylum coming from Iraq. In 1999 the project was extended to five other countries – Albania, Afghanistan, Morocco, Somalia, and Sri Lanka – but Morocco refused to implement the plan. Consequently the EU turned to the MEDA program (a product of the Declaration of Barcelona) and developed measures to prevent illegal immigration within the program's framework. Since then, however, the EU has failed to meet the initial objectives of MEDA – to reinforce the socioeconomic organizations and develop the democratic institutions of the countries of the southern and eastern Mediterranean. The conclusion of the presidency of the Euro-Mediterranean conference of foreign affairs ministers in November 2004 (Council of the European Union 2004) confirmed the lack of EU action on this issue by noting the many problems still to be resolved:

> In the light of the common problem of illegal migration to Maghreb countries and the subsequent transit migration to the EU, characterized by human suffering, there is a need for intensified cooperation that addresses root causes as well as negative effects of transit migration and the possibility of a dialogue with third countries to address the issue. This cooperation should involve all aspects of illegal migration, the fight against human trafficking and related networks as well as other forms of illegal migration, border management and migration-related capacity building. Support for capacity building and providing technical assistance to countries meeting their obligations under the Geneva Conventions could be considered.

The MEDA-CEPOL (European College of Police) program was initiated in Valence, France, in 2002, as a specific technical instrument of EU cooperation. The first phase of a wider program took place from March 1, 2004, to March 1, 2006. The function of the MEDA-CEPOL program is to reinforce migratory controls and anticipate the level of monitoring that is required in the majority of the Mediterranean transit or emigration countries. The EU police who are stationed in the majority of the countries of the southern and eastern Mediterranean are the principal monitoring instrument and are controlled by France. The fight against terrorism and illegal immigration has thus become a priority of the EU, preceding other concerns such as measures to restrict criminal networks involved in money laundering, drug trafficking, or cybercriminality.

THE MEDITERRANEAN: AN ELOQUENT LINE OF FRACTURE

Since the Seville summit in June 2002, cooperation between the member states of the EU has reached a new stage. In a document titled *Towards an Integrated Management of the Member States External Borders of the European Union* (May 2002), the European Commission defined four major requirements: to ensure mutual confidence between member states; to provide the resources necessary to counter terrorism; to guarantee a high level of security inside the EU after expansion (in particular, after new member states have been authorized to apply all of the Schengen assets of EU membership); and to increase the effectiveness of the fight against illegal immigration, in view of the principles of the right of asylum. However, the French Coordination for the Right of Asylum (CFDA) commented that

> this last reserve [is] quite formal because the remainder of the communication does not make at any time reference to the means under consideration for the respect of these principles. It would at least have been convenient to recall that, according to the convention of Geneva, the illegality of the crossing of a border cannot be applied to an applicant of asylum. This silence is characteristic of all European work relating to the control of the borders (CFDA 2004).

Thus, under the aegis of the Strategic Committee on Immigration, Frontiers and Asylum (SCIFA), which is composed of those responsible for border control for the twenty-seven member states of the EU, a common management plan for the EU's external borders is being worked out progressively. Increased illegal migrant flows in the Mediterranean often lead European Convention countries to intensify police and military presence on their external borders, and, if necessary, to use high-tech military equipment to prevent illegal migrants from reaching Schengen space. In addition, operational cooperation at the external borders is reinforced, both between member states and with neighbouring states.

Joint Member-state Operations at EU External Borders

During 2003 the SCIFA coordinated seventeen pilot projects for monitoring external EU frontiers. In the long term these various cooperative projects, initiated by the sharing of the costs of frontier checks during the conference in Thessaloníki, Greece, in 2003, are expected to lead to the creation of an EU border-police force. An EU agency based in Warsaw, Poland, and established in May 2005 does not carry out external frontier checks, but, via its own personnel as well as detached national experts, it coordinates and assists the external border-check operations of member states. Previously a similar structure had been based in Germany for land borders. Specialized agencies may also be created for air and maritime borders in Italy and Greece, respectively.

The Mediterranean and eastern member states of the EU are very interested in the creation of an EU border-police force. Currently, because of their geographical position and the length of their borders (maritime and terrestrial), Spain, Italy, Greece, and Poland, in particular, carry out most of the monitoring of illegal migrants on behalf of the majority of the member states. In March 2003 the Greek president proposed a more equitable sharing of the monitoring function based on four criteria: the geographical locality of a country, the nature of its borders, the degree of illegal migratory pressure it experiences, and the quality of its control measures. However, his proposal created a division between member states. Moreover, the European Commission noted that, although each member state financially guarantees security provisions at its external borders, the commission does not have the financial resources to enhance these provisions. Thus, pending the creation of an EU border-police force, cooperation between member states of the EU is organized at their borders.

As for maritime control, Spain coordinated two operations called Ulysses I and II, both of which included the participation of France, the United Kingdom, Italy, and Portugal. The first monitoring operation, from January 25 to February 8, 2003, extended from the Strait of Gibraltar to the Strait of Sicily and was carried out by naval forces exclusively. Eleven ships carrying 326 immigrants were intercepted during Ulysses I. The second operation, from May 27 to June 2, 2003, which focused on the archipelago of the Canary Islands, used the aerial and marine patrols of the British Royal Air Force (*Nimrod*) and the French Marine Nationale (*Atlantic*) to support interventions by the Spanish Guardia Civil and a corvette of the Portuguese navy. Seven boats carrying 139 immigrants were intercepted. According to CIVIPOL, although the legal framework was not adapted "to make it possible for ships of Member States to intervene in waters of another State and under its control, … the operation Ulysses 2 in the Canaries of May 2003 showed the dissuasive effectiveness of the use of the Surmar patrols (heavy planes with the long operating range of anti-submarine fighters), of *Nimrod* of the Royal Air Force and *Atlantic* of the Marine Nationale" (2003, 27 and 87). Considering the resources that were used, the operation was indeed similar to a military deterrent force.

At the end of 2003 another project, Neptune, was implemented to prevent ships carrying illegal migrants from evading the maritime patrols in the central and eastern Mediterranean. Coordinated by Italy, the project included the goal of identifying those responsible for the maritime movement of illegal migrants in order to freeze their resources and prevent them from operating.

Joint Operations of Member States and Third Countries

The member states of the EU have continued to appeal to nearby third countries that serve as points of origin for illegal migrants, or allow them to transit through their territory, to participate in the fight against illegal immigration, with the promise of important financial assistance for doing so. Within the EU framework "twinning conventions" have often been established between the first fifteen member states and subsequent EU applicant countries such as Cyprus and Malta. At external border posts, stickers or signs that read "Co-financed by the European Union" indicate the existence of such a convention, a process in which liaison officers play an important role. At the time of the Kosovo crisis in 1998, which generated a large flow of exiles from Albania, to Italy, member states sent logistical personnel and police brigades into Albania, to ensure that humanitarian aid reached the country and to reinforce the monitoring of Albanian ports.

Another example of joint operations between member states of the EU and third countries is the monitoring of the Channel of Otranto. Set up by Italy, this mission also includes France and Spain in maintaining security in the western Mediterranean. To some extent it preceded one of the missions of the European Maritime Force (Euromarfor) (Foucher 2000, 86–87).

An EU program, ARGO, was then established to facilitate administrative cooperation involving issues of external borders, visas, asylum, and immigration from January 1, 2002, to December 31, 2006. It "should be regarded only as one modest precursor of broader activities in this field" (point 3 of preamble). This program highlighted the desire of member states of the EU to control and "influence the movements" of a great number of foreigners coming from third countries. For instance, in the Spanish-controlled North African territories of Ceuta and Melilla, the shore road between Tangier and Ceuta that connects several monitoring stations was financed mainly by the EU. Further, since February 2005 the Spanish Guardia Civil and the Moroccan Royal Gendarmerie have alternately supervised (one week per month) the coasts located around Nador (Morocco) and Almeria (Spain).

These first steps toward the creation of an EU border-police force underline member states' increasing use of the EU framework agreement to put pressure on neighbouring third countries, to consolidate the requests for asylum controls at their borders, to restrict the number of foreign arrivals in their countries, and to implement a common policy of deporting people under certain circumstances. The fortress-like walls built around the Spanish possessions of Ceuta and Melilla, which border on the Strait of Gibraltar, reveal the type of border configuration toward which the external borders of the EU seem to be converging.

Frontier Spaces under a "Benevolent" Eye

Since 1998 the Spanish Guardia Civil has deployed an arsenal of methods aimed at slowing down the entrance of illegal migrants from Morocco through a system known as the Sistema Integrado de Vigilancia Exterior (Integrated System of Exterior Vigilance, or SIVE). It has evolved "from a system of control [that was] semi-mobile and exclusively terrestrial to a very flexible device including air and maritime intervention units" (Migreurop 2004). Thirty-four hundred additional agents have been recruited since 2001, and during 2004 three towers equipped with radar and thermal and infrared cameras were erected to reinforce the work of the Guardia Civil. Spanish border police use these very powerful technological instruments to monitor all movement in the Strait of Gibraltar, including movement beyond Spain's maritime borders. Each monitoring station can detect movement within a ten-kilometre operating range and maritime patrols in the contiguous zone are used increasingly to monitor coastal roads. (Beyond the twenty-four-mile limit, the monitoring of member states' external borders can complicate the process of determining maritime borders, especially when the coasts involved are opposite rather than adjacent.) Finally, since the end of 2003 the Guardia Civil has used sensors that are so powerful they can detect heartbeats from a distance.

Each suspicious movement that is detected can be sent in real time via satellite to various naval and land border-police units. Suspect boats trying to reach the Spanish coast are then intercepted and any foreigners on board are detained in refugee internment centres. People of Moroccan nationality are often sent back to Morocco in less than twenty-four hours. (On a personal note, one of the authors of this chapter was reminded of the existence of this border when he crossed between Algeciras (Spain) and Tangier (Morocco) in August 2002, and he observed a young man crouching behind an isolated table where an agent of the boat company stamped passports. This young man had failed in his attempt to reach Spain, a fact that is often forgotten in the routine of the Spanish borders.) The CIVIPOL (2003) report on controlling the EU's maritime borders predicted that these kinds of detection technologies would reduce "to ten percent the chances of success of one *patera* [smuggling boat] to unload its passengers without being located and being hailed either at sea or on the shore" (27). Still, hundreds of Guardia Civil agents continue to regularly search the wooded zones of the Spanish coastal road between Algeciras and Barbate for those who may have gotten that far.

With the reinforced and enhanced monitoring in the centre of the Strait of Gibraltar, boats carrying illegal migrants, known as *pateras*, were forced to take much longer routes, via the Alboràn Sea or the Atlantic Ocean. This change in sea routes was indicated by an increase in the number of drownings beyond the Strait of Gibraltar. In June 2003, in response to this change, the SIVE was equipped with mobile radar on vehicles, which allowed it to widen its sphere of activity to include a large part of the Andalusian coast from Huelva to Almeria (a distance of approximately 500 kilometres), and in 2005 the Andalusian border gained six additional fixed radar towers. The SIVE was also deployed on the archipelago of the Canary Islands, with three fixed radar-tracking stations and a mobile station located on Fuerteventura and Lanzarote, the two islands closest to the Moroccan coast. Spain's objective in extending its borders is to cover its maritime spaces in great detail "and to closely control the bodies and their movements at the borders where the power of the State in fact is most seriously put to challenge" (Migreurop 2004).

Thus, in addition to its role in the fight against drug trafficking, the SIVE is now a major element in monitoring the movements of illegal migrants and preventing them from reaching the southern borders of Europe. "During the first eleven months of the year 2003, the rescue services at sea 'assisted' nearly 5,500 people, a figure [that is a] very clear increase compared to the previous years" (Bejarano 2003, 51). Since 2004 Spanish authorities have justified the installation of various monitoring devices, at a cost of nearly XEU 140 million (using funds partly granted by the EU), by noting that they make it possible to save lives in the open sea. However, these electronic devices can fail in fog or high seas. For example, on December 23, 2004, these devices failed to detect thirteen men in a boat drifting off the island of Fuerteventura, all of whom died from exposure. Another example was a boat that was "transport[ing] . . . forty-three people, four of whom had to be hospitalized because of their serious state of hypothermia" (Agence France-Presse 2004). The writer Tahar Ben Jelloun (2003) blamed Spanish authorities for some of these shipwrecks. In a posthumous plea on behalf of fifty people who drowned on October 25, 2003, only 500 metres from Cadiz harbour, he called attention to the fact that the Guardia Civil waited one hour before intervening. These few examples emphasize how the use of new technologies contributes to changes in strategies employed by those who transport illegal migrants, in many cases increasing the risk involved for those desperate to reach the EU's shores.

CAMPS FOR FOREIGNERS ON THE BORDERS OF EUROPE

Beginning in 2003, several member states of the EU began to consider externalizing their asylum procedures in third countries. The government of the United Kingdom initiated this process in June 2003, when it proposed to the European Council of Thessaloníki that transit-processing centres be created in third countries. In addition to these centres for asylum applicants, the British proposal recommended that regional protection areas in the countries of origin or departure be installed, in order to offer "better protection to the people transferred close to their homes, and to develop legal ways by which real refugees will be able, if necessary, to come to Europe" (http://www.statewatch.org/news/2003/apr/blair-simitis-asile.pdf). Although the British proposal was not adopted, various European Commission statements that were issued later underlined that the British idea had become a serious element in the evolving asylum and immigration policies of the EU.

On August 12, 2004, the idea of externalizing the EU's asylum procedure re-emerged. Otto Schilly, the German minister of the interior, and Giuseppe Pisanu, the Italian minister for foreign affairs, proposed creating transit centres in Libya, under the euphemistic name of "immigration gates," in order to avoid new human dramas off the Mediterranean coasts. Thus humanitarian reasons became the pretext for the establishment of foreigners' camps in third countries. However, these proposed transit centres caused serious concerns for many. On one hand, Libya has not ratified the Geneva Convention on Refugees; on the other, many feared that such camps would cause some asylum candidates to take longer and more dangerous maritime routes to reach Europe, to avoid having to go into a transit centre.

Opposition from other member states to the proposal was not as hostile as expected, although discord existed between certain member states. Statements from the European Commission during 2004 emphasized the willingness of states such as Belgium, Spain, France, and Sweden, which were opposed to this proposal and to the earlier British proposal, to seek a settlement with the initiators, Germany, Italy, and the United Kingdom. In the absence of a consensus, it was suggested that such a policy could be included within an intergovernmental framework, like Schengen space itself, in order to overcome the opposition of some member states. As for preventing asylum-seekers from crossing illegally from Libya, a partial solution was achieved when EU sanctions against Libya were lifted on October 11, 2004. The EU could now supply Libya with the necessary equipment to control illegal immigration along its coastline and land borders. Tripoli asked for and received helicopters, fast patrol boats, radar, and apparatus equipped with night glasses to monitor its coastline (approximately 1,800 kilometres) and to stop flows of migrants from crossing its land borders (approximately 4,300 kilometres). The European Council commented on April 14, 2005, "It is essential to initiate cooperation with Libya as regards to migration" (http://www.coe.int/).

Clearly, the commitment undertaken in 1999 at Tampere, Finland, by the member states in favour of "an integral and total application of the Convention of Geneva" to the EU's system for asylum is crumbling. Various principles of externalization (visas, liaison officers, foreigners' camps, and so on) are likely to reinforce the imbalance that already prevails between the rich member states that are rarely confronted with having to welcome asylum applicants and the poor states that receive the majority of the refugees and displaced people. The various transit-centre proposals constitute implicit attempts to circumvent international agreements that the EU states have judged to be too constraining. They are the extension of a logic that is already largely at work, according to which asylum-seekers are no longer viewed as people who may be in need of protection but rather as a danger from which Europe must protect itself. The concept of asylum-seekers being locked up in camps evokes images of immigration as a criminal offence. Indeed, it is becoming difficult to know where the borders of the EU are located. The security approach being taken by member states opens the door to would-be migrants being given a numerical identity and being subjected to migratory "traceability" (Dana 2004). Thus practices that have been part of the world of fiction for many years – biological methods of identification such as fingerprint, iris of the eye, facial, or voice recognition – are becoming standard practices in the fight against illegal immigration. The member states have confirmed their willingness to implement high standards of control over certain immigrant populations, primarily by giving them the means to return more easily to their countries of origin. However, as Agamben (2004) points out

> One could not . . . exceed certain thresholds in the control and the handling of the bodies without penetrating in a new biopolitic era, without taking another step in what Michel Foucault called a progressive animalization of the man brought into play through the most sophisticated techniques.

The expanded physical area of migratory monitoring around the EU and elsewhere in the Western world (Australia, Canada, and the United States) underlines the international dimension of the immigration controls that have been established by these countries. This evolution is a consequence of the process of externalizing asylum and immigration policies. Although mainly used in the field of economics until the beginning of 2000, the term "externalization" is now used by multinational companies that establish subsidiaries in developing countries, as well as in referring to the delocalization of migratory controls in third countries.

However, the migratory controls that have been used by the member states of the EU since the beginning of the 1990s have never included a preplanned and coordinated strategy of action on this issue. Rather, individual member states adjust their policies according to their means, particular situations and crises, and the level of migratory flows at their borders. The EU's visa policy, the law authorizing a network of liaison officers throughout the world, the system of fines against those who are involved in transporting illegal migrants, and the significant technological devices deployed at external borders have led to a system in which the EU's territory can still be accessed, but doing so involves increasingly long, difficult, and dangerous routes for the increasing number of asylum-seekers who must resort to entering that space illegally.

An exhaustive description of the procedures and technical devices for controlling migratory flows from third countries that exist on the maritime border of the Mediterranean was not the principal objective of this chapter. Rather, the objective was to analyze tendencies, what Marie-Claire Caloz-Tschopp (2004) has referred to as "tensions at the borders of Europe." In the end the member states of the EU have sought to protect themselves from international flows of migrants by sanctifying the space they control.

LITERATURE CITED

Agamben, Giorgio. 2004. "No to Biopolitic Tattooing." *Le monde* (January 11), 16.

Agence France-Presse. 2004. Dispatch. [online]. www.afp.com [consulted December 23, 2004].

Bejarano, José. 2003. "A Littoral Almost Impossible to Control." *Courrier international* (La Vangardia) 684, 50–51.

Ben Jelloun, Tahar. 2003. "Died Without Burial, Demolished by Misfortune." *Libération* [Paris] (November 19), 15.

Bigo, D. 1998. "L'immigration à la croisée des chemins sécuritaires." *Revue Européenne des migrations internationales* 14:1, 25–46.

Bigo, D., and E. Guild 2003. "The Visa: Instrument of the Remote Setting of the 'Undesirables.'" *Cultures & Conflits,* 49–50. [online]. www.conflits.org/ [consulted December 23, 2004].

Caloz-Tschopp, M.-C. 2004. *Les étrangers aux frontières de l'Europe : le spectre des camps*. Paris: La Dispute.

CFDA. 2004. "*Lourdes menaces sur le droit d'asile en Europe : un bilan de quatre ans de rapprochement des politiques d'asile.*" [online]. cfda.rezo.net/Europe/rapport-02-04.html [consulted October 20, 2005].

CIVIPOL. 2003. *Etude de faisabilité relative au contrôle des frontières maritimes de l'Union européenne*. Brussels: CIVIPOL.

Clochard, O., and M.-K. Doraï. 2005. "Aux frontières de l'asile : les réfugiés non palestiniens au Liban." *A contrario* 3:2, 45–65.

Council of the European Union. 2004. "Pesidency Conclusions for the Euro-Mediterranean Meeting of Ministers of Foreign Affairs" (14869/04, Presse 331). Brussels: Council of the European Union, Press Office. [online]. ue.eu.int/ueDocs/cms_Data/docs/pressdata/en/er/82876.pdf [consulted November 30, 2004].

Dana, Diminescu. 2004. "The Difficult Exercise of Freedom of Movement." Paper presented at Rethymno, School of Social Sciences, University of Crete, Gallos Campus. [online]. www.transitmigration.org [consulted October 23, 2004].

Daoud, Z 2002. *Gibraltar improbable frontière, de Colomb aux clandestins*. Paris: Séguier, Les Colonnes d'Hercule.

European Commission. 2001. "Communication of the Commission to the Council and the European Parliament (Concerning a Common Policy as Regards to Clandestine Immigration)." No. 672, final. Brussels: European Commission.

European Commission. 2002. *Towards an Integrated Management of the Member States External Borders of the European Union*. Brussels: European Commission.

European Commission. 2003. "Communication of the Commission to the Council and the European Parliament." No. 152, final. Brussels: European Commission.

European Council. 2005, Press Release, 2,652nd Council Meeting – Justice and Home Affairs – Luxembourg. [online]. www.consilium.europa.eu/ueDocs/cms_Data/docs/pressdata/en/jha/84618.pdf [consulted October 30, 2005].

Foucher M. 2000. *La République européenne*. Paris: Belin.

Guild, E., and D. Bigo 2003. "The Setting Apart of Foreigners: The Logic of the Schengen Visa." *Cultures & Conflicts* 49–50. [online]. www.conflits.org/ [consulted December 23, 2004].

Le Bourhis, K. 2001. *Les transporteurs et le contrôle des flux migratoires*. Paris: L'Harmattan.

Maschino, M. 2003. "La loterie des visas". *Le monde diplomatique*, 4–5.

Migreurop. 2004. *SIVE: Electronic Shielding of the Spanish Borders*. [online]. www.migreurop.org/ [consulted September 16, 2004].

Razac, O. 2000. *Histoire politique du barbelé : la prairie, la tranchée, le camp*. Paris: La fabrique.

Zappi, Sylvia. 2003. "Au Sénégal, M. Sarkozy plaide pour un retour au pays des clandestins." *Le monde* (December 16), 8.

CHAPTER 2

WHOSE SECURITY? DILEMMAS OF US BORDER SECURITY IN THE ARIZONA–SONORA BORDERLANDS

Julie A. Murphy Erfani

INTRODUCTION: INEFFECTIVE US BORDER CRACKDOWNS AND ACCELERATING CRIME

Recent US government crackdowns on illicit crossings of the southern border with Mexico have helped to spawn a revolution in social networking among groups concerned with cross-border migration and national and human security. Current US border-security policy and practice have also helped to trigger crime waves associated with human and narcotics trafficking, which have in turn diminished the personal security of people who live in and transit though the borderlands. Paradoxically, federal immigration enforcement policies aimed at increasing governmental control over people crossing the southern border of the United States have actually inspired a complex array of informal networks, both legal and criminal, that exercise increasing control over everyday life and movement through US–Mexico border regions. Indeed, social networks and local government networking on both sides of the border are displacing the central government's control over national and human security in these regions. Thus, far from recentring immigration control in the hands of the central government, as the legal doctrine of state sovereignty would dictate, recent US border policies, such as Operation Gatekeeper in California and the Arizona Border Control (ABC) Initiative, have decentred control and spurred into action a larger cast of local actors and organizational agents of change in the municipalities, counties, and states in the various border regions on both sides of the line (see the maps in figures 2.1 to 2.6).

The Arizona–Sonora borderlands, especially since September 11, 2001, represent the quintessential example of a civil and criminal social networking revolution, a self-defeating federal border crackdown, and crime waves that threaten the personal security of residents and migrants. The Arizona–Sonora border situation raises key questions about current US border-security policy: Whose security is being enhanced by the stepped-up border surveillance of federal authorities when the personal security of people residing and moving through the region is threatened by increasing crime? Why has the increase in national-security measures rendered ordinary people less secure?

The argument is made in this chapter that flawed federal immigration policy and intensified organizational life in the Arizona–Sonora borderlands pose two basic dilemmas for US border-security policy in the region. The first dilemma is the fact that intensified federal border surveillance has proven to be self-defeating, given that border crackdowns spawn more civil-society networking. Such social networking has proliferated in the absence of a national guest-worker policy that distinguishes migrant workers from criminals and potential terrorists. The escalation of social networking among smugglers and migrants has prompted the federal government to become more involved in border surveillance, even though it has had little success in controlling illicit border-crossing behaviour. Social networks of human traffickers, migrants, migrant assistance organizations, and US civilian militia volunteers subvert, interfere with, and/or compete with the federal border patrol to control movement through the borderlands. In the context of this politicized organizational landscape, enhanced federal surveillance appears to be increasingly self-defeating at a time when the border's ability to filter criminals and potential terrorists is even more imperative. In effect, federal border crackdowns have engendered more social networking, politicized informal organizations, and resulted in a border that is more porous than ever before to all types of people and goods, including criminals and contraband, such as narcotics and weapons.

The second dilemma of current US national-security policy at the Arizona–Sonora border is its crime-accelerating side effect on the borderlands. This policy has exacerbated the amount of crime related to drug and human trafficking, which in turn has affected everyone from national park rangers to ordinary Phoenix residents, who are subjected to racial profiling. The continued inability of the federal government

countries and peoples, and security is based upon intercultural human contact and cross-cultural integration of common interests across borders. From this perspective border-crossing and border security are scripted according to broader concerns for human security. In fact, from this vantage point, the emergence of a transnational space of borderlands conceived as a zone of multicultural exchange and cross-border movement and cooperation makes both human security and border security possible. Those groups advocating amnesty and an assured path to US citizenship for undocumented migrants seek to construct a border region that entails a relatively unobstructed cross-border movement of people.

In the Arizona–Sonora context a growing number of migrant-assistance activists and organizations have embraced this social construction of borderlands security. A number of non-governmental migrant assistance networks in Tucson, Phoenix, Ambos Nogales, and Douglas–Agua Prieta have actively sought to reconstruct the discourse on border-crossing and border security in Arizona and Sonora in the language of protection of basic human rights and human security, regardless of national origin or legal status. For instance, Derechos Humanos, a human rights NGO in Tucson, enlists US attorneys as advocates for the human and legal rights of undocumented Mexican migrants. Humane Borders, a faith-based NGO also based in Tucson, networks to place water stations along the southern Arizona and northern Sonoran border regions in order to reduce migrant deaths from dehydration as crossers walk through remote parts of the desert. No More Deaths (No Más Muertes), an NGO with a statewide network, organizes and operates migrant assistance camps on both sides of the border to aid migrants in distress in the Arizona–Sonora wilderness. BorderLinks and Frontera de Cristo (Healing Our Borders), two more faith-based NGOs based in Ambos Nogales–Tucson and Douglas–Agua Prieta respectively, focus on cross-border cultural exchange and community outreach with a transnational human rights orientation.

For these pro-migrant organizations, cross-border migration and issues of border security are defined in terms of human security and human rights. For them border security is derived from the protection of human rights and human security in a borderland region of intercultural exchange, in which the human rights to life, health, safety, a living wage, and cultural dignity must be defended by people on both sides of the border, regardless of the national origin or formal legal status of border-crossers. Rather than viewing the border as a strict boundary dividing nationalities, countries, and ethical responsibilities along territorial lines, these NGOs view it as a porous borderland of interaction, in which the human and national security of the two nations are inextricably interdependent. Two prime examples of the social construction of a borderland region appeared in the unexpectedly large pro-migrant demonstration of March 24, 2006, and the 200,000-person pro-migrant demonstration of April 10, 2006, both of which took place on the streets of downtown Phoenix. In the demonstration on March 24 protestors rejected US House of Representatives Bill HR4437, which proposed to make it a felony for undocumented people to live and work in the United States. Protestors' signs called for "Safe, Humane, and Just Borders" and for "A Path to Permanent Residency" for undocumented migrants. On April 10 one of the key chants of undocumented Mexican migrant demonstrators was "*Somos América*" ("We are America"). The essence of that statement is a conception of the borderlands according to which anyone who contributes work to a society is rooted and belongs in that society.

Proponents of the third perspective on the social construction of security embrace a binational notion of a "smart border" that effectively regulates border-crossings with the dual objectives of balancing security concerns and advocating economic integration via cross-border commerce, labour movements, and trade. Smart-border proponents envision multiple levels of government on both sides of the border working cooperatively to filter out criminals and terrorists while retaining a border porous enough to permit ongoing economic integration via flows of shoppers, tourists, labourers, goods, and commerce in general. The most vocal proponents of this perspective are local government officials, particularly the governors of Arizona and Sonora, the mayors of Phoenix and Tucson and of various Arizona–Sonora border towns, and key segments of the private business sectors on both sides of the border. In Sonora, tourist industry representatives, whose revenues depend on tourists from Arizona favour this approach, while in Arizona the smart-border concept is advocated primarily by business interests and organizations in industries dependent on migrant labour, such as construction and services (restaurants, hotels, and resorts), as well as other labour-intensive industries such as landscaping. The president of the Arizona Contractors Association, for instance, has publicly embraced a smart border implemented in conjunction with a national guest-worker policy. A federally approved and locally implemented guest-worker policy would not only require federal and local officials on the US side of the border to cooperate significantly more than they have in the past, but it would also require cooperation, at both local and national levels of government, between the United States and Mexico, a form of cooperation that is currently latent at best.

However, as the remainder of this chapter illustrates, civil society on the Arizona side of the borderlands is so mobilized around, and divided on, issues of border security and cross-border migration that a smart-border security policy is unlikely to emerge or succeed. Despite some support among local-government officials and some private-sector actors, an effective Canada–US style of smart border, with multiple levels of government cooperating on both sides of the border, has not successfully emerged in the Arizona–Sonora border area. The actions, or social agency, and the relative political clout of competing and divided local civic groups and social networks have effectively blocked the emergence of a culturally integrating cross-border region. Thus, despite strong structural market forces and cross-border trade between Arizona and Sonora, various local political actors have effectively disrupted, and continue to disrupt, the emergence of a culturally integrating cross-border region with a smart border. Instead, both personal-security and national-security conditions have increasingly deteriorated for residents of the borderlands. This increasing insecurity and lack of cultural integration in the Arizona–Sonora borderlands corroborates the theory of borderlands studies advanced by Emmanuel Brunet-Jailly in this volume.

BORDER COUNTY INSECURITY: ANTI-MIGRANT VIGILANTES IN COCHISE COUNTY

Since 1999 civilian anti-migrant vigilantes have increased the levels of economic and physical insecurity of those who live in and transit through the Arizona–Sonora borderlands bounded by Cochise County, Arizona. In 1999, when the US Border Patrol's Operation Safeguard 99 finished sealing the urban border at Nogales, and then again after the terrorist attacks against the United States on September 11, 2001, Cochise County became ground zero for the organizing of armed civilians and vigilantes dedicated to patrolling the southeastern Arizona side of the

US border for undocumented migrants. The stated purpose of these vigilantes and armed civilians is to publicize and bolster the border patrol's failed mission to stop undocumented migrants from crossing the Arizona–Sonora border. According to *The Militant* (June 26, 2000), anti-immigrant organizing began in 1999, when a Douglas rancher and Sierra Vista businessman, Roger Barnett, and twenty other ranchers signed a proclamation declaring that "if the government refuses to provide security, then the only recourse is to provide it ourselves" (cited in Border Action Network 2002). In the same year, Cochise County Concerned Citizens (CCCC), a citizens' support group allied with vigilante groups, was founded by Larry Vance (Border Action Network 2002, 4). The American Patrol's website (www.americanpatrol.com) reported that the CCCC contended that the US government had failed to defend American citizens from "foreign invasion" and called for the deployment of military troops or the National Guard at the US border (cited in Border Action Network 2002, 4). The Cochise County Board of Supervisors made a similar request of Jane Hall, then governor of Arizona, in May 2000, calling for deployment of the National Guard as administrative support for the US Border Patrol (Associated Press 2000). As well, as noted by Reuters wire service on May 16, 2000, the CCCC teamed up with a California-based anti-migrant organizer, Glenn Spencer, and the American Patrol group in California to proclaim a "shadow Border Patrol" to monitor federal border-patrol operations.

In the summer of 2000 a flyer and the website of Ranch Rescue, a Texas-based vigilante group founded by a rancher, Jack Foote, began recruiting armed civilians to come to Arizona to hunt "hordes of criminal aliens" (cited in Border Action Network 2002). After 9/11 Ranch Rescue stepped up its operations in Cochise County and in October 2002 it organized Operation Hawk, a paramilitary operation complete with armed volunteers dressed in camouflage fatigues.

The Cochise County towns of Tombstone, Douglas, and Sierra Vista also saw a post-9/11 rise in anti-migrant organizations that identified undocumented labourers from Mexico as threats to US national security. Beginning in late 2001, Chris Simcox, a recent arrival in Arizona from California and the editor of the local newspaper, *The Tombstone*, organized a volunteer civilian militia called Arizona Homeland Defense, later renamed the Minutemen, to patrol the Arizona border. In November 2002 Simcox declared: "I'm vigilant in providing homeland security. We're going to show America how this can be done by sane, responsible people" (Gannett News Service 2002). Along these same lines, during the spring of 2004 a homemade, handwritten anti-migrant sign appeared on the outskirts of Douglas, Arizona, proclaiming: "Terrorists love open borders. Remember 9-11." In Sierra Vista, home to the US Army's Fort Huachuca, soldiers were deployed to repair parts of the border fence, and the fort's sophisticated monitoring technologies found local applications in border surveillance (House 2005).

Many long-time residents of Cochise County expressed dismay and worry about this influx of armed volunteers from out of state, who would likely alienate their border neighbours just to the south. The border towns of Douglas and Agua Prieta have developed urban economies that revolve around their proximity to the US–Mexico border. Douglas, Arizona, is a small town of 14,312 people (as of the 2000 Census) and many of its merchants rely on cross-border shoppers from Mexico, who walk from Agua Prieta through the US Customs checkpoint daily to shop in Douglas supermarkets and other retail establishments. The Douglas economy also includes a private ranching and cattle-raising industry, and a number of the area's private ranches are situated right at the international border. (The Mexican Consul at Douglas, Miguel Escobar, cited Ron Tracy's as one such ranch in the Douglas area.) According to Mark Adams of Frontera de Cristo, the town's overall economy, once dependent on copper mining, now depends as much on commercial ties with cross-border Mexican shoppers, Mexican migrants, and human smugglers as it does on the economic and employment benefits provided by the extensive numbers of US Border Patrol personnel, whose salaries in the Douglas area amount annually to US$ 36 million.

In 2005, for example, Border Patrol personnel decided to boycott the Hungry Bear Café, a small food establishment in Douglas that was owned by a woman who had emigrated legally from Agua Prieta, after one of the restaurant's waitresses, also a legal immigrant, broke off an abusive relationship with a Border Patrol agent who frequented the restaurant. In retaliation, Border Patrol personnel who regularly patronized the restaurant stopped eating there, and the waitress was arrested on site by Border Patrol agents and incarcerated for three days in the immigration jail in Florence. The restaurant suffered financially until the boycott ended later that same year.

Agua Prieta is adjacent to Douglas on the Mexican side of the line. It is a larger town of 61,944 people (as of the 2000 Census) who are mainly employed in commerce and services, both legal and illicit, associated with the town's geographical location on the international border. Spurred on by the ABC Initiative crackdown in March 2004, the town's *casas de huéspedes* (guest houses) have continued to boom as migrants, smugglers, and returnee migrants who are deported to Mexico by the US government frequent them. The town's hotels, restaurants, and bars also cater to migrants, small-scale smugglers, and organized criminal traffickers of both humans and narcotics. Some hotels act as fronts for money-laundering by smugglers. In May 2004, for example, a man named Paredes, the owner of a large hotel in downtown Agua Prieta, and three members of his family were shot and killed in broad daylight in the hotel's restaurant. Paredes was the apparent victim of drug traffickers with whom he was competing for control of the drug-smuggling routes through southeastern Arizona (Associated Press 2004).

The cost of living in Agua Prieta, as in most border towns in Sonora, is quite high in relation to the low-wage structure and, due to the high cost of groceries, ordinary residents customarily walked to Douglas to buy groceries. However, anti-migrant organizing in Douglas and Cochise County in general since 9/11 has strained relations between the residents of the twin border-towns (Associated Press 2005). This has been particularly the case since April 2005, when Chris Simcox deployed civilian vigilante Minutemen volunteers, some of whom carried weapons, to patrol thirty-seven kilometres of desert between Douglas and Naco, Arizona, to the west. During that time retail business in Douglas dropped significantly as cross-border Mexican shoppers in Agua Prieta diminished in number in response to the Minutemen's presence (Associated Press 2005).

Residents and migrants who live in or transit through Cochise County, Douglas–Agua Prieta, and the Naco area must face the everyday insecurities generated by the actions of these anti-migrant vigilantes. Given the vigilantes' tendency toward racial profiling, many residents of Douglas, a town that is 92 percent Latino, live with the fear of being targeted by them. Local municipal authorities, as well as immigrant assistance networks, have attempted to publicize and mediate these increasing insecurities among both residents and migrants. For example, when the Minutemen deployed border patrols in April 2005, Ray Borane, mayor of Douglas, publicly stated his concern: "There was a lot of concern expressed right at the beginning. There is a sense of fear in Douglas among residents, a fear of being discriminated against. There was and is an aura of tension" (Associated Press 2005). Local humanitarian networks, such as the Center for Recuperation and Rehabilitation from Drug and Alcohol Addictions (CRREDA) in Agua Prieta, work with the Douglas-based group Frontera de Cristo (Healing Our Borders), a binational Presbyterian border ministry in Douglas–Agua Prieta, the Just Coffee cooperative of Agua Prieta, Humane Borders in Tucson, and Christian Peacemaker Teams in Douglas, to aid migrants with donations of water, food, and clothing. These humanitarian networks also work to bring about greater cross-border cultural understanding and improve conditions of human security in general for migrants and residents in a politically polarized landscape.

Problems of increasing tensions and insecurity posed by anti-migrant vigilantes and by the dangers of border-crossing in remote areas have sparked expanded networking by humanitarian assistance organizations in the Douglas–Agua Prieta area. In 2005 CRREDA, Frontera de Cristo, and No More Deaths organized and operated a binational migrant assistance camp in the desert about twenty kilometres east of Agua Prieta, toward Naco (see figure 6.1). Three days into the encampment, in early March, several unmarked trucks manned by Chris Simcox's Homeland Defense (Minutemen) volunteers appeared on the US side of the border in front of the camp. Simcox told a reporter that he had learned of the camp's location from a contact in the US Border Patrol (Ibarra 2005). According to Simcox, he and his companions were there "helping out the Department of Homeland Security, being their eyes and ears, spotting and reporting" (Ibarra 2005), and this particular outing was a "dress rehearsal' for the Minutemen's deployment the following month, April 2005, west of Douglas–Agua Prieta. The face-to-face confrontational posture of the vigilantes in military attire vis-à-vis camp volunteers was symptomatic of the increasingly tense borderlands environment. The potential for violent confrontation and the implied danger of such encounters in the wilderness have continued to grow in the context of the Cochise County border, as vigilantes from Tombstone, Sierra Vista, and Douglas increasingly deploy as armed civilian forces. When the author interviewed the previous Mexican Consul at Douglas, Miguel Escobar Valdez, in May 2004, he decried anti-migrant vigilante activity in Cochise County and mentioned having had to notify next of kin in Mexico of migrants who died while crossing in the Agua Prieta–Douglas area.

The federal, locally funded Mexican migrant assistance corps, the Grupo Beta, aids stranded migrants who lose their way on the Mexican side of the border, although its operatives, who are officially prohibited by the Mexican government from carrying arms, increasingly find themselves in greater danger as armed human traffickers replace small-scale smugglers and armed drug traffickers become more prone to violence as they attempt to evade enhanced US Border Patrol surveillance.

SONORAN WILDERNESS INSECURITY: MIGRANTS, PARK RANGERS, AND NATIONAL PARKS AT RISK

During 2004 a key route for migrants crossing the Arizona–Sonora border—and, for many of them, dying en route—was through desert wilderness from the Sonoran town of Altar to Sasabe, Arizona, and then through the Tohono O'odham Nation Reservation near Sells. In 2005 two popular routes were from Sasabe to Three Points, near Tucson, or from Sasabe through the Buenos Aires National Wildlife Refuge and then on to Arivaca, near Tucson (see figure 6.2). In Mexico the town of Altar had become a major staging ground for migrants planning to cross. Migrants gathered there and then travelled in vans and pickup trucks across the border to Sasabe, a tiny town in the middle of the desert west of Nogales. Two hundred and twenty-four migrants died that year in the US Border Patrol's Tucson sector alone, with heavy concentrations of deaths occurring on the Tohono O'odham Nation Reservation, particularly just east of Sells (see figures 2.5 and 2.6).

Founded in June 2000, Humane Borders is a faith-based humanitarian network that currently maintains seventy-three water stations for migrants, which are marked with blue flags and are found throughout the desert wilderness of Pima County and outside Agua Prieta on the Mexican side of the border. The Pima County Board of Supervisors cooperates with Humane Borders and contributes funds to its network of water stations. Although from 2002 to 2004 many migrants died near Sells, the Tohono O'odham Nation does not permit Humane Borders to place water stations on its land. It did, however, partner with the federal DHS in the ABC Initiative, Phases I and II, in 2004-05 (US DHS 2005). The federal Department of the Interior also partnered with the DHS to implement the ABC Initiative on the various national wildlife refuges, national forests, and national monument lands scattered across southern Arizona at the border. However, several of the Department of the Interior's wildlife agencies, specifically the Fish and Wildlife Service and the National Park Service, as well as wilderness land preserves, allow Humane Borders to situate and maintain water stations along highly travelled migrant routes through federal preserves, in an effort to decrease the number of migrant deaths from heat exhaustion and dehydration (by far the most common cause of migrant death in Arizona).

Indeed, the largest percentage of the land along the Arizona border with Sonora consists of federal lands, including wildlife refuges, a national forest, national preserves, a Native American tribal reservation, a US Air Force and Marine Corps gunnery range, and US Bureau of Land Management and other federal lands leased to private ranchers (see figure 6.2). Since about 2000 the Cabeza Prieta and Buenos Aires National Wildlife refuges and the Organ Pipe Cactus National Monument, along Arizona's southwestern border, have become major transit sites for undocumented migrants, as well as for US Border Patrol surveillance and enforcement operations.

Researcher John Slown wrote an article in 2003 about the federal Department of the Interior's Fish and Wildlife Service's Comprehensive Conservation Plan for the Cabeza Prieta refuge and the endangerment of the Sonoran pronghorn antelope. In the introduction to his article, Slown described the Cabeza Prieta refuge as follows: "Imagine a dry-as-dust land baked by 118 degree summer heat, crossed by a single road and facing 25,000 trespassers each year." He also reported that at the Cabeza Prieta refuge the border patrol has placed sensors on known migrant paths, which have recorded 4,000 to 6,000 crossings per month during the peak crossing months of April, May, and June each year (Slown 2003).

In 2004 a park ranger at the Buenos Aires refuge expressed to the author as much concern about border-patrol vehicles' destruction of the refuge's wilderness character and wildlife habitat as about similar destruction resulting from migrant foot traffic and trash, and from the vehicles of human and narcotics traffickers. However, John Slown, in his discussions with another park ranger at the refuge, was struck by the ranger's overwhelming concern for the well-being of the refuge's wildlife, which was well beyond any concern for the lives of the many migrants who cross through it each day. That said, satellite images comparing the vegetation cover of the refuge in 1986 and in 2001 indicated increasing degradation of Buenos Aires's wilderness habitat (Slown 2003).

Despite increasing humanitarian social networking, water-station installations, and migrant assistance camps, the lives of migrants are increasingly threatened as they enter ever more remote stretches of desert wilderness on foot. Threatened as well are the wilderness habitats and national park rangers stationed and working on remote public lands. The personal insecurity and dangers faced by park rangers have increased in recent years as heavily armed narco-traffickers cross the border via public preserves, either to evade heightened US Border Patrol surveillance on the Arizona side or to evade Mexican law enforcement on the Sonoran side. In August 2002, for example, a known narcotics trafficker operating in the Sonoyta area under the alias "El Zarco" shot and killed National Park Service ranger Kris Eggle with an AK-47 weapon at Organ Pipe National Monument, the federal preserve immediately east of the Cabeza Prieta wilderness refuge. Eggle was killed helping federal border-patrol agents pursue two narcotics traffickers who had fled over the Arizona border while being pursued by Mexican authorities. In effect, the park ranger was called upon to act as if he were a US Border Patrol agent, even though his role was clearly to protect the refuge's wildlife and habitat. His killer was a suspect in a hit squad execution on a Sonoyta ranch in retribution for a drug-related debt (Associated Press 2002, August 16). In direct response to his murder, the National Park Service decided to build a major vehicle barrier in a reinforced concrete base along the entire fifty-kilometre length of Organ Pipe Monument's southern boundary with Sonora. As of October 2005, that barrier was still under construction, and the National Park Service had announced further plans to build a second barrier at the Coronado National Memorial, on the border just west of Douglas (Associated Press 2002, December 8).

Since the late 1990s, when the Clinton Administration sealed off most Arizona border-crossings in urban areas, particularly at Nogales, organized criminal traffickers have increasingly smuggled people, narcotics, and weapons through US national preserves and public lands, which are generally the most remote areas of the Arizona borderlands. Since 9/11 heightened US Border Patrol activity in Arizona has further increased the organized criminal smuggling presence in national preserves and diverted still more border-crossings and smuggling onto these preserves. Consequently, the risks, hazards, and insecurities of being a National Park Service ranger in southern Arizona have increased substantially, as have national parks' expenditures on what is now referred to as homeland security carried out by National Park Service personnel. After the murder of Kris Eggle in Organ Pipe, the service increased the number of park rangers working at the monument and on other preserves in southern Arizona. At Organ Pipe alone, the number of rangers went from three at the time of Eggle's murder in 2002 to fourteen in 2005 (Reese 2005, 2).

Underscoring the mounting threats faced by park rangers, a report by the Fraternal Order of Police in 2003 ranked Organ Pipe National Monument as the most dangerous park in the United States (cited in Reese 2005, 1). Speaking in December 2002, a former assistant director of the Federal Bureau of Investigation commented that the narco-traffickers, human smugglers, and potential terrorists whom park rangers are expected to arrest are more prone to violence than ever before (Gehrke 2002). Currently, rangers in the borderlands parks of southern Arizona usually carry weapons—M-16s, AR-15s, and/or side arms—in order to perform their dual set of duties: preservation of, and information-sharing about, wildlife and wilderness habitats; and national-security, Border Patrol–like functions of stopping drug traffickers, human smugglers, and undocumented migrants, and arresting violent criminals (Gehrke 2002; Turf 2004). For example, in early February 2004 Thane Weigand, chief ranger at Coronado National Monument just west of Douglas, described his experience of supervising groups of armed park rangers dressed in camouflage, wearing bulletproof vests, and carrying powerful flashlights, who were spending nights waiting for smugglers in remote parts of the park's Huachuca Mountains. As for the park rangers' new national security duties, Weigand said, "We have a responsibility to provide homeland security. Being on the border, we don't have a choice" (Turf 2004).

The National Park Service's increased spending on security since 9/11, especially in parks in Arizona and elsewhere in the US Southwest, has severely strained its budget and had deleterious effects on the entire national park system. Organ Pipe, for example, hired nine new protection rangers at a cost of US$ 900,000 and has continued to build the vehicle barrier along its border at a cost of US$ 7 million, but those expenditures did not include funds to repair damaged habitats or care for park resources and wildlife (US National Park Service 2004). Threats to the park and its wildlife were highlighted in January 2004 when Organ Pipe was named one of the ten most endangered parks in the country (US National Park Service 2004), a rating based on the scale of damage to habitat and wildlife that had resulted from hundreds of kilometres of illegal trails and roads being carved through the wilderness preserve, the draining and polluting of water sources, and huge amounts of trash being discarded by traffickers, undocumented migrants, and border patrol agents crossing through federal park lands. Overall, the National Park Service manages nearly 600 kilometres of land along the US–Mexico border, but since September 11, 2001, the US Congress has allocated US$ 120 million to the National Park Service to enhance security, and the parks have spent US$ 21 million more on security alone. Even with such security expenditures, park rangers report that smugglers' equipment typically rivals their own, and includes radios, cell phones, and often guns (Turf 2004). In July 2005 the US House of Representatives Resource Committee commented that park security expenditures allocated to block potential terrorists, human and narcotics traffickers, and undocumented migrants from crossing through border parks have diverted too many funds away from park maintenance and other necessities (Talhelm 2005). In 2005 security-related operating costs for the National Park Service soared to about US$ 40 million in annual recurring costs (US Newswire 2005).

Organized crime in southern Arizona parks has accelerated as US border crackdowns have rendered organized criminal trafficking of humans and narcotics ever more lucrative. Since 9/11, the US government has responded to this situation by calling on the National Park Service to supplement the DHS's border-patrol duties, but without budgetary compensation. The resulting militarization of national park rangers has diverted designated money, resources, and attention away from their fundamental roles of securing and preserving wilderness habitats and wildlife for all national parks in the United States. With US$ 48 million spent by the National Park Service for security-related construction costs alone at five park locations (including the vehicle barriers at Organ Pipe and Coronado), parks such as those at Carlsbad Caverns, the Grand Canyon, Zion, and Bryce Canyon have suffered a dramatic decline in basic upkeep, visitor services, and preservation of park resources (US Newswire 2005).

Thus, during the past five years, US national security policy and related crackdowns at the Arizona border have not only made the Sonoran wilderness more dangerous, but also made the people who live in and transit through it feel less secure.

URBAN BORDERLANDS INSECURITY: CONFLATING ORGANIZED CRIMINAL SMUGGLERS AND UNDOCUMENTED IMMIGRANTS IN THE PHOENIX METROPOLITAN AREA

In the face of heightened US national security following 9/11, metropolitan Phoenix has peaked as an urban focus for international criminal smuggling operations. Organized criminal human traffickers, especially those who hold undocumented migrants hostage until their smuggling fees are paid, have operated in increasing numbers in the metropolitan area since security policy was enhanced on the Arizona border in the late 1990s. The scope of these criminal operations is illustrated by the many migrant drop houses operated by criminal traffickers throughout metropolitan Phoenix. A spokesperson for the US Immigration and Customs Enforcement (ICE) agency recently called Phoenix "a transportation hub for smugglers" (Gonzalez and Johnson 2005). Clearly, unresolved federal issues of how to regulate undocumented migration and implement homeland security have contributed to accelerated criminal human smuggling activity in Arizona, with metropolitan Phoenix bearing the brunt of it. The lack of a federal guest-worker policy to regulate undocumented migration has also helped to spawn criminal industries of fake ID production and automobile theft, both of which flourish in metropolitan Phoenix and grow out of organized criminal trafficking in humans (Wagner 2005).

Accelerating human smuggling, undocumented migration, and homeland security issues have essentially split the organizational and policy landscape of metropolitan Phoenix and the state of Arizona into two opposing camps. In one camp are local residents who prefer to have relatively free movement across the border, or a smart-border system that would filter out criminals and terrorists while regulating legal guest workers. In the other camp are those who favour a border closed almost entirely to immigrants and migrant labourers. In a poll of 600 Arizona voters conducted from October 6 to 9, 2005, 68 percent said that they believed that some undocumented workers with no criminal record should be allowed to stay in the United States (Carroll 2005, A1, A19). In other words, most respondents did not want all undocumented migrants sent home, even though 79 percent of these same respondents felt that undocumented migrants were a burden on the state, given their use of social services. In contrast, a minority of those polled, 28 percent, stated that undocumented workers should be sent home, and another 4 percent said that they didn't know. As for opinions on national security, an overwhelming majority of those polled was skeptical of national border security. Nearly two-thirds believed that the border was not secure and, more specifically, 64 percent believed that the United States had not been successful in securing the border. Eighty-five percent of the 600 respondents stated that the possibility of terrorists entering the country through an unsecured border was a major concern. Only 34 percent believed that the United States had been moderately successful in securing the border (Carroll 2005, A19).

The division in Washington, DC, over immigration policy has led to a deep division between local-government and political officials in metropolitan Phoenix. In one camp are those state officials who want to implement a smart-border policy. In the other are local officials who tilt toward closing the US border to Mexican immigrants entirely. The state's Democratic governor, Janet Napolitano, has been placed in the awkward position of trying to mediate these two opposing stances, while still providing border security and maintaining favourable trade relations between Arizona and Sonora. The governor has essentially opted for a multi-level governance approach to border security whereby state and local officials would work with federal DHS agencies to implement a smart border capable of filtering out organized criminal smugglers and potential terrorists. Some local officials, however, have taken an avowedly anti-migrant stance, and the federal DHS has offered little in the way of cooperation with the governor or with Arizona law enforcement. For example, until she declared a state of emergency on Arizona's southern border on August 15, 2005, Governor Napolitano was unable to get the Phoenix branch of ICE that was assigned to targeting criminal smugglers and drug traffickers in Phoenix to cooperate with state agencies. Until then the ICE's Phoenix office had stonewalled her proposal to share a dozen Arizona Department of Public Safety officers with ICE to assist the federal agency in targeting human and drug traffickers in metropolitan Phoenix (Wagner 2005, A18). In general ICE and DHS agreed to increase cooperation only after the governor declared a border emergency.

While Governor Napolitano was battling with ICE officials in Phoenix to have them cooperate with local law enforcement in targeting smugglers, she signed a state bill that gave local police the authority to arrest "coyotes" (human smugglers), especially those in metropolitan Phoenix who coerced migrants into forced labour or prostitution. It went into effect on August 12, 2005, just three days before her border-emergency declaration. As noted earlier, her declaration resulted in ICE agents cooperating with local police to arrest coyotes (Scutari 2005, A1, A4), but Maricopa County Attorney Andrew Thomas, a Republican in charge of criminal prosecutions in metropolitan Phoenix, went one step further. He immediately attempted to expand the scope of the coyote law by broadly reinterpreting it to support arresting all undocumented migrants (Kiefer 2005, August 21, B1, B7). In effect Thomas embraced the side of the immigration debate in Arizona that essentially favours closing US borders to all migrant labour. He stated publicly that he believed that Arizona's conspiracy statutes gave him the authority to prosecute undocumented migrants under the coyote law (Kiefer 2005, August 21, B1, B7).

Upon Thomas's announcement, Maricopa County Sheriff Joe Arpaio initially articulated his own different approach to enforcing the coyote law on the streets of metropolitan Phoenix: "I want the authority to lock up smugglers, but I am not going to lock up illegals hanging around street corners. I'm not going to waste my resources going after a guy in a truck when he picks up five illegals to go trim palm trees" (Kiefer 2005, A4). Less than a month later, however, Arpaio asked County Attorney Thomas to clarify certain points of the law, specifically, whether county sheriff's officers could and should ask suspected undocumented migrants their nationality; whether officers should arrest migrants not suspected of being smugglers; and, if so, where the sheriff's office should incarcerate so many people (Kiefer 2005, September 30). Thomas responded that undocumented migrants could indeed be arrested if the sheriff's office had evidence that they had "conspired to be smuggled with a given coyote," although they "would have to have corroborating evidence" (Kiefer 2005, September 30). That evidence could include other witnesses' testimony and proof that the migrant had paid the coyote to be transported. Sheriff Arpaio then articulated what that policy would entail in terms of everyday operations:

> You arrest a smuggler, you have 50 guys there. We would have to hold those people as witnesses. We had no authority to hold them because we'd have to call the feds, and then they would have to hold those

> people . . . It gives me the authority now to arrest everybody involved in that situation and not have to rely on the feds. (quoted in Kiefer 2005, September 30)

The resource implications of Thomas's interpretation of the coyote law for Maricopa County and its taxpayers are essentially twofold. First, the county's "Tent City" jail would have to be expanded to accommodate such arrests, which could result in many undocumented migrants, as well as legal residents arrested mistakenly, being held in tent city jails in a metropolitan area known for its hot climate. Second, in the event of arrests of large groups of people, Maricopa County would have to hire private attorneys on contract at public expense in order to assign every suspected "conspirator" a separate attorney and avoid later conflicts of interest given the limited number of attorneys in the public defender's office (Kiefer 2005, September 30).

Thomas's decision to broaden the scope of the coyote law to allow state and local officials to arrest and prosecute undocumented migrants as "co-conspirators" in their own smuggling will likely not improve border security. Rather, it has the potential to increase racial profiling of legal residents by Maricopa County Sheriff's deputies, increase false arrests of legal Latino residents in metropolitan Phoenix, and divert scarce resources away from the full-fledged pursuit of organized criminal smuggling gangs. Arresting groups of fifty migrants at a time, as Sheriff Arpaio suggested, would quickly inundate the county's jails and strain its budget with outsourced public-defender expenses to private attorneys. Diverting county law-enforcement resources away from criminal smuggling rings would simply undermine the intent of the coyote law: to target criminal networks of human traffickers. Since these are the same networks that local and federal officials warn are capable of smuggling terrorists and weapons of mass destruction into the United States, Thomas's distortion of the coyote law stands to irreparably harm its local-level contribution to a smart border that could filter out such terrorists and criminal networks. Indeed, Thomas's conflation of undocumented migrants with criminal smugglers replicates at the local level the failure of the US government to formulate a national immigration policy on undocumented migration that would distinguish government regulation of migrant labourers from the prosecution of terrorists and the criminal smuggling networks capable of aiding terrorists. Giving local police the authority to arrest undocumented migrants as co-conspirators of coyotes will not make residents of Arizona and of the United States, in general, more secure from criminal smugglers, potential terrorists, and armed vigilantes.

However, Thomas displayed his penchant for prosecuting undocumented migrants as criminals and his political support for anti-migrant vigilante groups when he declined to prosecute army reservist Patrick Haab. On April 10, 2005, while the Minutemen were deployed in the Douglas area, Haab held seven men at gunpoint in classic vigilante fashion, threatening to kill them, at a remote rest stop at Sentinel on Arizona Interstate 8 highway. The men were later found to be undocumented migrants. Maricopa County sheriff's deputies immediately arrested Haab on seven counts of aggravated assault with a deadly weapon, and Sheriff Arpaio publicly defended the arrest, saying that no one can force people out of their cars at gunpoint without probable cause to arrest them (Anglen and Carroll 2005). However, several days later Thomas declined to prosecute Haab, claiming that Arizona citizens have a right to make a citizen's arrest of anyone suspected of a felony (Rotstein 2005). Instead, Thomas charged one of Haab's seven victims with a felony crime as an alleged human smuggler and the other six with being his co-conspirators (Rotstein 2005).

Notwithstanding that Arizona has an important and continuing history of close economic ties with Sonora, Mexico, Andrew Thomas and the anti-migrant social networks that have promoted Proposition 200, which mandates that all Arizona state employees deny public welfare benefits to undocumented migrants, repeatedly act at the local level to undermine the implementation of a smart Arizona–Sonora border that would filter out criminals rather than migrant labourers. The governor of Arizona, and other officials such as state Attorney General Terry Goddard, favour a smart border that would sustain the process of US–Mexico economic integration while filtering out criminal smugglers and potential terrorists. According to a University of Arizona study, both the governor and the attorney general valued the fact that residents of Sonora comprise 90 percent of the Mexican cross-border shoppers, who spend about US$ 1 billion a year in Arizona (cited in Higuera 2005). For political and ideological reasons, however, the attorney for Maricopa County seems willing to open a Pandora's box of possible false arrests not only of Mexican shoppers but also of Latino residents of metropolitan Phoenix. Thus residents and those who move through the urban borderlands of Phoenix are considerably less secure because of inflammatory legal opinions and federal immigration policies that allow some local Arizona officials, such as Thomas, to treat undocumented migrants as criminals.

CONCLUSION: LOCAL CULTURES OF BOUNDARY ENFORCEMENT AND THE UNDERMINING OF A SMART BORDER POLICY

One segment of Arizona's local culture, its anti-migrant networks and activists, is currently working to undermine the emergence of a Canada–US style of smart border based upon multi-level governance at the Arizona–Sonora border. Instead of employing their local political clout to construct a smart border capable of filtering out organized criminal traffickers and terrorists, these anti-migrant activists are organizing to label and pursue ordinary migrants as criminals. This trend reflects the segment of local civil society that is intent on national security being contingent upon the enforcement of a strict boundary between the United States and Mexico.

This local trend was aggravated at the national level in early 2006 with the passage by the US House of Representatives of Bill HR4437, which made it a felony for an undocumented person to live and work in the United States. These attempts to treat all undocumented migrants as criminals harm smart-border practices by threatening to divert law-enforcement attention and scarce resources away from pursuing organized criminals and human traffickers toward targeting multitudes of ordinary migrants. Such strict boundary-enforcement proposals are not only prohibitively expensive but also potentially counterproductive. From a national security perspective, devoting too many government resources to apprehending ordinary migrants leaves the US border less secure vis-à-vis organized criminals and terrorists.

Nevertheless, as of April 12, 2006, the Arizona legislature gave final approval to Bill 1157, making undocumented migrant status in Arizona a crime: a Class 1 misdemeanour for a first illegal entry into Arizona and a felony after the first offence. Ironically, Cochise County Sheriff Larry Dever, who helped two Arizona Republican state senators push the bill through the legislature, later commented that it is essentially "meaningless" for his purposes because it contains no funding to build additional jails to hold illegal migrants (Ruelas 2006). He also complained that local sheriffs' and county attorneys' offices lack the funding and resources required to convict first-time trespassers of a misdemeanour in order to convict them of a felony for a second offence. As a result Dever declared his support for those law-enforcement officials who had written to Governor Janet Napolitano asking her to veto the bill, which they see as pure politics and as having essentially no impact on illicit immigration or border security (Ruelas 2006). Notwithstanding their view of the bill as meaningless, one anti-migrant legislative activist, Russell Pearce, declared, "This is common-sense legislation. . . . It's about time we started standing up for the legal residents, the legal citizens of the United States, and enforce our laws [and] protect our neighborhoods [*sic*]" (cited in Newton 2006). The Arizona Coalition for Migrant Rights, which helped to organize the massive migrant rights' demonstration of April 10, 2006, immediately issued a call via MigrantRights.org for coalition supporters to urge the governor to veto the bill. For these activists the struggle to construct security in Arizona must include the right of migrants not to be labelled *a priori* and targeted as criminals.

This case study of the Arizona–Sonora border corroborates arguments advanced by the theory of borderlands studies articulated by Emmanuel Brunet-Jailly in this volume. Brunet-Jailly's theory posits that local border culture and local political clout play essential roles in the emergence of a borderland region that is culturally emerging and integrating. As the theory suggests, in the case of Arizona the local political culture, and the political clout of anti-migrant activists and networks, have effectively blocked the emergence of a smart border and of an integrating borderland region, despite the extensive cross-border market forces at work in the area.

Figure 2.1 Arizona–Sonora Border Towns

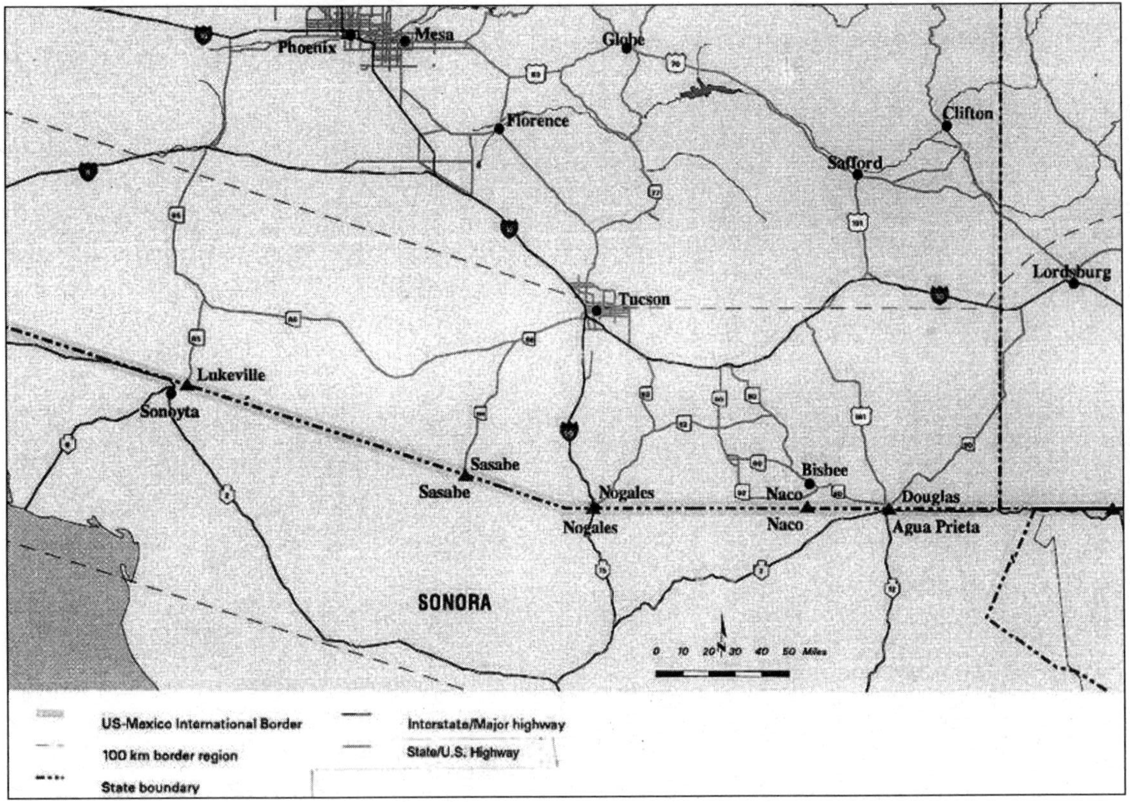

Source: Barton-Aschman and La Empresa, 1997

Figure 2.2 Federal Lands and Indian Reservations in Arizona

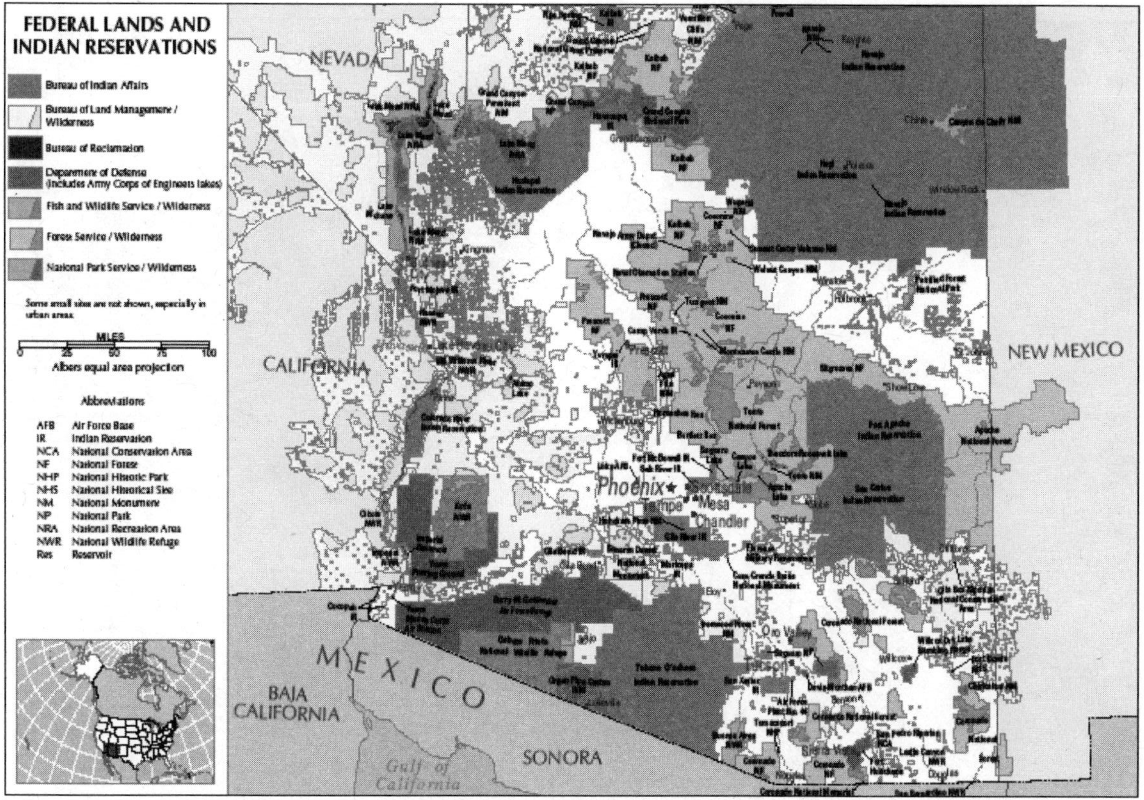

Source: *The National Atlas of the United States of America.*

Figure 2.3 Migrant Deaths in the Tucson Sector, 2003

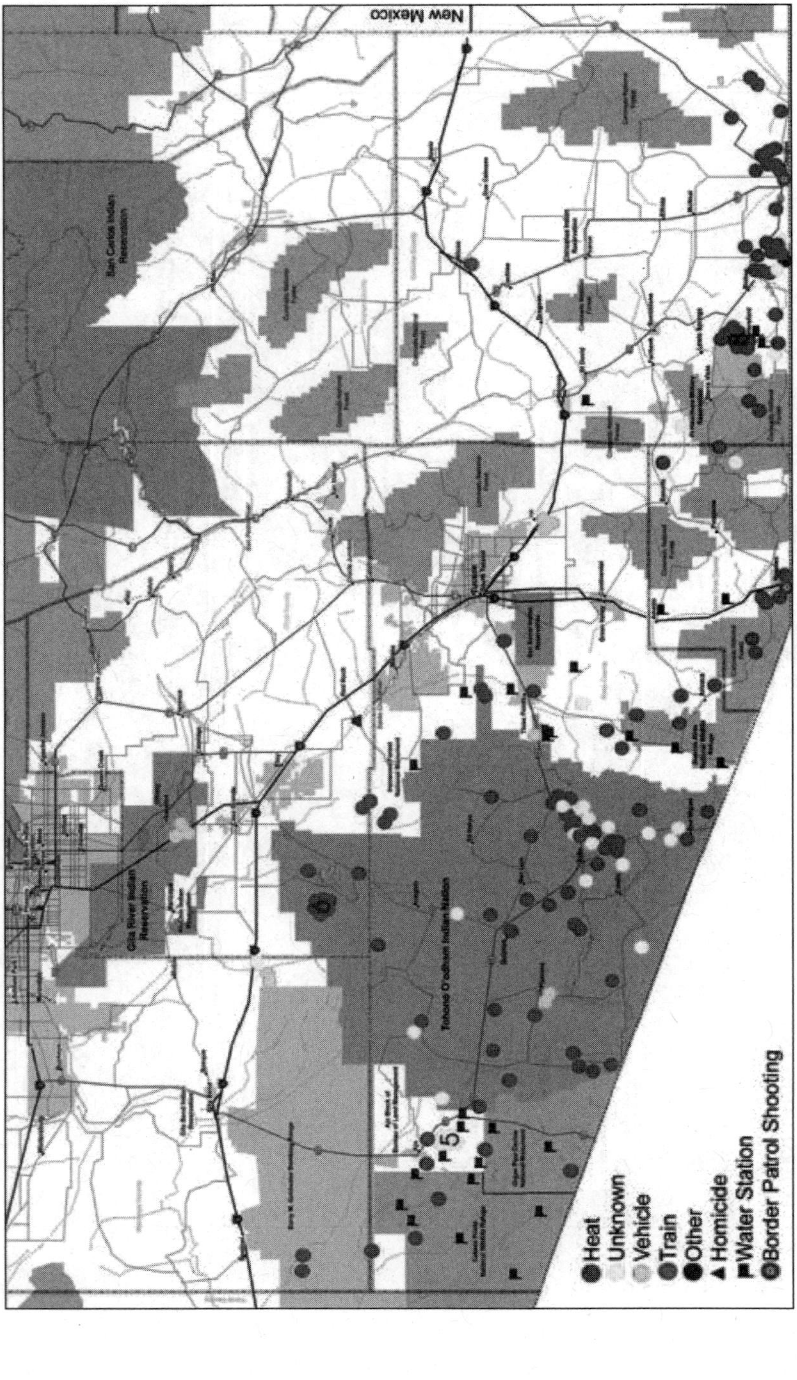

Source: Human Borders, Tucson, Arizona

Figure 2.4 Migrant Deaths in the Tucson Sector, 2004

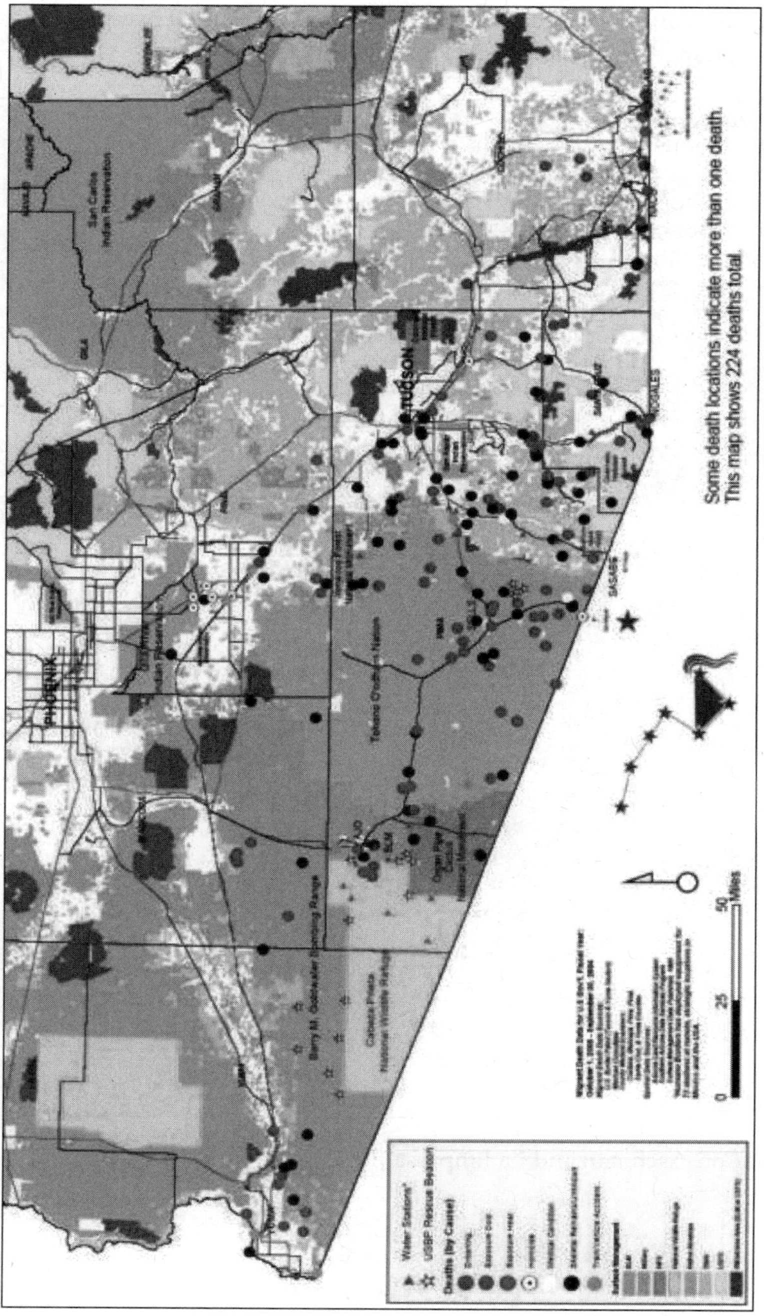

Source: Humane Borders, Tucson, Arizona

Figure 2.5 Migrant Deaths at One Day's, Two Days', and Three Days' Walking Distance from Sasabe to Three Points, Arizona

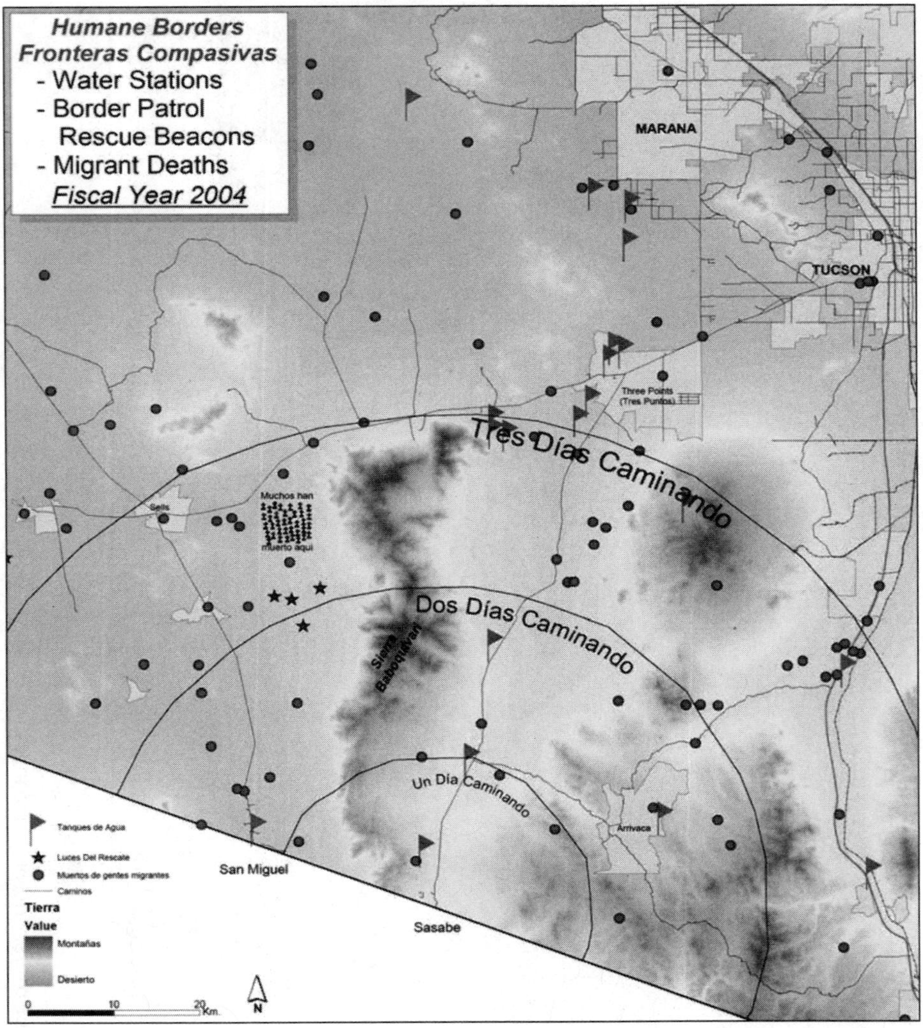

Source: Barton-Aschman and La Empresa, 1997

Figure 2.6 Migrant Deaths in California and the West Desert of Arizona, 2000–04

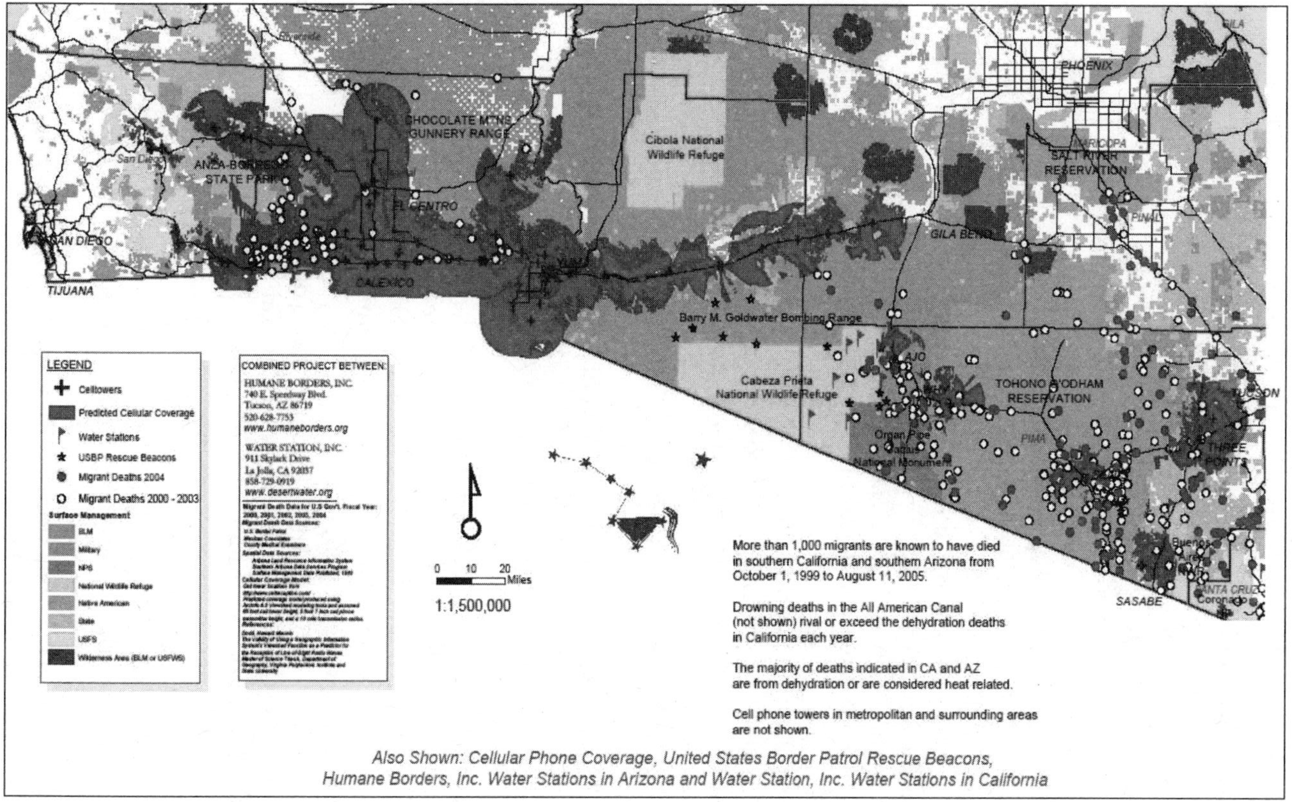

LITERATURE CITED

Anglen, Robert, and Susan Carroll. 2005. "Case Sounds Vigilante Alarm." *The Arizona Republic* [Phoenix] (April 13), B1–B2.

Associated Press. 2000. "Supervisors Formally Ask Governor for National Guard" (May 16).

———. 2004. "Killings in Border Town Likely Drug Turf War" (May 7).

Associated Press, State and Local Wire. 2002. "Mexico Says Ranger Killed By Man Fleeing Botched Attack" (august 16).

———. 2002. "National Park Service Plans to Build Vehicle Barriers Along Border" (December 8).

———. 2005. "Minuteman Project Still Creating Tension, Hurting Douglas Businesses" (April 15).

Border Action Network. 2002. *Hate or Heroism: Vigilantes on the Arizona–Mexico Border: A Report by Border Action Network*. Tucson, AZ: Border Action Network.

Brunet-Jailly, Emmanuel. 2004. "NAFTA, Economic Integration, and the Canadian–American Security Regime in the Post-September 11, 2001 Era: Multi-level Governance and Transparent Border?" *Journal of Borderland Studies* 19:1, 123–43.

———. 2005. "Theorizing Borders: An Interdisciplinary Perspective." *Geopolitics* 10, 633–49.

Carroll, Susan. 2005. "Most in Poll Would Let Immigrants Stay." *The Arizona Republic* [Phoenix] (October 19), A1, A19.

Gannett News Service. 2002. "Founder of Armed Border Patrol Group Rejects 'Rambo' Label" (November 25).

Gehrke, Robert. 2002. "Park Rangers Being Called Upon to Deal with Crime as well as Critters." Associated Press (December 28).

Gonzalez, Daniel, and Weldon B. Johnson. 2005. "Four Migrant Drophouses Found in Valley: Wealthy Areas Not Immune." *The Arizona Republic* [Phoenix] (March 17), B1–B2.

Hawley, Chris. 2005. "In Altar, Teeming with Transients, Small Town Shares Arizona's Conflicts over Impact of Illegal Immigration." *The Arizona Republic* [Phoenix] (August 21), A1, A20.

Higuera, Jonathan J. 2005. "Historic Economic Ties." *The Arizona Republic* [Phoenix] (August 20), A18.

House, Billy. 2005. "Border Agents Get Help from Above: Unmanned Aircraft Arriving in Arizona Next Month." *The Arizona Republic* [Phoenix] (August 31), B1.

Ibarra, Ignacio. 2005. "'No More Deaths Camp' an Oasis for Migrants." *Arizona Daily Star* [Tucson] (March 2).

Kiefer, Michael. 2005. "Law Agencies Cool to New 'Coyote' Law: Units Say They Will Abide by Federal, Not State, Requirements." *The Arizona Republic* [Phoenix] (August 21), B1, B7.

Kiefer, Michael. 2005. "Smuggled Can Be 'Conspirators': 'Coyote' Opinion Adds Teeth to Law." *The Arizona Republic* [Phoenix] (September 30), B6.

Newton, Casey. 2006. "Senate OKs Arrests of Immigrant Trespassers: Bill Sent to Governor." *The Arizona Republic* [Phoenix] (April 13).

Reese, April. 2005. "National Parks: Policing Parks Can Be Dangerous—and Sometimes Deadly." Greenwire, Environment and Energy Publishing, LLC.

Rotstein, Arthur H. 2005. "Army Reservist Who Held Migrants at Gunpoint Won't Be Prosecuted." Associated Press, State and Local Wire (April 21).

Ruelas, Richard. 2006. "Sheriff: Migrant Bill Worthless Without Funding." *The Arizona Republic* [Phoenix] (April 14), B12.

Scutari, Chip. 2005. "US to Aid Border Fight: Homeland Security Heeds Governor's Plea to Help Combat Smuggling." *The Arizona Republic* [Phoenix] (August 23), A1, A4.

Slown, John. 2003. "Taking Refuge." *American Planning Association,* April 21. [online]. www.fws.gov/southwest/refuges/plan/refuges.pdf [consulted April 14, 2006].

Talhelm, Jennifer. 2005. "Border Security Stretches National Parks' Budget, Resources." Associate Press, State and Local Wire (July 8).

Turf, Luke. 2004. "Searches for Migrants, Drugs Divert National Park Resources." *The Tucson Citizen* (February 8).

United States Department of Homeland Security. 2005. *Fact Sheet: Arizona Border Control Initiative—Phase II*. Washington, DC: Government Printing Office.

United States National Park Service. 2004. *Organ Pipe Cactus National Monument Named to List of Ten Most Endangered National Parks*. Washington, DC: Government Printing Office.

US Newswire, Flagstaff, Arizona. 2005. "Congressional Hearing Examines Health of Southwest National Parks, Says NPCA" (October 13).

Wagner, Dennis. 2005. "Border Governors Unite: Arizona–Sonora Duo Tackle Immigration." *The Arizona Republic* [Phoenix] (August 20), A1, A18–A19.

CHAPTER 3

BORDER ACROBATICS BETWEEN THE EUROPEAN UNION AND AFRICA: THE MANAGEMENT OF SEALED-OFF PERMEABILITY ON THE BORDERS OF CEUTA AND MELILLA

Xavier Ferrer Gallardo

Ceuta and Melilla, two North African territories under Spanish sovereignty, automatically became parts of the European Union (EU, then known as the European Communities, or EC) in 1986, when Spain joined it. Ceuta has a surface area of 19.48 square kilometres and a total perimeter 28 kilometres long, of which 8 kilometres constitute its land border with Morocco; Melilla comprises an area of 13.41 square kilometres and has a total perimeter of 20 kilometres, of which 11 kilometres constitute its land border with Morocco. As of January 2005 Ceuta was inhabited by 75,276 people and Melilla by 65,488 people. These two geopolitically contested territories of the Maghreb were turned into unique fragments of the EU on the African continent and, as a consequence, the nature of their borders with Morocco was transformed.

This chapter discusses the peculiar border regime that has governed people and commodity flows across the borders of Ceuta and Melilla since 1986. It highlights the progressively acrobatic mode in which the EU's borders with Morocco have been managed, and it argues that the administration of the border between these two cities and Morocco has dramatically accentuated the conflicting logic of softening and fortification in which the EU's external borders are entrenched. The causes and consequences of this accentuation are examined by taking into account both structural and agency levels of analysis. This research is informed by the scanning of the relevant literature on Spanish–Moroccan border dynamics, a selective scrutiny of Spanish and Moroccan newspapers, both local and national, and two research field trips to the frontier area in January 2003 and February 2006.

The range of issues investigated here is related to the four analytical dimensions suggested by Emmanuel Brunet-Jailly's border model: market forces in the borderlands; the policy activity of multiple levels of government; local cross-border political clout; and local cross-border culture (Brunet-Jailly 2005). Thus the aim is to show how EU structure has impinged on the daily border practice of Ceuta and Melilla, and how, in turn, this interaction between structural and agency factors has engendered an acrobatic border model.

The first section of this chapter contextualizes the frontier by outlining the historical evolution of Ceuta's and Melilla's borders with Morocco, from the Reconquista of the Iberian peninsula up to Spain's accession to the EU in 1986. The second section discusses the border regime deployed in the two cities since 1986, in particular, the exceptional "Schengenization" of Ceuta and Melilla, the increasing but selective impermeability of their perimeters that has resulted, and the anomalous patterns of cross-border mobility. The third section examines the implications of acrobatic border management and the conclusion highlights the capriciousness of the EU's external border practices.

HISTORICAL EVOLUTION OF THE BORDERS OF CEUTA AND MELILLA

Almost 800 years of the Muslim presence in the Iberian Peninsula separated the arrival of Tarik in Gibraltar in the year 711 and the fall of the Kingdom of Granada into Christian hands in 1492. The year 1492 and the tears spilt by Boabdil represent the symbolic end of the Reconquista, as well as the fixing of a relatively stable frontier between Christianity and Islam in the western Mediterranean. The existence of a mobile, permeable and at times non-existent border between Christian and Muslim domains evoked the idea of the Iberian Peninsula as a huge frontier territory of Christian, Jewish, and Muslim interaction. The Christian Reconquista, and its associated symbolic purification of the Iberian space, gradually transported the frontier zone toward the Strait of Gibraltar, where it has remained fixed ever since.

The Iberian seizure of Maghrebian territories, and thus the preliminary setting of today's frontier, took place within the logic of the Reconquista. Ceuta fell into Portuguese hands in 1415 and into Spanish hands in 1668, while Melilla was conquered by Castile in 1497. The seizure of Ceuta and Melilla was followed by the construction of a series of mostly Castilian strongholds on the North African coast—Mers el-Kebir, El Peñón de Vélez de la Gomera, Orán, Bougie, and Tripoli—referred to as the *Fronteras de África* (Driessen 1992, 17). The main difference between the mobile Iberian borders of the Reconquista and those established in the African continent resides in the fact that the former were borders of expansion, while the latter, at least at the beginning, were borders of contraction. The shift from a policy of expansion to a strategy of contraction must be read within the historical context of Columbus's discovery of the Americas, which also took place in 1492. Spain's interest shifted toward the Atlantic and hence the seizure of these territories was not followed by a policy of expansion throughout the African continent.

Figure 3.1 Ceuta and Melilla

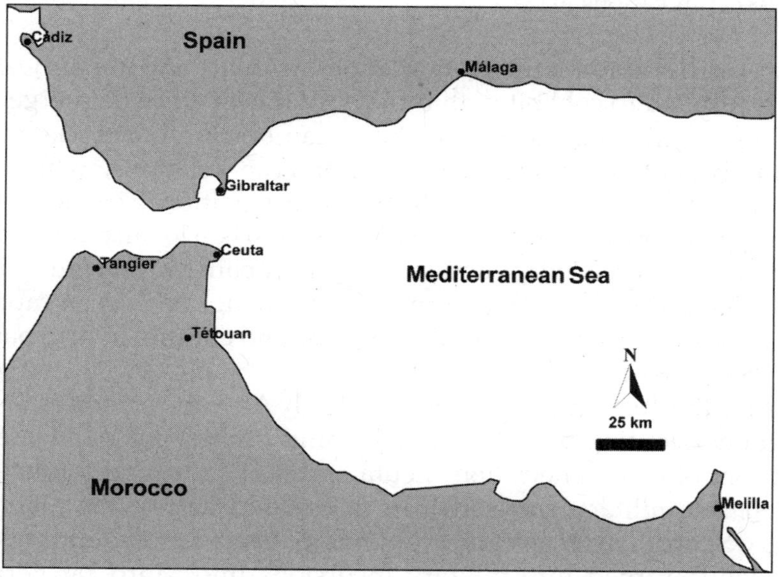

Source: Sergi Cuadrado 2006

As Rézzette (1976, 13) wrote,

> The Spanish settlement on the northern coast of Morocco from the beginning had a double offensive–defensive purpose: to observe

> the Moors in their own territory, in order to ward off their eventual preparations for the reconquest of the Iberian Peninsula; and to furnish Christian ships refuge from pirates and protection from storms.

Later the enclaves of Ceuta and Melilla also served as key outposts for colonial penetration. From the time of the Iberian seizure of Ceuta and Melilla until the colonial penetration into northern Morocco, as Driessen (1992, 34) points out,

> both Spanish and Moroccan authorities perceived and represented the Spanish–Moroccan frontier for more than four centuries as a hard and fast line of division between "civilisation" and "savagery," a divide that was mainly defined in terms of religion. In daily life, however, it was a zone of interaction between two different cultures, which, in spite of religious antagonisms, knew very well how to deal with one another in various ways.

Notions of division and interaction, of permeability and impermeability, have continued to cohabit within the border ever since it emerged.

These conflicting border dynamics can be closely associated with the ambivalent nature of Spanish–Moroccan relations, which have constantly swung back and forth between traditional friendship and fierce opposition, between peace and war, between loyalty and distrust, and between shared legacy and current discrepancies. Obviously it is in the border region that all these ambivalent swings have been captured, giving rise to the social, economic, political, and cultural hybrid patterns of border societies.

From the Iberian seizure of the North African territories to their subsequent development, first into dynamic trading posts and later into bases for colonial penetration, Ceuta and Melilla basically functioned as *presidios* (military garrisons). In the second half of the nineteenth century, Spanish defensive interventions in the areas surrounding Ceuta and Melilla turned into military incursions into Moroccan territory. Gradually these incursions modified the size of the territories that Spain still kept in North Africa. The official delimitation of the borders of these enclaves dates back to conventions signed in 1859 and 1862, in the case of Melilla, and in 1860, in the case of Ceuta (López García 1991). The Spanish–Moroccan agreements that comprised the Treaty of Tétouan (1860) entailed the territorial stabilization of Ceuta and Melilla, enabling their subsequent economic and social development (Cajal 2003, 170). This treaty also established the creation of a neutral zone around the enclaves in order to ensure peace and to protect the frontier territories. This neutral zone, 500 metres wide, still lies between Spain and Morocco, following the land perimeters of Ceuta and Melilla.

In 1863 Ceuta and Melilla both acquired free-port status, and intense trading activity came to complement their garrison function. By that time the Spanish interest in northern Morocco had increased considerably: the roads of colonial penetration were being paved. The Africanismo movement provided the ideological ground for further Spanish involvement and military intervention in North Africa. In the early twentieth century the Anglo-French geopolitical equilibrium enabled the establishment of the Spanish Protectorate of Northern Morocco. It was to last from 1912 until 1956, and its political, military, commercial, and sociocultural implications clearly had an impact on the enclaves and their borders.

During the years of colonial intervention (1912–56), despite being fully permeable, the perimeters of Ceuta and Melilla divided the African territories under Spanish sovereignty from the Spanish-protected territory of Northern Morocco. Although the two enclaves were highly interconnected with their hinterlands, their status remained distinct from that of the protectorate. To a certain degree this distinctiveness explains why, after the end of the Spanish–French Protectorate of Morocco in 1956, the enclaves remained in Spanish hands. Ever since Morocco has identified Ceuta and Melilla as integral parts of Moroccan territory, still to be decolonized. Spain, however, considers the enclaves to be as fully Spanish as any Spanish city in the Iberian Peninsula. Spanish and Moroccan perceptions and interpretations regarding the status of the enclaves are obviously contradictory. However, as Cajal (2003, 155) has argued, both the point of view of Rabat and that of Madrid seem to be reasonable within their respective internal logics.

The end of the colonization of Morocco in 1956 substantially changed the significance of the two Spanish enclaves and, consequently, of their borders with decolonized Morocco. Ceuta and Melilla remained under Spanish sovereignty and followed the successive political guidelines traced by Madrid. Accordingly, until 1975 the enclaves were ruled under the terms established by the fascist dictator Francisco Franco. Especially during the first years of his dictatorship, commercial activity within the enclaves underwent an important development, due partly to tax benefits and partly to the inward orientation of the Spanish economy. After Franco's death, in 1975, the enclaves were brought into line with the restitution of democracy in Spain. The Spanish Constitution of 1978 introduced the possibility of a certain degree of political autonomy for the enclaves, although it was not put into practice until 1995, when the Statute of Autonomy for Ceuta and Melilla was approved.

Spain's accession to the EU in 1986 involved another turn of the screw with respect to the enclaves, introducing a second border reconfiguration in thirty years. Ceuta and Melilla were still under Spanish sovereignty, and thus they automatically became parts of the EU, but their traditionally anomalous status remained and, to some extent, was even emphasized. Among their peculiarities, it is important to note that they did not become parts of the EU's customs territory. As Gold (1999, 23) has noted, the two cities "ha[d] certain preferential arrangements with the EU as a whole, and additional preference arrangements with peninsular Spain, whereby goods of Ceuta or Melilla origin qualif[ied] for exemption from duty." Agricultural exports from the EU to Ceuta and Melilla were financially assisted because the EU's Common Agricultural Policy (CAP) was not implemented in the two enclaves (Planet 1998a, 47).

READJUSTMENT OF THE BORDERS SINCE 1986

The year 1986, when Spain joined the EU, was unquestionably a major point of inflection within the history of the Spanish–Moroccan border: it is when the contemporary rethinking of the border started. Next came its "Schengenization," in 1991, and then, in 1995, the beginning of two simultaneous processes: the militarization of the enclaves' perimeters and the liberalization of trade in the area, the latter being due to culminate in the establishment of the Euro-Mediterranean Free Trade Area in 2010. In the course of these historical developments the Spanish–Moroccan border has been and is being reconfigured according to conflicting logics of softening and fortification. Moreover, these contrasting trends have been accentuated in the particular cases of Ceuta and Melilla. In order to see why this has occurred, we must delineate the main aspects of the readjustment of the borders between the EU and North Africa.

Even after Spain joined the EU the traditional geopolitical controversy regarding the status of Ceuta and Melilla persisted. Despite the new EU dimension acquired by the enclaves, the discrepancies kept on being discussed (or not) at a bilateral level. In contrast, the borders between the enclaves and Morocco clearly became of concern to the EU and therefore their management acquired an EU dimension. While the arguments, discourses, and political statements regarding the status of Ceuta and Melilla remained practically invariable, the meaning and significance of the enclaves, to the extent that they became EU territories, changed dramatically. Their borders were to be readjusted to the new situation, a readjustment that was translated into geopolitical, functional, and symbolic transformations. Spain's accession to the EU carried with it the implementation of a rethought border regime, which entailed the redefinition of the terms on which cross-border interaction between the enclaves and their Moroccan hinterland was to develop.

Prior to 1986, Spain needed to undertake a range of legal modifications in order to fulfill the requirements of EU accession. The incorporation of the Schengen Agreement was among these. In October 1985 a new Ley de Extranjería (immigration law) came into effect. As Gold (2000, 93) explains, "The main focus of the new law was to increase government powers to deal with non-EU foreign nationals already in Spain, rather than to improve border controls." The law impinged considerably on the Muslim population of Ceuta and Melilla, since, under its terms, an important section of the Muslim community in the enclaves was not given the right to Spanish nationality. Consequently the majority of the Muslim population reacted against the new immigration law, and important protests took place in both Ceuta and Melilla. The law enabled much easier acquisition of Spanish nationality by non-EU immigrants of Latin American, Filipino, Andorran, Sephardi, or Gibraltarian origin than by those of Moroccan origin. As Soddu (2002, 26) argues, the law condemned to illegality the Muslim populations whose forebears had settled in the enclaves more than one hundred years before. As a reaction to the protests and claims of the Muslim community, an extraordinary process of regularization was undertaken in 1987. This process shed light on the increasing demographic and political weight of the Muslim populations of Ceuta and Melilla. Their new status as EU citizens blurred some boundaries between the Muslim and Christian inhabitants of Ceuta and Melilla, whereas new boundaries emerged between these EU Muslims, on the one hand, and the Moroccans who inhabited the borderlands on the other side of the fence.

After the regularization processes concluded in 1991, Spain's compliance with the Schengen Agreement required the implementation of tight border controls. The borders became Schengen land borders and therefore their management needed to be adjusted to Schengen control standards. The adoption of visa requirements for Moroccan citizens in 1991 had a remarkable impact on Spanish–Moroccan border dynamics. The control mechanisms were reinforced and the patterns of cross-border mobility were significantly altered. From that moment onward Moroccan citizens were not allowed to cross the new Spanish/Schengen–Moroccan border without a visa, with an exception introduced later regarding "desirable" inhabitants of the Moroccan borderlands. Significantly, May 19, 1991, was the day when the first clandestine migrants died while trying to cross the Straits of Gibraltar. Ever since then the number of would-be immigrants who have died between the Pillars of Hercules has grown dramatically.

The particular characteristics of the enclaves, which are absolutely dependent on the cross-border interaction with their hinterlands, implied that the Schengen regime was put into practice in a selective mode. The border was rendered more or less impermeable, but with an eye to the future sustainability of the enclaves. Thus an exception to the Schengen regime was made to enable the daily cross-border flow of "desirable" migrants—workers, consumers, smugglers—against the general pattern of denial of access to non-EU citizens. Under the terms of this discerning regulation, the Schengen borders in North Africa are currently closed to the vast majority of Moroccan citizens yet open to some under certain conditions. In the case of Ceuta, Moroccan citizens from the neighbouring region of Tétouan are allowed to enter the enclave without a visa for a period of up to twenty-four hours. The same border regime is deployed 300 kilometres eastward, in Melilla, where, like the citizens from the region of Tétouan, those who inhabit the region of Nador are allowed to move back and forth across the border. This atypical deployment of the Schengen border regulations in Ceuta and Melilla seems to have been specifically designed to ensure the economic and, hence, the political sustainability of the enclaves.

Needless to say, this selective "Schengenization" of the enclaves has not only impinged on the cross-border flow of people but also influenced the cross-border flow of commodities. The daily cross-border flow of people and the illicit flow of commodities are intensively interconnected and, to a certain extent, function as two sides of the same coin.

The economic gap between Spain and Morocco increased extraordinarily after Spain joined the EU. The resulting structural asymmetries stimulated illegal flows of goods and people across their borders. In the case of Ceuta and Melilla, cross-border commercial interaction with Morocco was notably characterized by its smuggling dimension and now constitutes a sustaining pillar of the enclaves' economy. The dynamism of the irregular flow of goods across the borders is mainly motivated by three factors: the special tax regime of the enclaves, the economic differential between the two sides of the border, and the exception to the Schengen Agreement that allows the daily cross-border flow of Moroccan citizens under certain conditions. The fact that Morocco does not recognize the borders as legitimate implies the non-existence of official customs controls, so the flow of commodities across the borders takes place under a forced veil of legal obscurity.

On several occasions Morocco has officially complained about the negative consequences of these illicit cross-border flows, but in practice smuggling seems to be tolerated. Officially, commercial interaction between the enclaves and their hinterland is almost non-existent, yet, as Soddu (2002, 38) has pointed out, the volume of commercial interaction across the borders of the enclaves is estimated to be notably higher than the total volume of legal exports from Spain to Morocco. In northern Morocco, as Planet (2002, 275) has noted, the illicit cross-border flows entail "unfair competition for national production, obstruction of the creation of industrial units, discouragement of foreign investment and loss of jobs." This by no means contributes to overcoming the economic underdevelopment of northern Morocco, which, in turn, stimulates Moroccan emigration toward the EU, both motivating and somehow curiously justifying the EU's current model for its external borders.

The free-port status acquired by Ceuta and Melilla in 1863, their beneficial tax status, and the strategic location of their harbours have given rise to what Planet (2002, 268) has called a hypertrophy of the commercial sector. A very small part of what Ceuta and Melilla import is consumed in the enclaves, while 80 percent of it flows across the borders (*El País*, 2005) and the territories function as the main (atypical) bazaars of the Maghreb. Planet (2002, 269) has explained how the enclaves' extraordinary commercial activity is organized through a binary scheme (legal and illegal) that benefits from their tax structures: on the one hand, legal economic activity related to the redistribution of goods to locals and tourists; and, on the other, illegal or informal economic activity through which goods are redistributed outside the enclaves.

Hajjani (1986, as cited in Planet 2002, 275) identified three different types of smuggling to Morocco via the enclaves: (1) occasional smuggling of tobacco, alcoholic beverages, or electrical household appliances, performed sporadically by foreign workers, students, and civil servants, and generally by those, whether Spanish or Moroccan, who can easily enter and leave the enclaves; (2) subsistence smuggling, consisting of the illicit cross-border flow of consumption goods such as batteries, chocolate, canned milk, and perfumes, carried on by inhabitants of the surrounding Moroccan cities, who go back and forth across the border several times a day (called *matuteros* in Spanish); and (3) large-scale smuggling of electronic equipment, such as satellite dishes and of other expensive goods, carried on by organized networks of professionals. This typology coincides roughly with the three varieties of smugglers described by McMurray (2001, 116–17) as being involved in smuggling between Melilla and Nador, and can be extrapolated to the case of Ceuta and Finideq. McMurray (2001, 123) differentiated between weekend smugglers (or amateurs), everyday smugglers, and the "big boys," and he pointed out that "it is difficult to name an item that is not smuggled across that border into Morocco." In Ceuta and Melilla the very existence of the border equates to economic opportunity, and the border functions as a valuable resource for many of those who make a living from it, rather than as an obstacle to be overcome.

It seems clear that an extensive and vigorous economic network is fully dependent on the selectively sealed-off borders of Ceuta and Melilla. However, the economic model based on the existence of the present border regime might be altered in the near future. The EU's "Barcelona process," initiated in 1995, fixed the establishment of a Euro-Mediterranean Free Trade Area as one of its main goals. This raises the question of how the accelerating liberalization of Euro-Mediterranean trade is going to impinge on the network of interests that is currently based on the very existence of the border.

BORDER ACROBATICS

In sharp contrast to the trend toward liberalization of Euro-Mediterranean trade stands the fact that the borders of Ceuta and

Melilla continue to be physically reinforced. Thus, in the near future, the free flow of commodities across their borders will coexist with the militarized fencing off of the enclaves. From the perspective of free trade, the fortification of the borders seems to be clearly focused on filtering people's mobility.

Although the project of rendering the borders impermeable dates from 1992, the sealing off of the enclaves' perimeters was not a tangible reality until 1995. The palpable fortification of the enclaves coincided with their being declared Autonomous Cities within the Spanish constitutional framework. The initiation of the Euro-Mediterranean Partnership also took place in 1995. The fencing off of Ceuta's and Melilla's borders with Morocco was accelerated in that year, due partly to the increasing social tension that had been generated in the enclaves. By that time the inefficiency of the existing border controls had become apparent. During the early 1990s the continual arrival of sub-Saharan and Algerian migrants, who were neither repatriated nor allowed to cross legally to continental Europe, engendered chaos. An increasing number of migrants were trapped in the two cities, waiting for a legal response to their situation. The enclaves functioned as waiting areas from which, sooner or later, they would be able to cross to the Iberian Peninsula. The authorities in Ceuta were unable to deal with the situation, which culminated in migrant riots and xenophobic protests (Gold 2000; Soddu 2002). Despite the improved controls and the increased militarization of the perimeter, the border remained permeable to the illegal flow of people after 1995 and was not made impermeable until 1999. Notwithstanding that, and even though chaos and incompetence were slowly disappearing, the illegal entry of immigrants through the militarized border fence persisted. By that time, as Gold (1999, 27) observed, there was little evidence that the fences reduced illegal access to the enclaves because, particularly in some specific sections of the perimeter, the terrain made it difficult for the fence to be fully effective. Fortification techniques continued to be developed, but so did ways of subverting them.

The borders of both Ceuta and Melilla are now intensively militarized. Somehow the enclaves have restored their medieval fortress dimension, combining it with high-tech control mechanisms. The land perimeter of Melilla consists of 10.5 kilometres of double-metal fencing. The outer fence is 3.5 metres high and the inner fence reaches six metres. Both fences are equipped with barbed wire. A road between the two fences allows the circulation of border-patrol vehicles. The surveillance system consists of 106 video cameras, a microphone cable, and infra-red surveillance. The border patrols in Melilla are composed of 331 police officers (273 in 2002) and 676 members of the Guardia Civil (European Commission 2005). In the case of Ceuta, 316 police officers and 626 Guardia Civil officers control its 7.8-kilometre double-metal fence by means of the same technical equipment as that found in Melilla (European Commission 2005).

The Moroccan side of the border is not as strictly patrolled as the Spanish side. There are several reasons for this asymmetry. The Moroccan perception of the borders as illegitimate is, needless to say, far-reaching. Moreover, the dissimilar economic and technical potential, as well as the different roles regarding migration dynamics played by Spain and Morocco, also entail different border requirements and political responses. However, the improvement in Spanish–Moroccan diplomatic relations after José Luis Rodríguez Zapatero became prime minister in 2004 has given rise to enhanced cross-border cooperation at a variety of levels. This enhancement is occurring after a dark period of diplomatic misunderstandings between the two countries, which reached its zenith during the crisis over the disputed territory of Isla Perejil in July 2002 (Planet and Hernando de Larramendi 2003; Szmolka 2005). As far as border control is concerned, Spanish–Moroccan collaboration in the fight against terrorism, illegal immigration, and human trafficking has notably increased.

In 2005 the implementation of the Sistema Integrado de Vigilancia Exterior (Integrated System of External Surveillance, or SIVE), together with the expansion of collaboration between the Spanish and Moroccan authorities, resulted in a 37 percent reduction in the number of would-be migrants reaching the Spanish coasts (the Canary Islands and the Iberian Peninsula) compared to 2004 (European Commission 2005). The consequence of this decrease was an extraordinary increase in migratory pressure at the borders of Ceuta and Melilla. The strengthening of controls by the Moroccan police (both Gendarmerie and Mehanis) became apparent during the tragic events that took place at the borders during late August, September, and October 2005. During these months successive attempts were made to break through, as numerous groups of migrants tried to scale the fences using hand-made ladders. Hundreds made it across, but many more were repelled. This violent merging of border "subversion" and border "protection" ended with the death of fourteen people, all of them citizens of sub-Saharan countries.

The medieval-style practices of border subversion have been repeatedly employed by illegal migrants since the borders started to be made impermeable. During this episode, however, the number of attempts, as well as their proportions, grew considerably. These practices were described in Spanish and Moroccan media as "border assaults" (*L'Opinion* 2005; *El Telegrama de Melilla* 2005; *Aujourd'hui Le Maroc* 2005) and as "organized massive attacks" (*El País* 2005), and the Spanish Delegado del Gobierno in Melilla announced that the border of that enclave was being assaulted by means of an organized military strategy (*El País* 2005). In both Ceuta and Melilla the militarization of border controls seemed to go hand in hand with the militarization of border discourses. These events were followed by the reinforcement of the border fences (*El Faro de Ceuta* 2005; *El País* 2005) and of the patrols by both Spanish and Moroccan police and army units (*El Mundo* 2005; *Le Matin* 2005). As a consequence the episodes of "massive" border subversion stopped. Nevertheless, clandestine migrants continued to enter the enclaves, following a more complex pattern of entry and using more subtle crossing techniques, such as swimming.

The functional reconfiguration of the Spanish–Moroccan border and its new role as a regulator of flows is characterized by what Anderson (2001, 3–4) has described as the "selective permeability" of borders and their "differential filtering effects." On the one hand, the border became more permeable to the flow of goods and capital, due to the logics of globalization and the preparations for the Euro-Mediterranean Free Trade Area. On the other hand, the border became less permeable to the flow of some types of labour migration, in harmony with the idiosyncrasy of a selectively fortified EU (or "Fortress Europe"). This new border role entailed, as Nevins (2002, 7) has pointed out, "maximizing the perceived benefits of globalization while protecting against the perceived detriments of increasing transnational flows." Anderson (2001, 30) has further observed that "this seriously impedes the free movement and exchange of labour, and is generally accepted by neoliberals despite the fact that it contradicts their free-trade, anti-state ideology."

The peculiar border regimes of Ceuta and Melilla appear to be designed in accordance with their anomalous status. The atypical and paradoxical management of their borders with Morocco seems not only to embrace EU guidelines regarding external borders but also to take into account the special regulatory system required to sustain them. For this reason the "selective permeability" of the borders of Ceuta and Melilla and their "differential filtering effects" (Anderson, 2001, 3–4) are exceptionally amplified. Their border regimes are rooted in a precise acrobatic equilibrium between the bridging and barrier functions of borders. To the extent that the enclaves are "total" frontier territories, the border functions as their main resource, the preservation of which requires the deployment of acute contradictory policies of softening and fortification. At the present moment a contradictory situation is apparent. Strict control on illegal migration contrasts sharply with "tolerance" for the illicit flow of commodities. At the same time some kinds of cross-border mobility are allowed, and even encouraged, because they seem to be indispensable to the enclaves' economies.

The EU's external border regime seems to be entrenched in the same contradictory logic. The trend toward the free flow of goods across the external border is increasing, the control of cross-border flows of some people across the external perimeter has been notably tightened, and yet at the same time the free flow of certain types of migrants is allowed, even encouraged.

Van Houtum and Pijpers (2005, 1) have suggested an alternative metaphor for the EU's model of its external borders. In their view the "European Union follows a geostrategic logic which, much more than a Fortress, resembles the management of a Gated Community." In other words, the EU external border model resembles "a form of housing found mainly in developing countries with large internal income differences, such as Mexico, Brazil and Venezuela" where "the affluent gate themselves off from the rest of society in an enclave, primarily driven by fear (of crime) and the need for welfare protection and security" (Van Houtum and Pijpers 2005, 6). The simultaneous desirability and undesirability of immigration aimed at protecting the internal comfort zone (Van Houtum 2003) has engendered a contradictory regime of external border controls. The peculiar border management of Ceuta and Melilla may well coincide with the "Gated Community" model suggested by Van Houtum and Pijpers, although it is deployed in a very intense manner. The selectively permeable militarized border regime of these two territories seems to be a small-scale representation of the EU's model of sociospatial bordering.

CONCLUSION

As mentioned, the Euro-Mediterranean Partnership process, also known as the "Barcelona process," was initiated in 1995. From that moment onward the border between Spain and Morocco has been in the middle of a slowly integrating Euro-Mediterranean diagram of cooperation. Each of the three themes of the Declaration of Barcelona—political and security partnership, economic and financial partnership, and partnership in social, cultural, and human affairs—has impinged decisively on the current nature and significance of the Spanish land borders with Morocco. The establishment of a Euro-Mediterranean Free Trade Area by the target year of 2010, one of the major goals of the declaration, will particularly modify the patterns of commercial mobility across the Spanish–Moroccan border. The borders of Ceuta and Melilla will lose some of their barrier components, although others will remain. At the moment, however, the selectively permeable militarization of Ceuta's and Melilla's borders appears to be a symbolic performance, with clearly exclusive sociospatial implications that are aimed at marking the limits of the emerging identity of the EU, rather than a product of rational border regulation.

This chapter has attempted to provide grounds for questioning whether the EU is being built on foundations that are capricious and, in the long term, unsustainable. It is often said that much can be learned about the cores of territories by scrutinizing their peripheries. With this in mind, this chapter has attempted to shed light on the rapidly evolving borderland that lies between Morocco and the two Spanish enclaves in North Africa. In this regard, the core of the border model suggested by Emmanuel Brunet-Jailly (2005, 11)—that is, "the implicit recognition that agency and structure are mutually influential and interrelated in the shaping of emerging and integrated borderlands"—has provided a constructive and articulating analytical instrument for illustrating how the border changes derived from the EU's top-down model for the structure of its external borders has merged with the role played by border agents in the field.

In the end this chapter reveals that the relative structuring effect of EU border-security policy is key to understanding the negotiated fortification of border towns. The case is made that, in the cities of Ceuta and Melilla, the mutual influence between top-down structural border readjustments and the response to them by the border agency have engendered a situation within which the four analytical dimensions proposed by Brunet-Jailly (2005)—market forces, multiple levels of governments, local political clout, and local culture—interact according to an acrobatic pattern. In turn, this pattern is rooted, geopolitically, functionally, and symbolically, in the anomalous attributes of the territories of Ceuta and Melilla. The resulting acrobatic pattern is characterized by the asymmetric and at times highly contradictory sociospatial bordering practices of softening and fortification, which are marked by remarkable instances of selectivity. This phenomenon, observed at the periphery of the EU, surely tells us much about its core.

LITERATURE CITED

Aujourd'hui Le Maroc. 2005 [online]. www.aujourdhui.ma (October 6) [consulted November 17, 2005].

Anderson, J. 2001. "Theorizing State Borders: 'Politics/Economics' and Democracy in Capitalism." *CIBR Working Papers in Border Studies*. Belfast: Centre for International Borders Research, Queen's University.

Aziza, M. 2003. *La sociedad rifeña frente al protectorado español en Marruecos*. Barcelona: Edicions Bellaterra.

Ballesteros, Ángel. 1990. *Estudio Diplomático sobre Ceuta y Melilla*. Córdoba (Argentina): Marcos Lerner Editora.

Bennison, A. 2001. "Liminal States: Morocco and the Iberian Frontier between the Twelfth and Nineteenth Centuries." *Journal of North African Studies* 6:1, 11–28.

Brunet-Jailly, Emmanuel. 2005. "Theorizing Borders: An Interdisciplinary Perspective." *Geopolitics*, 10:4, 633–49.

Cajal, M. 2003. *Ceuta, Melilla, Olivenza y Gibraltar ¿Dónde acaba España?* Madrid: Siglo Veintiuno de España Editores.

Cardenas, S. 1996. "The Contested Territories of Ceuta and Melilla." *Mediterranean Quarterly* 7:1, 118–39.

Delmote, Gilles. 2001. *Ponts et frontières entre l'Espagne et Maghreb*. Paris: L'Harmattan, Histoire et Perspectives Mediterranéennes.

Driessen, H. 1991. *The Politics of Religion on the Hispano-African Frontier—A Historical Anthropological View*. Albany: State University of New York Press.

———. 1992. *On the Spanish–Moroccan Frontier: A Study in Ritual, Power, and Ethnicity*. New York and Oxford, UK: Berg.

———. 1996a. "At the Edge of Europe: Crossing and Marking the Mediterranean Divide." *Borders, Nations and States*, eds. L. O'Dowd and T. Wilson. Aldershot: Avebury, 179–98.

———. 1996b. "The 'New Immigration' and the Transformation of the European-African Frontier." *Border Identities. Nation and State at International Frontiers,* eds. T. Wilson and H. Donnan. Cambridge: Cambridge University Press, 96–116.

———. 1999. "Smuggling as a Border Way of Life: A Mediterranean Case." *Frontiers and Borderlands. Anthropological Perspectives,* eds. M. Rosler and T. Wendl. Frankfurt am Main: Peter Lang, 117–31.

El Abdellaoui, M., and N. Chikhi 2002. "Structure et transformations des espace urbains frontaliers: cas de Finideq." *Urbanisation et urbanisme dans les montagnes rifaines (Maroc),* ed. Groupe de Recherches Géographiques sur le Rif. Tétouan (Morocco): Publications du G.R.G. Rif. Série Études spatiales, no. 1.

El Faro de Ceuta. 2005. [online]. www.elfaroceutamelilla.com (October 4) [consulted November 17, 2005].

El Mundo. 2005. [online]. www.elmundo.es (September 29) [consulted November 17, 2005].

El País. 2005, September 1, 29; October 5, 9.

El Telegrama de Melilla. 2005. [online]. www.eltelegrama.com (October 6) [consulted November 17, 2005].

European Commission. 2005. *Technical Mission to Morocco: Visit to Ceuta and Melilla, On Illegal Immigration, 7th October to 11th October 2005, Mission Report.* Brussels: European Commission.

Evers-Rosander, Eva. 1991. *Women in a Borderland: Managing Muslim Identity Where Morocco Meets Spain.* Stockholm: Stockholm Studies in Social Anthropology.

García Flórez, Dionisio. 1998. "Ceuta y Melilla en la política española. Perspectivas de futuro." *UNISCI Papers* 13. Madrid: Universidad Complutense.

Garcia-Ramon, M., et al. 1998. "Voices from the Margins: Gendered Images of 'Otherness' in Colonial Morocco." *Gender, Place and Culture* 5:3, 229–40.

Gold, Peter. 1999. "Immigration into the European Union via the Spanish Enclaves of Ceuta and Melilla: A Reflection of Regional Economic Disparities." *Mediterranean Politics* 4:3, 23–36.

Gold, Peter. 2000. *Europe or Africa? A Contemporary Study of the Spanish North African Enclaves of Ceuta and Melilla.* Liverpool: Liverpool University Press.

Hajjaji, T. 1986. *Le phénomene de la contrebande au Maroc. Memoire du Cycle superieur*. Rabat (Morocco): École Nationale de l'Administration Publique.

Hernando de Larramendi, Miguel. 2004. "Las relaciones hispano-marroquíes durante los años noventa." *Atlas de la inmigración marroquí en España,* ed. B. López García. Madrid: Universidad Autónoma de Madrid Ediciones.

Hess, A. C. 1979. *The Forgotten Frontier: A History of the Sixteenth-century Ibero-African Frontier.* Chicago and London: University of Chicago Press.

Labatut, B. 1985. "Ceuta et Melilla: tensions sur la société et la politique de défense espagnoles." *Studia Diplomatica* 38:4, 409–27.

Lazrak, Rachid. 1974. *Le Contentieux territorial entre le Maroc et l'Espagne.* Casablanca: Dar el Kitab.

Le Matin. 2005. [online]. www.lematin.ma (October 6) [consulted November 17, 2005].

Lería Ortiz de Saracho, Manuel. 1991. *Ceuta y Melilla en la polémica.* Madrid: Editorial San Martín.

López García, B. 1991. "Entre l'Europe et l'Afrique, Ceuta et Melilla." *Revue du Monde Musulman et de la Méditerranée* 59–60, 165–80.

———, ed. 2004. *Atlas de la inmigración marroquí en España.* Madrid: Universidad Autónoma de Madrid Ediciones.

———, A. Planet, and E. Bouqentar. 1994. "La questione di Ceuta e Melilla." *Limes* 2, 171–74.

L'Opinion 2005, August 13. [online]. www.lopinion.ma [consulted November 17, 2005].

McMurray, D. 2001. *In and Out of Morocco: Smuggling and Migration in a Frontier Boomtown.* Minneapolis: University of Minnesota Press.

Martín Corrales, Eloy, ed. 2002. *Marruecos y el colonialismo español (1859–1912). De la guerra de África a la "penetración pacífica."* Barcelona: Edicions Bellaterra.

Morales Lezcano, Victor. 1986. *España y el Norte de Africa: El Protectorado en Marruecos (1912–1956).* Madrid: Universidad Nacional de Educación a Distancia.

———. 2000. *Las fronteras de la península ibérica en los siglos XVIII y XIX. Esbozo histórico de algunos conflictos franco-hispano-magrebíes.* Madrid: Universidad Nacional de Educación a Distancia.

Nevins, J. 2002. *Operation Gatekeeper: The Rise of the "Illegal Alien" and the Making of the US–Mexico Boundary.* London: Routledge.

Nogué, J., and J. Villanova, eds. 1999. *España en Marruecos (1912–1956). Discursos Geográficos e Intervención Territorial.* Lleida: Milenio.

Pennell, C. 2002. "Law on a Wild Frontier: Moroccans in the Spanish Courts in Melilla in the Nineteenth Century." *Journal of North African Studies* 7:3, 67–78.

Planet, A. 1998a. *Melilla y Ceuta: espacios frontera hispano-marroquíes.* Melilla: Ciudades Autónomas de Melilla y Ceuta/UNED Melilla.

———. 1998b. "Espacios-frontera y dinámicas de cooperación en el Mediterráneo occidental: el caso de Melilla." *Regiones y ciudades enclaves. Relaciones fronterizas, cooperación técnica y al desarrollo en Iberoamérica y Mar de Alborán,* ed. R. Cámara. Seville: Servicio de Publicaciones de la Ciudad Autónoma de Melilla, 17–27.

———. 2000. "Melilla y Ceuta: espacios-frontera hispano-marroquíes (1975–1995)." *Homenaje al profesor Carlos Posac Mon,* Vol. 3. Ceuta: Instituto de Estudios Ceuties, 351–56.

———. 2002. "La frontière comme ressource: le cas de Ceuta et Melilla." *La Méditerranée des réseaux. Marchands, entrepreneurs et migrants entre l'Europe et le Maghreb,* ed. J. Cesari. Paris: Maisonneuve et Larose Française, 267–81.

———., and M. Hernando de Larramendi 2003. "Maroc–Espagne: la crise de l'îlot du Persil." *Afrique du Nord Moyen-Orient. Espace et conflits,* dir. R. Leveau. Paris: Les Études de la Documentation, 133–40.

Remiro Brotons, Antonio. 1999. "Ceuta, Melilla, représentations espagnoles et marocaines." *Hérodote* 94, Paris: La Découverte, 54–76.

Rézette, R. 1976. *The Spanish Enclaves in Morocco.* Paris: Nouvelles Éditions Latines.

Ribas-Mateos, Natalia. 2005. *The Mediterranean in the Age of Globalization. Migration, Welfare and Borders.* New Brunswick, NJ: Transaction Publishers.

Soddu, Pietro. 2002. *Inmigración Extra-Comunitaria en Europa: El Caso de Ceuta y Melilla.* Ceuta: Archivo Central, Ciudad Autónoma de Ceuta.

Szmolka Vida, Inmaculada. 2005. *El conflicto de Perejil: la información y la opinión periodística sobre Marruecos en tiempos de crisis.* Ceuta: Ciudad Autònoma de Ceuta, Archivo Central.

Van Houtum, H. 2003. "Borders of Comfort: Spatial Economic Bordering Processes in the European Union." *New Borders for a Changing Europe: Cross-border Cooperation and Governance,* eds. J. Anderson, L. O'Dowd, and T. Wilson. London: Frank Cass.

———, and Roos Pijpers. 2005. "Towards a Gated Community." [online] www.eurozine.com [consulted November 17, 2005].

Zurlo, Yves. 2005. *Ceuta et Melilla. Histoire, représentations et devenir de deux enclaves espagnoles.* Paris: L'Harmattan.

CHAPTER 4

FAYUCA HORMIGA: THE CROSS-BORDER TRADE OF USED CLOTHING BETWEEN THE UNITED STATES AND MEXICO

Mélissa Gauthier

Borders, regardless of their location, represent lucrative zones of exchange and trade, often illicit and clandestine. Along the US–Mexico border there is a lively trade taking second-hand clothing into Mexico through a complex system of smuggling, which is locally known as *fayuca*. Although used clothing is a restricted import in Mexico, it is sold everywhere in urban markets. This chapter details the "unauthorized" flow of used clothing across the US–Mexico border in light of ethnographic fieldwork conducted in the twin cities of El Paso, Texas, and Ciudad Juarez, Chihuahua, over a period of twelve months between 2003 and 2005.

To begin, a conceptual distinction put forward by Van Schendel and Abraham (2005) between political legitimacy, or "legality," and social legitimacy, or "licitness," is introduced. This distinction is particularly useful for understanding the various processes involved in what these authors call "the criminal life of things." This chapter will reveal the interplay between the strict, state-based aspects of borders and their market-level aspects, and illustrate how borders and flows can operate at either the structural or the agency level. The second section of this chapter outlines the decades-long development along the US–Mexico border of a dynamic, informal recycling of second-hand goods, including the *fayuca* of used clothing. The next two sections focus on the overall political and legal environment that structures and regulates the unauthorized flow of used clothing between the United Sates and Mexico. Attempts to regulate cross-border flows have involved the monitoring of the border-crossings of Mexican traders by the US

Department of Homeland Security (DHS), the use of regulations under the North American Free Trade Agreement (NAFTA) with reference to used clothing, and local authorities' attempted disruptions of these flows. The final section is an ethnographic description of the actual cross-border trade in second-hand clothing between El Paso and Ciudad Juarez.

UNAUTHORIZED FLOWS IN BORDERLANDS

The study of "illegal flows"—flows of commodities, persons, and ideas that have been outlawed by one or more state—makes up the general framework of this chapter. Borderlands are the classic sites of research into unauthorized flows because flows are more visible there than in any other observation sites (Van Schendel and Abraham 2005, 47). The theoretical perspective adopted here is that proposed by Van Schendel and Abraham in the introduction to their edited book on illicit flows and criminal things, in which they call for a radically different way of conceptualizing illegal transnational flows. These authors proposed a more subtle approach to the issues of legality and illegality, one that draws upon a conceptual distinction between what states consider to be legitimate ("legal") and what people involved in transnational networks consider to be legitimate ("licit"). As Van Schendel and Abraham (2005, 4) suggest, "Many transnational movements of people, commodities, and ideas are illegal because they defy the norms and rules of formal political authority but they are quite acceptable, 'licit,' in the eyes of participants in these transactions and flows." By introducing the concept of social legitimacy (or licitness) and setting it against political legitimacy (or legality), they are encouraging us to adopt analytic perspectives that privilege the participants in international illicit activities, which, they argue, allows for the development of contrasting explanations and understandings of the causes, meanings, and processes involved in what they call "the criminal life of things" (6).

Van Schendel and Abraham (2005, 15) define "transnational criminal activities" as "forms of social practice that intersect two or more regulatory spaces and violate at least one normative or legal rule." Regulatory spaces refer to zones within which particular sets of rules prevail, rules that may be generated by states or otherwise socially produced and that are usually formulated directly in response to specific practices, typically some combination of the consumption, production, exchange, or distribution of commodities. Van Schendel and Abraham (2005, 15) refer to the notion of the "life cycle" of the commodity, which can be outlined through a sequence of linked activities that are exemplified by the image of the commodity chain (see also Hansen 2002):

> The traditional commodity chain approach does not, however, consider consumption a vital omission in the case of the transnational illicit. While in general the movement of any capitalist commodity continues until the moment of exhaustion, in the case of illicit goods, movement/consumption might also mean crossing over a key regulatory threshold. The vector of consumption, the passage of the commodities from one agent to another, is also often an act of *transformation* as well as an act of exchange.

In other words, according to Van Schendel and Abraham, consumption cannot be detached from exchange and transformation, and movement constitutes an inherent quality of commodity chains. Production, movement, and consumption, they argue, are bound by and happen within regulatory spaces. Each transformation carries with it new meanings, which might translate the illegal good into something quite legal, or vice versa. "What determines legality and illegality at different points of the commodity chain is the particular regulatory scale the object finds itself in" (Van Schendel and Abraham 2005, 17). Thus the origins of regulatory authority must be identified, whether they are political (legal and illegal) or social (licit and illicit). Studying illegal flows in borderlands from this kind of theoretical perspective can shed light on the everyday practices (production, exchange, consumption, and distribution) and local networks that actually make it possible for "illegal" commodities to cross regulatory spaces.

This approach stands in sharp contrast to the current discourse on illegal flows, which is based on constructing multiple contrasts between flows and borders. One particularly interesting contrast identified by Van Schendel and Abraham (2005, 41) is that between stimulus and reaction:

> In the discourse on illegal flows, agency rests with the flows. They are described as permeating borders, subverting border controls, penetrating state territories, seeking markets, and finding customers.

> Borders, on the other hand, are presented as passive, vulnerable, and reactive. Whatever changes occur at states borders are in response to proactive, indeed aggressive, attempts by proponents of illegal flows to violate them. These changes are defensive, geared toward restoring a level of national security that is in danger of being lost.

This vision of states as merely reactive, as just holding back against the increase of illegal transnational flows, is misleading, according to Van Schensel and Abraham (2005, 59), because, as they correctly point out, it downplays the extent to which "states actually structure, condition, produce, and enable clandestine border crossings." In contrast, the border model proposed by Emmanuel Brunet-Jailly in this volume provides space for agency and structure to interact, thus allowing us to develop a more accurate picture in which borders and flows can work at either the structural or the agency level.

Accordingly, this chapter is as much about understanding how and to what extent illegal flows shape and reproduce borderlands as it is about understanding how state borders condition and reproduce illegal flows. Thus it contributes to the general theoretical framework elaborated by Brunet-Jailly in terms of balancing the market-level aspects of borders and the strict, state-based aspects of borders. Moreover, these two different and sometimes contradictory aspects of borders and flows echo Van Schendel and Abraham's conceptual distinction between what people involved in transnational networks consider to be legitimate ("licit") and what states consider to be legitimate ("legal").

The underground cross-border flow of used clothing between the United States and Mexico is often described by the local expression *fayuca hormiga,* which means "ant trade." This border metaphor nicely captures the complexity of these transnational networks of "ant traders," who respond to the local-market demand for used clothing from the United States, and it conveys the determination and persistence that they must demonstrate on a daily basis to subvert the official rules. As Van Schendel and Abraham (2005, 4) suggest, the "'armpit smugglers' or 'ant traders' who cross borders all over the world with small quantities of goods may together account for huge quantities of contraband, but they do not represent global syndicates of organized crime." This chapter sketches a contrasting portrait of ant traders as "quintessential free traders," but from below, who trade with little regard for national and border regulations (Staudt 2001, 124). This portrait also illustrates the agency of these economic actors, which has arisen from the economic culture of this border region.

THE ECONOMY OF RECYCLING ON THE US–MEXICO BORDER

Since the mid-1960s the economy of the border region has been highly influenced by the booming *maquiladora* industry in northern Mexico. *Maquiladoras* are foreign-owned assembly plants that take advantage of a commercial agreement, established in the mid-1960s, through which they are allowed to import supplies from other countries without paying duties, assemble the product in Mexico, and export it back without paying duties aside from the value added (Vila 2000, 255). The proximity of Mexican border cities to high-level consumerism in American border cities has fuelled the development of a significant trade in used goods from the United States. During the Maquiladora Period (1967–86) vast amounts of second-hand goods (cars, stoves, clothes, etc.) began to flow from the United States into the border cities of Mexico (Heyman 1994, 191), and a good opportunity for small-scale entrepreneurship in these border cities consisted of informal brokering of used goods into Mexico (Spener and Roberts 1998, 93). Because much of this activity took place extra-legally and clandestinely, it is difficult to estimate the overall value of the goods or the number of people employed. However, qualitative accounts of this brokering activity led Spener and Roberts (1998, 86) to conclude that it was a vital part of the regional economy (see also Anderson and de la Rosa 1991; Hellman 1994).

One of the most revealing of these accounts was Joan Anderson and Martin de la Rosa's study "Economic Survival Strategies of Poor Families on the Mexican Border." The authors showed how, as compared to the interior of the country, the border maintained a more dynamic economy, sustained by tourism and the *maquiladora* industry, during the economic crisis of the early 1980s (Anderson and de la Rosa 1991, 66). Moreover, their study revealed the different ways in which the border environment favourably influenced coping strategies, one of the most important being the existence of an "economy of discards" from the United States (54). This economy of discards became a crucial survival strategy in the border region and included, for example, construction materials, appliances, automobiles, and materials such as used tires, which were in demand for use not only on cars, but also as retaining walls for houses, fences, and stairways. As Anderson and de la Rosa (1991, 66) noted, "Trash is recycled in practical ways to improve the quality of life within the context of poverty." But the type of discards from the United States most widely used by low-income border families was second-hand clothing. Indeed, in almost all of the study's cases families reported relying mainly on used clothing (59).

As Martin Medina (2006, 1) points out, the US–Mexico border is one of the few places in the world where an industrialized country shares a common border with a developing country. This economic disparity has created opportunities on both sides of the border for an intense cross-border flow of goods, including recycled materials, in both directions. Thus many different kinds of materials are recovered and transported across the border informally. Medina has analyzed this complex system of cross-border recovery, involving scavengers and businesses, by describing some of the recycling activities that have developed over the past several decades in the El Paso–Juarez area. Medina (2006, 8) views this entire cross-border movement of discarded materials as beneficial to both countries and argues that these cross-border activities should be supported by public policy.

Commercial dealers in American border towns, such as El Paso, that specialize in selling used clothing in bulk to Mexican cross-border traders are an integral part of this dynamic informal recycling system. However, as this chapter reveals, the cross-border trade of used clothing gets little support from public policy. As a result the importation of used clothing occurs through a complex system of smuggling, which is locally called *fayuca*. Those who participate in the *fayuca* trade in used clothing are often called *fayuqueros*.

Pelayo and Parra (1994, 7) defined the concept of *fayuca* as a popular expression used along the northern Mexican border to designate the introduction, not the importation, of new and used merchandise for consumption:

> *Esta tiene como objetivo el comercializarlas a nivel detallista y consumidor en pequeña escala, con fines de abastecimiento para consumo local y como complemento del producto nacional.* [Its objective is small-scale

commmercialization at the retail level, as a source of supply for local consumption and as a complement to national production.]

Over the past several decades *fayuca* networks have gradually made their way into the interior of Mexico (Staudt 1998, 54) and this extension of the *fayuca* practice at the national level has gradually converted it into a euphemism for smuggling (Pelayo and Parra 1994, 7). Several decades ago, however, the *fayuca* trade was apparently immersed in the formal economy, without the connotations of illegality that are currently attached to it (Pelayo and Parra 1994, 6).

BORDER CROSSINGS AND TRADE REGULATIONS

The United States is the world's largest exporter of used clothing, both in volume and value. American exports of used clothing have grown significantly over the past fifteen years. In 2005 the United States exported US$ 300 million worth of used clothing (United Nations 2006) compared to US$ 174 million in 1990 (Hansen 2004, 3). The largest single source of garments fuelling the global trade in second-hand clothing is the donations that American consumers make to charitable organizations such as the Salvation Army and Goodwill Industries. After selling half, or less, of the donated garments in their thrift shops across the country, these charities dispose of their massive overstock at bulk prices, selling it to commercial used-clothing dealers that, in turn, export it throughout the world (Hansen 2002, 227).

Different countries subject imported American second-hand clothing to various trade policies, ranging from liberalization to protectionism. The Mexican government has adopted numerous protectionist policies concerning the importation of used clothing for resale in Mexico over the past several decades, but used clothing has remained a highly desired commodity in Mexico and currently its popularity is greater than ever.

The clothing is retailed in stores and warehouses on the US side of the border before being smuggled across the border into Mexico through the *fayuca* system. This *fayuca* of used clothing is an illegal practice that could not survive without its legal counterpart in El Paso: used-clothing wholesalers. Indeed, it is made possible by the presence in downtown El Paso of many purveyors of this second-hand product. These wholesalers of American used clothing range from family-owned businesses, which have operated over several generations and sell almost exclusively to Mexican buyers, to larger textile recyclers and graders of used clothing, which export throughout the world. Most of the El Paso wholesale dealers carry on long-term business relationships with regular buyers of used clothing from Juarez, who each week must cross the border to the El Paso warehouse in order to sort their weekly stock of used clothing. Thus the business relationship over time strongly depends on the capacity of their Mexican customers to cross the border from Juarez to El Paso on a regular basis.

Most do this by means of a border crossing card known as a "laser visa." The laser visa allows Mexican nationals to enter the United States for up to thirty days at a time but restricts their mobility to within forty kilometres (twenty-five miles) of the border and legally prohibits their employment in the United States. (In Arizona, Mexican citizens can travel within 120 kilometres [seventy-five miles] of the border with their laser visa.) Laser visas are usually issued to individuals who can meet residency and financial-solvency requirements and who make frequent visits to the United States for different reasons, including business, shopping, and visiting relatives and friends. The Juarez traders who use a laser visa to cross the border in order to stock up on used clothing at the wholesalers in downtown El Paso comply with all the terms of the border-crossing cards, as the visas allow them direct access to their sources of used clothing. The cross-border sourcing activities of traders who lose their laser visa or have it stolen can be paralyzed for weeks due to the procedures required to replace it. Their cross-border activities can now also be affected by the new measures relating to the laser visa that have been implemented by the DHS. In the new context of increased border security, many politicians and community leaders from states along the border with Mexico have been concerned that securing the homeland may come at the economic expense of their communities.

Founded in 1986, the Border Trade Alliance (BTA) is a non-profit organization that serves as a forum for participants to address key issues affecting trade and economic development in North America. Working with entities in Canada, Mexico, and the United States, the BTA advocates on behalf of policies and initiatives designed to improve border affairs and trade relations among the three nations. It has urged the DHS to reform the regulations surrounding the use of laser visas and extend the permissible period of entry and the geographic entry area "to be more reflective of the social and economic realities of the border region" (BTA 2006). In August 2004 the DHS announced that all Mexican nationals holding laser-visa cards would be allowed to visit border cities for up to thirty days, an increase from the previous limit of seventy-two hours. The BTA continues to call for the extension of the distance limitation of 40 kilometres (25 miles), or 120 kilometres (75 miles) in the Nogales–Tucson corridor, "to more accurately reflect the realities of today's cross-border trade" (BTA 2004).

Border-security measures related to human mobility include the United States Visitor and Immigrant Status Indicator Technology (US VISIT) program. Its entry procedures require that everyone crossing US borders be fingerprinted and photographed. They apply to all foreign travellers except for most Canadian citizens, who do not need a visa or passport to enter the United States, and most Mexican visitors who apply for admission to the United States using a BCC (laser visa) within the 25-mile-wide "Border Zone."

In contrast, the laser-visa reform is a measure of accommodation that can help to distinguish between legitimate commuters and individuals intending to enter the United States with the intention of harming the nation. After all, "securing" the border is about identifying and separating legitimate from illegitimate flows of people and submitting them to very different regulatory regimes. The US embassy in Mexico (2004) has referred to the laser-visa reform as "part of the on-going cooperation and dialog between the governments on making the shared border both more safe and more efficient." In other words, the imperatives of the new border-security agenda that emerged after the events of September 11, 2001, must be balanced with the realities of growing cross-border trade under NAFTA. In the case presented in this chapter, there is no clear evidence that border-security policies are impinging on local shoppers and *fayuqueros* crossing the border into the United States using their laser visa. Moreover, the ever-tightening control that *fayuqueros* face when they re-enter Mexico seems to demonstrate Mexico's lack of concern with national security in this specific case.

The concern raised most frequently by Mexican authorities is the adverse effect of used clothing imports on the domestic textile and garment industries, an argument that is often coupled with hygiene and public health issues. According to the president of the Mexican

National Chamber of the Textile Industry (Canaintex), "Used clothing is totally insalubrious so, not only to protect the productive chain, but also to protect people's health, it is necessary to eliminate the illegal importation of those products" (*Vanguardia*, March 21, 2006).

Many similar accounts of the Mexican textile industry lobbying the Mexican government to end the importation of used clothing from the United States by denouncing its negative impacts on the production of Mexican clothing have appeared in local newspapers. In 1992 a coalition of businessmen presented a petition asking the Mexican authorities to legislate against the entrance of *ropa usada* (used clothing) from the United States. The coalition argued that *fayuca hormiga* ("ant trade") was harming the production of Mexican clothing and that the Secretaria de Comercio y Fomento Industrial (Secretariat of Commerce and Industrial Development, or Secofi) was ignoring its petition because thousands of people were involved in this activity at the border. The coalition's efforts were intended to denounce the fact that the trade in used clothing had never been under control at the border (*El Norte*, May 30, 1992).

The *fayuca* of American used clothing, which is part of a larger market of contraband clothing in Mexico—fifty percent of all clothing sold is said to be contraband (mostly from Asia) or pirated (*El Sol de México*, May 9, 2005)—has become a matter of serious concern to Mexican authorities in recent years. Allegations of corruption against Mexican customs authorities, as well as law-enforcement operations surrounding the unauthorized entrance of used clothing into Mexico, are the focus of intensive coverage by local newspapers. Moreover, Mexico's trade restrictions on imports of used clothing give rise to contrasting discourses from Mexican and American political officials. According to the Legal Counsel for International Trade at the Mexico Embassy in Washington, DC: "We cannot say that in order to clean up the corruption in Mexico we are going to make a free trade on a product such as used clothing. If there is corruption in Mexico we certainly will fight it and we are fighting it" (*San Antonio Express-News*, August 22, 2005). However, the deputy assistant US trade representative for North America declared, "Any restrictions that Mexico has in place we would like to eliminate. There are very few prohibitions. That makes used clothing unique" (*San Antonio Express-News*, August 22, 2005).

Indeed, used clothing was considered a very specific case in NAFTA negotiations and documents. Section 9 of Annex 300-B states,

"The Parties have established a Committee on Trade in Worn Clothing, comprising representatives of each Party." Initially, this committee's mandate was to "assess the potential benefits and risks that could result from the elimination of existing restrictions on trade between the Parties in worn clothing, including the effects on business and employment opportunities, and on the market for textile and apparel goods in each Party." This specific section of NAFTA also states,

> A Party may maintain restrictions in effect on the date of entry into force of the NAFTA on the importation of worn clothing, unless the Parties agree otherwise on the basis of the recommendations presented to the Commission by the Committee on Trade in Worn Clothing.

A report of the NAFTA Committee on Trade in Worn Clothing, published in 1997 and made available by the Canadian Department of Foreign Affairs and International Trade, confirmed that the American and Mexican representatives to this committee first met informally in April 1994, and that all three parties (Canada being the third party) attended a formal meeting held two years later in Mexico City (NAFTA Committee on Trade in Worn Clothing 1997). This report does not, however, provide any information on the work accomplished by the NAFTA Committee since 1996. Although NAFTA has incontestably brought a freer flow of "legitimate" commodities among the United States, Mexico, and Canada, thus creating new opportunities in Mexico for commerce to capture markets inside the country, *fayuqueros* have continued to respond to strong consumer demand for all sorts of contraband goods, such as used clothing, that continue to fall outside the scope of NAFTA regulations.

USED CLOTHING: AN ILLEGALLY IMPORTED COMMODITY IN MEXICO

The Mexican government has legally restricted the trade in used clothing to those holding an import license *(permiso previo)* from the Dirección General de Comercio Exterior (Directorate of External Trade) of the Secretaría de Economía (Ministry of the Economy). This import license is intended to be used to regulate and control the entry of certain products such as used goods, but apparently the Secretaría de Economía has never received a request for an import licence. Moreover, among the Mexican authorities there seem to be different interpretations of the regulations on trade in used clothing. In an interview given to a Juarez journalist in November 2003, the head (*administrador*) of the customs office in Juarez did not seem to know the exact reasons why the importation of used clothing was regulated in Mexico (*El Diario*, November 24, 2003). After claiming sanitary reasons ("because, it could bring a lot of diseases"), he rapidly changed his mind when informed that sanitary authorities did not have jurisdiction over the import of used clothing. Only after some investigation was the *administrador* able to say that the importation of second-hand clothing in Mexico was regulated by the Secretaría de Economía.

An official of the Secretaría de Economía interviewed by the same journalist did confirm that his office was in charge of delivering import licences for used clothing, but he indicated that in twelve years no one had ever applied for such a licence: "Nobody has presented a solicitude, which means that nobody is authorized to import used clothing" (*El Diario*, November 24, 2003). According to this official, it would be very difficult for traders to fulfill all of the specific requirements for an import licence. For example, they must provide information on the country of origin of the clothes and the classification of the garments, according to their material, in order for the customs tax to be fixed, as well as detailed fiscal information, which, because most traders operate informally, would be very difficult. The official concluded by assuming that the licence would probably be denied anyway: "The Mexican textile industry would probably go against it, but this is unsure until someone makes an application" (*El Diario*, November 24, 2003).

It is practically impossible to evaluate the total amount of used clothing that is brought from El Paso to Juarez every day, but in 2003 an underestimated five tons of used clothing was said to be smuggled across the border each day (*El Diario*, November 24, 2003). It is also very difficult to estimate the total amount of used clothing that is impounded by Mexican authorities. They regularly confiscate huge quantities, up to twenty-five tons (*El Norte*, December 29, 2001) and sometimes as much as fifty tons (*El Norte*, March 3, 2001). The authorities usually destroy used clothes as a sanitary precaution due to concerns about infections and pests (*El Paso Times*, October 10, 1999), but they impound smaller amounts of as little as sixty to one hundred kilograms (130 to 220 pounds). Because it is up to agents to confiscate used clothing that they believe is destined for resale in Juarez, they must be convinced that the clothes are for personal use. "It has to be justified by the person's size and the length of the travel," according to one Mexican customs official in Juarez (*El Paso Times*, October 10, 1999).

The real target of the Mexican customs authorities remains the larger importers of used clothing. At the beginning of 2004 the "brand new" *administrador* of the border customs in Juarez announced the imminent installation of sensors to detect overloaded vehicles and video cameras to register licence plates at the moment of entry in Juarez (*El Diario*, February 2, 2004). The official was very confident that the new system would help in detecting the *fayuca hormiga* of used clothing through the international bridges and put on file the vehicles used by the *fayuqueros*. Smugglers caught in this illegal activity can receive steep fines. In addition to the import tax, at 35 percent, they can be fined an amount equivalent to 70 to 100 percent of the value of the used clothing, which can be as much as 20,000 pesos, or US$ 2,000 (*El Paso Times*, October 10, 1999). Their car may also be confiscated until they pay, and their used clothing imports are seized.

This seizing of second-hand clothes is coordinated in some cases with the municipal government of Juarez. Municipal public security agents recently impounded 850 kilograms (about 1,900 pounds) of used clothing and footwear. The merchandise and the vehicle in which it was transported were then turned over to the Procuraduría General de la República (Office of the Federal Attorney General); the amount of import taxes evaded in this specific case was estimated to exceed 25,000 pesos, or US$ 2,500 (*El Diario*, April 25, 2006).

The municipal government seems to be increasingly involved in law-enforcement operations directed at used-clothing *fayuqueros*. The involvement of municipal authorities at this level stands in sharp contrast, however, to their administrative role in the regulation of municipal commerce. Although used clothing is a restricted import in Mexico and thus imported illegally across the border, it is "legally" sold along Juarez curbs and street markets. In fact a significant number of the used-clothing vendors are licensed by the municipal government and have vending permits issued by the Dirección de Comercio Municipal (Directorate of Municipal Commerce) of the City of Juarez. These vending permits allow the sale of brand-new and second-hand goods, contraband or not. Street-market leaders usually play an active role in securing vending permits on behalf of used-clothing vendors. As well, there are only a few municipal inspectors to enforce vending regulations in the hundreds of popular markets (*tianguis*) dispersed across the city (*colonias*).

Some of these markets in Juarez are under the leadership of the Comité de Defensa Popular (Popular Defense Committee, or CDP), one of the most important of the several popular organizations that operate in northern Mexico. As Staudt (1998, 50) has explained, "Under CDP leadership, settlers 'invaded' publicly and privately owned land to create new *colonias*. CDP leaders maintain a dense, top-down organization reinforced with weekly meetings." During the 1980s the CDP's clientele in Juarez included a large number of the cross-border traders in used goods (Lau 1991, 47). According to Staudt (1998, 191), the CDP is well known in Juarez for providing protection for informal traders and *fayuca* commerce. Indeed, some of the CDP's leaders were actively involved in the development of an underground structure for the importation and freight transport of foreign goods throughout the state of Chihuahua during the 1980s. The CDP remains a powerful actor in the informal economy of Juarez, playing an active role as a mediator between the state and local civil society. The CDP in Juarez is certainly one of the most powerful illustrations of what Brunet-Jailly (2005, 633) calls "the political clout of borderland communities."

Although the importation of used clothing into Mexico has evolved into a practice that is categorized as "illegal" by the state, this cross-border trade enjoys widespread "social legitimacy" in borderland communities, due to its local economic importance to the survival of Mexican border consumers. As even a former head of the customs office in Juarez has acknowledged, the only way to avoid smuggling is to allow the import of used clothing: "Anyway, they are going to cross it [the border], the necessity is too important because people need to purchase inexpensive clothing" (*El Diario*, November 24, 2003).

Furthermore, as Martinez (1994, 313) has pointed out, smuggling ordinary goods is "an illegal activity that borderlanders easily rationalize" because they see it as a necessity for carrying on daily life and as an essential component of the unique economic integration of the border region. Martinez (1994, 53) also observes that

> while government intervention is expected for the purpose of enforcing national tariff laws or keeping out undesirable products, borderlanders also expect officials to be flexible and tolerant, allowing a certain amount of illegal traffic to go on in order to maintain the delicate interdependence between the two sides of the border.

Thus smuggling or illegal cross-border flows open up a significant space of negotiation between structure and agency in these borderlands.

THE CROSS-BORDER TRADE IN USED CLOTHING BETWEEN EL PASO AND CIUDAD JUAREZ

The present-day market in Ciudad Juarez for recycled and refurbished clothing is vast. Mexican traders travel daily to El Paso to purchase used clothing by the pound at several warehouses downtown. Currently, the most important commercial used-clothing dealer in downtown El Paso is the Mid-West Textile Company. Founded in 1982, Mid-West Textile has grown into one of the largest graders of used clothing in North America, grading more than 22 million kilograms (50 million pounds) of clothing every year in its processing plant. One of Mid-West's main suppliers is Noamex, Inc., of Brooklyn, New York, which makes periodic shipments to the Texas communities of El Paso, Laredo, McAllen, and Brownsville. Mid-West also deals directly with the local Goodwill Industries by buying the overstock of used clothing from the nine Goodwill stores around El Paso.

Mid-West Textile's plant has more than 200 employees trained in processing, sorting, and grading clothing in large volumes on the basis of quality, style, and fabric. They sort the clothing into 600 classifications, some of which are intended for industrial use as rag, some for the "vintage" clothing market, and some for export. The garments meant for export are compressed into bales (*pacas*), weighing between 45 and 635 kilograms (100 and 1,400 pounds), which are then wrapped in waterproof plastic and bound with metal straps. The company ships 90 percent of these used clothes throughout Asia, Europe, and Africa (*El Paso Times*, October 10, 1999; *El Diario*, November 24, 2003).

Although Mid-West does not directly export to Mexico, the company sells 10 percent of its used clothes by the pound from its sales centre, mostly to Mexican buyers from Juarez. According to the cross-border traders from Juarez, its sales centre is one of the most popular warehouses of *ropa usada* (used clothing) because of its variety of choice and its wholesale prices.

Many Juarez traders cross the border legally into El Paso with their laser visa once or twice a week to buy second-hand clothing at the warehouses, where they sort the bales of used clothing on the spot.

Each bale contains a particular type of garment (such as Polo Men, Blouse Poly, Skirt Denim, Legging, Polo Lady, Jeans) and can weigh as much as 450 kilograms (1,000 pounds). Traders who purchase a larger number of bales can count on the services of *surtidoras* (sorters) to help them in the sorting process. Some *surtidoras* cross the border into El Paso every day to come to the sales centre, where they receive a certain amount of money for each bale they sort for the regular buyers. The sorting process consists of throwing away any garment that is too discoloured or outmoded or has too many holes and then identifying the remaining clothes according to two categories. The "number one" category is generally for brand-name clothes that have been worn only once or twice or have arrived intact, price tags and all. They have a higher resale price and usually end up displayed on hangers or body forms in Juarez market stalls. Clothes assigned to the "number two" category are of lower quality and are sometimes sold directly on the floor at a lower price.

Purchasing the stock in El Paso is the most straightforward part of the used-clothing trade. The real uncertainty and expense comes with bringing the used clothes back to Mexico. Ciudad Juarez and El Paso are linked by four separate bridges. Entry to Mexico via the international bridges is screened through a red light/green light random system of car and pedestrian inspection, operated by the Mexican customs authorities. A green light means an automatic customs clearance while a red light leads to an inspection. Considering that the proportion of green lights is said to be 95 percent of the total (*El Diario*, November 27, 2003), the probability of crossing with used clothing without being stopped is relatively high. Thus numerous women from Juarez who buy used clothing in the El Paso warehouses lug their best finds to the international bridge and sneak them across the border, usually by presenting themselves as shoppers (Staudt 2001, 127) and trying to minimize the size of their bags, or by making more frequent trips in order to avoid the customs agents' attention. Nonetheless, the probability of having to pay informally for their imports in the form of *mordidas* (bribes) to the Mexican customs agents is never excluded. Other buyers smuggle the used clothing across the border by folding their purchases in clothes baskets in the trunks of their cars, with fabric softener sheets to mask the smell of mothballed used clothes, in order to make it look as if they are coming back from doing their laundry in El Paso if they are stopped for a car inspection. Those who travel south by bus into the interior of Mexico to sell used clothing must usually pay a set of bribes for their imports, which can range as high as double the worth of the used clothing, at a number of government checkpoints (Hellman 1994, 155).

The Juarez vendors who do not want to risk crossing with used clothing on their own can rely on a network of *pasadores* (smugglers) dedicated exclusively to the process of smuggling such merchandise across the border. The *pasadores* offer their services in exchange for a certain amount of money, which depends on the amount of used clothing to be taken across the border. The *pasadores,* who are almost all men, act as packers, loaders, and drivers, and they use mini-vans for their smuggling activities. These vehicles, known as *venaditas* in the argot of the *fayuca,* usually have tinted windows, missing back seats, border plates, and reinforced suspensions in order to carry their cargos of used clothing, which can weigh as much as 450 kilograms (1,000 pounds). The *pasadores* have contacts among Mexican customs officials, who allow them to make numerous trips in their *venaditas* from El Paso to Juarez, and they smuggle a large volume of used clothing every day in exchange for bribes. However, these bribes only certify their border crossing (*pasada*) and are no guarantee of safe passage once they arrive in Juarez, where they may face other forms of extortion. They are always at risk of being stopped by officers of the Policia Federal Preventiva (Federal Preventative Police) and having to pay them an extra *mordida.* Failure to pay can lead to the confiscation of their entire cargo of used clothing and the vehicle in which it is being transported.

The traders' cross-border sourcing and smuggling activities are a response to Mexican consumers' demand for second-hand clothing from the United States. These activities are also essential to a vast network of Juarez vendors who prefer to rely on local sources of used clothing, either because they do not have laser visas or because the weekly volume of used clothing they purchase is too small. Some used-clothing vendors sell their merchandise in front of their houses, while others manage to get stalls at one of the numerous Juarez markets. Vendors usually display the clothes, which have been washed and ironed, on hangers to add value to the garments. Their strategy is to de-emphasize the second-hand nature of the clothes while displaying their American origin as much as possible. The thrift stores' price tags or the brand-name labels still attached to some garments in the "number one" category are never removed, in order to keep every trace of their foreign origin intact, which appears to be very meaningful to their marketing.

Most low-income Mexican border consumers cannot afford to purchase new brand-name clothes in El Paso and rely instead on the local markets for smuggled second-hand name-brand clothes, which are marketed as fashionable American garments and can be purchased at lower prices than locally produced garments or branded copies made in China. Whether consumers come into the *segundas* (flea markets) with the intention of buying in order to resell or to shop for a special item to complement their wardrobe, consumers are selective when purchasing second-hand garments, just as wholesalers of *ropa usada* are selective when sorting bales of used clothes in the warehouses of El Paso.

CONCLUSION

The borderlanders who introduce used clothing into Mexico clandestinely or who pay bribes to Mexican custom officers in order to do so are carrying on a local tradition that began in the nineteenth century. As Oscar Martinez (1994, 314) has noted, "Over time, the only changes in the contraband game have been in the volume of the merchandise making its way from one country to the other and in the strategies invented to circumvent the law." Although Mexico's interaction with American used clothing goes back several decades, trade in this commodity did not begin to flourish along its boundary with the United States until the mid-1960s, when many commercial used-clothing dealers in American border cities, most of them family-owned businesses, started in the trade. This period in the borderlands corresponds to the accelerated industrialization that was fuelled by the establishment of *maquiladoras* in Mexican border cities.

Many less industrialized countries, including Mexico, restrict the importation of second-hand clothing, while others control the volume or limit it to charitable purposes rather than resale. As Hansen (2004, 5) points out: "Regardless of import rules, and because borders are porous, smuggling and other illegal practices accompany the trade." Van Schendel and Abraham (2005, 60) have criticized current discourses on the cross-border movement of commodities prohibited by states for overlooking "the fact that it is consumer demand within the state territory that fuels unauthorized transborder flows." Goods that the local economy cannot supply and that the state considers undesirable become contraband as a result of state action. Moreover, the conceptual distinction between political legitimacy (or legality) and social legitimacy (or licitness), which Van Schendel and Abraham (2005) highlight in the introduction to their book, is rarely encountered in the discourse on unauthorized cross-border flows.

This conceptual distinction is especially relevant in the case of the unauthorized flow of used clothing across the US–Mexico border. It allows us to differentiate cross-border flows that are illegal because they defy formal political authority, yet are quite acceptable ("licit") in the eyes of the participants involved in these flows. This cross-border trade of used clothing is among those kinds of activities that large populations require for their livelihood, housing, and so on. In short, these activities have widespread legitimacy, even where they are illegal. As Josiah Heyman and Alan Smart (1999, 21) wrote in the introduction to an influential book on states and illegal practices, "Many illegal-labelled activities have much legitimate life in society (or in particular groups), and under such circumstances the state response can constitute bad law, adding to illegality and persecution." By categorizing used clothing as an illegitimate commodity and maintaining restrictive import trade policies on it, the Mexican government contributes to the creation of alternative markets, and to opportunities for the importation and distribution of this foreign commodity across the Mexican border.

The economic activities of the ant traders involved in the *fayuca hormiga* of used clothing "challenge state attempts to regulate the movement and flow of commodities, to define what are and what are not marketable goods" (Donnan and Wilson 1999, 88). This chapter has illustrated the agency of these economic actors that arises from the economic culture of the border region, and how ant traders bypass the multiple activities of governments and increase the economic integration of the border region. It does not, however, merely exemplify the agency that borderlanders demonstrate to get around state attempts to interrupt illegal cross-border flows. Its contribution to the theoretical framework outlined by Emmanuel Brunet-Jailly in the introduction to this volume also resides in its effort to illustrate how borders and flows can work either at the structural or at the agency level. Consequently this chapter has further highlighted the extent to which states' borders produce and enable clandestine border crossings.

ACKNOWLEDGEMENTS

Field research for this paper was first initiated in Ciudad Juarez in the summer of 2003 and continued between January and September 2005. Financial support for this research was provided by the Social Sciences and Humanities Research Council of Canada (SSHRC) through the research project "*De la récupération. Analyse ethnographique de la seconde vie des objets de consommation*" (2002–05), directed by Jean-Sébastien Marcoux (HEC Montréal), and a CGS Doctoral Scholarship (2004–07).

At the University of Texas at El Paso, I thank the Center for Inter-American and Border Studies (CIBS), to which I was affiliated in 2003, and Josiah McC. Heyman, Chair of the Sociology and Anthropology Department, for his thoughtful comments on this chapter and his continuous support of my research.

I am also grateful to all the people of Juarez who dedicate themselves to the cross-border trade in used clothing and have shared their experiences with me.

LITERATURE CITED

Anderson, Joan, and Martin de la Rosa. 1991. "Economic Survival Strategies of Poor Families on the Mexican Border." *Journal of Borderlands Studies* 6:2, 51–68.

Border Trade Alliance. 2004. *Extension of Time Limit on Admission of Certain Mexican Nationals*. [online]. www.thebta.org/keyissues/homelandsecurity/documents/Responseto30dayrule-FINAL.pdf [consulted April 24, 2006].

———. 2006. *Advocacy: Homeland Security and Secure Trade. Laser Visa / Border Crossing Card Reform*. [online]. www.thebta.org/keyissues/homelandsecurity/HomelandSecurity.cfm#laser [consulted April 24, 2006].

Brunet-Jailly, Emmanuel. 2005. "Theorizing Borders: An Interdisciplinary Perspective." *Geopolitics* 10:4, 633–49.

Donnan, H., and T. M. Wilson. 1999. *Borders: Frontiers of Identity, Nation and State*. New York and Oxford, UK: Berg.

El Paso Times. "Clothes Sold by Pound Attract Mexican Buyers." November 12, 1997.

El Sol de México. 2005. "Es ilegal 50% de la ropa que se vende en Mexico." [online]. www.elsoldemexico.com.mx/impreso/050509/finanzas/1finanzas.asp [consulted May 02, 2006].

Hansen, K. 2002. "Commodity Chains and the International Secondhand Clothing Trade: *Salaula* and the Work of Consumption in Zambia." *Theory in Economic Anthropology*, ed. Jean Ensminger. Walnut Creek, CA: AltaMira Press, 221–36.

———. 2004. "Helping or Hindering? Controversies around the International Second-Hand Clothing Trade." *Anthropology Today* 20:4, 3–9.

Hellman, J. 1994. *Mexican Lives*. New York: The New Press.

Heyman, J. McC. 1991. *Life and Labor on The Border. Working People of Northeastern Sonora, Mexico, 1886–1986*. Tucson: University of Arizona Press.

———. 1994. "The Organizational Logic of Capitalist Consumption on the Mexico–United States Border." *Research in Economic Anthropology* 15, 175–238.

———, McC., and A. Smart. 1999. "States and Illegal Practices: An Overview." *States and Illegal Practices*, ed. Josiah Heyman. New York and Oxford, UK: Berg, 1–24.

Lau, Rubén. 1991. "El Sector Informal y el CDP." *Nóesis* 6–7, 45–51.

Martínez, O. 1994. *Border People: Life and Society in the US–Mexico Borderlands*. Tucson: University of Arizona Press.

Medina, Martin. 2006. "Achieving the MDGs through the Informal Recycling Sector: A Case Study in Northern Mexico." Paper presented at the workshop on Solid Waste, Health, and the Millennium Development Goals, CWG–WASH, Kolkata, India, February 1–5.

Mid-West Textile Company [online]. www.midwest-textile.com [consulted April 4, 2006].

NAFTA Committee on Trade in Worn Clothing. 1997. "Report to the NAFTA Free Trade Commission" [online]. www.dfait-maeci.gc.ca/trade/nafta-alena/report2-en.asp [consulted April 24, 2006].

Office of Textiles and Apparel. 2006. North American Free Trade Agreement, Annex 300-B, Textile and Apparel Goods, Section 9: Trade in Worn Clothing and Other Worn Articles. [online]. otexa.ita.doc.gov/nafta/300bsec9.htm [consulted April 24, 2006].

Pelayo, Alonso, and Antonio Parra. 1994. *El Contexto Fronterizo de la Economía Informal* (Cuadernos de trabajo 23, Unidad de Estudios Regionales). Juárez: Universidad Autónoma de Ciudad Juárez.

San Antonio Express-News. 2005. "Illegal Resale Trade in Mexico Offers *Ropa Usada* for Dirt Cheap Prices." [online]. www.mysanantonio.com/news/mexico/stories/MYSA082205.1A.ropa_usada.86a9009.html [consulted April 12, 2006].

Spener, D., and B. Roberts. 1998. "Small Business, Social Capital, and Economic Integration on the Texas–Mexico Border." *The US–Mexico Border: Transcending Divisions, Contesting Identities*, eds. David Spener and K. Staudt. Boulder, CO: Lynne Rienner Publishers, 83–103.

Staudt, K. 1998. *Free Trade? Informal Economies at the US–Mexico Border*. Philadelphia: Temple University Press.

———. 2001. "Informality Knows No Borders? Perspectives from El Paso-Juárez." *SAIS Review* 21:1, 123–30.

United Nations. 2006. *International Trade by Commodities Statistics* [online]. www.intracen.org/tradstat/sitc3-3d/ep269.htm [consulted April 30, 2006].

United States Embassy, Mexico. 2004. "US Department of Homeland Security Expands Use of the Laser Visa/Border Crossing Card" [online]. mexico.usembassy.gov/mexico/ep040810borderstay.html [consulted April 24, 2004].

Vanguardia. 2006. *"Ropa usada, basura para EU negocio en México"* [online]. noticias.vanguardia.com.mx/d_i_521768_t_Ropa-usada,-basura-para-EU-negocio-en-México.htm [cited April 4, 2006].

Van Schendel, Willem, and Itty Abraham, eds. 2005. *Illicit Flows and Criminal Things. States, Borders and the Other Side of Globalization*. Bloomington and Indianapolis: Indiana University Press.

Vila, P. 2000. *Crossing Borders, Reinforcing Borders: Social Categories, Metaphors and Narrative Identities on the US–Mexico Frontier*. Austin: University of Texas Press.

CHAPTER 5

A NEW NORTHERN SECURITY AGENDA

Lassi Heininen and Heather N. Nicol

The Arctic has become a region of renewed and heightened geopolitical interest to decision-makers since the end of the Cold War. Despite the continuation of traditional security concerns within the region, attention has recently begun to shift from the military issues of strategic security that were previously tantamount to security within the region, such as the creation of the Distant Early Warning (DEW) system, to the broader challenges of achieving "human security," countering the risks imposed by global warming, and addressing the impact of new and pressing environmental threats on circumpolar environments.

In part the new environmental agenda is a result of the recognition of the growing impact of global sources of pollution, global warming, and military contamination on the circumpolar North. However, it is also a result of the growing awareness of the need to apply the concepts of sustainable development that originated in the 1980s, from forums such as the Brandt Commission (1980, 1983) or the Palme Commission (1982). The Brandt Commission is sometimes credited as the first international body to promote the idea of "comprehensive security" (although Olof Palme was one of the first to coin the phrase). This idea has comprehensive implications for three types of security needs, especially following the end of the Cold War: economic, environmental, and human. In discussing "Common Security" the Brandt Commission urged the transformation of traditional military-based notions of security to include a broader focus on "human security," which would require greater international cooperation, transparency, disarmament, and demilitarization. Notwithstanding the impact of the terrorist attacks on the United States on September 11, 2001, this new approach to defining security has had a catalytic impact on the structure of international relations within the circumpolar North as attention has shifted from maintaining strategic control of territory to promoting environmental cooperation and multilateralism (Center for Globalization Negotiations, Brandt 21 Forum 2006).

This chapter addresses the transformation of the security agenda, which has led to an integrating Arctic region where local agency influences broader issues and decisions. Indeed, the relationship between local agency and broader issues and decisions is reflected in the reconception and redefinition of "security," moving away from an exclusively state-centred and militarized geopolitical discourse to a more humanistic definition. This new definition is becoming increasingly relevant in the twenty-first century (Heininen 2004b) because the agencies responsible for human security have also changed. New regional actors and the new regional dynamic now focus not just on security in the sense of military policy but also on other aspects of security, such as the challenges and threats posed by long-range transboundary pollution. For example, a recently published scientific assessment of human development within the circumpolar North (Arctic Council, 2004) identified three main themes, or trends, in international relations and geopolitics within the region at the beginning of the twenty-first century, namely: increased circumpolar cooperation by indigenous peoples' organizations and subnational governments; new efforts toward region-building, with nations as major actors; and the development of a new relationship between the Arctic and the outside world, including both consideration of traditional security policy and threats to the environment and human populations.

Thus, while geopolitical discourse in the North has, until quite recently, focused almost exclusively upon either military or defence activities and the use of natural resources, changing definitions of human security are now influencing not only how security is defined but also how the parts of this globalized region relate to each other and to the outside. The result has been both a greater emphasis on the development of a comprehensive conceptualization of security and the development of new types of regional relationships. A restructuring and redefinition of the North–South relationship is reflected, for example, in the recently launched "northern dimension" policies of many of the circumpolar states, where foreign policy discussions revolve around distinctive attributes of the northern regions of Arctic states.

In order to appreciate the extent to which changes in the definition of security have influenced the circumpolar North, this chapter begins with a general exploration of the definition of "security," and the implications of changing security definitions and perceptions for the region. This is followed by a further exploration of the broad definition of "security" and the changes that the new approach has engendered in international relations within the circumpolar North, for example, its role in shaping international and interregional cooperation, and new external structures for cooperation, such as the "northern dimension" policy of the European Union (EU) or its counterpart within Canada's foreign policy. Ultimately the goal is to identify the relationships between structure and agency in the process of circumpolar integration and the redefinition of "human security" within the North. More specifically, the question to be answered is: how has the relative power of structure and agency varied across time and space according to specific political, geographical, and cultural conditions?

We go on to examine what is meant by "environmental security," and what effect it has on regional and national borders. We also consider whether public concern about transboundary pollution and recent academic discourse on risk threat can be translated into action, and, if so, whether they push officials to implement changes in the definition of security. To this end we explore the way in which broadly defined or comprehensive security has become integral to redefining transnational regions, boundaries, and corresponding recent foreign policies in the circumpolar North. In the final analysis this allows us to speculate about the specific boundary effects of such changes throughout the region and to ask whether the analytical frameworks identified in the introduction to this volume are relevant to our study of transnational border processes. That is: how has the transformed security agenda led to an integrating Arctic region, where local agency influences broader issues and decisions in previously impossible ways?

In addressing these issues we have used some very specific methodological approaches. We have examined official documents and working papers, newspapers, and commentaries on comprehensive and northern security, including documents such as *Canada and the Circumpolar World: The Northern Dimension of Canada's Foreign Policy* (Department of Foreign Affairs 2000) and the EU's two Northern Dimension action plans (European Union 2000, 2004), as well as the texts and discourse of more informal government workshops on global warming and regional governance. We have interviewed civil servants, decision-makers, and other actors at national, regional, and local levels, and collaborated on the nature of discourse deployed at regional meetings and workshops in which they participated (particular attention was paid to so-called active research methods). In light of this analysis, we suggest that, if questions of security are addressed broadly, both in academic discourse and political terms, then there are many ideas about the meaning of security and what should, or should not, be a "security" issue. The problem is to identify how changing definitions have been promoted by, and incorporated into, political and academic debate. For example, how does the concept of "comprehensive security" differ from that of traditional security?

REDEFINING SECURITY

There are many kinds of security in practice, many different understandings of it, and many different ways to define and conceptualize it. Because the concept appeals to basic human instincts—everyone wants to be secure and different people invariably have different security needs—security is relative and socially constructed (Westing 1988). Moreover, it is defined on the basis of subjective and objective assessments of specific threats and risks faced by a people, a society, a region, or a state, and therefore has both a spatial context and a social context. Such risks can be construed as emanating from outside but also as originating from within. Thus security can be understood as an intersubjective construction and a process of securitization, much as Vuori (2004, 5) has suggested. Security affairs and matters are complicated and multifunctional, existing on many different levels and in many different contexts, which makes "security" a broad concept. It includes traditional notions about a nation-state's predominant need for military security, which some, perhaps prematurely, now consider outdated, and for environmental security, which includes interpretations of risk and threat in a modern society. Indeed, as Miller (2001) has asserted, the end of the Cold War made room for increased attention to what were previously neglected subjects. He observes (Miller 2001, 32) that

> a good example is the connection between environmental problems, resource scarcities, and conflict . . . [D]uring the 1990s discussion

> of these issues was reinvigorated. A burgeoning literature explores possible causal linkages that lead from environmental concerns to conflict, examines particular cases in great detail, and explicitly considers the extent to which the environment deserves to be regarded as a security problem.

The new approach to security also stresses human rights, traditional society, social equity, and civil society, envisioning a sort of human and civil security that encompasses health and well-being. Today this concept of security is accepted as a given and is used normatively. The United Nations Commission on Human Security, for example, observed that "as security challenges become more complex and various new actors attempt to play a role, we need a shift in paradigm. The focus must broaden from the state to the security of people—to human security." This includes, by definition, policies in the areas of (1) protecting people in violent conflict; (2) protecting people from the proliferation of arms; (3) supporting the security of people on the move; (4) establishing human security transition funds for post-conflict situations; (5) encouraging fair trade and markets to benefit the extremely poor; (6) working to provide minimum living standards everywhere; (7) according higher priority to ensuring universal access to basic health care; (8) developing an efficient and equitable global system for patent rights; (9) empowering all people with universal basic education; and (10) clarifying the need for a global human identity while respecting the freedom of individuals to have diverse identities and affiliations (United Nations Commission on Human Security 2001).

Accordingly, this means not only security in the context of practical issues such as health, standard of living, and general well-being, as well as a life in peace without tension, conflict or war, but also in terms of values such as political freedom, democracy, respect for citizens, and freedom from a range of threats and risks, such as natural disasters, pollution, hunger and starvation, disease and illness, and terrorism. "Human security" can also be interpreted to include cultural survival, human rights, freedom of expression, and security of communication (see, for example, UNEP/GRID-Arendal 2004; Menshikov 2004). If we draw upon the theory of "low" politics that deals with environmental, social, and cultural issues or the desire to strengthen civil society, such agendas clearly emphasize the importance of the environment and its protection. Here the focus is not on controlling a region or gaining hegemonic military and political control but rather on reaching a socially stable, peaceful situation and an environmentally sustainable order (Chaturvedi 2000).

Quite apart from traditional military security, the new comprehensive circumpolar security discourse, which includes people and society, deals with practical environmental issues and access to resources, as well as the social and economic conditions of circumpolar peoples. It asks new questions, such as, how do we clean up the environmental mess when the mess is a product of Cold War efforts to secure military security? Nuclear waste in the Barents Sea region and pollution from radar stations of the North American DEW line system are both parts of this mess, and both resulted from efforts to "securitize" the North in traditional military terms, ultimately creating threats to the health and well-being of Arctic populations.

This new security discourse also asks if public concern about transboundary pollution and recent academic discourse on risk threat can be transferred into action. A perfect example of this is the so-called Murmansk speech, given by the former Soviet president Mikhail Gorbachev in the city of Murmansk in the Soviet North in 1987 (Gorbachev 1987). Gorbachev opened the door to new cooperation by making specific proposals for promoting environmental protection and reducing the potential harm of nuclear weapons in the circumpolar North, which subsequently became a powerful rhetoric embedded in a broader definition of security after the Cold War. Furthermore, there is considerable concern about depleting ozone layers, climatic change in the North, and the presence of heightened levels of persistent organic pollutants. Several questions must be answered. Will this concern translate into action to protect northern populations from these previously developed risks and, if so, what kind of action? Will the new security discourse on global warming, environmental degradation, pollution, and other emerging threats push Arctic officials to implement changes in problem definition as far as achieving security is concerned? Will new and effective frameworks for transnational cooperation be established? These questions are vital to understanding the current state of circumpolar geopolitics and the new security agenda, and they, along with the issue of what a change from traditional to comprehensive security entails, form the starting point of our discussion.

TRADITIONAL MILITARY SECURITY IN THE ARCTIC

As noted, traditional security generally means national security based on the territory of the sovereign state. To say that security guaranteed by the power of a state and its military organizations is the core of a unified state system would not be an exaggeration (see, for example, Buzan 1991). It has also been called weapons-oriented or unilateral competitive national military security, meaning that security is ultimately guaranteed by the military or a military deterrent (Newcombe 1986). In this sense traditional security emphasizes power, political and military, as a tool to achieve national security, and power is viewed as vital to ensuring the state's national interest. Moreover, security is almost exclusively concerned with establishing the authority of state governments and centres (Laitinen 2005), particularly to maintain control over national territory and natural resources, even beyond national borders in some cases.

The problem posed by this view is evident in figure 5.1, which outlines one set of potential nuclear and military "threats" in the North, particularly in the Barents Sea region (Heininen and Segerståhl 2002). Although military security initiatives have been developed to protect the national interests of northern states, the fallout is potentially transnational in character, raising new questions about cross-border relations. For example, tensions between Nordic countries and the former Soviet Union were heightened in the early 1990s over perceived levels of nuclear contamination in the Barents and Kara seas, as well as the fear of nuclear accidents from neglected Russian nuclear fleets. Nuclear waste threatened not only human health but also fish stocks and maritime resources. For small nations dependent on northern resources and fishing grounds, the stakes were high indeed. Diplomatic explosions followed a sharp rhetorical exchange in which Norway accused the former Soviet Union of "threatening" the environmental security of its citizens.

Indeed, although traditional thinking about the importance of the North in terms of military security dominated definitions of human security in the region until the end of the Cold War, the threat of military activities did not end with the collapse of the Soviet Union. In some instances it was heightened. Different kinds of military activities emerged within the region that changed the way in which both the strategic importance of the region was calculated and human security

Figure 5.1 Nuclear Problems in the Barents Sea Area

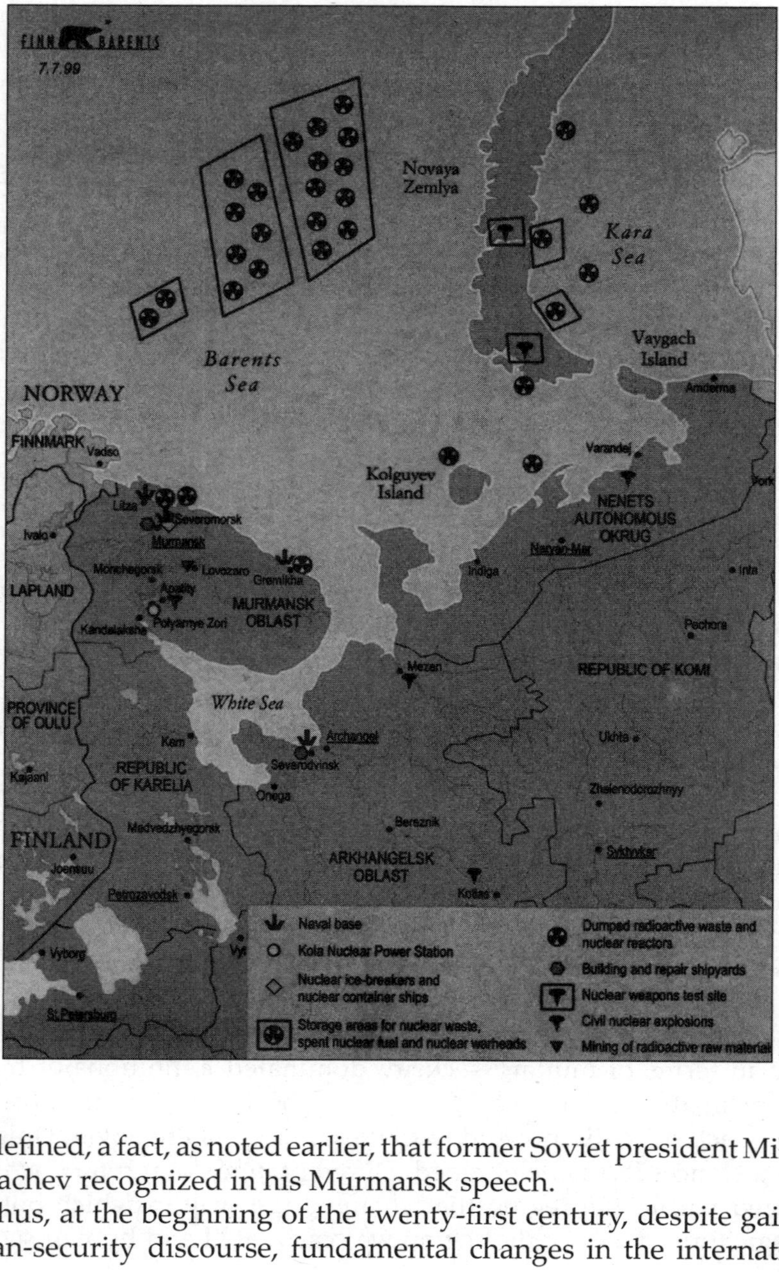

was defined, a fact, as noted earlier, that former Soviet president Mikhail Gorbachev recognized in his Murmansk speech.

Thus, at the beginning of the twenty-first century, despite gains in human-security discourse, fundamental changes in the international system, and the obvious influence of globalization, security is still largely structured according to the concept of traditional security policy. Indeed, a recent Arctic human development report, written under the auspices of the Sustainable Development Working Group (SDWG) of the Arctic Council, reconfirmed that the circumpolar North still has a high strategic importance both militarily, especially for the United States and the Russian Federation, and economically (Duhaime 2004; Heininen 2004b) due to the use of, and competition over, the region's rich resource base, especially strategic resources such as oil and gas. Moreover, the appearance of the military and the construction of new infrastructure or training areas remain common within the region even today. For example, Norway and the North Atlantic Treaty Organization (NATO) planned to expand a military training area for testing missile systems, and for bombing and military exercises, in the traditional summer reindeer herding area in Lakselv in northern Norway (Nelleman 2003, 1–2).

Events such as these highlight the close relationship between the environment and traditional security (Galtung 1982; Westing 1988). The need to reduce environmental pollution and the risk to northern populations has recently drawn attention to what has been called the "armies' war" on the environment in peacetime, forcing recognition that armies are not only "normal" polluters but also "protected" polluters, in that they generally operate outside environmental legislation (Renner 1991; Finger 1991).

Further evidence of the transnational character of military risks and the resilience of military security, despite an overall paradigm shift, includes increased potential for industrial and military accidents of the sort suggested by the nuclear problem in the Barents Sea area. As strategic northern resources come under increased pressure, the potential for heightened levels of transnational pollution and environmental catastrophe due to industrial or military accidents expands the risk. Complicating the matter is the fact that since 9/11, public demand for a greater military presence in the North, and for a stronger military representation in national security political decision-making, has increased.

Moreover, even though there has been a recent shift in thinking about military security and military technology, from the paradigm of "quantity" to that of "quality," the latter has meant changes in warfare that emphasize not just quality but also "mobility." An example is the

US National Missile Defense (NMD) system, which has significantly affected the circumpolar North, leading, on one hand, to fewer military bases, troops, and radar stations in fewer geographical locations, and, on the other hand, to a more intensive military presence, including testing and training, in some northern areas suited to such activities. As large and sparsely populated areas, northern peripheries are potentially suited to deploying, operating, and testing arms systems, including nuclear-weapons systems, as well as military training and manoeuvres. This dualism of demilitarization and remilitarization has meant that while military bases are closed and numbers of troops are decreased in some regions, other regions, including new regions, are being used for military purposes (see Heininen, forthcoming).

Thus, even as greater environmental threats posed by military security are recognized, a lack of military security is perceived as potentially leaving the region open to increased terrorist threats. In this sense it is important not to underestimate or oversimplify the issue by saying that circumpolar military threats are simply a legacy of the Cold War, a "Russian problem," or even a northern European problem. The close relationship between the Arctic and the outside world is always present (as illustrated by figure 5.1). A substantial part of the radioactive contamination of the Barents Sea region with technetium-99 is a result not only of atmospheric nuclear tests but also of nuclear activities in southern latitudes, especially from nuclear reprocessing plants in Sellafield in the United Kingdom and Chelyabinsk in West Siberia (Heininen and Segerståhl 2002).

In fact, the multidimensional processes that generate military and environmental risks in the North operate through a large number of actors, both Russian and non-Russian, who are interested and active in nuclear issues, including those who smuggle components of nuclear or other weapons of mass destruction in and out of the region. This makes nuclear security, if properly understood as part of comprehensive security, particularly complicated, because nuclear threats are usually associated with both military and civilian activities, even though nuclear power was originally developed for military purposes. In the Arctic region, especially in the Russian north, there is no clear dividing line between military and civilian security issues, so nuclear safety in the Barents Sea area, whether based on environmental protection or human security issues, must be implemented through international cooperation, which will require strong political will and a long period of international negotiations. Moreover, official policy discussions on nuclear safety related to military sources, as well as unified states and intergovernmental organizations engaging in political discussions to negotiate agreements—such as the agreement creating the Barents Euro-Arctic Region (BEAR), or the Agreement on Military Environmental Cooperation (AMEC) between Norway, Russia, and the United States—will be ineffective without the technical ability to clean up pollution and environmental catastrophes. This can be problematic, however, as the case of threats from radioactive contamination in the Norwegian Sea has shown.

ENVIRONMENTAL SECURITY AND TRANSNATIONAL CO-OPERATION

Although military security is rooted in normative ideas about national sovereignty and territory, it has a transnational character and scale of influence. Indeed, individual nation-states no longer have the ability to contain the environmental fallout from traditional security activities. However, there are other, equally important, environmental threats and risks that originate from non-military sources. In the context of this volume, a new relationship between structure and agency has clearly emerged within the circumpolar North that is reflected in political structures at the international, national, and subnational levels. For example, there has been a perceptible trend toward a new security agenda that considers the impact of globalized threats on the northern physical environment. Although in other regions globalization is often interpreted as increased flows of trade in goods and services, globalized threats within the circumpolar North include long-range air and sea pollution, climate change, and global warming. Global warming would not only affect northern communities and their cultures, infrastructures, and regional identities, but also threaten sea and air transportation routes, as well as food security and indigenous lifestyles (Paci et al. 2004). In one sense this new security dimension has opened up a new regional dimension in environmental cooperation, one that includes new intergovernmental and supranational governmental agencies to implement a transnational environmental agenda. This approach stresses that peoples, societies, and the environment are as vital to comprehensive security as geography and political systems are. Moreover, peoples, societies, and environments are local as well as regional, with the potential to be transformative in terms of both security and transnational or cross-border initiatives to advance comprehensive regional security agendas.

This recent round of environmental cooperation, framed by transnationalism, was given new life in 1987 when, as noted earlier, Mikhail Gorbachev called for the peoples and countries of Arctic states to cooperate. Shortly afterward Nordic countries such as Norway and Finland issued a similar call when they too began to define their northern policies. These events began a new kind of international process, one outcome of which was the signing in 1991 of the Arctic Environmental Protection Strategy (AEPS) by the "Arctic Eight," the states (Canada, Denmark, Finland, Iceland, Norway, Sweden, the United States, and the former Soviet Union) that cover the northernmost parts of the globe defined as the Arctic (see figure 5.2). The AEPS was initiated by Finnish diplomatic efforts and its content was greatly influenced by Canada. The signatories meet regularly in order to craft policies to increase the protection of the Arctic from environmental degradation through coordinated efforts.

The AEPS was clearly an environment-focused initiative. Transboundary pollution and the need for environmental protection in the North were among the main reasons for this international cooperation, which extended across what were then the borders dividing the two major ideological blocs of the Cold War. The AEPS now includes the following programs and working groups: the Arctic Monitoring and Assessment Program (AMAP), established in 1991 to "monitor identified pollution risks and their impacts on the Arctic ecosystem"; the initiative for the Protection of the Arctic Marine Environment (PAME); a program for Emergency Preparedness and Response (EPPR); and an agreement on the need for Conservation of Arctic Fauna and Flora (CAFF). Cooperation later expanded into other aspects of multilateral decision-making in the North, particularly through the AEPS Task Force on Sustainable Development.

The momentum created by the AEPS consensus on resolving northern development challenges also contributed to the formation of the Arctic Council in 1993 (Arctic Council 1996). The AEPS Task Force on Sustainable Development was transformed into the Arctic Council's Working Group on Sustainable Development (SDWG), while the council assumed the role of overseeing and continuing the work of the AEPS, but with a broader and continued focus on foreign policy.

Figure 5.2 Arctic Monitoring and Assessment Program Area

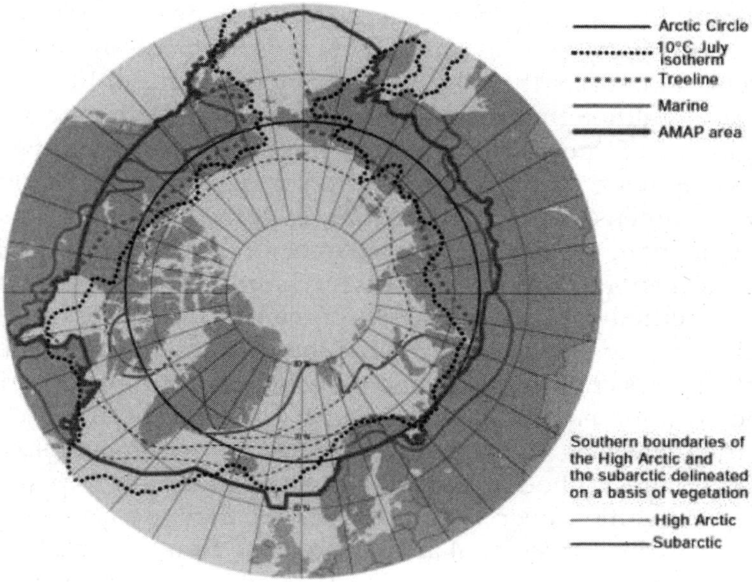

Source: *Arctic Council. Arctic Monitoring and Assessment Report*. Oslo: Arctic Council, 1997.

The AEPS, the Arctic Council, and other similar northern initiatives, such as the Barents Euro-Arctic Council (BEAC) initiated by Norway in 1993, contributed to this broader foreign-policy focus by spurring the EU to develop its own "northern dimension" in foreign policy as part of its external and transboundary policies. The aim was to deal with issues specific to the three member states of the EU that are among the "Arctic Eight" (Denmark, Finland, and Sweden), as well as to other northern European countries (Iceland, Norway, and Russia), other countries in the Baltic Sea region (Estonia, Latvia, and Lithuania), and their immediate neighbours (Poland and Germany). The growing recognition of the importance of the North thus encouraged recognition of a broader process of internationalization and even globalization, transforming or breaching international borders in keeping with the EU's other northern neighbours and member states.

It was also in keeping with broader developments throughout the circumpolar North, where the ultimate shape of regionalism and region-building within the Arctic reflected a new internationalism based upon such issues as sustainable development and indigenous representation, rather than the old security discourse of the Cold War. In this sense, although the rise of the circumpolar North may represent the beginning of a new North–South metaphor concerning dependency and development, it also represents, to some extent, the rise of a new East–West dimension among the countries of the Western Hemisphere. This is evident in the activities of the Arctic Council's Arctic Monitoring and Assessment Program (AMAP), which aims to create a transnational space concerned directly with environmental security issues (Arctic Council 1997). In effect the AMAP is the instrument that defines the Arctic Council's environmental mandate in the circumpolar region.

The idea of environmental security is relevant for the North given the increasing number of complicated environmental conflicts occurring there. Although these are mainly due to the expanded use of, and competition over, natural resources, they are also partly due to the rich variety of regional actors and those from outside the region with different interests. Arctic political communities are beginning to play a more important role in the process of defining translational and cross-border cooperation. For example, northern indigenous peoples' definitions of "human security" often differ appreciably from those of southern majorities. Northern indigenous peoples hope not only to decrease the influence of, and their dependence on, non-regional actors and outside forces, who interpret the region as a potential military arena or a reserve of natural resources, but also to promote sustainable development in the region (Heininen, Käkönen, and Jalonen 1995). Competition, or even conflict, between indigenous peoples and the respective Arctic states has the potential to continue, especially in the context of the Arctic Council, as when the council attempts to define "sustainable development" and, more especially, to implement it in the Arctic as both a main goal and another pillar of its agenda (Heininen 2004a).

This observation is even more cogent for the oil-dependent states and centres of the Northern Hemisphere because of their heightened demand for hydrocarbon resources and the evidence of large, untapped oil reserves in the circumpolar region. The geopolitics of oil and other strategic resources has no doubt played a considerable role in the efforts of both the United States and Canada to maintain control over vast northern regions in North America. Recent debate has focused on the perceived need to drill for oil in the Arctic National Wildlife Refuge (ANWR), regardless of its designation as a protected area, a debate that has created ripples of reaction throughout the United States, as well as within the political and indigenous communities of Canada. The ANWR debate highlights the degree to which issues other than ballistic missiles and nuclear submarines have become incorporated into northern security discourses. The focus of the debate is clearly the issue of energy security versus the protection of natural wilderness and the Central Arctic and Porcupine caribou herds. Even more important, from this perspective, is the fact that oil exploitation in the wildlife refuge may potentially threaten human security, specifically the livelihoods of the Gwich'in people, who are situated in the Canadian Arctic proximate to the ANWR and are partly dependent on the Porcupine caribou herd that calves inside it. The ANWR dispute looms as a cross-border issue, pitting the discourse of US energy security against those of sustainable development, food security, and comprehensive human security. The Gwich'in claim that the destruction of ANWR habitat, specifically in the area of the coastal calving grounds, may well result in the decimation of the caribou herds, which cross international borders in the spring and fall, and the destruction of their traditional food base and culture.

This dispute not only pits country against country but also pits each country's distinctive geopolitical discourse and understanding of human security against the other. Indeed, the predominant US view of the North American circumpolar North lacks a more general or even geographical perspective, as well as a focus on human security. Counter to the northern European approach, for example, US interests in the region are not multilateral and are limited almost exclusively to environmental concerns, as evidenced by the nature of its participation in the AEPS and the Arctic Council, and by the structure of scientific research emanating from US foundations that focus on the North. Furthermore, the goals of the United States are strategic, as illustrated by its North Europe Initiative (NEI) of the 1990s and early twenty-first century. A policy directed toward the Baltic Sea region and northwestern Russia, the NEI was promoted as an effort to engage northern Europe in a democracy project, couched in the discourse of human security (see Shearer 1997; Talbott 1997). In reality it focused on strategic geopolitical goals, such as erasing East–West divisions by increasing stability in northern Europe, with a plan to include the Baltic states in NATO, to support their inclusion in the EU, and to engage Russia in new dialogues.

This returns us to the question raised at the outset of this chapter: have new security agendas been translated into changes in problem definition within the North and has concern been translated into action? In this sense it is important to understand how broader concerns such as human or civil security, constructed with reference to the environment, are addressed within the region. This is particularly relevant to such basic areas as achieving food security under conditions of rapid climate change, which challenge the ability of indigenous peoples to secure traditional or country food. Although food security means "the continued and predictable availability and access to food, derived from northern environments through indigenous cultural practices" (Paci et al. 2004, 1), indigenous peoples have recently become conscious of, concerned about, and active around toxic threats and impacts of climate change in the North in general.

Accompanying this new area of concern and activism is an emphasis on human security, directly in terms of programs aimed at human security issues and indirectly through environmental protection measures, such as activities to decrease and stop transboundary pollution, lessen the impacts of climate change, and increase the capacity for human responses to climate change. Moreover, environmental protection in the North can be understood as an implementation of a global public good, and a practical and timely vehicle for region-building in the North, especially in the context of the Arctic Council. Human security within the integrated Arctic must also be understood in terms of the political structure, agenda, and culture of indigenous peoples, and their local and regional initiatives. These initiatives are distinct from those of the South and require regional cross-border cooperation. The border between North and South is less likely to be breached as regional integration increasingly suggests a sort of East–West solidarity on specific economic, environmental, and security issues.

THE RELATIONSHIP BETWEEN SECURITY AND GOVERNANCE

New multiple, increasingly globalized (especially North–South-oriented), and long-range environmental problems, such as nuclear waste and climate change, have fostered a renewed interest in the environment and contributed to the creation of a supranational forum for discussion of environmental protection, the Arctic Council, and to the various environmental treaties that now prevail in the circumpolar North. This international cooperation has made new forms of more internationalized governance very relevant, not just in decreasing the impact of environmental problems but also in governing how natural resources are used and by whom. The circumpolar North does not have a comprehensive international regime of the same type that covers the Antarctic, nor does it have legally binding agreements to control the use of natural resources. However, some international agreements are now in place to protect the environment and promote sustainable development. The Arctic Council aims "to increase stability" and promote "sustainable development," while the signing of the Stockholm Convention on persistent organic pollutants (POPs) relates to environmental problems due to long-range (air and sea) pollution and the recent problems of traditional livelihoods. It was, all in all, an interesting success story on fruitful cooperation between northern indigenous peoples and the Arctic epistemic community (Arctic Council 2002; Flöjt 2003).

Equally significant are the other political, legal, and institutional changes in governance that have occurred during the past few decades and have initiated changes in the relationship between northern peoples and government processes. Some of the first initiatives in the restructuring of governance began as early as the Cold War, when, for example, Greenland obtained "home rule" through the processes of decolonization and devolution. Since then new ways of governing have been identified within the northern regions by both national and subnational governments. Among the main trends affecting governance of Arctic resources have been the transfer or devolution of power to local decision-making and the widening involvement of residents in ownership and development of lands and resources (Caulfield 2004, 135–36), such as the Land Claims and Self-government Agreement (2004) between the government of the Tli Cho people, the government of the Northwest Territories, and the government of Canada, or the establishment of the Canadian Territory of Nunavut in 1999.

Events such as this suggest that devolution is a significant force that will likely continue to develop and influence the regions. This leads us to consider another interesting issue, the relationship between security and governance, particularly the problem of developing a regionally based capacity for response to security affairs, even security policy, within the circumpolar North. In order to effectively examine the issue a definition of security must be adopted that is embedded within the region, one that includes development, environment, societies, peoples, identities and interests, culture, democracy, and the rights of citizens. In short it requires consideration of how and by whom security is to be defined regionally, and how it can be implemented. However, is it possible to define security based on a region (Heininen 2004a, 38–39)?

Currently, regional governance is characterized by a dualism, or even gaps. On one hand, international organizations and forums in the North, such as the Arctic Council and BEAR, were established after the Cold War to facilitate transboundary and functional cooperation in the fields of "low" politics, in order to increase stability and security, as part of a general stability policy, the "peace project," spearheaded by the West. These external political structures have dealt with environmental protection, including nuclear safety, but not with traditional security policy or military security policy (see Arctic Council 1996). As a result northern regional actors and residents were excluded from activities that dealt with the environment and regional development, as well as from security-policy planning. This was both problematic and sensitive since security was still interpreted to mean only traditional security based upon a state, guaranteed ultimately by the military, and discussed and defined by governments and foreign-policy elites. On the other hand, these new international bodies, especially the BEAC and the AMEC, include concrete and international agendas for nuclear safety in the Arctic, where radioactive contamination and the nuclear problem were caused mainly by military activity during the Cold War (Heininen and Segerståhl 2002). As early as the 1980s many governments, and even some citizens, of the Nordic countries considered themselves as stakeholders in the international nuclear negotiations process, although in most cases they remained outside the formal negotiation process. In the early 1990s a change in problem definition occurred in the relationship between the military and the environment when the environmental impacts of the military, especially radioactive contamination, were implicitly included in the political agendas of governments (Heininen 2004c).

Therefore it can be argued that an effort to define a "regionally based" security has emerged in northern Europe, which is particularly persuasive in terms of reflecting how a "circumpolar North" has resulted from new constructions of threats and new definitions of security. Although international cooperation is needed to implement the concept of comprehensive security, including nuclear safety, a common political will is the first requirement. This remains a sensitive and complicated question for the international system and its traditional security structure, as well as a challenge for northern peoples.

THE RELATIONSHIP BETWEEN THE CHANGING DEFINITION OF SECURITY AND CIRCUMPOLAR BOUNDARIES

Why has the changing definition of security produced a corresponding alteration in the function of boundaries in the circumpolar North in recent years? Has the change been equal everywhere? To answer these questions it must be noted that, according to traditional "realist" schools of political geography, the purpose of a boundary or even an explicit border is to differentiate between or separate peoples, cultures, and regions. This is quite different from the function of a borderland, which serves as a crossing point and zone that connects peoples, cultures, and regions. The latter is better understood when counterpoised against the realist perspective, which represents what might be called the perspective of the "new geopolitics," and recognizes that actors, spaces, and identities play an increasingly relevant role in the construction of borders (Paasi 1996, 1998). Indeed, a borderland can act as much as a bridge as it can a border between two or more actors, joining rather than separating and facilitating increased interdependence, not just between actors but between the unified state and the globalized world.

This particular understanding of borders is relevant to the circumpolar North because national borders in the North are rather recent, being generally associated with the colonization and militarization of the Arctic and established by events in the nineteenth and twentieth centuries. These recently superimposed international borders divide societies and cultures that were historically united or in close cooperation with each other and reinforce the assertion that cross-border cooperation must be understood through analytical lenses that measure the specific cultures of borderland communities.

Moreover, because the circumpolar North consists of both the Arctic Ocean and numerous smaller regional seas and what might be considered as "rimlands," the role of its maritime boundaries, or, in some cases, the lack thereof, is as important as the role played by its land boundaries. However, although northern sea areas are important and strategic, in many cases maritime boundaries remain poorly defined and are sometimes managed by border practices predicated on trans-boundary cooperation that precedes the contemporary era. This historical cooperation remains a strong tradition within the region and applies to more than just maritime boundaries. In some places within the region cooperation has produced opportunity and conditions for maintaining cultural networks and establishing cultural crossroads. These cultural crossroads facilitate frequent travelling, exchanges of goods and experiences, trade, and migration between communities as well as across national borders (Heininen 2004b, 207–08). Indeed, since the 1980s regional cooperation between counties and municipalities has been viewed in many northern subregions not only as a realistic possibility but also as a new resource for regional development.

Another major complication within the international system of circumpolar countries, and especially the northern Arctic or sub-Arctic parts of each northern state, is their perception as "peripheral places." Traditional thinking about security has historically dominated relations between the region and the outside world. It can be argued that for centuries, the North has remained, literally, a geographical frontier, particularly in terms of interconnections, communication, and trade between peoples and communities. After the First World War, but especially after the Cold War, many of its borders became more pronounced, more like boundaries, due to growing strategic military and other types of security concerns, while former frontiers and borderlands were divided by national borders, reinforced by foreign and defence policies. The resulting state territories and new borders were increasingly controlled by state actors in response to the ideological and political divisions of the Cold War, which can only be described as the militarization of the Arctic.

These political barriers did not, however, put an end to trade and other forms of functional cooperation across national borders in such places as the North Calotte (the region comprising Nordland, Troms, and Finnmark in Norway, Lapland in Finland, and Norrbotten in Sweden). There the ideological divisions of the Cold War and the increasing scrutiny paid to borders in the North neither did, nor could, stop long-range air and sea pollution originating elsewhere from becoming a serious problem for the region.

There are grounds to argue that northern borders are now becoming easier to cross and less strategic. Accordingly, it is clear that the political clout of borderland communities is an important analytical lens through which to understand the relationship between structure and agency in maintaining border functions. Indeed, northern borders are becoming more like borderlands and less like fences, in the sense that they are being increasingly perceived as areas where transnational flows from trade, culture, and science are encouraged. More and more frequently these northern frontiers are bridged by municipal and regional linkages, growing together across a border, as has been the case with the twin towns of Haparanda (in Sweden) and Tornio (in Finland), which lie on either of the Torne/Torniojoki River.

Such bridging is not new but goes back to a tradition of regional cooperation in the circumpolar North before the implementation of modern national borders. Before the Cold War the indigenous peoples of North America, for example, were known to navigate the circumpolar North and actively connect with their counterparts in northeastern Asia. After the fall of the Soviet Union some researchers suggested that the circumpolar circle had been "made complete once again," referring to the historical tendency of circumpolar navigation among indigenous peoples. Thus it is possible to argue that a borderland model has begun to replace a borderline model in the contemporary circumpolar North, and that this represents, to some degree, a renaissance in regional and local cooperation. At the same time the contradiction is that the North remains situated in a world where it is historically perceived as a "frontier," a region unified by virtue of its emptiness and remoteness rather than by its linked human populations and activities. Whether new security parameters have changed the nature of border linkages and, if so, whether the change has been effective throughout the North are questions to be answered.

REGIONALISM IN NORTHERN EUROPE AND THE SOVIET UNION

For Russia and its predecessor the Soviet Union the idea of a "northern dimension" to foreign policy developed somewhat later than in Europe or North America. The North was traditionally a military and resource or industrial frontier, meaning that it served as a region, or the field of play, for the Soviet industrial and military economies.

Support for a northern dimension or for broader human-security concerns, supportive of a more comprehensive and internationalized circumpolar North stems from Gorbachev's Murmansk speech in the late 1980s. The current political discussion of relations between the EU and Russia, corresponding to that of the EU's "northern dimension," stresses the importance of the North to the Russian state, particularly in the aftermath of the collapse of the Soviet Union. Russian President Vladimir Putin proposed this kind of northern policy at the Russian Security Council's meeting in Salechard in April 2004 (ITAR-TASS 2004). Important to the latter development is the identification of the need for a long-term northern policy by the new Russian Federation and a more academic discourse that addresses the urgency of redefining the role of the Russian "North" as more than a geostrategically important resource reserve (Veniamin 2001; Golovnev 2001, 45–48).

All these interests and approaches coalesced in one way or another with the formation of the Arctic Council, and with international linkages that attempted to transcend the state-focused nature of Arctic governance in order to come to terms with a new host of transnational threats to human security after the Cold War. Among the most important of these were threats to the environment and to quality of life that stemmed either from industrial activities and traffic originating in the South or from southern agendas dictating the industrial and military uses of northern territories and resources. Recognition of these new threats subsequently produced action. For example, environmental and "quality of life" issues led to a sense of urgency that prompted the AEPS, and the subsequent recognition of sustainable development as the other pillar and main aim of the Arctic Council. This was perhaps the most important aspect of the "northern dimension" discourse that began in the 1990s and continues today, with its focus on science and technology, its emphasis on empirical research, and its targeting of the circumpolar North as a field for concerted international cooperation.

The recasting of the imperative for northern cooperation in environmental terms cannot be overestimated. Not only has it given rise to the type of regional definition supported by figure 5.2 in this chapter and identified a new security threat—climate change, POPs, and other forms of environmental degradation—but it has also become a vehicle for building regional consensus. Today few, if any, Arctic countries contest the need for action on environmental issues. This new security agenda has meshed North American and European approaches and security concerns within the circumpolar North in unprecedented ways and has led to the development of the EU's Northern Dimension strategy, the Arctic Council's definition of the circumpolar North through the AMAP, and various environmental treaties to which all the circumpolar nations have responded. In North America, Russia, and Europe the result has been a reorganization of international relations and new approaches to foreign policy based upon the acceptance of a broader circumpolar North as a field for cooperation.

THE EUROPEAN UNION AND THE CIRCUMPOLAR NORTH: THE NORTHERN DIMENSION AND THE NEW SECURITY AGENDA

The EU's Northern Dimension (EUND) policy responded to the new comprehensive human-security agenda in ways that were mindful of the security and geopolitical realities of the Cold War period. From the EU's point of view, its northern strategy is a framework and process for coordination, even management, of cross-border cooperation across its borders and for continuous dialogue on cooperation between the EU and its neighbours in northern Europe, specifically, the Russian Federation, Norway, Iceland, and Greenland (European Union 2003). (Greenland counts as a neighbour of the EU because, although it is under the rule of Denmark, itself a member state of the EU, Greenland left the European Communities in 1985.) Originally the EUND was implemented within the framework of the EU member states, the Europe agreements with the Baltic states (Estonia, Latvia, Lithuania, and Poland), the Partnership and Cooperation Agreement with Russia, and the European Economic Area regulations involving Iceland and Norway. Geographically it targets a broad and diffuse area extending from Greenland in the west to the Urals in the east, and from the Arctic in the north to the southern coast of the Baltic Sea. It also covers northwestern Russia and the Baltic, and the regions of the North, Norwegian, and Barents seas, all areas with a significant northern or circumpolar, even Arctic, environment. Thus the EUND crosses several international borders as it "addresses the specific challenges of those regions and aims to increase cooperation between the EU member states, the EU applicant countries and Russia" (European Union 2003). Indeed, of the EU's external and cross-border policies, the EUND is directed specifically toward northern Europe and the Arctic.

In keeping with its new concern for comprehensive and human security, the "areas for cooperation" under the EUND include the environment, nuclear safety, and energy cooperation. Indeed, the EUND now has five key priority areas: (1) economy, business, and infrastructure, to promote closer integration of markets and economic integration with the Russian Federation; (2) human resources, education, scientific research, culture, and public health, to develop and promote opportunities for residents of the Northern Dimension region, particularly in the areas of science, technology, and tourism; (3) the environment, nuclear safety, and natural resources, to meet some of the well-identified environmental challenges that are beyond the capacity of any one country to resolve; (4) cross-border cooperation, to promote economic development and achieve social, educational, and health goals; (5) justice and home affairs, to promote security in the context of fighting cross-border crime, human and drug trafficking, and illegal immigration. These key priorities are aimed at addressing "the special regional development challenges of northern Europe" such as "harsh climatic conditions, long distances, particularly wide living standard disparities, environmental challenges, including problems with nuclear waste and waste water management, as well as insufficient transport and border crossing facilities" (European Union 2004).

However, the EUND is not the same as the AEPS, nor does it define the Arctic Council or the structure of regional cooperation among the "Arctic Eight." Rather, it operates through existing EU financial instruments such as Poland and Hungary: Assistance for Restructuring their Economies (PHARE), Technical Aid to the Commonwealth of Independent States (TACIS), or the various EU regional programs known as Inter-Region (INTERREG) to finance specific projects (European Union 2000, 2004). Initially one of its important focal points was the Baltic Sea region, but more recently there has been a shift in political focus. With recent rounds of EU enlargement attention has moved away from the region (with the exception of the Kaliningrad Oblast) toward northwestern Russia and the Arctic, including Greenland. The second EUND action plan, which ends in 2006, focuses on "cross-cutting issues" and "key priorities." For example, as a result of the most recent enlargement into central and eastern Europe the EU–Russia dialogue has become critical for "strengthening stability, wellbeing and sustainable development in Northern Europe." To that end the EU and the Russian Federation agreed on four common spaces: economic cooperation; freedom, security, and justice; external security; and research, education, and culture (European Union 2000, 2006). Thus, based on these common spaces, it may be that Russia is not only a strategic partner but also a more equal partner both in European politics and, especially, in dealing with the EUND. The four common spaces will also form the main structure of the forthcoming action plan and other EUND political declarations.

In the final analysis the EUND ensures that the EU's environmental requirements as posed by the AEPS and the Arctic Council are met, and that necessary actions are taken to monitor POPs and other environmental threats. This process is evident in the heightened interest in building capacity for cooperation in nuclear safety and environmental issues between Russia and the EU, with a focus on "sustainable development," in terms of resource use, and on "securing the border," while harmonizing legislation, standards, and procedures in the interests of protecting and promoting civil society and environmental security. The latter is of particular interest to the countries bordering the shallow Baltic Sea, due to intensive and growing sea traffic, especially heavy oil transportation from Russian oil terminals to the Atlantic Ocean. Correspondingly, the EUND has played a constructive role as a practical political tool for functional cooperation in many fields in the EU–Russian relationship. The forthcoming EUND action plan has the potential to create cross-cutting themes of research and development and "tech-knowledgy" (for example, environmentally friendly and secure energy production, technology, and distribution) to bring to this relationship and to common European activities in general (Heininen 2005b).

Although in European political rhetoric Russia is considered part of Europe, the reality is different. Before the EU enlargement of 2004 the only borders between member states of the EU and the Russian Federation were the Finnish–Russian border, which was more of a boundary than a borderland, and the Estonian–Russian border, also more of a boundary because there was no ratified treaty between the two countries. As a result visa freedom between the EU and Russia was a difficult issue for the EU, especially as Russia was stricter and less flexible in border-crossing arrangements. Although an agreement to make those arrangements easier was reached at the EU–Russian Summit in the fall of 2005, border crossings remain a challenge in the context of the EUND, given its goal of decreasing the importance of national borders in northern Europe.

Is the EU–Russian border defined as a boundary or a borderland? Furthermore, how are the national borders of northern Europe defined and how do people interpret them? The models of "soft borders," such as the Euregio Karelia, the Euro-Region formed by Russia and Finland in 2000, are both relevant and effective. They have increased the porosity of the EU's national borders, turning them into a sort of borderland, and enhanced communication across them, increasing cooperation and furthering confidence between borderland populations, and building regional cooperation, as in the case of the Finnish–Russian border, the first common EU–Russian border (Heininen 2005a). Other Russian regions such as St. Petersburg and the Kaliningrad Oblast are also defining their geopolitical location as linking Russia with the West, as being "a Russian gateway to Europe," "a window onto Europe," or "a bridge between Russia and Europe" (Valuev 2003). The Euregio Karelia is not only a part of the EUND but also a concrete example of the EUND's impact on the external and cross-border policies of the EU. The alternative vision of the Euregio Karelia has been used to change the meaning and interpretation of national borders by integrating the regions through a cooperative process rather than by trying to change physical borders (Cronberg 2001).

A more advanced example of a borderland that emphasizes connections across national borders and between municipalities, which are today generally more active in international cooperation and regionalism, is the previously mentioned case of Haparanda (in Sweden) and Tornio (in Finland), located on the border at the mouth of the Torne/Torniojoki River, at the north end of the Gulf of Bothnia. This entity, which is referred to as a "Euro City," represents local bottom-up transboundary cooperation in northern Europe. Although the plan, known as På Gränsen/Rajalla (At the Boundary), is to build a common town centre, there is already a substantial level of cooperation between the two towns, including joint investments in fire and rescue services, a common sewage treatment plant, combined district heating networks, a common international language school, a Euro college with an international study program, and mutual cultural and leisure activities, such as combined tourist agencies and a Green Zone golf course across the national border.

The cooperation between Haparanda and Tornio started in the 1960s, when their citizens began to engage in practical activities such as transboundary shopping and cross-border employment. This informal cooperation slowly became part of a system of official institutionalized cooperation, supported by the authorities of both towns and including common use of a swimming pool and the choice to attend school in either town. In 1987 the two town councils established the Provincia Bothniensis with a common governor to promote increased cooperation between Haparanda and Tornio, and the use of the euro in Haparanda's shops and its community budget, even though Sweden was, and remains, outside the euro zone (see Zalamans 2001; Ronkainen and Westman 1999).

In general, northern counties, provinces, municipalities, and other subnational governments, together with non-governmental organizations (NGOs), are currently attempting to be more visible in different international circles. In the context of northern Europe several counties are active in international cooperation. For example, the North Calotte Council promotes and develops interregional cooperation between the northernmost counties of Norway and Sweden along with the northernmost province of Finland (as mentioned above), just as the Northern Forum does for the circumpolar North region. In the 1990s some subnational entities, such as the province of Lapland (in Finland) and the Komi Republic (in Russia), created a regional "foreign" and economic policy. In northern Europe the notion of a "Europe of Regions" and transboundary regionalism via the model of Euro-Regions includes East–West cooperation across the national borders between subnational units in the Nordic states and northwestern Russia. The kind of cooperation found in Haparanda–Tornio has also promoted integration across the national borders among the Nordic countries and been used as a model for intermunicipal cooperation in northern Europe. Furthermore, the Euregio Karelia has the potential to facilitate both cooperation and development in northwestern Russia. This concept of "northernness" can be viewed as representing the rise of northern regional and local actors into the realm of international cooperation due to the emergence of northern issues onto the political agendas of the Arctic states (Heininen 2005a).

This interpretation of a border and "de-bordering" process makes it possible to redefine a region and create a new kind of virtual region. This is not, however, a completely new idea. Since the 1980s there have been ideas and proposals for creating new economic zones, such as the Rio Grande on the US–Mexico border and the Magic Mill on the Finnish–Russian border, as well as activities by civil organizations, international academies such as the Kuhmo Summer Academy, and the Finnish–Russian international research project dealing with national borders, the *Karjalat katsovat toisiaan*. Thus, long before the EUND was developed, Finland's need for a northern policy was discussed in sessions of the Kuhmo Summer Academy (Heininen and Käkönen 1996) from the perspective of a Finnish–Russian borderland that emphasized connection instead of separation.

The twin towns of Haparanda–Tornio provide a unique laboratory for border research. They have been studied to determine how a border, or a borderland, influences the identity and culture of a region as well as the human and social understandings of its people (Zalamans 2001). They also illustrate how a common history of long and rich cooperation can produce close and peaceful relations between peoples. In this case it occurred simply because for centuries there was no border in the Torne/Torniojoki River valley, most people spoke Finnish, and Saami (Lapp) people lived on both sides. Even after Finland ceased to be ruled by Sweden and became a Grand Duchy of Russia, in 1809, the national border that was established was more of a borderland than a boundary, meaning it was easy to cross. Although today the goal of saving money is one of the main reasons for collaboration, the decision-makers and authorities in Haparanda and Tornio have been in the vanguard of border cooperation on politics, social issues, economics, and governance, lobbying for changes to national legislation in both Finland and Sweden (Heininen 2004b, 207–08).

NORTH AMERICA AND ITS NEIGHBOURS

The restructuring of the northern security discourse and the character of its geopolitical underpinnings must be understood in the context in which the circumpolar world is situated, that is, internationalism, particularly if notions about border security are to be addressed. Historically, conventional ideas about the strategic military and defence role of the circumpolar North have been oriented to its regional structure, or lack thereof, which has also helped to define its relationship to the South. As noted earlier, the circumpolar North has had, and still holds, great strategic importance in military terms. Yet there is not one "North" but many, because, by definition, the security agenda implies that the North is divided into states, despite being an empty wasteland that stands unguarded, unobserved, and open. In this sense it has been traditionally perceived as a fragmented geopolitical region rather than a coherent and integrated northern context.

The Arctic became a region of renewed and heightened interest to decision-makers after the Cold War ended and attention shifted from security issues related to its geostrategic significance to the problem of human security, as well as new and pressing threats on its circumpolar environments. In Europe the concept of a "northern dimension," initially developed in Finland and subsequently promoted by Finland and Sweden, gained acceptance as a basis for foreign policy development in the EU. In North America, however, the story is somewhat different. In Canada, for example, although the concept of a northern dimension to foreign policy can be traced back to the 1940s, it remained relatively dormant until the late 1980s and early 1990s, when new attitudes and a new receptivity toward indigenous cultures were incorporated into Canada's political agenda (Royal Commission on Aboriginal Peoples 1996). This culminated in the development of a northern dimension for Canadian foreign policy, an explicit set of ideas and approaches to northern Canada and its neighbours that differed from that of the south.

Indeed, North Americans have engaged more actively with the idea of a northern dimension than northern Europeans have. The North has always been important, symbolically, to their concept of nationhood, defined by the broader military security paradigm that existed until the end of the Cold War and viewed as a front line of the Cold War's military theatre, though more so, perhaps, in the United States than in Canada. Canada's engagement with the North was, to a large extent, limited to strategic considerations based on the more widespread view of the Arctic as a frontier sparsely populated by traditional peoples living ancient lifestyles and outside the mainstream of Canadian life, but also as a region rich in natural resources. This attitude shifted substantially in the 1980s and 1990s, as changing geopolitical concerns and definitions of security, increased attention to environmental issues, and a new sense of the legitimacy of the Arctic as a homeland for traditional societies replaced Cold War concerns. By the late 1980s Canada was actively attempting to establish an international political forum on cooperation in the Arctic. In 1991 both Canada and the United States signed the AEPS, and, although the strategy took longer to establish than initially expected, in 1996, with the support of the "Arctic Eight," the Arctic Council was formed, institutionalizing new attitudes about environmental issues and governance in the Arctic.

This signalled the beginning of a Canadian foreign policy approach to the Arctic that culminated in a new emphasis on the environment, human security, and sustainability in the circumpolar North, as well as building upon a distinctive Canadian approach to Arctic issues. The process continued during the early 1990s, contributing to the development of a new and focused direction for Arctic geopolitics. Indeed, many of the specific protocols and programs of the AEPS were shaped by Canadian concerns. One example is the CAFF agreement. However, it was also clear by the late 1980s and early 1990s that, by participating in the AEPS, Canada had assumed an influential role that suffered from too little in the way of foreign policy to fall back on. The Canadian North had never been an arena for the development of international relations, except in reaction to very specific events. One of these events, the Cold War, prompted a closer military alliance with the United States in the Arctic and the establishment of the DEW line. It also generated Canada's ongoing struggle to infer sovereignty over the High Arctic when challenged by the United States and various European governments. Still, cases in which the Arctic entered into Canada's foreign affairs agenda were limited, punctuated an approach to the North that was otherwise largely determined by neglect, and generally incorporated into domestic and defence concerns as a "frontier" or "periphery." This was the situation until Mikhail Gorbachev's Murmansk speech in 1987, after which the Arctic assumed new proportions in foreign policy and regionally, as emphasis shifted away from maritime definitions of the region to a broader political and environmental constituency. The Canadian government observed that a clearly defined northern dimension to its foreign policy would help to establish "a framework to promote the extension of Canadian interests and values, and would renew the government's commitment to cooperation with its own northern peoples and with its circumpolar neighbours to address shared issues and responsibilities" (Department of Foreign Affairs 2000). In other words, the northern dimension of Canada's foreign policy was now the gateway for the incorporation of new ideas about the relevance of human security in the context of the environment and civil society, framed in reference to the northern territories and peoples of Canada, Russia, the United States, and the Nordic countries. The Canadian government asserted that the challenges were mainly in the area of transboundary environmental threats, such as POPs, climate change, and nuclear waste, which were having increasingly dangerous effects on the health and vitality of northern peoples, lands, waters, and animal life (Department of Foreign Affairs 2000).

In terms of transnational engagement, however, different security discourses indicate significant differences between Canada's "northern dimension" and the EU's. The EUND is a vehicle for continuous dialogue on cooperation between the EU and its neighbours, especially the Russian Federation, and on the coordination of cross-border cooperation across the EU borders. Moreover, its goal is to focus on the sectors in which the "value added" is expected to be the greatest, the so-called priority sectors. A comparison of the first and second *Northern Dimension Action Plans*, for example, reveals a greater focus on energy cooperation, human resources, and social issues such as education, public health, and the environment in the second plan. In contrast, although Canada's foreign policy uses many of the same terms as those of the EU, particularly the notion of "northern dimensionality," the Canadian policy has its own design and procedure, with a slightly different emphasis. Its objectives mesh with those of the EUND to the extent that it recognizes the potential for forging new bilateral and multilateral linkages with Russia, especially in the area of defining and implementing broad-based human security and environmental concerns. However, the EU's international juggling act is somewhat different: the EU member-states and Greenland have been given, or have earned, a strong, almost equal position within the EUND, which has played an important role in garnering support for the EUND initiative and its specific policies.

Currently, then, the "northern dimension" structures the EU's relations with Canada in specific and different ways than in previous decades, and it generally fosters cooperation, particularly in the area of the environment and civil society. The EUND's second action plan (2004) is a specific example of this new relationship. It signalled the EU's intention to work more closely with the United States and Canada, structuring this interaction in the context of a trans-Atlantic agenda and a joint statement on northern cooperation with Canada. This initiative had the potential for both greater cooperation on a trans-Atlantic agenda and greater divisiveness, given the degree to which the United States and Canada were ultimately linked by it. It had implications for Canada precisely because the EU's rationale and instruments for including the

United States within its general Northern Dimension program were closely associated with the rationale for including Canada. As well, because both Canada and the United States are viewed as potential partners in a trans-Atlantic relationship, both Canada and the United States were marginalized as fears of US hegemony rose. Indeed, Browning (2002) has asserted that "one result of this has been that when the Action Plan came to define the scope of the Northern Dimension, the United States and Canada were excluded." Sergounin (2002) has also suggested that fear of US hegemony precipitated reactions whereby both Canada and the United States were discouraged from institutionalizing their presence within northern Europe or within the EU's northern dimension, except on a case-by-case basis.

Still, within the EU, endorsement of regionalism as a "Pan-Arctic" or circumpolar event remains a realistic possibility that may even prove to be a new resource for northern development. Historical and even mythical referents, including the images of the Hanseatic League and of Norse adventurers and explorers, conjure up a vision of a North linked, East to West, by nature and tradition, and they create new enthusiasm for the EUND in the context of a broader circumpolar project. This open support for transnational linkages is consistent with Canada's northern foreign policy.

In the United States, however, the idea of a northern dimension was not part of normative geopolitical discourse. The North was originally synonymous with Alaska, at least until the Cold War, when the region assumed geostrategic proportions in the fight to contain Communism and construct the DEW line. These heightened geostrategic sensitivities to the North, particularly its new importance to US military security, structured US attitudes to the Arctic, and indeed US–Canada Arctic relations, for decades to come. Americans looking north tended to see the region as a foreign place rather than a national frontier and a depopulated place synonymous with the ends of the Earth. Perhaps this is why the NEI, launched in 1997 as the first new US northern policy following the end of the Cold War, referenced a northern but "Europe-centred" and "strategic" policy framework (see, for example, Shearer 1997; Talbott 1997). The policy paid little attention to the circumpolar world of North America, giving a slightly different twist to the concept of a "northern dimension" and situating it squarely within the realm of a foreign policy for those outside of the US North. Thus US ideas about northern security gave rise to specific and limited stereotypes and policies regarding human security in the North, as well as a clear lack of focus on the circumpolar North as a broad region or international forum in which to deploy more general ideas about comprehensive security. In the US security regime borders are firm, traditional, and transgressed only by concern with specific security sectors such as pollution, climate change, or military and resource use. In effect the boundary between the United States and its circumpolar partners is defined, to a large extent, by internationalism and continental foreign policy, rather than a "northern dimension" policy. This retains the strategic importance of US borders and borderlands within the North and locates translational cooperation squarely at the national level, in Washington, DC.

The approach taken by US decision-makers, at least federally, with respect to the circumpolar North was distinctively different from that taken by Canadians and Europeans, although there was overlap with the EU's focus on eastern and northern European states. The US has recently revised its approach, however, discarding the NEI and developing the Enhanced Partnership in Northern Europe (e-PINE). Its emphasis on this aspect of foreign policy is once again in sharp contrast to Canada's approach. At the state level US policy-makers are less inclined to make policies that promote a formal relationship and linkages with the Arctic Circle, and, indeed, they have secured an agreement from the Arctic Council nations that the council will not be used as a forum for the making of binding policy. The US approach to participation in the Arctic Council is driven by a number of specific issues rather than by a sense of geographical regionalism. Indeed, national security, economic development, and scientific research are important US interests in the region. According to the official political rhetoric, a true US Arctic policy "emphasizes environmental protection, sustainable development, human health, and the role of indigenous people" (Department of State 2006), but it is specific to US peoples and places, not Pan-Arctic indigenous organizations or transnational issues above and beyond the environment. Consequently, in theory the US position toward the circumpolar region remains traditional in the sense that it is based upon a state-centred agenda in which security and national interests are emphasized, although with recognition of the broader context of globalization.

The United States has other understandings of the North that are very different from those of the rest of the Arctic Council nations. For example, until very recently a "northern dimension" foreign policy within the United States meant concern with the Baltic states and "security" issues. However, the development of the NEI in 1997 was designed to address the issues of a new geopolitical order in the wake of the ending of the Cold War and the dissolution of the Soviet Union. Since then the US approach to the North has had two very separate sets of initiatives and policy directives, administered by two separate State Department programs. In one case the NEI and now e-PINE have been steered toward meeting the more general policy goals of building democratic and stable societies and promoting free markets. There has been a focus on the subnational level—broadened out to include actors such as NGOs, transnational corporations, multilateral organizations, and others—as well as an expanded definition of security interests that encompasses a broad-based concept of human security, including "energy, environmental cooperation, nuclear safety, coordination with international financial institutions, development of civil society and democratic infrastructure, legal reform and cooperation on law enforcement, and health and infectious diseases" (US Mission to the EU 1999). In the second case a separate US State Department entity administers its participation in the Arctic Council, but it has virtually no overlap in personnel, program, or policy development with the e-PINE. There is no single "northern dimension" to US foreign policy.

It seems, then, that the US government is less interested in the dynamics of northern civil society today than it has been in previous years. It also seems less interested in indigenous society or indigenous representation than in monitoring the Arctic environment or assessing the potential for Arctic oil reserves. Somewhat ironically, although its definition of broadening the basis of civil society has recently been modified to include private oil companies' assessments of environmental issues in drilling for Alaskan oil, currently the United States is more interested in the Russian North. Russia's huge oil resources may trigger close energy cooperation between the United States and Russia, which will likely entail a dramatic increase in the amount of oil being transported from the Barents Sea area to North America and central Europe.

At the state-to-state level the US may be said to approach the circumpolar North from a position of hegemony and an attitude of "What's in it for us?" Because of its state-centred focus conceptions of a US "northern dimension" do not, by definition, consider cooperation with Canada beyond a narrow set of initiatives based on the environment and health. In this sense the United States cannot claim to have a northern dimension to its foreign policy, nor does it recognize the need for a geographical approach to northern environments. Its concept of a "northern dimension" remains an issue-based approach in which traditional security and strategic concerns dominate.

Yet, although the United States has not responded well to the concept of a transnational agenda within the circumpolar North, and continues to situate itself in terms of traditional geopolitical discourse and security concerns at the regional level, it has still engaged in active cooperation. Alaska is, to some extent, a model for interregional and grassroots initiatives and cooperation between indigenous and civil organizations and universities, which in turn have led to the establishment of academic, indigenous, and institutional linkages. In recent years there has been considerable cross-border cooperation, ranging from formal agreements on energy, environment, and boundaries to participation in broad-ranging initiatives to develop a University of the Arctic, to encourage scientific research within the circumpolar North, and to engage indigenous Alaskans in the process of strengthening civil society. The state of Alaska has expressed its interest in participating in the Arctic Council in five priority areas: finding common solutions to common problems; advancing a better understanding of the Arctic environment; bettering the lives of Arctic peoples; focusing on the issues of Native peoples (as distinct from Arctic peoples); and advancing the use of technology to deliver services to remote areas (Ramseur 1999). The University of Alaska is currently active within the region, particularly in higher education. including curricula and applications of information technology in the Arctic context, such as the Bachelor of Arctic Studies program.

Thus Alaska's participation in the circumpolar North is through traditional institutions—that is, institutions of the state government, universities, research foundations, and indigenous peoples' organizations—rather than translational venues. Although there are avenues for indigenous participation based on regional affiliation, such as the Inuit Circumpolar Conference and the Inuit Tapisariat, US and Alaskan decision-makers have pushed for the inclusion of indigenous peoples on narrower terms, in the context of their role within US national or subnational institutions, with the intent of countering a more broadly based Pan-Arctic definition. Arctic issues are more narrowly defined as well, mainly in the areas of the environment, health, and education.

Nonetheless, the Alaskan perspective is more highly regionalized and features more prominently in the definition of the "northern dimension" than the US national perspective.

It is clear that the formal role of the United States as defined by the US government and its goals in the Arctic Council are based on decreased cooperation. As for the US approach to the North American circumpolar region, at the level of nation states there is only a tenuous link between the promotion of civil society and human security beyond the context of environmental issues. Indeed, there is neither a region nor a geopolitical discourse that connects people and places, outside of a narrowly and empirically defined environmental agenda. The State Department's expertise consists of personnel previously assigned to border security and the Immigration and Naturalization Service, and its interest in the work of the Arctic Council is limited to concern with scientific, environmental, and technical issues affecting the state of Alaska.

However, although the failure of the United States to engage on the level of the circumpolar North has been criticized by Canadians and Europeans, it has given Canada an opportunity to navigate the Arctic Council to some extent freed from the confines of a formal and separate bilateral relationship with the United States on indigenous issues. Canada has given particular support to initiatives to strengthen the role of indigenous peoples in regional government, and it has cooperated with transnational NGOs such as the Inuit Circumpolar Conference and the Inuit Tapirisat.

The general thrust of US northern policy with respect to Europe, however, could have consequences for Canada in respect of international institutions and policies connecting the circumpolar North outside of the Arctic Council agenda. If, as was previously suggested, the NEI and its replacement, the e-PINE initiative, are more strategically defined than the EUND Action Plan, there may be significant consequences for Canada's involvement in northern Europe. For example, to some extent NEI membership in Europe was linked to membership in Western institutions such as the EU and NATO, which became re-envisioned as a "community of values" (see Browning 2002). The EU and European countries were quick to appreciate this problem, and indeed Browning claims that there were attempts to marginalize the NEI and, presumably, subsequent initiatives for fear of US definition and hegemony within the region. Consequently, the notion of comprehensive security through building a "northern dimension" in foreign policy and its relationship to US circumpolar strategies cannot be understood without reference to the broader framework of Arctic international cooperation and new human security concerns.

Today international relations are framed by the context of a multinational circumpolar context and globalization. At the same time, Canada has its own set of foreign-policy objectives and emphases that must be accommodated, not the least of which is its bilateral relationship with the United States. For Canadian policy-makers it is less a question of how multilateralism within Arctic cooperation will affect the equally important bilateral relationship with the United States than it is one of how to situate the bilateral Canada–US relationship in the increasingly globalized and regionalized context of a circumpolar North and a new "North–South metaphor."

This situation helps to explain why, over the past decade, a different type of translational structure and border management regime has, arguably, existed among North American nations compared to those of northern Europe, the EU, or Russia. In North America since the ending of the Cold War, transboundary cooperation in the North, coupled with a new emphasis on regionalism, has reinforced rather than diminished the prominence of the international system. Thus, boundary cooperation in a large part of the region is defined through a series of treaties, agreements, and cooperative initiatives made at the state-to-state level. Border management has become instrumentalized by a series of sectoral and comprehensive national and international agreements, rather than by translational policies targeted to border areas or local scales, although this is less true in northern Europe or the EU, even in their border relationships with Russia.

Still, in the long run this may prove not to be a particularly effective means of promoting security. New developments in information and communication technology, which have the potential to provide northern populations greater access to health and education services, are limited to some extent by the correspondingly limited potential for aggregate demand within the current circumpolar international order. Yet, although such technology is not restricted in application to the strengthening of civil society, its ability to contribute to civil society in the North is clearly constrained in large measure by policies that reinforce the fundamental divisions inherent in the Westphalian international order.

CONCLUSION

The repercussions of this shift in boundary cooperation and border management have had a significant impact on the international organization of the region, from the late 1980s, when Mikhail Gorbachev called for cooperation in the Arctic, via the signing of the AEPS in 1991, to the formation of the Arctic Council in 1996. The council assumed a new role of overseeing and continuing the work of the AEPS, but with a broader focus on foreign policy and a new emphasis on the need for coordinated international effort to achieve the goals of sustainable development within the circumpolar North.

The consensus in favour of "sustainable development" was influenced by the acceptance of the broader definition of "human security" described earlier in this chapter. This consensus was based on a variety of considerations, most of which were triggered by a series of new security challenges in the region, including the visible gap between standards of living and environmental quality; environmental concerns raised by global climate change and pollution, including POPs and nuclear waste; and the legacy of the military contamination of sensitive circumpolar environments (Heininen 2002).

Clearly, much of the reinvigoration of northern issues in recent years has come from an emerging circumpolar perspective that is based on a new multinational geopolitical discourse. Although geopolitics, interpreted as traditional security policy (the military control of geographical spaces), as well as geopolitical discourses of natural resource use, has always played a dominant role in defining the relations between "North" and "South" by contributing to the structure of the relationship between the Arctic and the outside world, the new geopolitical discourse, and new set of foreign policy practices and themes within the circumpolar North, are very specific about the need to achieve the broad goals of "human security" and "sustainable development." A new and globalized "human security" geopolitical discourse or model has now appeared within the region (Heininen 2004b; Chaturvedi 2000), which brings us back to the point raised at the outset of this chapter, namely, that this new discourse finds its focal point in the Arctic but extends to cooperative agreements and institutions outside the region. Thus, although the politics of the Cold War dictated that the Arctic region be treated as part of a broader strategy of exclusion and confrontation, it is clear that the politics of globalization and the diffusion of power now highlight the importance of the circumpolar region as an area for inclusion and cooperation. (Heininen 2004b)

New security discourses have affected transnationalism and resulted in new foreign policy and cooperative mechanisms. The "northern dimension" policies of Canada and of the EU, and to a lesser extent of the United States, are similar in that they address what were previously state-centred, specifically national issues with more internationalized thinking about regional cooperation. All of these actors have a stake in recasting and internationalizing the geopolitical and territorial dimensions of the new circumpolar region. At the same time, they are required to translate such reterritorialization into state-centred rhetoric and practice. It is not, therefore, simply a problem of individual countries "fitting in" or "falling out" in terms of acceptable practice, but one of reinventing region-building from the bottom up. New alignments are forming as NGOs and governmental organizations adapt to the fact that, until now, region-building in the North has been a state-dominated, top-down activity. Seen in this way, contestation, competition, and even conflict and negotiation are necessary parts of the region-building process, not outcomes. This is consistent with the new northern European focus on sustainable development within the Arctic and the development of strengthened northern civil societies.

The concept of a circumpolar region is mutual and overlapping. Policy frameworks recognize, participate in, and otherwise involve the Arctic Council. Although there are grounds for debate, even disagreement, between member-states of the Arctic Council over the degree to which it should move beyond specific environmental goals, the council's explicit goal includes sustainable development, while the goals of its member-states include to some degree the establishment of regional institutions. This is vital to achieving the ultimate goals of a "Pan-Arctic" space and transnational institutions, as well as an important first step, one that cannot be divorced from the redefinition of new ideas about security and the significance of overcoming regional obstacles. It seems, then, that the northern hierarchy of, and discourses on, threat pictures now has a separate agenda on security. This new agenda is slowly but surely changing the calculus of security within the circumpolar region and is a substantial development in a region where little consideration was previously given to human security concerns. As Heubert (2004) has asserted, the circumpolar North was a geographical region summed up by harsh conditions and isolation of the North, and it was treated accordingly.

In the process of redefining security within the region, traditional borderlines are being redrawn, either literally or conceptually, while new assessments about security needs and vulnerabilities are privileging one type of security over another. This is particularly true in the transformation of the international and foreign policies that have been developed in relation to the circumpolar North following the ending of the Cold War, in response to new and more comprehensive definitions of security, as compared to traditional security practices (see, for example, Walt 1991; Derghoukassian circa 2003). "Northern dimension" frameworks represent a new and more comprehensive process for redefining security in the North. Of particular consequence, however, is that in doing so they prescribe a new approach to the definition of transnationalism and the role of borders in comprehensive security (Huebert 2004, 21). If definitions of security have undergone transformation, then northern geopolitical discourse has changed accordingly. It has moved from an exclusively state-dominated and militarized or defence-oriented discourse to one that is more humanistic in definition, with corresponding attention paid to developing what Emmanuel Brunet-Jailly (in the introduction to this volume) describes as increasingly coordinated cross-border "policy activities of multiple levels of government on adjunct borders." New definitions of security have brought renewed interest in policy activities at multiple levels, which have allowed and in fact made room for greater participation and cooperation within the circumpolar North. These responses are in direct proportion to the new perception of increasing levels of environmental threats within the circumpolar North, and they affect not only the structuring of translational relationships across borders but also the significance and role of national borders themselves.

In relation to the theme addressed in this volume, the changing relationship between structure and agency in transnational or cross-border relations, we suggest that the relationship between structure and agency has been influential in creating the conditions for a new security context within the integrating North. Our discussion of circumpolar security and transnationalism thus reinforces the theoretical framework presented by Brunet-Jailly, in which he argues that borders need to be understood in terms of four equally important and analytical lenses: economic flows across borders; structural frameworks and policy activities of multiple levels of governance (as opposed to "government"); the political strategic importance of specific borderland communities; and the cultures of those borderland communities. Although market forces and trade flows have set the stage for the tension between resource-focused and more comprehensive types of security agendas, the cross-border forces of integration reflect the influence of other processes. Among the most important of these are the shifts in engagement between multiple levels of government as an international agenda becomes contextualized within the policy frameworks of national governments, NGOs, and indigenous communities. As noted previously, the Arctic Council, for example, incorporates NGOs, indigenous institutions, and national governments in its transnational agenda.

The new concept of "human security" in the North also relies upon transnational, cross-border cooperation, reflecting other aspects of a changing structure–agency relationship that results from changes in other types of structure–agency relationships. We have observed, for example, that the role of borderland communities has been affected by the restructuring of regional cross-border cooperation at the level of both regional governance (for example, Euregio Karelia) and municipal governance (as in the case of Haparanda–Tornio), down to shared recreational facilities such as golf courses. The agency for cooperation in all of these cases has been subnational groups, but it is a form of cooperation conditioned and facilitated by new translational agreements such as the AEPS. Instrumental to this political cooperation on human security issues are the transnational nature of borderland culture—circumpolar culture being a construction of the 1990s—and the restoration of community and cultural linkages across old Cold War barriers.

In this sense our model of the four analytical lenses holds true within this study. The notion that the relative power of structure and agency varies across time and space according to specific political, geographical, and cultural conditions has been demonstrated in this chapter. This indicates that the borders within the circumpolar North have responded to forces of globalization in ways that are increasingly sensitive to emerging comprehensive security agendas.

Still, although it can be argued that each of the four analytical lenses is present in the circumpolar North, their importance and intensity varies. Local cross-border culture, which has a strong presence in many northern regions, is the background to, and may also be a precondition for, local cross-border political clout: this is either already dominant or, at least, the political will to strengthen it exists. Market forces and trade flows are clearly relevant to the region, due to globalization and the political, cultural, economic, and other significant flows it creates, each of which in turn creates a challenge for resource governance and democracy in the North. Finally, the idea that the policy activities of multiple levels of government are important is an apt description of the current state of northern geopolitics following the ending of the Cold War and the subsequent transition period, but it reveals nothing new or innovative about the situation.

What is missing from Brunet-Jailly's theoretical framework, and yet is relevant to comprehensive security in the North, is a discussion and discourse on the importance of long-range pollution and cross-border environmental problems. Are these issues relevant in borderland studies? This chapter suggests that, while borders within the circumpolar region have responded to forces of globalization in ways that are increasingly sensitive to emerging comprehensive security agendas, there are geographically specific outcomes associated with the integrating North. Market flows, for example, must be understood not only as goods and products but also as by-products of market and trade forces, such as the pollution generated by manufacturing processes in the South or the changes to global climate regimes resulting from hydrocarbon-based economies. The determining relationship between structure and agency in the case of northern market flows is not so much the characteristics of trade agreements or goods-first border infrastructures, but rather international environmental policy collaboration at the national and supranational levels. This collaboration, in combination with the political structure of local border communities and the degree to which civil or indigenous society is incorporated into transnational institutions, remains a key defining characteristic of cross-border cooperation within the circumpolar North.

LITERATURE CITED

Arctic Council. 1996. *Declaration of the Establishment of the Arctic Council*. [online]. www.arctic-council.org/en/main/infopage/190/ [consulted September 13, 2006].

———. 1997. *Arctic Monitoring and Assessment Report*. Oslo: Arctic Council.

———. 2002. *Arctic Pollution 2002*. Oslo: AMAP, Arctic Council.

Browning, Christopher. 2002. "Competing or Complementary Policies? Understanding the Relationship between the NEI and the NDI." Copenhagen Peace Research Institute Working Papers. [online]. www.diis.dk/graphics/COPRI_publications/COPRI_publications/publications/workingpapers.htm [consulted September 13, 2006].

Brandt Commission. 1980. *North–South: A Program for Survival*. Cambridge, MA: MIT Press.

———. 1983. *Common Crisis North–South: Cooperation for World Recovery*. Cambridge, MA: MIT Press.

Buzan, Barry. 1991. *People, States and Fear: An Agenda for International Security Studies in the Post–Cold War Era*. 2nd ed. Hemel Hempstead, UK: Harvester Wheatsheaf.

Caulfield, Richard A. 2004. "Resource Governance." *Arctic Human Development Report 2004*. Akureyri, Iceland: Stefansson Arctic Institute, 121–38.

Center for Globalization Negotiations, Brandt 21 Forum. 2006. *The Brandt Proposals: A Report Card*. [online]. www.brandt21forum.info/Report_Armaments.htm [consulted September 13, 2006].

Chaturvedi, Sanjay. 2000. "Arctic Geopolitics. Then and Now." *The Arctic: Environment, People, Policy*, eds. M. Nuttall and T. V. Callaghan. Amsterdam: Harwood Academic Publishers, 441–58.

Cronberg, Tarja. 2001. "Europe Making in Action: Euregio Karelia and the Construction of EU–Russian Partnership." *Focal Point North West Russia* [report from a think tank seminar]. Björkliden, Sweden.

Department of Foreign Affairs [Canada]. 2000. *Canada and the Circumpolar World: The Northern Dimension of Canada's Foreign Policy*. [online]. www.dfait-maeci.gc.ca/circumpolar/sec06_ndfp_rpt-en.asp [consulted September 13, 2006].

Department of State [US]. *US Arctic Policy*. [online]. www.state.gov/g/oes/ocns/arc/ [consulted September 13, 2006].

Derghoukassian, Khatchik. circa 2003. *After the Renaissance: The Reformation of International Security Studies in the Post–Cold War*. [online]. www.isanet.org/portlandarchive/ghougassian.html [consulted September 13, 2006].

Duhaime, Gérard. 2004. "Economic Systems." *Arctic Human Development Report 2004*. Akureyri, Iceland: Stefansson Arctic Institute, 69–84.

European Union. 2000. *The First Northern Dimension Action Plan (2002–2003)*. [online]. europa.eu.int/external_relations/north_dim/ndap/ap2.htm [consulted November 12, 2003].

———. 2004. *The Second European Union Action Plan (2004–2006)*. [online]. europa.eu.int/external_relations/north_dim/ndap/ap2.htm [consulted November 12, 2003].

———. 2005. *Guidelines for the Development of a Political Declaration and a Policy Framework Document for the Northern Dimension Policy from 2007*. [online].

www.ec.europa.eu/comm/external_relations/north_dim/index.htm [consulted September 13, 2006].

Finger, Matthias. 1991. *The Global Environmental Crisis and the Social Implications of Delaying Action* [mimeo]. Vancouver: NRF.

Flöjt, Mika. 2003. "Arktinen episteeminen yhteisö kansainvälisissä POPs-neuvotteluissa." *Politiikan tutkimus Lapin yliopistossa,* eds. M. Luomaaho, S. Moisio, and M. Tennberg. Rovaniemi, Finland: PSC Inter Julkaisuja, 359–79.

Galtung, Johan. 1982. *Environment, Development and Military Activity: Towards Alternative Security Doctrines*. Oslo, Bergen, and Trondheim: Universitetsforlaget.

Golovnev, Andrei. 2001. "Two Northern Stories Meet Two Northern Projects." *North Meets North: Proceedings of the First Northern Research Forum,* eds. T. Björnsson, J. Haukur Ingimundarson, and L. Olafsdottir. Akureyri, Iceland: Stefansson Arctic Institute and University of Akureyri. [available online at www.nrf.is]. [consulted September 13, 2006].

Gorbachev, Mikhail. 1987. Text of "Murmansk Speech." *Pravda* [Moscow], October 2, 1987.

Heininen, Lassi. 2002. "The Northern Research Forum—A New Design for Open Dialogue in the North." Paper presented at the conference Northern Veche. Proceedings of the Second NRF Open Meeting, Veliky Novgorod, Russia, September 19–22.

———. 2004a. "New External Political Structures in Northern Cooperation and Northern Governance: From Quantity to Quality." *Arctic Governance,* eds. T. Koivurova, T. Joona, and R. Shnoro. *Juridica Lapponica* 29. Rovaniemi, Finland: University of Lapland, The Northern Institute for Environmental and Minority Law, 27–42.

———. 2004b. "Circumpolar International Relations and Geopolitics." *Arctic Human Development Report 2004*. Akureyri, Iceland: Stefansson Arctic Institute, 207–25.

———. 2004c. "Changes in Problem Definition—The Interpretation of Nuclear Risk and Threat in the Barents Sea Region." Paper presented in the session "Geopolitical Categorizations and the Risk Society: 'Dangers' to 'Public Life' at the Border" (sponsored by Political Geography Specialty Group), Centennial Meeting of the Association of American Geographers, Philadelphia, March 14–19.

———. 2005a. "Northern European Geopolitics: Northern Dimension and 'Northernness'—An Essay." *Northern Sciences Review 2005—Northern Dimensions and Environments,* eds. L. Heininen, K. Strand, and K. Taulavuori. Oulu, Finland: Oulu University Press, 13–50.

———. 2005b. "About European–Russian Relations." Paper presented at the international conference Agenda 2007: The Northern and the Eastern

Dimensions of the EU's Policy in the Context of the Neighbourhood Strategy. Perspectives for the Northwest of Russia, St. Petersburg, Russia, October.

———. Forthcoming. "Changing Northern Security: Discussion on Traditional, Environmental and Human Security." *Proceedings of the Third NRF Open Meeting: The Resilient North—Human Responses to Global Change* [Yellowknife and Rae Edzo, NT, Canada, September 15–18, 2004], ed. J. Haukur Ingimundarson. Akureyri, Iceland: Stefansson Arctic Institute and University of Akureyri.

———, and Jyrki Käkönen. 1996. "Rajalta maailmaan. Tutkijoiden matka periferiaan. Rauhan-ja konflintintutkimuskeskus." *Tutkimustiedotteita*, 68.

Heininen, Lassi, Jyrki Käkönen, and Olli-Pekka Jalonen. 1995. *Expanding the Northern Dimension: The Final Report of the International Arctic Project of TAPRI*. Tampere Peace Research Institute Research Report no. 61. Jäljennepalvelu, Finland: University of Tampere, 141–58.

———, and Boris Segerståhl. 2002. "International Negotiations Aiming at a Reduction of Nuclear Risks in the Barents Sea Region." *Containing the Atom: International Negotiations on Nuclear Security and Safety*, eds. R. Avenhaus, V. Kremenyuk, and G. Sjöstedt. New York: Lexington Books, International Institute for Applied Systems Analysis, 243–70.

Huebert, R. 2004a. "Arctic Security: Different Threats and Different Responses." Paper presented at the Third NRF Open Meeting: The Resilient North—Human Responses to Global Change, Yellowknife and Rae Edzo, NT, Canada, September 15–18.

Huebert, R. 2004b. "Canada and the Circumpolar World: Meeting the Challenges of Cooperation into the Twenty-first Century: A Critique of chapter 4, 'Post–Cold War Cooperation in the Arctic: From Interstate Conflict to New Agendas for Security.'" *Omitted Arctic Security Issues*. Calgary, AB, Canada: Department of Political Science/Strategic Studies Program, University of Calgary.

ITAR-TASS News Agency. 2004, April 28. "Putin Says Northern Regions Need 'Intelligent Long-term Policy.'"

Laitinen, Kari. 2005. "Kansainvälisen politiikan imperatiivit—Kansallinen turvallisuus, järjestys ja turvallistaminen Yhdysvaltain globaalin valtapolitiikan selittäjinä." *Kosmopolis* 35:1, 43–57.

Menshikov, Vladimir. 2004. "'Hot Zones' of the Security of Latvian Population." Paper presented at the international conference Negotiating Futures—States, Societies and the World, Riga, Latvia, November 11–14 [mimeo].

Miller, Steven E. 2001. "International Security at Twenty-five: From One World to Another." *International Security* 26:1, 5–39.

Nelleman, C. 2003. "New Bombing Ranges and Their Impact on Saami Traditions." *POLAR Environmental Times*, 3.

Newcombe, Hanna. 1986. "Collective Security. Common Security and Alternative Security: A Conceptual Comparison." *Peace Research Reviews* 10:3, 1–8 and 95–99.

Paasi, Anssi. 1996. *Territories, Boundaries and Consciousness: The Changing Geographies of the Finnish–Russian Border*. Chichester, UK: John Wiley.

———. 1998. "Boundaries as Social Processes: Territoriality in the World of Flows." *Geopolitics* 3:1, 69–88.

Paci, J., et al. 2004. "Food Security of Northern Indigenous Peoples in a Time of Uncertainty." presented at the Third NRF Open Meeting: The Resilient North—Human Responses to Global Change, Yellowknife and Rae Edzo, NT, Canada, September 15–18.

Palme Commission. 1982. *Common Security: A Program of Disarmament: Report of the International Commission on Disarmament and Security Issues under the Chairmanship of Olof Palme*. Moscow: Progress Publishers.

Ramseur, David. 1999. *Statement to the Commonwealth North Arctic Council Forum, May 4, 1999*. [online]. www.commonwealthnorth.org/transcripts/arcticcouncil.html [consulted September 17, 2006].

Renner, Michael. 1991. "Assessing the Military's War on the Environment." *State of the World 1991*. ed. L. R. Brown. London: Worldwatch Institute.

Ronkainen R., and B. Westman. 1999. "Tornio–Haparanda—A Unique Result of City Twinning." *Vital North! Security, Democracy, Civil Society: The Calotte Academy*, eds. R. Grönick, L. Päiviö, and M. Waller. Helsinki: Finnish Committee for European Security and Hakapaino Oy, 10–15.

Royal Commission on Aboriginal Peoples. 1996. *Report of the Royal Commission on Aboriginal Peoples*. Ottawa: Royal Commission on Aboriginal Peoples.

Sergounin, Alexander. 2002. "The United States' Northern Dimension? Prospects for a US–Russian Cooperative Agenda in Northern Europe." PONARS Policy Memo No. 232, January 25.

Shearer, Derek. 1997. "The NHL—Creating a Zone of Stability in Northern Europe." Remarks by the Honourable Derek Shearer at the Conference on Regional Integration, Helsinki, Finland, October 8. [mimeo]

Talbott, Strobe. 1997. "What's New—Towards a New Hanseatic League? Strobe Talbott Speaks at Stanford on the New Russia," September 19. [mimeo]

UNEP/GRID-Arendal. 2004. *Poverty & Environmental Times* 2 (March).

United Nations Commission on Human Security. 2001. *Outline of the Report of the Commission on Human Security*. [online]. www.humansecurity-chs.org/finalreport/Outlines/outline.pdf [consulted September 13, 2006].

US Mission to the EU. 1999. *US–EU Joint Statement on Northern Europe, December 17,1999*. Brussels: US Mission to the EU.

Valuev, Vasiliy N. 2003. *Russian Border Policies and Border Regions*. [online]. www.ciaonet.org/wps/sites/copri.html [consulted September 13, 2006].

Veniamin, Alekseyev. 2001. "The Russian North at the Crossroads of Two Epochs." *North Meets North: Proceedings of the First Northern Research Forum*, eds. T. Björnsson, J. Haukur Ingimundarson, and L. Olafsdottir. Akureyri, Iceland: Stefansson Arctic Institute and University of Akureyri [available online at www.nrf.is] [consulted September 13, 2006].

Vuori, Juha. 2004. "Turvallistaminen totalitaarisessa poliittisessa järjestelmässä—Makrotason mallin ja mikrotason analyysin yhdistämisestä." *Kosmopolis* 34:3, 4–28.

Walt, Stephen M. 1991. "The Renaissance of Security Studies." *International Studies Quarterly* 35, 211–39.

Westing, A. 1988. "The Military Sector *vis-à-vis* the Environment." *Journal of Peace Research* 25:3, 257–64.

Zalamans, D. 2001. "Transboundary Regionalisation—The Case of Haparanda and Tornio." *Borders Matter: Transfrontier Regions in Contemporary Europe*. Border Studies, no. 2. Aabenraa, Denmark: Danish Institute of Border Regions.

CHAPTER 6

FROM IRON CURTAIN TO PAPER WALL: THE INFLUENCE OF BORDER REGIMES ON LOCAL AND REGIONAL ECONOMIES—THE LIFE, DEATH, AND RESURRECTION OF BAZAARS IN THE ŁÓDŹ REGION

Martin van der Velde and Szymon Marcińczak

The history of the Łódź region of Poland is closely tied to the development of the textile industry, and the region has even been labelled the "Polish Manchester" or "Textilopolis." Partly due to its location in central Europe, the Łódź textile industry has always been oriented toward the countries to the east of the Polish border. Its large bazaars, with their range of both Polish and foreign customers, could be regarded as the industry's offspring. Many kinds of bazaar developed, both formal and informal, some publicly operated and others privately operated. (The terms "bazaar" and "open-air market" are used synonymously in this chapter.)

Although Łódź has been located in the geographic centre of Poland since the Second World War, it has always been a focal point of trade with the former Soviet Union. Even after the collapse of the Soviet Union traders as well as buyers, especially from Belarus and Ukraine, continued to come to Łódź, crossing Poland's relatively permeable eastern border. This permeability began to decrease, however, when Poland applied for membership of the European Union (EU), and it continued to decrease as Poland prepared to become a party to the Schengen Agreement.

The bazaars of the Łódź region came into existence after 1989 and acquired considerable importance during the 1990s, along with bazaars elsewhere in Poland. It has been estimated that by 1998 the large bazaar in the Tenth Anniversary Stadium, a soccer stadium in Warsaw, accounted for no less than XEU 330 million in Polish exports, making it the country's fifth largest "exporter" at that time. Moreover,

Figure 6.1 Location of Łódź and Main Highways

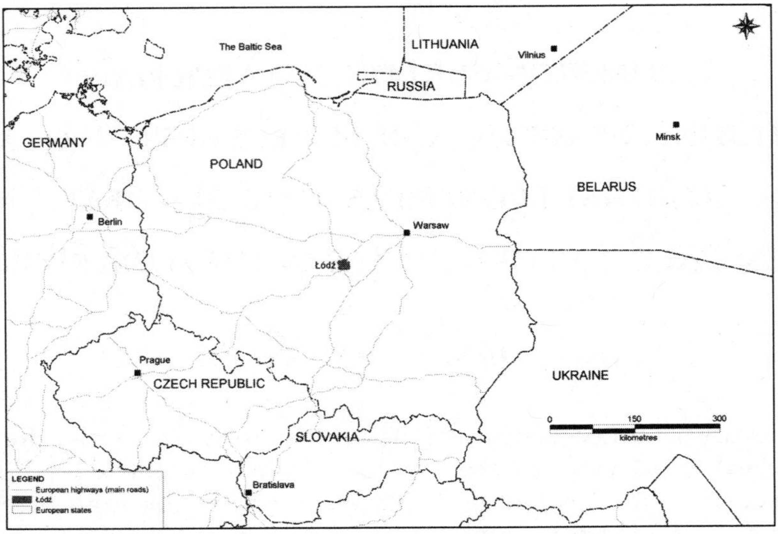

Figure 6.2 Location of Rzgów and Tuszyn

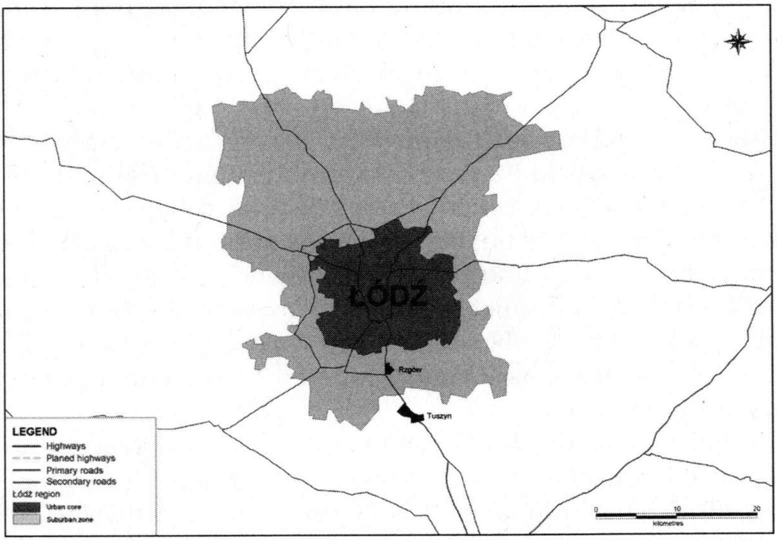

bazaars in Poland were estimated to provide a living for 130,000 people in the actual bazaars and their ancillary services. In the Łódź region, for instance, budget hotels were built close to markets, while people living near the larger bazaars rented out their yards as parking spaces and rooms in their house as accommodations for traders who wanted to stay overnight. After the eastern border was tightened it was estimated that this economic activity fell by no less than 50 percent. Recent trends, however, suggest that the bazaars are recovering. Bazaars have thus been a major factor in the Łódź region's economy. Not only have they served as outlets for locally and regionally produced textile products, but the taxes they pay have made up a major portion of the budgets of the municipalities in which they are located.

In this chapter we trace the effects of the "Schengenization" of the eastern border of Poland on the functioning of the larger bazaars in the Łódź region, specifically those in Tuszyn and Rzgów, and on the local and regional economies. We analyze not only the changes in the functions and customers of the bazaars due to the Schengenization process but also the responses and policies of local government and development agencies. Through this analysis of the implications of Schengenization at the local and regional levels we hope to contribute to a further understanding of broader developments in Europe. In order to explain the current position and past performance of these two bazaars we examined the development of the bazaars within the local, regional, national, and European contexts. As well as playing a historic role within central and eastern Europe, the Łódź region and its bazaars have been shaped to a great extent by their political and institutional context. In this case it was not only the local and regional institutions that were in play but also the decision of the Polish government to join the EU and, eventually, the Schengen Agreement. The fate of the bazaars has come to depend on the decisions made and agendas set by the Polish government and by the EU.

This chapter is based mainly on the ideas of structuration theory, in which "functional embeddedness" is an important issue. The structuration theory argues that people live in structures, according to organized sets of rules and resources that they have created, and that, as they enact them, they reproduce. Thus agents and structures are interdependent, they form a duality—that is, "the structural properties of social systems are both medium and outcome of the practices they recursively organize . . . Structure is not to be equated with constraint, but is always both constraining and enabling" (Giddens 1984, 25). In other words there is no independent dualism of structure and agency, for they are inseparably interconnected.

This metatheoretical perspective, which stresses micro–macro dialectics, soundly resonates with the methodological claims of Storper and Scott (1986). These authors argue that in any viable study of industrial change "the micro and macro levels must be simultaneously and actively present . . . but at the same time, it is necessary to keep to the forefront the intermediating *meso* level . . ." (14) of theory and empirical inquiry. In this chapter a meso level is represented by entities that have spatial (territorial) dimension, that is, municipalities in general and bazaars in particular. This is implied by the fact that it is feasible to comprehend a structure–agency interplay while examining its spatial or scalar manifestations. In the present context the focus is more on agency, in the sense that agency responses to structural changes are central, thereby fully recognizing that their enacted responses have structuring capacity. The agency aspect of structure, that is, the structural responses to agency—if the bordering practices of the EU and the national government of Poland can be regarded as such—are dealt with less fully.

The general line of argumentation is also in accordance with the framework of new economic geography, which gives greater emphasis to the spatial interactions between economic agents. Thus, instead of focusing on activities, the actors are given a more prominent role (Fujita, Krugman, and Venables 1999). In other words, according to Yeung (2003, 445)

> the context in which the multiplicity of identities and logics shapes the social practices of economic actors constitutes the key starting point in most recent studies of new economic geography . . . [and] context sets the contingent in which economic action can be analyzed . . . Thus the context of economic situation becomes a critical component in any geographical explanation.

Since the assessment of the actors is partly based on the regime theory (Stoker 1995), the actors (or their representatives) who were chosen have a coalition-building capacity.

This analysis attempts to combine the importance of the temporal, spatial, and institutional contexts with a strong focus on actors and their interaction in order to gain insight into the significance of the changing interpretation of the EU's eastern border, especially where it concerns the bazaar phenomenon. In doing so it incorporates the concepts laid out by Emmanuel Brunet-Jailly (2005) in his recent work toward a theory of borders, in which he clearly recognizes the multifaceted, multi-level, multi-actor, and integrated character of borders and borderlands. Notwithstanding his main focus on the border "region" proper, his general framework, which is aimed at mapping out the relative positions of different approaches, is useful in the context of this chapter, which focuses more on border "effects." Brunet-Jailly (2005, 634) defines four different analytical lenses: "(1) market forces and trade flows, (2) policy activities of multiple levels of government, (3) the particular political clout of borderland communities, and (4) the specific culture of borderland communities." These place the focus on economic issues, governance, organizational capacity and activism, and cultural issues, respectively. In the spirit of structuration theory both structure and agency are incorporated through all four lenses, and the different issues complement, enhance, and influence each other. In our analysis the lenses of political clout, market forces, and governance are used in particular.

The first section of this chapter describes the bazaar phenomenon in general, while the second section looks at the preparation for, and the implications of, Poland's acceptance of the Schengen Agreement, one of the institutional contexts of the bazaars. The third section elaborates on their regional setting by describing the development of the Łódź region, and the fourth focuses on the bazaars in the Łódź region and how the specific consequences of the Schengenization of the Polish border have been handled.

OPEN-AIR MARKETS

The bazaars discussed in this chapter represent one form of the broader phenomenon of open-air markets. The term "open-air market" may be somewhat misleading, as the bazaars in Tuszyn and Rzgów currently both function in partially covered structures. They are among the wide varieties of forms that together constitute a continuum, running from small, haphazard street-corner markets to large-scale, mall-like market halls.

Open-air markets have played and continue to play a major role in the distribution of goods throughout the world, and in that sense they have a long history. The term "bazaar," certainly in the early days, has been associated most often with periodic markets in less developed countries, and the bazaar phenomenon was first studied by cultural anthropologists. In studies of more developed countries bazaars are still often characterized as having an air of folklore, or, are put in the category of "garage sale."

Figure 6.3 Bazaars in Tuszyn and Rzgów

One of the first definitions of a bazaar was developed by Polanyi in 1957, as part of his examination of bazaars in terms of market relations (cited in Sik and Wallace 1999, 698). His straightforward definition of open-air markets as "places for the exchange of simple goods" was augmented by Bohannon and Dalton (1962), who included social, cultural, political, and economic characteristics as influencing factors for the manifestation of market relations.

There are two dominant approaches to the bazaar economy. The first regards the bazaar as a prototype of the competitive market. The second, ethnographic approach stresses their exotic and sometimes bizarre character, in the sense that at first glance the entrepreneurs operating in these markets often display almost irrational behaviour (Fanselow 1990). Both perspectives may apply to the open-air markets of central and eastern Europe described in this chapter. Although they can be regarded as a stage in the development of capitalist markets since the 1990s, these bazaars continue to exhibit an exceptional character that extends to their products, the sellers, and the buyers. Not only are strange, exotic, and bizarre combinations of products sometimes on display, but the traders and their customers also come from unexpected locations. Originally the markets in Warsaw and Łódź did not cater to Polish people. Instead customers came largely from eastern countries to buy products made in Poland, often in the many small factories that were set up by Poles around these markets. Today Vietnamese traders sell textiles imported from Asia and some bazaars have become centres for contraband from eastern countries.

Under the socialist regimes that dominated central and eastern Europe before the 1990s, open-air markets played an important complementary role in dysfunctional redistributive systems. Officially they were considered "as remnants of an outdated and unnecessary form of commerce or as a dangerous challenge to the socialized retail sector" (Sik and Wallace 1999, 697). After the fall of Communism they continued to play an important intermediary role between the collapsed socialist system and proliferating capitalism. As illustrated later, the markets of central and eastern Europe have become almost a substitute for, rather than a supplement to, the normal retail sector (Sik and Wallace 1999, 697). As Aidis (2003, 461) has noted, they are "officially despised yet tolerated." According to Rada (2006), it is even possible to speak of a cross-border bazaar economy stretching from the Józsefvárosi V Market (or "Chinese Market") in Budapest, to Tuszyn and, via the Tenth Anniversary Stadium in Warsaw, to the Seventh Kilometre (or Tolchok) Market in Odessa, Ukraine. Nowadays "they have developed from sites for illegal activities condemned as 'parasitical' by the former regimes (but nevertheless an important part of those regimes) to becoming increasingly open" (Sik and Wallace 1999, 701). Indeed, the existing open-air markets became the prototype of shopping malls (Shields 1992).

The past adaptation and current functioning of these markets have depended greatly on the interaction of the state and the market in the everyday life of citizens, an interaction that is applicable not only on the national (Polish) level but also on the European level. The success and/or failure of these markets have also depended to a large extent on traders and customers coming from abroad, especially from eastern countries. In this sense the security regimes that have been imposed on the Polish border with Belarus and Ukraine are of great importance to the open-air markets.

Notwithstanding the fact that these types of markets are increasingly claiming a regular position within the wholesale and retail system, there is still a penumbra of illegality surrounding them, supported by the fact that many of them may be characterized as examples of "raw" capitalism. This characterization implies that, although these markets do operate according to certain institutionalized rules, for a long time these rules were not formalized, so traders had to behave according to the rules, as when paying a fee to occupy a stall, without being protected by law. Furthermore, when these markets were first established they operated in what Elster, Offe, and Preuss (1998) have called an "institutional void," in which the state withdrew and other institutions were not prepared to regulate market forces, which may have contributed to their unregulated character. Huge profits were possible, but failure also lurked.

The topic of open-air markets is still very much a wasteland, which is remarkable considering that they are a form of intermediary between the market and the planned economy, as much in the socialist past as in the capitalist present. One exception to this "intellectual void" is a collection of academic papers on the issue of open-air markets in central Europe published in the *International Journal of Urban and Regional Research* in 1999. The core of this special issue was based on an extensive study carried out by Czakó and Sik (1999) in which they analyzed four open-air markets in Hungary. In their contribution to this special issue Sik and Wallace (1999, 701) attempted to systematize the structural changes that had influenced the development of the open-air markets of central and eastern Europe, formulating six major changes: (1) the deconstruction of the socialized retail sector, (2) the disappearance of bilateral international trade, (3) the opening of previously closed borders, (4) the "vanishing" of the strong and paternalistic state, (5) the growth of a "western" consumer culture, and (6) the rapidly decreasing standard of living. These six changes created a fertile bed for existing open-air markets. The skills of surviving in a Communist society also proved to be very valuable in dealing with these changes (Piirainen 1997).

However, within the context of this chapter the changing interpretation of the border is of particular interest. Immediately after the collapse of the Communist system the border controls were alleviated, resulting in increasing cross-border flows not only of sellers but also of buyers. To illustrate, in 1989 fewer than three million people from the former Soviet Union entered Poland, but a year later that number had more than doubled, and it continued to grow, to reach more than fourteen million in the peak year of 1997 (Stola, cited in Iglicka 2001a). Until 1989 travelling within the Communist bloc had been difficult because many national borders were completely sealed most of the time, and even travelling within each national territory was difficult. The high level of cross-border interaction after 1989 was induced for the most part by price differences between countries, in addition to shortages of products. These factors stimulated what some have called "shuttle migration," whereby migrants shuttled, or travelled, to certain places to sell products and stayed for some days before returning home (Iglicka 1999, 2001a, 2001b). According to Iglicka (2001a, 507), inhabitants of the former Soviet Union who were involved in this shuttle migration often gave up their jobs and positions because the differences in the currency exchange rates or the price differences between countries was much more profitable for them, and international commuting became their main source of income and, *de facto*, their "job." Similarly, the so-called suitcase traders, sometimes also referred to as "ants," travelled, literally, with their products in their suitcases (Sword 1999) because they sold only very small quantities on each trip. Notwithstanding that cross-border travel was possible, the borders were still barriers and thus also created opportunities for border traders (Thuen 1999). These traders earned a living by taking products across the border to sell and charging their customers extra fees as compensation for the risk they took (smuggling) or for the effort it took to get products back and forth across the border (transportation and other costs). When a border gets less permeable, as is currently the case in the Łódź region because of the implementation of the Schengen Agreement, this process becomes even more attractive to some traders.

Given that increased border permeability was an important contributor to the rise of bazaars, not only in the border regions but also further inland, in Warsaw and the Łódź region, it is not surprising that the tightening of the borders and the intensification of border control in the run-up to Poland's accession to the Schengen Agreement also had major consequences for the bazaars. Indeed, it may have been a fatal blow for them. In the case of the Warsaw bazaar it was estimated that the number of vendors fell from 7,000 in 1997, the year the first Schengen transitional measures were taken, to 5,000 in 1998. According to a report in the *New York Times* (Andrews 2001), sales fell from XEU 450 million in 1997 to XEU 200 million in 1998 to XEU 160 million in 2000, although this decline was also partly due to the financial crisis that began in Russia in 1998. Apparently, customers failed to return to the Warsaw bazaar immediately after its recovery, and its

> decline reflects changes in central and eastern Europe. New markets have usurped Warsaw's role as a shopping centre for Minsk, Kiev or Moscow. Asian producers selling through Poland's sizeable Vietnamese community have undercut Poland's sweatshops. And many companies now use Warsaw simply as a distribution centre.

The fact that stricter border regimes are not the only factor influencing the functioning of bazaars may be supported by the observation that, after an initial decline, the open-air markets of central and eastern Europe, at least in the Łódź region, seem to have regained some of their position. (This observation is dealt with more extensively in a later section of this chapter.)

To this point bazaars and open-air markets have been discussed only in general terms. The study by Czakó and Sik (1999) provides detailed information about four Hungarian open-air markets, but the data used in their study stemmed from a project carried out in 1995–96, and it is important to keep in mind that this was before the introduction of any transitional measures, such as introducing visas for certain countries, in anticipation of Hungary's accession to the EU and the Schengen Agreement were in place. In other words this report more or less described the heyday of open-air markets in central and eastern Europe. Nevertheless, since the observations presented on the bazaars in Tuszyn and Rzgów in a later section are more global and anecdotal, and the questionnaires that were used dealt only with buyers, the data collected by the Hungarian scholars are used here to gain some insight into the "who" and "what" of these open-air markets as they used to be.

The biggest bazaar in the Hungarian study was the famous Józsefvárosi V Market (or "Chinese Market") in Budapest, which is still functioning today on 12,000 square metres of land owned by the Hungarian National Railway Company, although it is still run by a private entrepreneur. Its turnover in 1995 was estimated at XEU 75 million. Almost half the traders in this Budapest market were Asian, an indication of the international orientation of the bazaars. This high proportion of Asian traders was exceptional, however. In the other markets two-thirds or more of the sellers were Hungarian. Eighty-six percent of the products sold in this bazaar were items of clothing. In that sense it is comparable with the bazaars in the Łódź region. The high proportion of trade in textiles in Budapest may have been a result of the large number of Asian textile traders present in the market. The majority of the products sold in the other three Budapest markets also involved textiles, albeit not in such high proportions. The second most important category involved the geographic origin of the products, in the West, as the bazaars were likely satisfying the growing culture of western-style consumption. A particularly interesting aspect of the research by Czakó and Sik (1999) is the comparison of price levels. The prices in general would be expected to be lower compared to the national level, and this was especially true for textile products, the prices of which were about half the level seen elsewhere. However, chocolate, cigarettes, and deodorant, all of which were western products, were just as expensive or even more expensive. Moreover, the price differences were remarkably constant over the four markets that were scrutinized, almost as if the prices were subject to some regulation.

Clearly, open-air markets in central and eastern Europe played an important role in the local, regional, and national economies, mediating between the incoming capitalist market and the fading socialist system. They were increasingly a substitute for "normal" retail and wholesale outlets, rather than playing their previous role as a supplement to them, and both traders and buyers exhibited a widespread geographical pattern. Thus, the changing regimes, especially at the eastern border of the current EU, may have had a major impact on these bazaars. The Schengen Agreement, which organizes and regulates the EU's outer border (or, more precisely, the outer border of Schengen territory) is discussed next.

THE SCHENGEN AGREEMENT

Initially, the removal of the Iron Curtain in the late 1980s enabled the inhabitants of central and eastern Europe to freely cross national borders. However, as a consequence of the aspirations of some countries in the region—Estonia, Lithuania, Latvia, Hungary, Poland, and Slovakia—to join the EU and the Schengen Agreement, this situation changed. In order to meet the requirements for joining, these countries had to virtually seal their eastern borders, as they would become the outer borders of the EU. This was achieved mainly by the introduction of visas for non-EU citizens.

The Schengen Agreement was originally signed in June 1985 by five countries: Belgium, France, Germany, Luxembourg, and the Netherlands. Its aim was, as it still is, the free movement of people, goods, and services within the EU in parallel with a harmonized system of external border controls. In other words, the opening up of internal EU borders is accompanied by the sealing of its external borders. Five years later, in June 1990, the Convention Implementing the Schengen Agreement was signed. Its key issues relate to measures designed to create a common area of security and justice, following the abolition of internal border checks (Rakowski and Rybicki 2000). The implementation of these measures gradually led to the establishment of a set of rules and norms, the Schengen *acquis*, that created a uniform visa system enabling non-EU citizens to travel across Schengen territory. The Schengen *acquis* became EU law with the adoption of the Amsterdam Treaty in 1997 (Rakowski and Rybicki 2000). The Schengen Convention entered into force on September 1, 1993, but its provisions could not be put into practice until the necessary technical and legal prerequisites, such as databases and the relevant data protection authorities, were in place. The convention thus took practical effect only on March 26, 1995, for the original parties to the Schengen Agreement, as well as for Spain and Portugal. Italy followed suit on October 26, 1997, Austria on December 1, 1997, and Greece on March 26, 2000. Meanwhile, a Schengen cooperation agreement had been concluded with the non-EU members of the Nordic Passport Union, Norway and Iceland, in 1996, and both these countries fully implemented the Schengen regime, beginning on March 25, 2001, the same day that the Schengen Convention also entered into force for Denmark, Finland, and Sweden, the three Nordic countries that are member-states of the EU. Thirteen other countries have signed up to the Schengen system but have not yet implemented it, including the member-states of the EU in central and eastern Europe, while two EU member-states, the United Kingdom and the Irish Republic, remain outside the system (SCADPlus 2005).

The visa is the main tool used to control the flow of migrants into the EU. It creates quotas and shapes the structure of the inflow by laying down prior numbers of permitted admissions and by imposing requirements on migrants that involve their personal history, income, and martial status. For individuals the process of obtaining a visa is usually problematic and at best time consuming. Apart from planning their trip beforehand, potential tourists must travel to a consulate, which may be quite remote from their place of residence. At the consulate they are interviewed, very often on detailed personal information, and have to pay for a visa without any certainty of receiving one. Those fortunate enough to be granted a visa may have to wait several weeks for it to be issued.

In preparation for signing the Schengen Agreement and in order to adjust its border-crossing policy to EU norms, the government of Poland introduced the Aliens Law in 1997. This law stopped the free movement of people across the Poland's eastern border, a movement that had been flourishing since the early 1990s. Individuals crossing the border were now required to possess a legal document stating their identity and a tourist voucher. Belarusians, Russians, and Ukrainians were affected the most by the new law, since citizens of neighbouring countries that were part of the ongoing "Schengenization" process were exempted from the this requirement, as were citizens of the existing member states of the EU. In order to diminish the negative impact of this policy, particularly the decrease in the number of visitors from the former Soviet Union, the Polish government allowed Belarusians and Russians to cross the border without vouchers for certain types of journeys, such as business trips or family visits, and also allowed Ukrainians who wished to stay in Poland for less than ninety days to travel without vouchers (Rakowski and Rybicki 2000). The situation became even more difficult after October 1, 2003, when visas were introduced for all travellers from non-EU countries. However, the Polish government, seeking once again to maintain the profitable influx of shuttle migrants from the former Soviet Union, introduced measures aimed at relaxing the emerging border congestion. According to Tokarz (2004), the "stream" method of visa-issuance is the most important of these measures, as it implies that the interviews formally required when applying are seldom carried out and, perhaps more significantly, a visa must be issued no later than two days after it is requested.

Thus since 1997 the former Iron Curtain has been gradually replaced by a "paper wall," created by visas, invitations, work permits, and so on. Furthermore, this process may be reinforced by future legislation. However, although Poland's "liberal" visa policy has been tolerated by the EU, it will inevitably change when Poland actually becomes part of the Schengen territory, which is scheduled to occur in 2008.

THE ŁÓDŹ REGION

A succinct description of the Łódź region is essential for understanding the environment in which the actors act—the bazaar managers in particular. Indeed, the absence of such a description may lead to spurious conclusions concerning the activities of individuals (Johnston 1986). Moreover, in order to achieve a proper insight it is necessary to use an extended time frame (Jones 2004). This is especially significant in the case of post-socialist urban regions, where the path-dependency narrative is very important (Andrusz, Harloe, and Szelenyi 1996). Therefore the Łódź region is described next, with a special emphasis on the development of the textile industry.

Łódź was granted city status in 1423, although at the time it was only a small agricultural settlement with no more than one hundred houses. It led an obscure existence until the nineteenth century, when its situation changed completely and it began to grow (Koter, Liszewski, and Suliborski 1996) due to the parallel development of a textile industry and the opening of eastern markets. This particular set of events was enabled by the political and economic context of the nineteenth century. An independent Polish state did not exist at that time, since, following partitions in 1772, 1793, and 1795, Polish territory was divided among three powers: Austria, Prussia, and Russia. However, from 1815 relative autonomy was given to the Congress Kingdom of Poland under Russian supervision. As part of this political entity, Łódź used the opportunity to respond to the growing demand for textile products, particularly from the army and from Russia. The Russian market gained importance when Russia imposed a protectionist customs duty on imported goods produced in Prussia in 1821 and established a customs union with the Congress Kingdom of Poland a year later. These factors eased Łódź's penetration of the vast markets of the Russian empire (Liszewski 1997).

This period of uncontrolled development ended in 1830 when, following the failure of the November Uprising and the removal of most of the Congress Kingdom's autonomy (Davies 1982), custom duties were imposed on the border with the Russian empire. During the ensuing period of relative idleness technological changes were implemented, such as the restructuring of the production process and the introduction of steam power (Liszewski 1997). Consequently, by 1851, when the customs duties were abolished, Łódź was a highly mechanized industrial city, producing high-quality textile goods, especially cotton products, that were competitive in the eastern market (Liszewski 1997). The introduction in 1877 of restrictive custom duties on goods imported into the Russian empire from western Europe (Owen 1985) led to an even more favourable market environment for Łódź industry, and from 1879 to 1913 about 70 percent of the region's textile production was sold on the Russian market (Puś 1987).

During the years between the two world wars three factors caused the collapse of Łódź's industrial production: its textile machinery was confiscated by the Germans; its entrepreneurs lost the capital and securities they had deposited in Russian banks; and the eastern markets were closed. After the Second World War the region, together with the rest of Poland, found itself under the political and economic supervision of the Soviet Union. The traditional eastern market was opened again, but it was a controlled opening with no appreciation of free-market forces. Moreover, Poland, like the other countries forced into the Soviet bloc, was compelled to join the Council for Mutual Economic Assistance (CMEA, also known in the West as Comecon), an organization overseen and controlled by the Soviet Union. For Łódź, the socialist era (1945–89) generally meant further industrialization, but with limited possibilities to control the structure of the process. In effect the industrial structure, as in other Communist states (Elster, Offe, and Preuss 1998), was subordinated to the idea of economies of scale. In practice, even though new industrial activities were introduced, such as chemicals, electrical engineering, and machine industry, Łódź remained strongly tied to textile production. Because this ongoing industrialization required a larger labour force, inhabitants of the hinterland, mainly the suburbs, found employment in Łódź factories (Jakóbczyk-Gryszkiewicz 1997, 228). However, it can be argued that, overall, this was a period of relative stability (Liszewsk 1997, 18).

The periods of prosperity and decline in the Łódź region were influenced by contemporary relations with the Soviet Union in general and by access to eastern markets in particular. As illustrated in the following section, this pattern seems to have prevailed in the economic performance of the region in general, and in the case of the Tuszyn and Rzgów bazaars in particular, in the years from 1990 to 2003, after the collapse of the Soviet system. Moreover, the region's present socioeconomic situation bears a heavy socialist legacy. The former mode of production, which implied strong ties between suppliers and their customers (Elster, Offe, and Preuss 1998), undermined the regional economy during the early years of transition. It not only influenced the internal economic structure of the region, since the collapse of one link created severe problems for the whole production chain, but also affected external trade relations. The almost exclusive reliance on the CMEA market before 1989 meant that the city and the region lost all their customers in the early days of the transition. By 1991 some 100,000 people were unemployed and numerous factories had closed. Łódź and its region shared the fate of many other urban industrial regions in central and eastern Europe (Kovács 2000, 3), and, in general, it was perceived as having no immediate prospects for development (Walker 1993).

Nevertheless, the region achieved a positive shift in its developmental trajectory by implementing a set of more or less successful projects (Dornisch 2002). Among these was the creation of bazaars on the outskirts of Łódź city by a consortium of private and public investors, including private businesspeople, city councils, and the Communal Bank of Łódź (Dornisch 2002). Two main factors facilitated their development. The first was the launch of two government organizations, the Enterprise Monitoring Department and the Debt Restructuring Department (Dornisch 2002). Apart from all kinds of other positive effects, this enabled individual actors to buy assets, especially machines, from liquidated factories and to start their own enterprises. This was of major importance to the inhabitants of Rzgów and Tuszyn, since the majority of the new textile entrepreneurs were former employees of Łódź factories who had backgrounds in textile production. The second factor was the phenomenon of the shuttle migration (also known as primitive mobility) from the countries of the former Soviet Union into Poland during the 1990s, after the collapse of Communism (Okólski 1996). This influx of "tourists" from the former

Soviet Union had many positive effects, including the development of specific sectors of the Polish economy. Indeed, the foreign demand for textiles and leather products was one of the main factors behind the boom in the private textile and shoe businesses (Okólski 1996). Thus these "tourists" proved to be the major stimulus not only for bazaars in the Polish borderland (Potrykowski 1998) but also for markets located in the heart of the country, such as the Warsaw bazaar (Okólski 1996) and the Rzgów–Tuszyn textile-trade strip.

Current development in the Łódź region is path dependent in nature. Employment in manufacturing industry still dominates total employment. In October 2005 51 percent of the Łódź labour force was employed in industry and of that proportion more than 30 percent was employed in the textile industry. The economy of the Łódź region is still influenced by the eastern markets, although to a lesser extent than before, thanks to the diversification of industrial activities and the development of a tertiary sector in the urban core. Given Poland's chronic balance of payments deficit, the eastern markets will remain of vital importance to development in the Łódź region.

THE BAZAARS OF TUSZYN AND RZGÓW

The history of the Tuszyn and Rzgów bazaars began in the early 1990s, when some local entrepreneurs, desperate to sell their products, started to set out their wares along the major north–south arterial highway that runs through the two municipalities. This, along with the growing influx of Russian visitors, stimulated the region's textile-producing and trading activities, which were soon flourishing. By 1993 representatives of local government and businesspeople from the region were active in seeking to improve conditions at the bazaars. They began by delimiting the number of bazaar locations.

In the case of Rzgów the local government provided a space and local businesses supplied the necessary funds, and this private–public collaboration led to the creation of a huge clothing bazaar known as PTAK (the initials of its founder's name). The bazaars in Tuszyn had a different origin. Instead of one market, seven markets were established. In contrast to Rzgów, in Tuszyn the biggest bazaar is on public land and is maintained by the local government, a situation that inevitably influences the flexibility of the venue.

Figure 6.4 Number of Stalls, 1995–2004

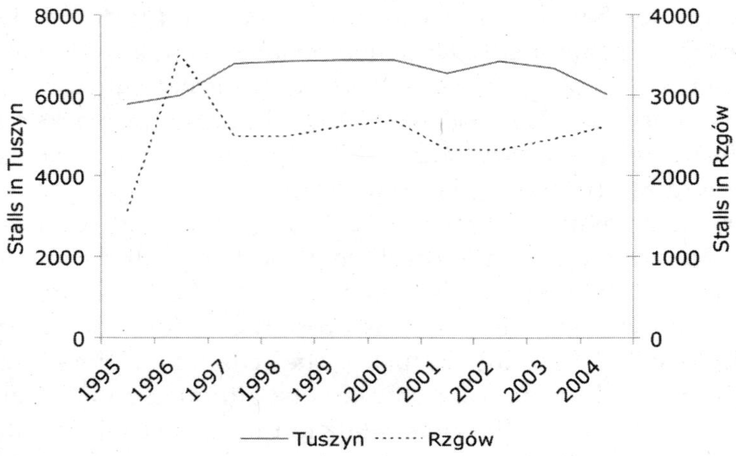

The bazaars in both municipalities flourished, as measured by the number of stalls, until 1998, but particularly in 1995–96. In late 1997, however, the Polish government introduced stricter border-crossing requirements for inhabitants of former Soviet republics, in order to fulfill the obligations arising from its forthcoming accession to the EU. This, according to Iglicka (2001a), immediately affected movement from Belarus and Russia, which in turn affected the sales at the big bazaars in eastern and central Poland. This issue caused heavy lobbying at the national level, and Polish traders and manufacturers ultimately forced the central authorities to lower the cost of tourist vouchers and the amount of money necessary to enter Poland (Iglicka 2001a). A second blow struck the bazaars in October 2003 when the further fulfilment of Poland's Schengen obligations led the government to introduce a visa requirement for inhabitants of former Soviet republics wishing to travel to Poland, further hindering international travel. However, despite these unfavourable circumstances, the bazaars have remained important to the local and regional economies. The taxes derived from them constitute a significant share of the municipalities' revenue.

The periods of prosperity and decline experienced by the bazaars have also had a crucial influence on the regional economy. This is

Figure 6.5 Share of Bazaar Taxes in the Revenues of Tuszyn and Rzgów, 1995–2003 (%)

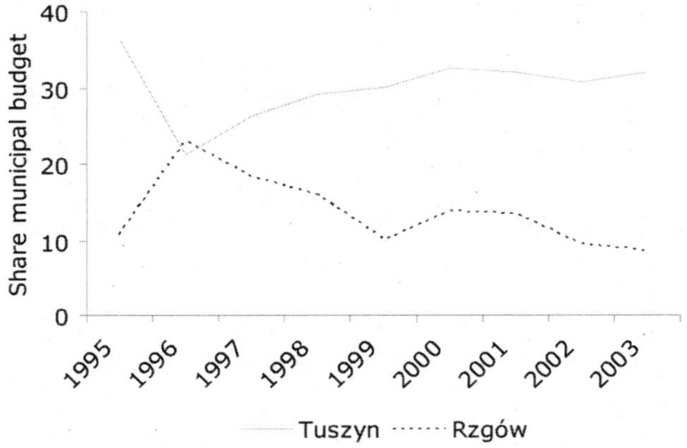

reflected, albeit indirectly, in the numbers of people employed in both municipalities, as well as in the structure of employment, which both demonstrate the region's dependence on eastern markets. In short, Poland's economic and political relations with, and the situation of, its eastern neighbours affect employment in the region.

Unfortunately, Polish employment statistics are biased in the sense that enterprises that employ up to nine workers have not been included in official statistics since 2000, a fact that is of great importance in that small enterprises constitute the predominant type of firm in the Łódź region. Consequently, a better measure of municipal economic performance and employment structure in Tuszyn and Rzgów is the number of enterprises in their industrial and service sectors (figure 6.6). The majority of industrial venues are related to the textile sector, and the service sector is dominated by bazaar-related activities.

Clearly, not all of the volatility in the bazaar economy is accounted for by changing border regimes, and in any case it is likely too early to observe the effects of the visa measures implemented by the government in 2003. However, in general a decline has been witnessed since 1997, especially in the industrial sector.

Figure 6.6 Number of Enterprises Operating in Industry and Services in Tuszyn and Rzgów, 1995–2004

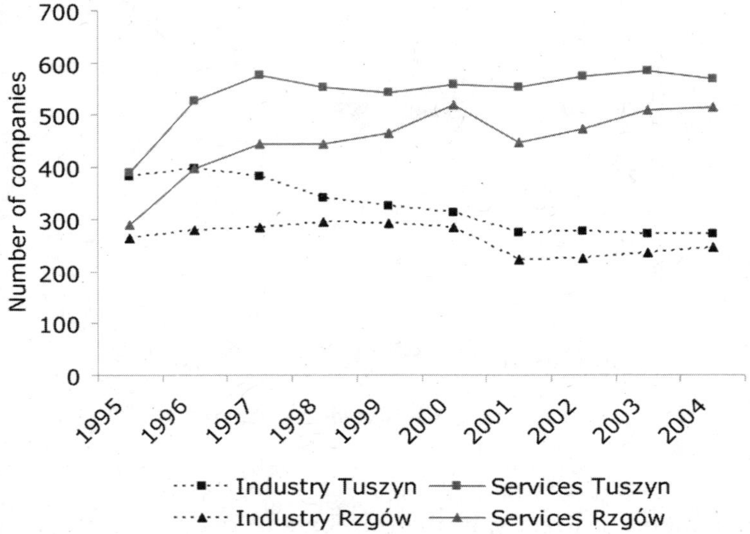

Customers of the Bazaars

Data from a study of four Hungarian markets at the end of the twentieth century (Czakó and Sik 1999) was presented earlier in this chapter to illustrate the "who" and "what" of open-air markets. Since that study was conducted, ten former Communist states in central and eastern Europe have been admitted to the EU (eight in 2004 and two in 2007), and many of these countries have had to prepare for their Schengen membership by tightening their border-security regimes and changing their attitudes toward illegal immigration. All of these events have had implications for the mobility of people and, as illustrated earlier, the market phenomenon relies to a great extent on people being able to travel to trading places. Given the continued dearth of scholarly literature on the topic, and in an attempt to start filling this empirical gap, we carried out a small-scale questionnaire project among the buyers at one of the larger markets in the Łódź region, the publicly run open-air market in Tuszyn.

Together the markets in Tuszyn occupy an area of about fifteen hectares and traders have at their disposal about 7,000 stalls. The market where the questionnaires were conducted had a little over 1,100 semi-permanent stalls. As at many of the area's markets, textiles and clothing were the most important products at this market, which was open from 3 a.m. to 11 a.m six days a week. The municipal authorities estimate that each year about seven million people visit the seven Tuszyn markets and spend about XEU 830 million, and that the markets contribute more than XEU 1.5 million in taxes to municipal revenues.

In order to get some basic insight into the behaviour and attitudes of bazaar customers, about 97 individuals were approached with a questionnaire while they were visiting the bazaar. Of course, firm conclusions cannot be drawn from such a small sample, but indications are possible. Two respondents were from Belarus and two were from another EU country, while one respondent was Israeli and another refused to answer. The remaining ninety-one respondents were quite evenly split between forty-five from the Łódź region and forty-six from the rest of Poland.

The first indication of changes in the regional composition of the local population may be that only two of the respondents came from countries outside the future Schengen zone, which in turn may be an early indication of the importance of the stricter border regime imposed in 2003. Although we are unable to prove it statistically, we believe that only a small proportion of the markets' customers come from countries of the former Soviet Union. This is supported by the observation that few of the private cars and small trucks in the surrounding parking lots had come from the East, though the share of buses from these countries is much higher.

However, the notion that fewer customers come from former Soviet republics does not imply that revenues have fallen. The two respondents from Belarus indicated that the amount of money they had spent in the market fell into the highest category, while the average for people from the Łódź region was about XEU 300 and that for people from the rest of Poland was XEU 800. (Please note that in figure 6.7 the złoty, the original Polish currency, is used, but in the text this currency is converted into euros, using an exchange rate of four złotych to one euro.)

In general, people were mainly interested in buying textiles and clothing. About three-quarters of the questionnaire's respondents had bought or were going to buy textiles. About two-thirds of the respondents indicated that low price was their main reason for coming

Figure 6.7 Expected Expenditures, Łódź and Rest of Poland (złotych)

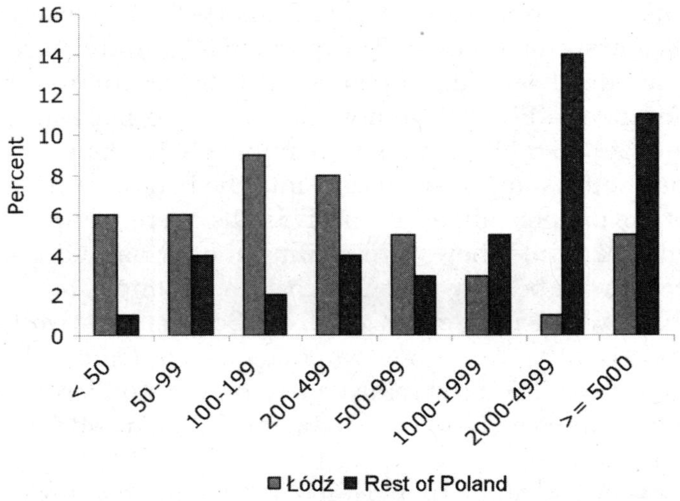

Figure 6.8 Visiting Frequencies, Łódź and Rest of Poland (%)

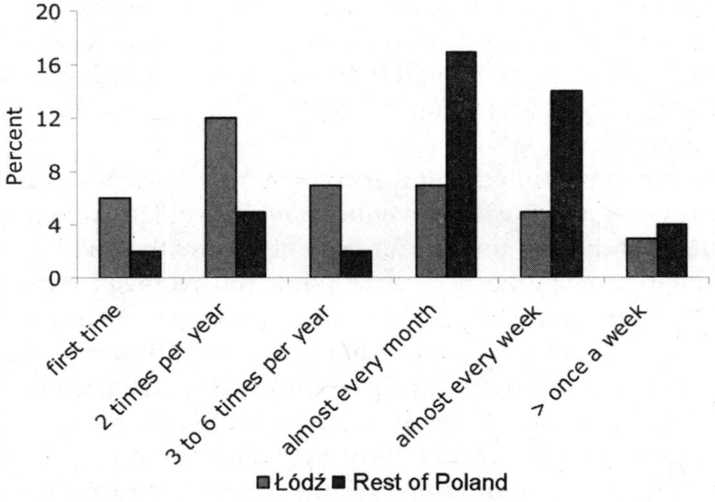

to the bazaar. This pattern was true for people from the Łódź region, as compared to those from the rest of Poland.

The biggest difference between these two groups involved whether they were buying products for personal use or for resale. Whereas two-thirds of the Łódź people who took part in the survey bought products for private use, two-thirds of respondents from the rest of Poland intended to resell their acquisitions. This may account for two other observations. Questions on the frequency of visits revealed that three-quarters of the visitors from outside the Łódź region came to the market at least once a month, while only one-third of the people living close by shopped at the market that frequently (figure 6.8). The age composition of the two groups was also quite different. About two-thirds of the respondents from the Łódź region were under forty, while about three out of every five respondents from outside the region were older than forty.

Before and After October 2003

One of the presuppositions of this chapter is that the implementation of visa requirements has likely influenced the functioning of the bazaars. This could be expressed in the ways in which customers perceive the bazaar. Indeed, some effect was noticeable in the questionnaire results, albeit the small number of respondents again requires caution. About half the respondents stated that they had not noticed much change in the bazaars. Of those, only a small majority rated the change as negative, and this tendency was more pronounced among respondents from the Łódź region. Although we must be particularly careful in our analysis, it seems that respondents' most frequent observation concerned the changing range of products, with positive and negative change being mentioned almost equally. Among those who indicated that things had changed for the worse, prices and suppliers were mentioned most often.

Another possible effect of new visa requirements is that people were travelling to other markets, especially those to the east of Łódź, closer to the Ukrainian and Belarusian borders, although this could not be substantiated from the questionnaire results. Respondents indicated that they visited the bazaars to the east and west of the Łódź region as often as they visited those in the Łódź region, and that since October 2003 the frequency of their visits had hardly changed.

Local Responses

A full and proper understanding of local responses to stricter visa requirements requires a prior theoretical contextualization. Thus we stress the need for a fusion of Giddensian structuration theory with the scalar approach (Brenner 2000; Cox 1996). Although the scalar approach is currently being contested (Marston, Jones, and Woodward 2005), its epistemological assets (Jones 1998) should be borne in mind: that is, that it requires a combination of societal structuration with geographical structuration. For our purposes scales can be associated with a set of overlapping institutions/organizations, from continental to local, that constrain and enable the activities of given actors (Marcińczak 2005). Obviously this approach narrows the meaning of institutions (Amin 1999, 367) at the same time as it highlights the crucial role of governmental and non-governmental institutions (organizations) of different scales. In doing so it sheds more light on how power is exercised in the interplay between structure/institutions and agency.

In response to the unfavourable economic changes brought about by new visa regulations local private–public coalitions implemented their own initiatives. In order to investigate such responses in-depth interviews were carried out with the mayors of Tuszyn and Rzgów, and with the manager of the PTAK market. Based on these interviews the conclusion can be drawn that the character of visits and the purchasing habits of the markets' customers have changed since 1997. In particular, only about twenty coaches now come from the former Soviet Union, as compared to the more than forty that used to come in the markets' heyday. Furthermore, only the driver and a few passengers are on board, with textile products filling the places formerly occupied by shoppers.

The first strand of local initiatives involved intensive marketing, especially commercials for PTAK on Russian television, on the internet, and in the press, as well as billboards welcoming "tourists" crossing the eastern border. Selected journalists and entrepreneurs from Ukraine were also invited to join a study tour introducing the business opportunities available in the PTAK bazaar and the Łódź region in general, which was organized in cooperation with the voivodship. (There are sixteen voivodships functioning as the first tier of subnational government in Poland. The idea underlying their inception was to create regional units with strong self-government.)

In addition to the individual actions of the PTAK management other initiatives were conducted in cooperation with different levels of local government. The municipal government of Rzgów made it easier for residence permits to be obtained, in order to allow local entrepreneurs to maintain their informal contacts. Then regular ("preferred") customers whose names had been placed on a computer database at the PTAK bazaar were allowed obtain visas more quickly and with fewer problems. Customers using this service were then obliged to shop exclusively at the PTAK bazaar, the process thus constituting a kind of loyalty program. To reinforce the exclusiveness of its customers' shopping activities the PTAK's management arranged with the company that provided transport from the border to the bazaar to ensure that these customers did not visit any of the borderland markets.

Since post-socialist growth coalitions are strongly influenced by national governments (Kulcsar and Domokos 2005), the PTAK's management sought partners from the voivodship council to take part in regional lobbying at the national level. An illustration of this mechanism was the struggle for national funds to develop Łódź Airport. Representatives of PTAK strongly supported this idea and stressed the need for regular flights between Łódź and the Ukrainian capital, Kiev. The PTAK's management also began the process of converting the bazaar into a more regular shopping mall in an attempt to attract not only more Poles but eventually also people from western countries. Our three in-depth interviews indicated that the enhanced strategy put in place after the initial stricter border controls were implemented in 1997 remained effective after visas were introduced in October 2003.

However, it should also be mentioned here that the municipality of Rzgów has since diversified the local economy by actively attracting other industries and by establishing a second bazaar close to the PTAK bazaar. These municipal initiatives were not greatly appreciated by the PTAK's management and the coalition between the two has weakened accordingly.

The situation of the Tuszyn bazaar has been somewhat different, to a large extent due to its public ownership, which inevitably narrows the range of possible activities. In Tuszyn only small-scale projects could be implemented, such as providing inexpensive meals for coach drivers, offering sellers discounts for renting stalls, and extending operating hours to create an almost 24/7 operation. However, because the Tuszyn municipality is responsible for the inhabitants at large, it also tried to protect the local economy. In 2005 the municipality joined the Association of European Textile Collectivities (ACTE) in an attempt to protect local textile producers and, more recently, the strong textile lobby in the Łódź region convinced the voivodship council to join the ACTE as well.

These activities indicate that coalitions were being built and strategies were being pursued in the Łódź region to battle the negative outcomes of the tightening of Poland's eastern border. Thus the interplay of structure and agency has been mediated by different institutions, as local actors, in addition to undertaking some actions on their own, have attempted to cooperate with organizations that have different territorial ranges and, consequently, different bargaining power.

CONCLUSION

In this chapter we have outlined the effects of the changing interpretation of the eastern border of Poland on the local and regional economies of the Łódź region, in an effort to create some empirical basis for further research. In that sense the material presented has a strongly descriptive character.

Clearly, the local and regional development of the Łódź region has a strong connection to developments on other levels of scale. It is by no means an isolated process—on the contrary, it is embedded in national, European, and global structures and processes, not only in the spatial sense but also in temporal and institutional senses.

First, the region is burdened with the powerful legacy of its socialist past. This past explains its relative monoculture, which is still predominantly based on the textile industry. The industry's hard infrastructure, in the form of available machinery, for example, kept the sector alive immediately after the collapse of Communism in the early 1990s, while its soft infrastructure, in the form of the expertise and craftsmanship of former textile workers, enabled the rise of new home-based companies. The local bazaars were the perfect outlet for their products. This may also account for the fact that, even in what is often called an age of post-industrialism, the industrial sector in the Łódź region grew, or at least remained stable. The survival strategies of its population, honed under socialist rule, proved to be useful in the post-socialist transition period.

Second, the development of the region is embedded within the overarching process of continuing integration within the EU in general and, in relation to border effects, the Schengen framework. Because the bazaars of the Łódź region attracted customers from outside Poland, any and all border measures that were implemented to impede their mobility affect the region's development. Indeed, the current cross-border policy within the Schengen framework, especially the visa requirements, may be viewed to a certain degree as a counterpart of former trade wars that excluded the Łódź region from its biggest market.

Based on these observations, the development of the region is strongly tied to the changing regimes at the border in general and at the eastern border in particular. The initial success of the region's bazaars, which was important to the regional economy, can largely be explained by the openness of the border in the early years of the economic transition. The differences between and within countries, both in prices and in mere availability, induced high levels of interaction, not only in flows of people but also in flows of goods. Moreover, the consequence of the institutional void that existed in those early days was the emergence of a form of "raw" capitalism.

Poland's accession to the EU and then to Schengen membership has led to a reinterpretation of the eastern border and, in effect, a process of tightening. Because the fate of the bazaars is so closely linked to the openness of the border, this process greatly influenced Łódź's regional economy, as revealed in the responses to our questionnaires and our in-depth interviews with three groups of actors—bazaar management, local government, and bazaar customers.

The management of the Tuszyn and Rzgów bazaars responded in quite different ways to the problems posed by the tightening of the borders, although both were closely linked to the institutional form of their respective bazaar. The management of the privately run PTAK bazaar actively and almost aggressively started to campaign in Belarus, Ukraine, and Russia, using every means available. They pampered their customers as much as possible; they formed a coalition with local government, based on their mutual interest in combating the decline in the number of visitors from the East; and they attempted to diversify by transforming the bazaar into a shopping mall, to increase its attractiveness to potential customers not only from the Łódź region but eventually also from western countries. Their reaction can be characterized as ex-ante and proactive. The response of the management conglomerate in Tuszyn seems to have been more ex-post and reactive. This was largely due the fact that it was a publicly run market and management had few options, although they may well have profited from the proximity of the PTAK bazaar and its activities in attracting new customers.

With regard to the municipalities, as previously noted, the local government of Rzgów worked quite closely with the PTAK's management in order to maintain the tax revenues it received from the bazaar. During the bazaar's most successful period these tax revenues accounted for over 20 percent of the municipal budget, and thus the death of the bazaar would have implied the virtual collapse of the municipality. In Tuszyn the local government has remained strongly dependent on the bazaars, with 30 percent of its budget coming from the tax revenues generated by these open-air markets. The municipality's most prominent action to date, as noted earlier, has been to join the ACTE in order to protect local textile production. Clearly there has been no change in Tuszyn's dependence on the textile industry.

As for the customers of the bazaars, the strategies of the cross-border sellers and buyers are particularly interesting. The fieldwork done at the Tuszyn bazaar revealed few customers from former Soviet republics and strongly suggested that the number of buyers from the East had already greatly diminished. Based on the responses to the questionnaires, those who still came from the East had changed their strategy, in that they bought greater quantities on each visit. Thus the seats on coaches that had been occupied previously by people were now filled with goods. Because sellers were not included in this research, it is difficult to know whether this strategy of buying bigger quantities has compensated for the loss of customers. However, it may be that the reinforcement of the eastern border has had far more consequences for the flow of people than for the flow of goods. To substantiate this supposition future research on this topic must include the sellers.

Finally, as the subtitle of this chapter suggests, the region has been on a rollercoaster ride as far as the eastern border is concerned. Until 1990, Poland's border could be characterized as an Iron Curtain that prevented almost all interaction with neighbouring countries. This was almost completely lifted during the first half of the 1990s. However, in the prelude to Poland's accession to the EU and the Schengen Agreement the border was slowly reinstated as a barrier, although this time it was better characterized as a "paper wall." The border remained permeable, but in a very selective way. The ability of non-EU citizens to cross it was now to be based on whether they belonged to the appropriate social networks, in which possessing the right expertise and attitude is crucial. The stronger actors will survive this new border regime, while the cross-border suitcase traders (the "ants") will be confronted with virtually impassable barriers and will likely die out. This situation will also affect the functioning of the bazaars in the future, and consequently the local and regional economies.

From an analytical point of view the Łódź region, as a region having to cope with systemic changes in border regimes, fits nicely into the framework of structuration theory. Some of the local and regional agency responses, in particular, have been brought to the fore in this chapter, while the structural responses to the implementation of the border regime were taken for granted. In order to fully grasp the structure–agency interplay in the context of the bazaar economy of the Łódź region, future research should include such structural responses.

ACKNOWLEDGEMENTS

During the preparation of this chapter Szymon Marcińczak was hosted by the Department of Human Geography of Radboud University Nijmegen, the Netherlands, an arrangement that was made possible through a Huygens Scholarship.

Both authors would like to thank the students from the Department of Geography at the University of Łódź who did the questioning of customers at the bazaar in Tuszyn.

LITERATURE CITED

Aidis, R. 2003. "Officially Despised yet Tolerated: Markets and Entrepreneurship in Post-socialist Countries." *Post-Communist Economies* 15, 461–73.

Amin, A. 1999. "An Institutional Perspective on Regional Economic Development." *International Journal of Urban and Regional Research* 23, 365–78.

Andrews, Edmund L. 2001. "Fate of a Polish Bazaar Shows Shifting Patterns of East Europe's Economy." *New York Times,* September 30.

Andrusz, G. D., M. Harloe, and I. Szelenyi. 1996. *Cities after Socialism: Urban and Regional Change and Conflict in Post-socialist Societies*. Oxford, UK: Blackwell.

Bohannan, P., and G. Dalton. 1962. *Markets in Africa*. Evanston, IL: Northwestern University Press.

Brenner, N. 2000. "The Urban Question as a Scale Question: Reflections on Henri Lefebvre, Urban Theory and the Politics of Scale." *International Journal of Urban and Regional Research* 24:2, 361–78.

Brunet-Jailly, Emmanuel. 2005. "Theorizing Borders: An Interdisciplinary Approach." *Geopolitics* 10, 633–49.

Cox, K. R. 1996. "The Difference that Scale Makes." *Political Geography* 15:8, 667–69.

Czakó, Á., and E. Sik. 1999. "Characteristics and Origins of the Comecon Open-air Market in Hungary." *International Journal of Urban and Regional Research* 23, 715–37.

Davies, N. 1982. *God's Playground: A History of Poland in Two Volumes, Vol. 2: 1795 to the present*. New York: Columbia University Press.

Dornisch, D. 2002. "The Evolution of Post-socialist Projects: Trajectory Shift and Transitional Capacity in a Polish Region." *Regional Studies* 36:3, 307–21.

Elster, J., C. Offe, and U. Preuss. 1998. *Institutional Design in Post-communist Societies: Rebuilding the Ship at Sea*. Cambridge, UK: Cambridge University Press.

Fanselow, F. 1990. "The Bazaar Economy or How Bizarre is the Bazaar Really." *Man (NS)* 25, 250–65.

Fujita, M., P. Krugman, and A. J. Venables. 1999. *The Spatial Economy: Cities, Regions and International Trade*. Cambridge, MA, and London, UK: MIT Press.

Giddens, Anthony. 1984. *The Constitution of Society: Outline of the Theory of Structuration*. Oxford, UK: Blackwell.

Iglicka, K. 1999. "Nomads and Rangers of Central and Eastern Europe." *Prace Migracyjne*, 27.

———. 2000. "Ethnic Division on Emerging Foreign Labour Markets in Poland during the Transition Period." *Europe–Asia Studies* 52:7, 1237–55.

———. 2001a. "Migration Movements from and into Poland in the Light of East–West Migration." *International Migration* 39:1, 3–32.

———. 2001b. "Shuttling from the Former Soviet Union to Poland: From 'Primitive Mobility' to Migration." *Journal of Ethnic and Migration Studies* 27:3, 505–18.

———. 2002. "Poland: Between Geopolitical Shifts and Emerging Migratory Patterns." *International Journal of Population Geography* 8, 153–64.

Jakóbczyk-Gryszkiewicz, J. 1997. "Functional and Morphological Changes in the Suburban Zone of Lodz." *A Comparative Study of Lodz and Manchester*, eds. S. Liszewski and C. Young. Łódź, Poland: University of Łódź Press, 223–35.

Johnston, R. J. 1986. *On Human Geography*. Oxford, UK: Blackwell.

Jones, K. T. 1998. "Scale as Epistemology." *Political Geography* 17:1, 25–28.

Jones, R. 2004. "What Time Human Geography?" *Progress in Human Geography* 28:3, 287–304.

Koter, M., S. Liszewski, and A. Suliborski. 1996. *Studium wiedzy o regionie lodzkim. Delimitacja potencjalnego wojewodztwa lodzkiego.* Łódź, Poland: LTN.

Kovács, Z. 2000. "Cities from State Socialism to Global Capitalism: An Introduction." *GeoJournal* 49, 1–6.

Kulcsar, L.J., and T. Domokos. 2005. "The Post-socialist Growth Machine: The Case of Hungary." *International Journal of Urban and Regional Research* 29: 3, 550–63.

Liszewski, S. 1997. "The Origins and Stages of Development of Industrial Łódź and the Łódź Urban Region." *A Comparative Study of Łódź and Manchester,* eds. S. Liszewski and C. Young. Łódź, Poland: University of Łódź Press, 11–35.

Marcińczak, S. 2005. "Motivations of Marine Euroregional Cooperation: The Case of the Baltic Sea Region." *European Spatial Research and Policy* 12, 25–46.

Marczynska-Witczak, E. 1989. "Changes in the Direction of the Polish Foreign Trade in Textiles during the Last Decade." *Problems in Textile Geography* 3, 55–70.

Marston, S. A., J. P. Jones III, and K. Woodward. 2005. "Human Geography without Scale." *Transactions of the Institute of British Geographers (NS)* 30, 416–32.

Okólski, M. 1996. "Recent Trends in International Migration: Poland 1996." *Prace Migracyjne* 16.

Owen, C. T. 1985. "The Russian Industrial Society and Tsarist Economic Policy, 1867–1905." *Journal of Economic History* 45:3, 587–606.

Piirainen, T. 1997. *Towards a New Social Order in Russia: Transforming Structures and Everyday Life.* Dartmouth, UK: Aldershot.

Potrykowski, M. 1998. "Border Regions and Trans-border Cooperation: The Case of Poland." *Social Change and Urban Restructuring in Central Europe,* ed. G. Enyedi. Budapest: Akadémiai Kiadó.

Puś, W. 1987. *Dzieje Łodzi przemyslowej. Zarys historii.* Łódź, Poland: Muzeum Historii Miasta Łodzi

Rada, Uwe. 2006. *Zwischen Börse und Basar, Die Zukunft der europäischen Stadt liegt in Osteuropa* [online] www.uwe-rada.de/themen/zukunft10.html [consulted March 13, 2006].

Rakowski, P., and R. Rybicki. 2000. "Wschodnia granica Polski po przystapieniu do Unii-Europejskiej." *Raporty i analizy* 7 (Cenrtrum Stosunków Miedzynarodowych), 6–22.

SCADPlus. 2005. *The Schengen Acquis and its Integration into the Union.* [online]. europa.eu/scadplus/leg/en/lvb/l33020.htm [consulted January 11, 2007].

Shields, R., ed. 1992. *Lifestyle Shopping: The Subject of Consumption*. London: Routledge.

Sik, E., and C. Wallace. 1999. "The Development of Markets in East-Central Europe." *International Journal of Urban and Regional Research* 23, 697–714.

Stoker, G. 1998. "Regime Theory and Urban Politics." *Theories of Urban Politics*, eds. D. Judge, G. Stoker, and H. Wolman. London: Sage Publications, 54–71.

Storper, M., and A. J. Scott. 1986. "Production, Work, Territory: Contemporary Realities and Theoretical Tasks." *Production, Work, Territory: The Geographical Anatomy of Industrial Capitalism*, eds. A. J. Scott and M. Storper. Boston, MA, and London, UK: George Allen & Unwin, 1–13.

Sword, —Thuen, T. 1999. "The Significance of Borders in the East European Transition." *International Journal of Urban and Regional Research* 23, 738–50.

Tokarz, B. 2004. "Ramy prawne systemu wizowego." *Monitoring polskiej polityki wizowej—Raport*. Warsaw: Fundacja im. Stefana Batorego.

Walker, A. R. 1993. "Łódź: The Problem Associated with Restructuring the Urban Economy of Poland's Textile Metropolis in the 1990s." *Urban Studies* 30:6, 1065–80.

Yeung, H. C. W. 2003. "Practicing New Economic Geographies: A Methodological Examination." *Annals of the Association of American Geographers* 93:2, 442–62.

CHAPTER 7

THE ECONOMIC COST OF BORDER SECURITY: THE CASE OF THE TEXAS–MEXICO BORDER AND THE US VISIT PROGRAM

J. Michael Patrick

Powerful forces of global economic integration, increasing cross-border trade and commerce, and recent acts of cross-border terrorism have renewed the interest of policy-makers and the public in the role of borders. In the United States, in response to the terrorist attacks on New York and Washington DC on September 11, 2001, President George W. Bush moved quickly to secure the nation's northern and southern borders. The borders were never officially closed, but the intense scrutiny and security imposed by the US Customs Services and the US Border Patrol brought cross-border traffic, both of people and of cargo, to a virtual standstill. Three- to four-hour waits to cross the border at major US ports of entry became common in the days and weeks following the 9/11 attacks. However, although the heightened security procedures remain in place, border crossings have already rebounded to their pre-9/11 levels at most southern ports of entry.

In the aftermath of 9/11 the chief national-security policy response has been to establish "smart borders." This technology-oriented response to securing US borders against terrorist incursions includes screening, biometrics, and information technology. Pre-screening of individuals and cargo as well as dedicated lanes on international bridges facilitate the separation and expedited crossings of low-risk individuals and cargo operators, allowing customs, immigration, and border-patrol officials to focus their attention and inspection where potential threats are the greatest. Automated methods for recognizing humans, using unique physiological characteristics (biometrics) such as facial, fingerprint, retinal, and vocal features, help to separate legitimate border-crossers from suspicious individuals. Information-technology programs and interoperational databases that collect, track, and coordinate data on individuals passing through US border ports allow the Department of Homeland Security (DHS) and other agencies to share information on suspicious individuals and activities in "real time." According to President Bush, the goal is to establish "smart borders" that pose little or no obstacle to legitimate trade and travel, while keeping pace with expanding trade and protecting the United States from threats of terrorist attacks, illegal immigration, drugs, and other contraband. Following the 9/11 terrorist attacks, the DHS implemented section 110 of the Illegal Immigration Reform and Immigrant Responsibility Act of 1996, known as the Automated Entry-Exit Control System, and renamed it the US Visitor and Immigrant Status Indicators Technology (US VISIT) program. Under the US VISIT program foreign visitors, students, and business travellers are tracked by using at least two biometric identifiers, such as digital fingerprints, iris scans, and digital photographs, when entering and leaving the United States.

The purpose of this chapter is to estimate the potential economic cost of the implementation of one component of the "smart borders" policy, the US VISIT program, to Texas border communities. Mexico is America's third-largest trading partner, accounting for millions of American jobs, while over 80 percent of US–Mexico merchandise trade crosses at US southern border ports of entry. Millions of Mexican border residents and others cross the border daily to shop and work. Any delays or disruptions to this cross-border flow of people and goods would have negative consequences for US border communities.

The first section following this introduction provides a general assessment of the importance of trade and commerce to the United States and to the Texas border communities, and it discusses the growing concern that a porous southern border poses a serious security risk. The second section examines the US VISIT program and the opposition the program faces in Texas border communities. The program's potential economic impact on Texas border communities is presented in the third section, followed by a discussion of those findings in the fourth. A conclusion and recommendations close the chapter.

The discussion in this chapter is based on review and analysis of published studies and reports on the economic impact of increased border waiting times due to increased congestion at US–Mexico ports of entry. Specifically it looks at the potential economic cost of the US VISIT program to Texas border communities. The studies and reports that are evaluated here have employed a variety of methodologies to acquire and analyze data and information, including input-output models and descriptive statistics. A brief discussion of the methodologies used is provided as part of the discussion of each study or report evaluated.

THE IMPORTANCE OF TRADE AND COMMERCE

Trade in goods and services with the rest of the world constitutes a significant component of the US economy. US trade increased 16 percent in 2004, to US$ 3.7 trillion, reflecting a stronger US economy as well as improved economic conditions in a number of US trading partners. The value of US goods and services traded in 2004 represented 25 percent of US GDP, up from 12 percent in 1970 and 20 percent in 1994. Canada, Mexico, and China are the leading trading partners of the United States, together accounting for 40 percent of US trade with the world (Office of the US Trade Representative 2004). US exports support 12 million American jobs, including one out of five manufacturing jobs. Workers in export-related industries receive, on average, 13–18 percent higher wages than the national average (International Trade Administration 2004).

The large flows of people and goods that cross the US border daily thus lie at the heart of the country's prosperity. At the same time, the sheer volume of this commercial and passenger traffic can provide opportunities for smuggling drugs, people, weapons, all types of contraband, and even terrorists. The relative ease with which the 9/11 hijackers entered the United States reveals how easy it is for its enemies to exploit this flow of people and trade (National Commission on Terrorist Attacks 2004). Thus the United States now faces the challenge of providing meaningful security on its borders while maintaining and enhancing the travel and trade that help to generate prosperity.

Nowhere is the tension between security and cross-border commerce more pronounced than on the US southern border with Mexico. Economic activity in the region has grown rapidly since the implementation of the North American Free Trade Agreement (NAFTA). US–Mexico trade has increased from just over US$ 100 billion in 1994, the first year of NAFTA, to over US$ 260 billion in 2004 (see figure 7.1). Of that amount, merchandise trade by all modes of surface transportation increased more than 150 percent from 1994 to 2004 (International Trade Administration 2004).

Figure 7.1: Total US–Mexico Trade, 1990–2004

Value (US$ billions)	Annual average	Change (%)
2000	247.6	23.9
2001	232.9	-3.3
2002	232.2	2.5
2003	235.6	2.5
2004	266.6	12.8
2005 (first half)	140.3	8.5
1990–2004	2,362.2	23.7

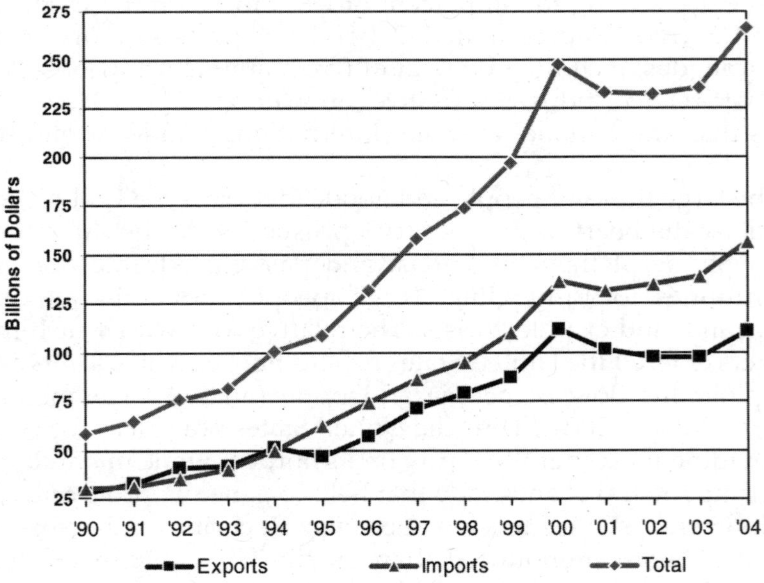

Source: Texas Center for Border Economic and Enterprise Development, Texas A&M International University.

Texas ports of entry, which account for over 80 percent of total US–Mexico overland merchandise trade, experienced an 86.7 percent increase in truck crossings from 1994 to 2004, while vehicle crossings increased 65.1 percent, pedestrian crossings increased 14.5 percent, and rail-car crossings increased 149.1 percent (see tables 7.1 to 7.4.) The Laredo port of entry accounts for 41 percent of all US–Mexico overland merchandise trade, with daily crossings of some 25,000 pedestrians, 41,000 vehicles, 9,000 trucks, and 1,119 rail cars.

Texas is the leading state exporting to Mexico, accounting for 14 percent of US exports to Mexico in 2004 (International Trade Administration 2004). The state's leading industrial metropolitan centres export tens of billions of dollars in computer and electronic products, vehicles and transportation equipment, machinery, and chemicals to Mexico annually, supporting thousands of skilled, high-paying jobs (see tables 7.5 to 7.7). Exports to Mexico account for one out of every ten Texas jobs. Texas is also a major importer of Mexican goods, receiving over US$ 100 billion in 2004. Leading Mexican imports include energy, machinery, vehicles and transportation equipment, and high-technology and telecommunication products (International Trade Administration 2004).

The degree of economic interaction and integration at the US–Mexico border is significant. Trade and commerce account for 30–40 percent of total industry sales and employment in Texas border communities (Texas Center for Economic and Enterprise Development 2005). Nearly four out of every ten jobs in the region are tied to trade and commerce activities with Mexico. A recent study by the San Antonio branch of the Dallas Federal Reserve Bank estimates that Mexican cross-border shoppers account for roughly 20 percent of total retail and wholesale sales in the Texas-border metropolitan communities of El Paso, Laredo, McAllen, and Brownsville. The study found that 49.4 percent of retail/wholesale sales (by value) in Laredo are made to Mexican shoppers (Federal Reserve Bank of Dallas 2004). (See table 7.8.)

Mexico's *maquiladora* industry, composed largely of multinational firms operating on Mexican soil, often in partnership with Mexican companies, is a significant generator of foreign-exchange earnings, and an engine of economic growth and industrial modernization. The industry dominates US–Mexico trade. Roughly 80 percent of the trade between the two countries is *maquiladora*-led intra-industry trade. Laredo is the *maquilas'* port of choice, handling 90 percent of the industry's output of vehicles and transportation equipment, electronics,

Table 7.1: Border Pedestrian Crossings, 1994–2004

Northbound	1994	1995	1996	1997	1998	1999	2000	2001	2002	2003	2004
Brownsville	3,189,878	2,953,747	3,045,123	2,897,296	2,784,246	2,623,605	3,102,297	3,198,168	3,044,681	2,765,884	2,715,080
McAllen	1,101,400	1,071,601	1,215,767	1,082,071	1,094,550	1,146,294	1,491,730	1,768,897	1,689,153	1,711,862	1,662,079
Laredo	3,837,723	3,387,789	3,278,329	3,183,533	3,149,623	3,798,716	4,768,564	4,596,023	4,756,757	4,466,739	4,642,340
El Paso	5,060,474	4,957,288	5,826,360	6,193,535	6,345,344	6,602,353	7,068,152	7,307,850	8,268,991	7,715,504	7,500,916

Southbound	1994	1995	1996	1997	1998	1999	2000	2001	2002	2003	2004
Brownsville	3,309,484	2,899,268	3,156,606	3,231,224	3,067,687	2,877,518	2,709,099	2,792,043	2,697,340	2,438,581	2,392,260
McAllen	1,204,284	1,052,767	1,167,887	1,328,699	1,307,005	1,275,302	1,350,631	1,376,333	1,310,776	1,347,550	1,354,404
Laredo	3,658,531	3,141,985	3,558,847	3,955,841	4,033,277	4,274,223	4,296,630	4,159,473	4,225,008	4,037,398	4,152,408
El Paso	4,822,217	4,196,671	4,615,409	4,573,153	4,895,467	5,302,707	5,503,418	5,504,661	6,039,402	5,411,956	5,930,117

Source: Texas Center for Border Economic and Enterprise Development, Texas A&M International University.

Table 7.2: Border Vehicular Crossings, 1994–2004

Northbound (Annual)	1994	1995	1996	1997	1998	1999	2000	2001	2002	2003	2004
Brownsville	5,409,042	5,161,274	5,696,885	6,103,548	6,215,573	7,040,061	7,279,489	6,991,739	7,463,926	6,872,032	6,753,606
McAllen	5,533,567	4,682,605	4,793,753	4,744,265	4,941,479	5,689,560	5,694,829	5,401,575	5,779,314	5,006,764	5,206,757
Laredo	7,441,134	6,990,743	7,135,678	7,034,579	7,642,793	8,384,721	8,036,434	7,657,231	7,488,576	7,104,801	6,968,532
El Paso	6,759,007	7,872,293	7,843,533	8,174,640	8,094,839	8,543,131	8,981,678	8,370,987	7,572,650	7,565,603	7,621,214

Southbound (Annual)	1994	1995	1996	1997	1998	1999	2000	2001	2002	2003	2004
Brownsville	5,984,902	5,592,958	5,830,043	6,152,801	6,951,202	7,458,871	7,584,703	7,247,571	7,529,858	6,873,466	6,727,312
McAllen	5,407,500	4,557,338	4,847,137	5,133,697	5,421,953	5,988,514	5,932,488	5,870,400	6,297,301	5,552,014	5,520,755
Laredo	7,289,017	6,626,142	7,675,065	8,018,127	8,333,735	8,685,103	8,805,944	8,613,606	7,188,388	7,025,241	6,967,107
El Paso	5,332,618	4,988,008	5,091,948	5,284,025	5,373,377	5,309,676	5,678,802	5,186,548	4,316,436	4,512,110	4,439,944

Source: Texas Center for Border Economic and Enterprise Development, Texas A&M International University.

Table 7.3: Border Truck Crossings, 1994–2004

North	1994	1995	1996	1997	1998	1999	2000	2001	2002	2003	2004
Brownsville	260,751	224,642	228,776	249,881	275,661	287,962	299,238	199,521	200,444	189,319	186,947
McAllen	164,900	166,218	205,017	234,600	262,693	325,225	374,150	368,395	390,282	406,064	454,351
Laredo	614,696	744,276	999,412	1,207,555	1,315,069	1,486,511	1,493,073	1,404,184	1,441,653	1,354,229	1,380,414
El Paso	N/A	N/A	N/A	N/A	N/A	N/A	N/A	666,910	704,199	659,614	723,669

South	1994	1995	1996	1997	1998	1999	2000	2001	2002	2003	2004
Brownsville	204,794	184,848	197,617	229,788	290,746	237,189	234,121	217,731	215,573	199,498	201,447
McAllen	152,659	122,969	181,877	212,648	232,552	266,244	304,161	295,630	302,169	331,990	392,306
Laredo	914,421	765,425	924,724	1,078,540	1,192,354	1,306,610	1,409,336	1,407,621	1,460,777	1,386,217	1,464,908
El Paso	N/A	N/A	N/A	N/A	N/A	328,287	349,096	344,023	307,203	281,589	292,288

Source: Texas Center for Border Economic and Enterprise Development, Texas A&M International University.

Table 7.4: Border Rail Crossings, 1994–2004

Northbound	1994	1995	1996	1997	1998	1999	2000	2001	2002	2003	2004
Brownsville	11,854	13,789	19,158	11,707	12,134	24,773	12,426	11,415	7,832	10,055	6,266
Eagle Pass	15,177	22,331	39,795	39,438	40,314	37,326	42,196	31,392	24,208	15,475	19,451
Laredo	39,871	59,377	85,592	93,967	92,829	115,771	151,083	167,376	174,862	174,837	170,248
El Paso	10,297	12,908	8,418	2,073	4,246	1,578	N/A	17,310	30,437	21,045	58,565

Southbound	1994	1995	1996	1997	1998	1999	2000	2001	2002	2003	2004
Brownsville	31,119	21,820	25,389	25,873	32,717	31,780	36,074	40,935	50,309	41,059	34,917
Eagle Pass	18,818	24,713	40,929	52,443	56,669	48,912	78,348	86,038	86,331	75,006	67,889
Laredo	121,166	109,385	133,314	152,227	148,009	168,116	184,498	182,244	190,974	219,362	238,266
El Paso	N/A	N/A	N/A	N/A	N/A	N/A	N/A	N/A	N/A	N/A	N/A

Source: Texas Center for Border Economic and Enterprise Development, Texas A&M International University.

Table 7.5: Texas Gross Domestic Product and Exports, Selected Years 1994–2004 (US$ billions)

	1994	1997	2002	2004
GDP	484.1	601.6	712.4	847.8
Total exports	59.9	84.3	95.4	117.2
Exports to Mexico	23.8	31.2	41.6	45.7

Source: Texas Department of Economic Development, Texas Comptroller of Public Accounts.

Table 7.6: Value of Texas Exports to Mexico by Sector, 2002 (US$ millions)

Texas	41,647
Computer and electronic products	10,565
Transportation equipment	6,368
Electrical equipment, appliances, and components	3,458
Chemicals and allied products	3,075
Machinery, except electrical	2,703
Plastics and rubber products	2,298
Petroleum and coal products	1,867
Fabricated metal products	1,842
Textile mill products	1,228
Primary metal manufacturing	1,170
Food and kindred products	1,164
Agricultural products	1,111
Paper and allied products	812
Miscellaneous manufactured products	780
Oil and gas	734
Total	**39,175**

Source: Texas Department of Economic Development.

Table 7.7: Importance of Exports from the Ten Leading Metropolitan Areas in Texas to Mexico: State Output, Earnings, and Employment, 2002 (US$ Billions Except Employment)

	Value of Texas exports to Mexico by sector in 2002	Output impact	Earnings impact	Employment impact (thousands)
Texas	41.6	100.4	25.8	985.6
Ten Metropolitan Areas	30.1	73.2	19.8	745.6
Dallas	10.8	26.7	7.5	278.1
Houston	6.2	14.7	3.6	135.5
Fort Worth–Arlington	4.8	11.4	3.0	114.6
Austin–San Marcos	3.4	9.0	2.6	92.0
El Paso	1.7	4.1	1.1	47.1
San Antonio	1.6	4.0	1.1	42.3
Brownsville	0.5	1.2	0.3	13.4
McAllen	0.4	0.7	0.2	10.3
Longview–Marshall	0.4	0.7	0.2	7.4
Beaumont–Port Arthur	0.3	0.6	0.2	4.9

Source: Derived from Texas Department of Economic Development and Texas Workforce Commission data, using the US Department of Commerce Regional Input-Output Modeling System (RIMS).

and machinery. In addition, Laredo is a leading port for US agricultural trade with Mexico, accounting for roughly 80 percent of US shipments of animal feed and animal and vegetable fats and oils, crude and processed (International Trade Administration 2004).

THE POROUS SOUTHERN BORDER

According to the Department of Homeland Security (DHS), approximately 1.1 million illegal immigrants were apprehended on the southern border in 2005. Apprehensions in 2006 were about 1 million (http://www.dhs.gov/ximgtn/statistics/). DHS estimates that between 150,000 and 600,000 succeed in entering the U.S. illegally every year (CBP Congressional Affairs Office, Department of Homeland Security

Table 7.8: Texas Border Retail/Wholesale Trade and All Industry Sales 1994–2004 (US$ millions)

	Brownsville		McAllen		Laredo		El Paso	
	Retail sales / wholesale	All industries	Retail sales / wholesale	All industries	Retail sales / wholesale	All industries	Retail sales / wholesale	All industries
1994	1,420.5	1791.3	2,813.2	4,595.5	2,866.9	3,368.5	8,855.6	13,242.3
1995	1,237.8	1,638.6	2,384.5	3,970.7	1,975.7	2,398.0	8,171.2	13,195.3
1996	1,249.3	1,686.0	2,581.7	3,519.6	2,253.5	2,800.6	8,335.4	13,230.4
1997	1,304.3	1,810.0	2,619.6	3,938.8	2,715.9	3,270.8	8,440.0	14,427.9
1998	1,385.2	1,911.1	2,774.3	4,071.6	2,900.0	3,497.8	8,398.0	14,821.2
1999	1,420.7	2,015.2	2,732.6	3,806.9	3,078.6	3,746.7	9,992.2	15,836.9
2000	1,558.1	2,196.3	2,873.8	3,657.2	3,236.1	4,010.6	9,572.2	15,216.6
2001	1,821.8	2,562.7	3,130.4	4,047.7	3,105.4	3,863.7	9,107.1	14,706.4
2002	1,844.3	2,407.9	3,410.6	4,535.6	3,413.2	4,033.9	9,433.6	15,758.9
2003	1,877.8	2,651.7	3,355.6	4,471.7	3,376.0	4,116.3	9,688.6	16,452.6
2004	1,941.2	2,542.0	3,670.3	4,820.2	3,577.5	4,422.8	10,843.8	16,783.2

Source: Texas Comptroller of Public Accounts.

2005)." As T. J. Bonner (2004), the president of the National Border Patrol Council, has stated,

> Prior to September 11, 2001, it was extremely easy to enter the United States illegally, either by sneaking across the border or by securing permission to enter temporarily and then never leaving. . . . With few exceptions, any individual who is determined to enter the United States illegally will eventually be successful.
>
> We cannot pretend that our homeland is secure if our borders are not . . . If it is so easy for impoverished and poorly educated people to illegally cross our borders, consider how much easier it is for well-financed and highly trained terrorists to do the same.

According to DHS officials, terrorist organizations such as al-Qaeda recognize the vulnerability of the US–Mexico border. In 2002 al-Qaeda's website noted, "In 1996, 254 million persons, 75 million automobiles, and 3.5 million trucks entered America from Mexico. At the 38 official border crossings only 5 percent of this huge total is inspected… These are figures that call for contemplation" (al-Qurashi 2004, 84).

In the decades leading up to September 11, 2001, protecting US land borders was not viewed as a national security issue. It was either a drug or a crime or an immigration problem, but not one rising to the level of national security. As a result many critical problems that had been previously identified by border communities, industry groups, the Government Accounting Office, academics, and even congressional committees were largely ignored. Issues such as deteriorating infrastructure, inadequate facilities, insufficient staffing at border ports of entry, poor intelligence, and dysfunctional immigration laws were repeatedly identified but never adequately addressed (House Select Committee on Homeland Security 2004). Since September 11 this has changed. Significant attention is now focused on the southern border, and security is the nation's number-one priority. Many community leaders on the southern border, however, are concerned that securing the homeland may come at the economic expense of their communities.

THE US VISIT PROGRAM AND TEXAS BORDER COMMUNITIES

According to the DHS, the US VISIT program is a top priority because it enhances security for US citizens and visitors while facilitating legitimate travel and trade across US borders. The program is part of a continuum of security measures that begins outside US borders and continues through a visitor's arrival (entry) in and departure (exit) from the United States. In those cases where a visa is issued by the Department of State, biometrics such as digital, inkless finger scans or digital photographs allow the DHS to determine whether the person applying for entry to the United States is the same person who was issued the visa by the Department of State at one of its embassies or consulates. Upon exiting the country a scan of the visitor's travel documents permits the DHS to determine if the individual has entered the country illegally or overstayed his or her visa (Department of Homeland Security 2004).

The US VISIT program's entry procedures were put in place at 115 airports and 15 seaports on January 1, 2004, and were implemented at the 50 busiest land ports of entry on December 31, 2004. As of December 31, 2005, all procedures were to be in place at all remaining land ports of entry. The exit portion of the program is now being tested at airports and seaports, but a date for implementation at the land ports has not been set.

The program's procedures apply to all foreign travellers with the exception of most Mexican visitors who apply for admission to the United States using a Border Crossing Card (laser visa) within the 40-kilometre (25-wide) "Border Zone." Visitors seeking to travel to the US interior must apply for an I-94 visa, which subjects them to US VISIT procedures. The visitor's biographic information and biometrics are electronically scanned, and the I-94 visa is processed in a matter of minutes, significantly reducing the time, according to DHS, previously required to fill out and process the I-94 application. DHS officials estimate that only 10–15 percent of visitors seeking to travel to the United States from Mexico actually go beyond the "Border Zone" and therefore become subject to US VISIT procedures.

Many officials and business leaders in Texas border communities are opposed to the US VISIT program because they are convinced that it will have a devastating impact on the border economy, the economy of Texas, and, indeed, the US economy overall. In August 2003, for example, the International Bank of Commerce, a leading southern Texas financial institution headquartered in Laredo since 1966, expressed the following views:

> [There are] fears that implementation of the US VISIT program at land border ports will bring commercial and tourist traffic from Mexico into the US to a grinding halt. Likewise, it will choke commercial exports from the US to Mexico. Any slowdown in terms of people and commerce between NAFTA partners will work to the competitive advantage of the Pacific Rim and the European Union (EU). Increases in trade friction have the same impact as higher taxes or tariffs. *US-VISIT will kill NAFTA* (McAllen Economic Development Corporation/ Chamber of Commerce 2003).
>
> The border communities oppose the implementation of the "exit and entry system" . . . It will destroy border economies . . . For industry time is money. Manufacturers, which are located on both sides of the border, will face increased costs from transport delays. Shipping and traffic delays caused by the system could result in the loss of thousands of jobs along the border. The US/Mexico border handles more traffic with 600,000 vehicles crossing per day and 3.5 million commercial trucks per year . . . Border communities rely heavily on retail trade and tourism. If border inconveniences continue, Mexican tourists will choose to spend their dollars elsewhere. The Mexicans play a huge part in the border retail market and provide substantial sales tax revenue to border communities.
>
> The US has benefited from the huge flow of trade, tourism, shoppers, commuters, and family members across our borders with Canada and Mexico. IBC is concerned that the attempted controls proposed by the Department of Homeland Security (DHS) will devastate the lucrative trade and people with absolutely no assurance the US VISIT will stop the entry of terrorists and other criminals. This will have a direct negative impact on our nation's Gross Domestic Product and cost the US a large number of jobs. The exit inspection process proposed by US VISIT does nothing to control suicide bombers who have entered the US and who died fulfilling their mission.

THE POTENTIAL ECONOMIC IMPACT OF THE US VISIT PROGRAM ON TEXAS BORDER COMMUNITIES

The issue of delays at the US–Mexico border is a common topic of discussion in the popular media and at binational meetings, such as the annual US–Mexico Border Governors' Conference. These sources of information, however, are based mostly on anecdotal accounts, and so provide a limited picture of the magnitude and consequences of border wait times.

The most comprehensive study to date on the economic impact of border waiting times was completed in June 2005 by the San Diego (California) Association of Governments (SANDAG). In that study SANDAG reported that daily waiting times of forty-five minutes at the ports of entry between the San Diego region and Baja California were costing the San Diego region US$ 1.4 billion in revenues, US$ 2.4 billion in output, and 32,821 jobs lost on an annual basis (SANDAG 2005). The study noted that, although cross-border travel generates significant revenues in the retail, hotel and lodging, and recreations sectors in the San Diego region, increasing congestion and delays at the border are constraining cross-border trips, resulting in output and employment losses. The study attributed the increased congestion and longer waiting times at the border to the growing numbers of border crossings and to stepped-up homeland security activity following the 9/11 terrorist attacks.

Few studies, to date, have attempted to estimate the economic impact that the US VISIT program may have on border communities, Texas, or the US economy. The results from available studies are summarized here.

The Perryman Group Study

The Perryman Group, an economic and financial analysis firm, was hired by the International Bank of Commerce of Laredo, Texas, to determine the impact of the US VISIT program. In its 158-page report (Perryman Group 2004) it concluded that,

> Analysis indicates that even under a conservative assumption regarding the delays (a 20 percent increase above the current level) the program could cost the US economy in excess of 375,000 jobs (0.2 percent of total), with more than 215,000 (0.2 percent of total) Texas positions lost. If delays prove to be more disruptive (up 75 percent), the job losses could top 1,400,000 (0.9 percent of total) in the US and 800,000 (0.8 percent of total) in Texas. Border areas would be particularly hard hit. Because much of this trade represents integrated production activity, the ramifications extend to US competitiveness on a global scale. While the intent of US VISIT is unarguably a very good thing, the current timetable and capacity for implementation is simply not appropriate and would be devastating to business activity on multiple fronts.

According to its report the Perryman Group developed a dynamic input–output model (USMRIAS), using available data, to assess the economic impact of the US VISIT program. Apparently, interviews with cross-border Mexican shoppers were not conducted as part of the study. Tables 7.9 to 7.14 summarize the Perryman Group's economic-impact assessment of the baseline 20 percent and 75 percent increases in delays on the Texas border economy and key metropolitan cities.

Table 7.9: Economic Impact Assessment (US$ Millions)

	Total expenditures	Gross product	Personal income employment	
Texas border	1,666.6	1,048.5	638.1	-19,199
Brownsville–Harlingen area	175.8	109.6	66.4	-1,998
McAllen–Edinburg–Pharr area	539.4	343.5	210.1	-6,308
Laredo area	339.4	219.3	133.3	-4,067
El Paso area	432.2	262.1	157.6	-4,628

Baseline: 20% Increases in Delays

Table 7.10: Negative Impact with 20% Increase (%)

	Output	Employment
United States	- 0.3	- 0.2
State of Texas	- 0.2	- 0.2
Texas Border	- 3.7	- 3.1

Table 7.11: Economic Impact Assessment 2003 (%)

	Proportion of gross product	Proportion of employment
Texas border	3.7	3.1
Brownsville–Harlingen area	2.0	1.7
McAllen–Edinburg–Pharr area	3.4	3.5
Laredo area	5.2	5.4
El Paso area	1.5	1.8

Baseline: 20% Increases in Delays

Table 7.12: Economic Impact Assessment (US$ Millions Except Employment)

	Total expenditures	Gross product	Personal income	Employment
Texas border	6,249.7	3,931.7	2,393.0	-71,994
Brownsville–Harlingen area	659.2	411.0	248.9	-7,493
McAllen–Edinburg–Pharr area	2,022.6	1,288.0	787.9	-23,655
Laredo area	1,272.6	822.4	499.9	-15,252
El Paso area	1,620.6	982.8	590.9	-17,354

Baseline: 75% Increases in Delays

Table 7.13: Negative Impact with 75% Increase (%)

	Output	Employment
United States	- 1.1	- 0.9
State of Texas	- 0.6	- 0.8
Texas border	- 14.1	- 11.6

Table 7.14: Economic Impact Assessment 2003 (%)

	Proportion of gross product	Proportion of employment
Texas border	14.1	11.6
Brownsville–Harlingen area	7.4	6.6
McAllen–Edinburg–Pharr area	12.7	13.2
Laredo area	19.4	20.3
El Paso area	5.7	6.9

Baseline: 75% Increases in Delays

The Perryman Group also reported,

> Assuming notable disruptions occur, bank deposits in the border region are projected to decline by [US]$ 2.285 billion (approximately 13.3 percent), which has a measurable impact on the ability of local banks to finance future growth.
>
> Housing values in the border region would decline by 2.8 percent to 10.6 percent depending on the severity of the delays, thus causing substantial loss of household wealth.

The University of Texas–Pan American Study

In December 2003 the Center for Border Economic Studies (C-BEST) at the University of Texas–Pan American conducted a study for which researchers interviewed 1,000 Mexican visitors over four days at four locations in McAllen (Hidalgo County) and Brownsville (Cameron County), in the lower Rio Grande Valley. The study's findings were noted under two categories: the economic impact of Mexican visitors and findings related to the US VISIT program.

Mexican visitors' expenditures varied by mode of travel. A typical car traveller averaged almost US$ 5,000 a year (US $182 per visit), a plane traveller spent about US$ 8,000 a year (around US$ 2,000 per visit), while bus travellers and pedestrians spent approximately US$ 1,100 a year (US$ 80 and US$ 20 per visit, respectively). C-BEST's researchers concluded that, given a total of 22.7 million Mexican border-crossers, total estimated expenditures by Mexican visitors amounted to US$ 1.4 billion in 2003. Using an input-output model (IMPLAN), the researchers estimated that these expenditures generated a total of approximately US$ 1.7 billion in output (sales), 41,000 jobs, US$ 560 million in wages, and US$ 203 million in business taxes. The researchers concluded that Mexican visitors' expenditures support 12 percent of total output and 10–15 percent of employment in the lower Rio Grande Valley.

Extensive delays (exceeding two hours) to enter the United States were generally not tolerated by visitors, and 70 percent of the study respondents indicated that such delays would cause them to reduce the frequency of their visits.

Texas A&M International University Studies

The Texas Center for Border Economic and Enterprise Development has conducted three studies related to the economic impact of the US VISIT program.

The first study by Texas Center researchers was conducted in August 2003. Using available border-crossing data and applying assumptions regarding cross-border Mexican shoppers' expenditure patterns (based on previous research), researchers estimated the impact of 1 percent, 5 percent, and 10 percent declines in cross-border expenditures on sales, employment, sales-tax rebates, and bridge revenues. It was assumed that a decrease in cross-border sales to Mexican shoppers would lead to decreases in employment and sales-tax revenues. In addition, decreases in cross-border trade, that is, commercial truck crossings (of 1 percent, 5 percent, and 10 percent), would lead to decreases in employment and bridge revenues. Both sales-tax rebates and bridge revenues are important sources of revenue for local government. At the border-region level a 5 percent (permanent) decline in cross-border commerce and trade would result in an (estimated) loss of US$ 380 million in sales, a loss of 7,745 jobs, an increase in the unemployment level to 11.2 percent (from 10.0 percent), and the loss of US$ 2.7 million in sales-tax rebates and $3.6 million in local-bridge revenues (see tables 7.15a and 7.15b).

Based on the assumptions used in this study, of the four border metropolitan communities, Laredo would be affected the most, in relative terms, by the US VISIT program. The researchers estimated that a permanent 5 percent decline in cross-border commerce and trade for Laredo would result in a 2.3 percent decline in local sales, a 2.6 percent decline in sales-tax rebates, a 5.0 percent decline in bridge revenues, the loss of 1,990 jobs, and a 3.0 percent increase in the unemployment rate (see tables 7.15a and 7.15b).

Historically, border communities have demonstrated strong resilience in the face of external shocks to their economies, bouncing back from devaluations of the Mexican peso as well as from government policies that delay or restrict the flow of people and commerce across the border. For example, the decline in cross-border Mexican shoppers in border communities following the devaluation of the peso in 1995 was roughly 6 percent, though it was higher in some communities than in others. A year later the number of cross-border shoppers had recovered to pre-devaluation levels. The fall-off in cross-border shoppers following the 9/11 terrorists attacks and the heightening of border security was roughly 5 percent during September and October 2001—though, again, it was higher in some communities than in others—yet by early 2002 the numbers of cross-border shoppers in most border cities had surpassed the levels seen before 9/11.

Table 7.15a: Estimated Impact of Permanent Decline in Border Crossings (Northbound and Southbound Pedestrian, Vehicular, and Commercial Trucks) of 1%, 5%, and 10% (Based on 2002 Data; Absolute Changes)

	Brownsville			McAllen			Laredo			El Paso			Border		
Decline in border crossings (%)	1	5	10	1	5	10	1	5	10	1	5	10	1	5	10
Sales (US$ Millions)	-9	-45	-89	-28	-140	-280	-19	-95	-190	-20	-100	-200	-76	-380	-759
Unemployed	228	1140	2280	594	2970	5940	398	1990	3980	366	1830	3360	1549	7745	15490
Unemployment rate (%)	10.8	11.5	12.3	14.1	15.0	16.5	7.2	9.1	11.5	8.3	8.8	9.4	10.4	11.2	12.3
Sales tax rebates (US$ Thousands)	-62	-310	-620	-196	-980	-1,960	-133	-665	-1,330	-140	-700	-1,400	-531	-2,655	-5,310
Bridge revenues (US$ Thousands)	-143	-715	-1,430	-156	-780	-1,560	-324	-1,622	-3,240	-103	-515	-1,030	-726	-3,630	-7,260

Table 7.15b: Estimated Impact of Permanent Decline in Border Crossings (Northbound and Southbound Pedestrian, Vehicular, and Commercial Trucks) of 1%, 5%, and 10% (Based on 2002 Data; Proportional Changes) (%)

	Brownsville			McAllen			Laredo			El Paso			Border		
Decline in border crossings	1	5	10	1	5	10	1	5	10	1	5	10	1	5	10
Sales	-0.17	-0.85	-1.70	-0.29	-1.45	-2.90	-0.46	-2.30	-4.60	-0.12	-0.60	-1.21	-0.21	-1.05	-2.10
Unemployed	1.54	7.24	13.5	1.89	8.76	16.1	5.75	23.37	37.85	1.49	7.03	2.19	1.98	9.20	16.85
Unemployment rate	0.2	1.0	2.0	0.3	1.5	3.0	0.6	3.0	6.0	0.1	0.5	1.0	0.4	2.0	4.0
Sales tax rebates	-0.14	-0.70	-1.40	-0.29	-1.45	-2.90	-0.52	-2.60	-5.20	-0.19	-0.95	-1.90	-0.33	-1.65	-3.30
Bridge revenues	-1.0	-5.0	-10.0	-1.0	-5.0	-10.0	-1.0	-5.0	-10.0	-1.0	-5.0	-10.0	-1.0	-5.0	-10.0

The impact on Texas of a permanent 5 percent decline in the state's exports to Mexico (see table 7.16) would result in an estimated loss of US$ 2.1 billion in export sales, a decline in the state's gross product of $5.1 billion and earnings of $1.3 billion, and a loss of 42,000 jobs.

Table 7.16: Estimated Impact of a Decline in Texas Exports to Mexico of 1%, 5%, and 10% (US$ millions Except Employment)

	Exports	Gross State product	Earnings	Employment
1% Decline	-417	-1,200	-258	-8,300
5% Decline	-2,100	-5,100	-1,300	-42,000
10% Decline	-4,200	-10,300	-2,600	-84,000

Table 7.17: Estimated Impact of a Decline in Numbers of Cross-Border Shoppers of 1%, 5%, and 10% on State Sales Tax Collections (US$ Millions)

1% Decline	-4.6
5% Decline	-22.9
10% Decline	-45.9

A shortcoming of the study is that its impact estimates are based on assumptions, which may or may not be true, about how cross-border Mexican shoppers and businesses would react to border-crossing delays caused by the implementation of the US VISIT program. In an attempt to address this shortcoming, Texas Center researchers surveyed cross-border Mexican shoppers in Laredo about their likely responses to delays at the border. Two different studies were conducted: one in April 2004, during Easter Week, and the other in December 2004, over the weekend before Christmas. Both periods saw a large number of cross-border Mexican shoppers in Laredo stores. According to local merchants and business owners, April, December, and July (when Mexican students are on summer vacation) are their busiest sales periods, accounting for up to 60 percent of their total annual sales.

Over the seven days from April 3 to 9, 2004, Texas Center researchers completed 595 random surveys with self-selected cross-border Mexican shoppers. Of those, 19 percent (113 surveys) were completed in Laredo's downtown business district, adjacent to the international bridge, and 81 percent (482 surveys) were completed at the Mall Del Norte, Best Buy, and two Wal-Marts in its uptown district. Expenditure patterns, based on whether respondents crossed the border by foot (pedestrian), car, or bus and whether they shopped at least once a week, once a month, or once a year, are presented in table 7.18.

Table 7.18: Cross-border Mexican Shoppers' Expenditures (Average), April 2004 (US Dollars and Numbers of Shoppers)

Total number of shoppers: 595

Mode of travel	Weekly	Monthly	Annually	Total	Average expenditure
Pedestrian	US$22 (38 shoppers)	27 (49)	76 (2)	2,311 (89)	25.97
By car	25 (96)	168 (194)	475 (158)	110,042 (448)	245.63
By bus	20 (7)	60 (27)	57 (24)	3,128 (58)	53.93

Combined total expenditures: US $115,481
Average expenditure per shopper: US $194.08

Pedestrians as proportion of total: 14.9%
By car as proportion of total: 75.3%
By bus as proportion of total: 9.8%

On December 18, 2004, Texas Center researchers completed 202 random surveys with self-selected cross-border Mexican shoppers. Of those, 16 percent (32 surveys) were completed in Laredo's downtown business district and 84 percent (170 surveys) were completed in the uptown district as above. Expenditure patterns are presented in table 7.19.

In both surveys, when cross-border shoppers were asked how they would react if the implementation of the US VISIT program were to result in border-crossing delays of more than an hour and a half, 40 percent responded that they would reduce their visits and expenditures by 30 percent.

Table 7.19: Cross-border Mexican Shoppers' Expenditures (Average), December 2004 (US Dollars and Numbers of Shoppers)

Total number of shoppers: 202

Mode of travel	Weekly	Monthly	Annually	Total	Average expenditure
Pedestrian	$26 (13 shoppers)	31 (13)	66 (1)	807 (27)	29.88
By car	38 (15)	301 (53)	645 (85)	71,348 (153)	466.33
By bus	24 (3)	58 (7)	68 (12)	1,294 (22)	58.82

Combined total expenditures: US $73,449
Average expenditure per shopper: US $363.61

Pedestrian as proportion of total: 13.4%
By car as proportion of total: 75.7%
By bus as proportion of total: 10.9%

Summary of Studies

The conclusion drawn from the studies, all of which were conducted before the implementation of the entry portion of the US VISIT program, is that significant economic harm, in lost jobs, income, and business activity, may occur in the border region if the program produces prolonged delays in moving people and merchandise across the border. As has already been described, trade and commerce with Mexico are vital not only to the economies of Texas border communities but also to the welfare of the state and national economies. Much of US–Mexico and Texas–Mexico trade involves the intra-industry shipments of key US industrial and agricultural products, including automobiles and automotive parts, electrical equipment, machinery, chemicals, and electronics—ranging from low-tech household appliances to high-tech telecommunications equipment and computers—as well as animal feed and animal and vegetable fats and oils. Significant border-crossing delays could disrupt the just-in-time delivery of essential products and parts, shutting down production lines at US automotive plants and other manufacturing facilities across the country, and producing negative rippling effects throughout the national economy.

Conservative estimates (see table 7.20) indicate that a 5 percent decline in border crossings, due to delays, would result in drops in gross sales (2.1 percent; US$ 380 million), employment (9.2 percent; 7,745 jobs), sales-tax rebates (1.7 percent; US$ 2.7 million), and bridge revenues (5 percent; US$ 3.6 million), the latter two being important sources of local revenue in Texas border metropolitan communities. Although these declines may seem negligible, their impact would be a blow to the border communities and the region, as per-capita income is only 60 percent of the state and national average, and unemployment is twice as high.

Table 7.20: Impact of 5% Decline in Border Crossings (North and Southbound Pedestrian, Vehicular, and Commercial Trade) 2002 (%)

	Brownsville	McAllen	Laredo	El Paso	Border
Gross sales	-0.9	-1.5	-2.3	-0.6	-2.1
Employment	-7.2	-8.8	-23.4	-7.0	-9.2
Sales tax rebates	-0.7	-1.5	-2.6	-1.0	-1.7
Bridge revenues	-5.0	-5.0	-5.0	-5.0	-5.0

Source: *US VISIT: A Preliminary Impact Assessment on the Border and Texas Economies, Texas Center for Border Economic and Enterprise Development*. Texas A&M International University (October 2003).

The Case of Laredo

On January 3, 2005, three days after the implementation of the US VISIT program at the nation's fifty busiest land ports, Asa Hutchinson, under-secretary for Border and Transportation Security at the DHS, announced that "the US VISIT Program [was] expediting the processing times for those visitors who [were] subject to the US VISIT procedures and land ports of entry" (Department of Homeland Security 2005). Hutchinson added that more than 16.9 million foreign visitors had been processed by the program without an adverse effect on waiting times.

A big test for the program is the port of Laredo, the busiest land port on the southern border, which handles 41 percent of all US–Mexico overland trade: 25,000 pedestrians, 41,000 vehicles, 9,000 trucks, and 1,119 rail cars cross the border at Laredo daily. The entry portion of the program was implemented at the Laredo bridges on December 31, 2004. The grave concerns that community leaders and business owners had expressed about long delays and lost sales did not materialize. Indeed, Gene Garza, port director for the Laredo District in the Customs and Border Protection Bureau of the DHS (in conversation with this author on April 4, 2005) asserted that the implementation of the US VISIT program had gone smoothly. Mr. Garza cited reduced, not increased, waiting times at Laredo's bridges and reduced time in processing I-94s, a process that requires travellers to submit to the program's procedures for securing biometric data. Mr. Garza also provided information on peak-crossing days during the Christmas holidays (December 17 to January 10) and Easter (the ten days ending on Easter Sunday) for 2004 and 2005 (see tables 7.21 to 7.24).

Table 7.21: Waiting Times to Process I-94 Visas, December 17 to January 10, 2004 and 2005

	Number of permits	Average waiting time
FY 2004	91,619	11–12 minutes
FY 2005 (with US VISIT processing)	93,981	3–4 minutes
Change (%)	+2.3	-67

Table 7.22: Waiting Time to Cross Bridge, December 17 to January 10, 2004 and 2005 (Minutes)

	Average	Maximum
FY 2004	24	95
FY 2005 (with US VISIT processing)	17	50
Change (%)	-29.2	-47.4

Table 7.23: Waiting Times to Process I-94 Visas, Ten-day Period Ending on Easter Sunday, 2004 and 2005

	Number of permits	Average waiting time
FY 2004	66,867	11–12 minutes
FY 2005 (with US VISIT processing)	68,873	3–4 minutes
Change (%)	+ 3.0	-67

Table 7.24: Waiting Time to Cross Bridge, Ten-day Period Ending on Easter Sunday, 2004 and 2005 (Minutes)

	Average	Maximum
FY 2004	10	44
FY 2005 (with US VISIT processing)	10	38
Change (%)	no change	-13.6

Conclusive evidence about the impact of the entry portion of the US VISIT program on Laredo and other Texas border communities awaits further study. However, the lack of negative news stories and commentary from border officials and the business community suggests that, at least initially, the US VISIT program is not delaying border crossings or disrupting economic activity.

CONCLUSION: THE ECONOMIC COST OF THE US VISIT PROGRAM TO TEXAS BORDER COMMUNITIES

Although the studies evaluated above confirm that trade and commerce, especially cross-border Mexican shoppers, are important to the border region, particularly Laredo, they also confirm that the implementation of the entry portion of the US VISIT program has had no measurable negative effect on the local border economies to date. The implementation of the exit portion of the program is the next challenge. As Mr. Garza acknowledged (in conversation in 2005), although it is not yet clear how the exit portion will be implemented, existing facilities and manpower are probably not adequate for the task.

Many border community leaders, including the ranking member of the US House Select Committee on Homeland Security (2004), feel strongly that the infrastructure at southern-border ports of entry cannot effectively handle the hundreds of millions of inspections now being conducted annually. In addition, they believe that

> the Southern Border's infrastructure cannot support the implementation of new border security programs (like [the] US VISIT Program) without harming the economies of border communities... There is a need to balance the competing tension between screening

> people and vehicles for terrorist weapons, contraband, smuggled immigrants, and other prohibited items with the need to ensure an efficient flow of commerce. Substantial investment [estimated at US $1 billion] in border infrastructure is needed to ensure national security while sustaining economic prosperity caused by increased cross-border trade over the last ten years.
>
> . . . Just as sufficient infrastructure is necessary to achieve both security and the efficient flow of commerce at the border, it is also necessary for the government to have the appropriate numbers of border agency personnel in order to achieve its trade and security goals. Government officials and community leaders have strongly asserted that staffing levels for all agencies responsible for border security are inadequate. Yet, three years since 9/11, no comprehensive staffing plan has been developed for the border. The number of border inspectors needs to be doubled to provide the needed level of security and support technological improvements.
>
> . . . Border communities, along with many DHS officials at the ports of entry, [are expressing] grave concerns over the implementation of the [U.S. VISIT Program]. These concerns are focused on insufficient infrastructure and staffing requirements needed to support this new security initiative. The Department of Homeland Security also needs to better coordinate the implementation of the US VISIT Program with border communities. For it to succeed, border communities' concerns must be addressed.

Two important facts driving renewed interest in understanding borders must be kept in mind. First, borders are complex, are intimately related to the nature of their physical and human environment, and are shaped by culture, society, markets, and state-sponsored and state-enforced laws and policies. Second, borders are barriers to trade and commerce. Nonetheless, the presence of effective policy-making at multiple levels of government (national, state, and local) can reduce the barrier effects of borders on trade and commerce. Borderland communities play a central role in informing and effecting multiple-level government activity in border regions.

RECOMMENDATIONS

Designing and Implementing Border Security Programs and Measures

The announcement by the DHS of the implementation of the US VISIT program brought cries of opposition from many border communities. This was not because they are opposed to secure borders but rather because they believed that the implementation of security policies and procedures would likely have an immediate and direct impact on their local economies and daily lives, which revolve around the steady and daily cross-border flow of people and goods, in the tens of thousands. Consequently community and business leaders in the border region wanted to have a say in the design and implementation of programs such as the US VISIT program. From the perspective of the border communities, the DHS and other federal (as well as state) agencies needed to seek input from and partnerships with border communities.

In his review of the "smart border" regime put in place after 9/11 on the border between the United States and Canada, Emmanuel Brunet-Jailly (2004, 136) noted that

> The federal governments of Canada and the United States dominate the key financial and regulatory decisions, and they sign international agreements. But in the end both depend on the local networks of public security agencies that span the border. Also, those security networks encompass both the functional agencies of both the public and private sectors.

Brunet-Jailly (2004, 137) concluded

> Indeed, a large number of the objectives listed in the Smart Border Declaration depend primarily upon the good will of lower-level security agencies, particularly, those of provincial and state governments and regional, county, and municipal governments . . . From an implementation perspective, it is clear that this security policy (Smart Border) cannot be effective without the active interest and participation of all of the concerned security agencies. (137)

Brunet-Jailly's perspective on the importance of "multi-level governance" for successful implementation of security measures on the US–Canada border is equally valid for the US–Mexico border. A poorly conceived and implemented US VISIT program would impede rather than facilitate legitimate travel and trade between the NAFTA partners—the United States, Mexico, and Canada. A healthy US–Mexico trade relationship is key to a growing and modernizing Mexican economy, and without this it would be difficult to stem the flow of illegal immigration and drugs crossing the southern US border.

The successful conceptualization and implementation of the US VISIT program may, arguably, require more, not less, input from the border communities. Only after repeated complaints from business leaders did the DHS seek, through public forums, media briefings, and advertising, to inform the border communities about the specifics of the program. The success of the program may be decided largely by the behaviour of residents, cross-border shoppers, shippers, business people, and local officials, who will have to adjust their personal and professional lives to meet its requirements. Involving those who will be affected directly by the program from the beginning may greatly improve the program's chances of succeeding. To date, this is a point that DHS officials in Washington, DC, appear to be slow to recognize. In order to address not only border security issues but also economic integration, immigration, social, health, and environmental issues in the border region, the federal government needs to develop a formal liaison mechanism, for example, an Office of Border Relations, that would involve the active participation of border-community representatives in the federal policy-making process.

Measuring the Economic Impact of Border Security Programs

Further research is needed to provide an accurate assessment of the potential economic impact of the US VISIT program and other border-security measures that affect the cross-border movement of people and goods. More in-depth and comprehensive survey work is needed to pinpoint the contributions that cross-border Mexican shoppers make to the border communities. For example, it is not clear what proportion of those who cross the border daily to go to work, take their children to school, attend college, or visit family and friends make purchases on the US side, or what impact they have on local sales and employment. Nor is it clear just how long they are willing to sit in line waiting to cross the border before they decide that it is more convenient to shop in Mexico. There is considerable anecdotal evidence to suggest that cross-border shoppers are willing to tolerate sporadic lengthy delays, up to an hour or more, but not persistently long delays. Research on the psychology of waiting suggests that waiting in line is more tolerable if it is understood to be a necessary part of the process of acquiring a good or service, accomplishing an activity, or achieving a goal (Maister 1985).

Cross-border shoppers know that the process of crossing the border inevitably involves waiting in line, for some period of time, to clear customs and immigration inspections. Research also shows that the fewer alternatives people have to waiting, whether going without or switching to an alternative source, the more tolerant they are of waiting. Given that most cross-border shoppers in Texas border communities are local, the option of driving hours to another less congested border crossing is not practical. Shopping in Mexico, however, is an option for many cross-border shoppers.

More research is needed to identify the threshold waiting times, those times beyond which daily and infrequent border crossers would decide to change their crossing plans, either postponing crossing to another time or choosing to cross fewer times. Evidence from the studies evaluated in this chapter indicate that a waiting time over one hour is the threshold point where many cross-border shoppers decide to cross less frequently. However, in most cases, these shoppers increase the size of their purchases when they do cross, so there is little overall negative effect on total expenditures. Much more research is needed to verify the threshold waiting times and their impact on the purchasing decisions of cross-border shoppers (both local and non-local) in order to get a more accurate estimate of the economic impact of waiting times.

Developing a Better Understanding of Borders

At the same time as forces of global economic integration accelerate to eliminate borders, countervailing forces for border security are gaining momentum to keep, reinforce, and expand borders. The growing debate over "open" versus "closed borders has sparked a renewed interest in the study of borders and borderlands. This renewed interest gives scholars a unique opportunity to advance their understanding of borders and borderlands through the development and testing of theories and models of borders.

LITERATURE CITED

Bonner, T. J. 2004. *How Secure Are America's Borders? Statement by National Border Patrol Council President T. J. Bonner*. Washington D.C., August 23.

Brunet-Jailly, Emmanuel. 2004. "NAFTA, Economic Integration, and Canadian-American Security Regime in the Post-September 11, 2001 Era: Multi-level Governance and Transparent Borders?" *Journal of Borderlands Studies* 19:1, 123–41.

Center for the Study of Border Economic Studies, University of Texas–Pan American. 2004. *The Economic Impact of Mexican Visitors to the Lower Rio Grande Valley 2003*. Edinburg: Center for the Study of Border Economic Studies, University of Texas–Pan American.

Department of Homeland Security [US]. 2004. *Fact Sheet: U.S.-Mexico Land Borders, US-VISIT.* Washington, DC: Government Printing Office.

———. 2005. "US VISIT Process Saves Visitors Time Crossing Land Border." *US-VISIT UPDATE*, January 4. Washington, DC: Government Printing Office.

Federal Reserve Bank of Dallas. 2005. *Business Cycle Coordination Along the Texas–Mexico Border*. Working paper 0502. Dallas, TX: Federal Reserve Bank.

House Select Committee on Homeland Security [US House of Representatives]. 2004. *Transforming the Southern Border*. Washington, DC: Government Printing Office.

International Bank of Commerce. 2003. *US VISIT (Entry and Exit System)*. Paper. Laredo, TX: International Bank of Commerce.

International Trade Administration [US Department of Commerce]. 2004. *Fact Sheet: Exports Are Important to the US Economy*. Washington, DC: Government Printing Office.

McAllen Economic Development Corporation and McAllen Chamber of Commerce. 2003. *US VISIT: A Threat to American Jobs and Economy*. Paper. Laredo, TX: McAllen Economic Development Corporation and McAllen Chamber of Commerce.

Maister, David. 1985. "The Psychology of Waiting Lines." *The Service Encounter*, eds. J. Czepiel, M. R. Soloman, and C. Surprenant. Lanham, MD: Heath and Company, Lexington Books.

National Commission on Terrorist Attacks Upon the United States. 2004. *Final Report of the National Commission of Terrorist Attacks Upon the United States*. Washington, DC: Government Printing Office.

Office of the US Trade Representative. 2004. *US Trade in 2004*. Washington, DC: Government Printing Office.

Perryman Group. 2004. *Stalling the Engine of Growth in a Global Economy: The Impact of Implementation of the US VISIT Program at US–Mexico Border*

Crossings on Business Activity in the US, Texas, and the Border Region. Laredo, TX: IBC.

al-Qurashi, Abu Ubayd. 2004. "America's Nightmares" (*Al-Ansar* [online], (February 13, 2002). *Imperial Hubris,* ed. Anonymous. Washington, DC: Brassey's Press.

SANDAG [San Diego Association of Governments]. 2005. *Estimating Economic Impacts of Border Wait Times in the San Diego–Baja California Region*. San Diego: SANDAG.

Texas Center for Border Economic and Enterprise Development, Texas A&M International University. 2003. *US VISIT: A Preliminary Impact Assessment of the Border and Texas Economies*. Laredo: Texas A&M International University.

———. 2004. *The Texas Border with Mexico: Opportunities and Challenges*. Technical Report no. 10. Laredo: Texas A&M International University.

CHAPTER 8

THE COSTS OF HOMELAND SECURITY

Tony Payan and Amanda Vásquez

The US–Mexico border has undergone several historical transformations. Between 1848 and 1920 the border went through an era best characterized by informality: there were no border guards, no customs controls, and no checkpoints. This era is best referred to as a frontier system. In general, although a line divided the two countries on the sand and the river banks, border controls were practically non-existent. The Mexican Revolution of 1910–21 brought a new era for the border, one better referred to as a customs system. In 1924 the Border Patrol was created, and customs and immigration personnel at border checkpoints became a regular and increasing fixture. By 1929 Mexicans required a visa to enter the United States and it became illegal to enter the country between ports of entry. Between 1920 and 1980 the US government more heavily regulated economic activities across the border, and cross-border immigration and mobility became increasingly restricted. Of grave concern was the alcohol smuggling along the border during the Prohibition era in the United States. This period was, in effect, a customs management system. The border, however, was to go through two more "border systems." Between 1980 and 2001 a law-enforcement border system focused on illegal drugs, illegal immigration, and general economic activity, particularly contraband. Not only were the laws more restrictive, but the penalties for violating the laws regulating cross-border activity also became more stringent.

While the other three historical systems blended one into the other, the third border system was to change abruptly into the fourth and present border regime. A key incident inspired these changes in 2001. In effect, the terrorist attacks of September 11, 2001, inaugurated a new era along the border, a regime in which security became the focus. Trade, immigration, illegal drugs, and all other cross-border interactions were redefined as matters of national security. As Robert Emerson (2004, 459) has observed, "Key incidents involve particular observations that play a central role in identifying and opening up new analytic issues and broader lines of theoretical development." The shift from a law-enforcement focus to a security focus in 2001 brought profound policy and practical changes to the US–Mexico border. These policies marked the most recent changes to the border's structure.

As during previous border systems, the "agents" of the border, that is, border residents and border crossers—from shoppers to business people to students to families and friends—were forced to modify their behaviour in order to maintain their daily activities and continue with their cross-border lives in the face of the new border system. As each transformation in border policy affected the structure of the border, that structure in turn affected the behaviour of nearly all border agents. Although the debate between scholars favouring "structure-based" approaches and those favouring "agent-based" approaches is not new, when it is applied to the border, scholars must question whether the nature of the border—the laws that govern the border, its physical appearance, and so on—is the primary determinant of how the border functions. In such an instance border agents (those who enforce the border and border crossers alike) would be governed by the structure of the border. In contrast an agent-based approach would assume that the agents are the primary determinants of how the border functions.

As the history of the border suggests, the nature of its structure has gone through four stages since its initial establishment in 1848. In this chapter we suggest that neither a structure-based nor an agent-based analysis is sufficient to explain what history shows about the border. Rather, a more holistic, albeit tautological, approach is more appropriate, wherein the structure of the border—at a minimum, the effectiveness of its functioning—is affected by border agents as much as the behaviour of border agents is affected by changes in the border's systemic structure. Clearly, each new border system has affected the borderlands in all four components analyzed in this volume: market forces and trade flows, policy activities at all levels of government, the political clout of the borderlands vis-à-vis their central governments, and the specific culture of the borderlands. Each was affected in two ways: (1) in the short term or the long term; (2) the degree of each new regime's effect on each of these aspects. This chapter explores these elements from the perspective of both structural change and agent adaptation in the move toward a security-based border regime after 2001.

Because structures imply new costs and create new benefits, we interweave our agent–structure debate with a cost–benefit analysis of the border. The creators and modifiers of the structure expect both, although they nearly always expect the benefits to exceed the costs. In this study we measure the overall US investment in the new border-security regime that emerged after September 11, 2001, the investment from which the new border structure materialized. After noting the overall investment in the new security-based border system, we assess the added burden on border residents stemming from the new security regime and attempt to establish whether this additional burden was a temporary nuisance or is a permanent ongoing cost. Most of these costs are quantifiable, although some, such as cross-border intimacy, are not. Most of the benefits of the new border-security strategy are also quantifiable. Finally we compare the added costs to the benefits measured in terms of increased national security. If quantifiable national-security policies produce decreased drug flows, fewer undocumented border crossers, less contraband (other than drugs), and fewer terrorists coming across the border, while promoting greater and safer trade between the two countries, one may conclude that US investment in new border-security strategies was successful. As we move through this cost–benefit analysis, we insert the narrative concerning the adaptation of agents to the new structures in regard to some of the four elements central to the theoretical premises of this volume.

To assess the total costs of the new border-security environment on the US–Mexico border major statistical data kept by various organizations that monitor both private and public spending were compiled and analyzed. Various interviews were conducted with officials and community leaders, in order to gather their impressions of the changed security-based border system and the hidden costs to the border community. Similar interviews were conducted with researchers and border residents, in order to assess their impressions of the costs of the new regime and how they had adjusted to the new-border security structures. Finally, research done on the benefits of the new homeland security regime was surveyed.

THE INVESTMENT

With every border regime has come the creation of new laws and new bureaucracies, or the reorganization of the bureaucracies already operating on the border. Every historical border era represented an escalation of monetary, personnel, and equipment resources dedicated to "bringing order to the border," "enforcing border laws," or "securing the border." The advent of the security era on the US–Mexico border was no exception. As a response to the terrorist attacks of September 11, 2001, the US Congress passed the USA PATRIOT Act, a law designed to enhance the authority of law-enforcement agencies to fight terrorism. In 2002 Congress moved on to reorganize the border bureaucracies, passing the Homeland Security Act, which effectively established the Department of Homeland Security (DHS). The DHS pooled together 22 different agencies, a workforce of some 180,000 bureaucrats, and a budget of over US$ 40 billion in 2005 (General Accounting Office 2005; Department of Homeland Security 2005a). In regard to borders, title IV of the Homeland Security Act created the Office of the Undersecretary for Border and Transportation Security, grouping all border agencies under that position. In sum, starting a few weeks after 9/11 some of the most important security initiatives coming out of the new laws, in addition to bureaucratic reorganization, were directed at securing US borders. This was done despite the fact that none of the terrorists had used either the Mexican or the Canadian border to enter the United States.

The border security initiative of the new DHS was broken down into programs, and three of these were particularly important. The first was the Customs Trade Partnership against Terrorism (C-TPAT), which began in November 2001. C-TPAT was designed to secure the supply chain from the factories of Mexican *maquiladoras* to the transportation companies to US importers. All producers, carriers, and importers must register with US Customs for pre-clearance before their merchandise and personnel get to the border, which, in turn, expedites their crossing at the port of entry.

The second important initiative was the National Targeting Center, which was to gather statistics on all border crossers (people, vehicles, and transactions) for the purposes of detecting higher-risk crossers or transactions and allowing targeted inspections of those with a higher probability of being associated with criminal or terrorist elements. It integrated government, commercial, and law-enforcement databases into an evolving statistics-producing mechanism to make the latest criminal trends on the border available to law-enforcement officers on the ground. The targets identified as higher risk are screened on arrival at the port of entry, while those deemed of lower risk are only randomly checked.

The third effort was the United States Visitor and Immigrant Status Indicator Technology (US VISIT) program. The system has been initiated at airports and seaports across the nation, but it is still under test at some land ports of entry along the US–Mexico border. The system scans travel documents and takes fingerprints and pictures of the border crosser. The data are then run through databases to determine whether the individual is a criminal or a terrorist. This system also keeps track of all border-crossing information on any one individual over time.

Many other programs and agencies were "beefed-up," adding personnel, introducing higher technologies, and adding equipment. One such agency is the US Border Patrol and its various programs on the ground along the border.

The new laws, the reorganization, and the myriad new border-security initiatives, as well as the additions to existing programs, have resulted in two measurable changes: (1) increased costs for border security; (2) increased burdens on border communities from Tijuana–San Diego to Matamoros–Brownsville.

The new investments in border security following 9/11 are best measured by observing the increased expenditures on border security. The total border-security budget in comparative perspective shot up from US$ 19.7 billion in the fiscal year 2001 to US$ 40.2 billion in fiscal 2005 (see table 8.1).

The number of personnel dedicated to securing the border also increased at the federal level. Table 8.2 shows the increase in expenditures on manpower to perform border duties. On February 7, 2005, US President George W. Bush presented his budget to Congress, requesting a 4.8 percent increase in Customs and Border Protection funding, for a total of US$ 6.7 billion for fiscal 2006.

More stringent border management is commonly associated with this investment. Not only was there an entire bureaucratic reorganization to respond to national security needs, but the resources poured into making the border more efficient also grew considerably. It may be appropriate to emphasize that these investments and policies changed

Table 8.1: Total US Federal Government Expenditures on Border Security, Fiscal Years 2001–06 (US$ Billions)

FY2001	FY2002	FY2003	FY2004	FY2005	FY2006
19.7	23.2	31.2	36.2	40.2	41.1

Note: As the Department of Homeland Security was not created until 2003, comparable estimates for the programs now organized under it were provided by the White House for the fiscal years 2001 and 2002. The figure for the fiscal year 2006 is the amount requested by the White House.

Sources: Department of Homeland Security. "2004 Budget in Brief" (2004); Office of Management and Budget. "Department of Homeland Security" (2006).

Table 8.2: Total US Federal Government Expenditures on Personnel Performing Duties on Border Security, Fiscal Years 2003–06

FY2003	FY2004	FY2005	FY2006
2.3	5.99	6.3	6.7

Note: As the Department of Homeland Security was not created until 2003, the figure for fiscal 2003 represents an estimate of the Customs budget. The figure for fiscal 2006 is the amount requested by the White House.

Sources: Department of Homeland Security. "2004 Budget in Brief" (2004); Office of Management and Budget. "Department of Homeland Security" (2006).

the structure in question; that is, they changed the nature of the border. However, one may first question whether the agents, specifically the border residents—businesspeople, families, school and university students, and even criminals on either side of the border—simply conformed to the changes or whether their behaviour has come to affect the nature of the border. After exploring the agents' reactions one may then question whether the costs of the new border are beneficial, not beneficial, or neutral. Having reviewed the fiscal costs of increased security, we now analyze the costs of the new border-security regime on the US–Mexico divide.

THE COSTS

Measuring the costs of compliance for US–Mexico border businesses requires a breakdown of two important economic sectors operating on the border: (1) the local retail business, in which some 246 million Mexican cross-border shoppers spend as much as US$ 7.5 billion a year, according to a study done by the Center for Border Economic Studies of the University of Texas–Pan American (Ghaddar and Brown 2005); and (2) the substantial cross-border import/export trade, which has a total value of US$ 260 billion a year. The very day after 9/11 changes in security and policy were reportedly evident along the border. Commuters accustomed to crossing at the international port of entry every day, for business, school, or personal visits, found themselves stuck in lines with hours to wait. Some consumers and commuters found it more beneficial to simply stay at home and wait for the chaos of the tragedy to pass. The effects of 9/11 were noted throughout the border region, particularly in the major cities of the four border districts, that is, El Paso, Nogales, San Diego, and Laredo.

In the city of El Paso, Texas, crossings of privately owned vehicles declined by more than six million between 2001 and 2002 (City of El Paso 2001–02). Prominent local leaders interviewed in May 2004, at the annual Border Security Conference at the University of Texas at El Paso, estimated that declines in border crossings due to policies or effects stemming from 9/11 may have translated into 50,000 fewer sales or transactions in the city. According to estimates by the Texas Workforce Commission, jobs in wholesale and retail businesses fell by 300 in 2001, following a three-year increase, and fell another 200 in 2002. If these estimates are reliable, the aftermath of 9/11 produced notable damage within El Paso's economy.

There are rival hypotheses to these occurrences, however. According to the City of El Paso (2001–02), trade stimulated by the North American Free Trade Agreement (NAFTA) and the growth of the *maquiladora* industry were major components of economic prosperity for the city. Another hypothesis is that during 2001, the entire nation experienced economic decline that could be attributed to a variety of causes, ranging from decreased consumer confidence following 9/11 to economic trends that were initiated during the previous Clinton Administration, trends that would have affected general trade and the *maquiladora* industry, and translated into losses in the El Paso economy, whether 9/11 occurred or not.

Yet a third hypothesis argues that 9/11 and its aftermath had no significant impact on the local economy. According to the City of El Paso (2001–02), trade with Mexico continued at a high rate throughout 2001 and into 2002, accounting for 43.8 percent of all Texas exports, and imports through El Paso alone totalled more than US$ 22.3 billion in 2001. The city reported economic growth trends from 2000 to 2002 and projected continued growth through 2016. Thus, despite immediate declines in border crossings and economic growth following 9/11, El Paso finds itself back at its level of normalcy.

Debates regarding the impact of 9/11 on local economies extend to other border cities as well. As the long lines at ports of entry passed, the border economy returned to its previous levels of normalcy. Studies conducted by the offices of Economic Development at the University of Arizona and Arizona State University found a slight decline in the level of northbound truck crossings between August and September 2001, but by October levels had returned to "normal" (Wright, Howard, and Davis 2002). However, the number of passenger-vehicle crossings declined three million in Texas, nearly two million in California, and nearly 500,000 in Arizona between August and September. These had not attained normalcy by October, but they have done so by now (Wright, Howard, and Davis 2002).

Based on the significant change in numbers between August and October 2001, economic indicators should reflect negative changes in the economy of the Arizona border. Rival hypotheses make this assertion difficult, however. According to the Arizona Department of Commerce, the entire state experienced economic decline, profiled through declines in individual household income and decreased growth in retail sales (University of Arizona Economic and Business Research Center 2005). Subsequently, as with the case of El Paso, explanations range from the impact of 9/11 to the nationwide trend in economic decline that began during the latter half of 2001. While the declines are difficult to attribute to the effects of 9/11 and the corresponding costs of security on the border, the indicators clearly demonstrate that economic prosperity in Arizona has progressed since 2001 and has returned to levels of normalcy observed in 1999 in most areas.

Like El Paso and Nogales, San Diego reported immediate effects after 9/11. Information released by the US and Foreign Commerce

Service and the US Department of State indicated that waiting times at international ports of entry increased to between two and four times, prompting a decline of 27,000 pedestrian crossings and 28,000 private-vehicle crossings, and that this decreased number of crossings, in combination with decreased consumer confidence, resulted in a 30 percent loss in business for 96 percent of businesses in San Diego during the first three months following September 11, 2001, while 56 percent of San Diego businesses experienced losses of 50 percent or more and 21 percent experienced losses of 60 percent or more (Department of Commerce 2005). International trade flowing through ports along California's borders fell by more than US$ 11 million in net exports (State of California 2004). The months following 9/11 were difficult for the border economy.

It would be unfair, however, to present this data without acknowledging that there had been a downward trend in international trade through California ports since 2000, long before 9/11. Between 2000 and 2001 net exports through these ports fell by more than US$ 50 million. As with the other border districts, one must question whether the effects attributed to 9/11 have been inflated. Since that time San Diego has returned to pre-9/11 levels of growth and trade. Although the effects of 9/11 may have been difficult at first, they were by no means detrimental to long-term growth.

Unlike the other three border districts, Laredo does not seem to have experienced significant loss in the aftermath of 9/11. Between 2001 and 2002 exports to Mexico through the Laredo port increased by US$ 3.4 billion and imports from Mexico increased by US$ 0.4 billion (City of Laredo 2004). At the same time the city reported a US$ 0.1 billion increase in local wages. These increases are difficult to explain when compared with the effects experienced by the other three border districts, but it is possible to hypothesize that the extraordinary level of trade normally experienced in Laredo may have cushioned economic decline, allowing for a slowdown of growth but not permitting a substantial decline. It appears as though Laredo's local economy was able to sustain a path of normal development despite the changes surrounding September 11, 2001.

Before moving away from the local economy, it must be noted that new policies were implemented at international ports of entry. On October 17, 2001, when authorities implemented level-one procedures for border monitoring, the US and Foreign Commerce Service and the

US Department of State suggested that these procedures may have interrupted the normal flow of goods and prevented it from returning, and they further suggested that the new procedures would prevent future growth and progress that would facilitate the movement of goods and people across the border (Department of Commerce 2005). Although border procedures will likely never return to their previous state and, in this sense, have attained a new "normal," the border economy and border crossings have returned to their normal levels. Moreover, all four of the border cities reported efforts to improve and facilitate border crossings. Efforts to facilitate crossings do not necessarily have to be abandoned with the introduction of new technology. Rather, technology may help to provide a safer, more efficient method of crossing.

Returning to the agent–structure debate, one may argue that the ability of border crossers to maintain levels of local commerce may serve as a strong argument in support of the agent-based approach. Although the policies following September 11, 2001, clearly changed the structure of the border, border crossers seem to have adapted and restored local commerce to its previous level. Thus changing the level of commerce, in turn, affects the face of the border, and this area demonstrates an interdependent relationship between agent and structure.

Impact on the Trucking Business

One of the most important costs for the import/export business stemming from 9/11 and the new border-security initiatives is centred on the trucking business. Although consumer levels quickly returned to normal in the United States, trucking industries and importation firms were overwhelmed by the burdens of extensive inspections at international ports of entry. After 9/11 the US government quickly acted to secure all international crossings and ensure that illegal weapons and aliens did not slip through the cracks, further threatening the well-being of the nation. Cargo entering the United States through the southern border was of particular concern, for the process involves many actors, and accountability for the loads is difficult to secure, which leaves this cargo vulnerable to illegal infiltration.

A number of actors are involved in the importation process that dominates the southern border. Products to be imported originate with manufacturers and other commercial organizations, but these organizations may outsource the transportation of their products to other firms. Transportation firms arrange for the movement of goods from their point of origin into the United States. These transportation firms may further outsource actual transportation by contracting individual drivers to transport cargo loads across the border. This multitude of actors makes accountability difficult. Without a central source of accountability it is possible for drug cartels and terrorist networks, for example, to infiltrate the process by persuading individuals at corporation loading docks, employees of transportation firms, or individual drivers to smuggle anything from drugs to humans to dangerous weapons.

Customs agents at international ports of entry along the southern border have long understood the need to monitor shipments. Following 9/11 experts quickly recognized the importance of devising a program that would entice actors to have a central system that would not only be more accountable for goods being transported but would also better meet security goals. To this end inspection policies were implemented at ports of entry that sought to increase and improve levels of inspection, in hopes of minimizing the smuggling of illegal goods or individuals. These increased levels of inspection in turn increased border waiting times and increased difficulties for the trade process.

C-TPAT sought to control international trade and limit the possibility of security threats that might penetrate the border through seemingly routine trade (Customs and Border Protection 2005). As noted earlier, the nature of the import process along the southern border makes it vulnerable to manipulation by drug cartels and terrorist networks, and disconnection between truckers, importers, and producers leaves wide gaps in the trade processes that are vulnerable to infiltration and corruption.

C-TPAT was designed to create a network of partners, or companies, that would agree to take certain precautions to ensure that safe, untainted loads were secured from start to finish. If the Department of Homeland Security could be assured that the loads being transported were secured, the level of inspection could be reduced enough to provide for a more timely border-crossing process. Today C-TPAT is a partnership whose membership consists of companies that have fulfilled a series of requisites, designed to ensure that cargo loads will not be penetrated by drug cartels, terrorist networks, or any other network that may pose a threat to national security. Participants must first provide evidence that they and their partners have obtained C-TPAT certification from the government, and, subsequently, demonstrate sufficient capacity to meet security criteria. The primary objective of these criteria is to ensure that participants "conduct a comprehensive assessment of their international supply chains" from the "point of origin (manufacturer/supplier/vendor) through the point of distribution" (Customs and Border Protection 2005). At the point of origin, C-TPAT requirements include container security: specifically, containers must undergo physical inspections prior to loading on all surfaces; container seals must be controlled and secured by designated employees who are trained in identifying "compromised seals and containers"; and, before transportation, these containers must remain stored in a manner that prevents access by unauthorized individuals.

Securing the loaded container consists of a number of "physical access controls" that prevent access by unauthorized individuals. C-TPAT stipulates that employees and management must comply with specific guidelines for background checks, and that these checks must be performed before new employees are hired. In order to monitor individuals who have access to containers the manufacturer or vendor must employ an employee identification system that designates the areas to which employees are granted access, as well as points within the facility that monitor the movement of employees within restricted areas. Equally important to the process is the monitoring of visitors. C-TPAT requirements stipulate that photo identification is necessary for all visitors. Photo identification must also be presented by all those making deliveries to the facility, and deliveries are to be routinely screened for safety. Theoretically, securing access to cargo loads will help to prevent tampering or manipulation of cargo contents. Even after the load has left the point of origin, partners must take steps to ensure that the load remains safe. Safeguarding documents containing information regarding the load and verifying the weight and marks of loads at the point of distribution, compared with the figures recorded at the point of origin, are important to the security process (Customs and Border Protection 2005).

These C-TPAT stipulations seem to be logical and reasonable: it seems only appropriate that a firm would have full control over the load at all times. However, the changes that must be made to accommodate these requirements place cost burdens on firms, as they are not easy to fulfill. Partnerships and proposals have been rejected, which has disrupted the previously existing normal flow of trade. Firms that choose not to accept these changes incur costs of time when their loads undergo extensive inspections at international ports of entry. Although the US Bureau of Customs and Border Protection has attempted to accommodate the flow of trade by providing a system to facilitate international crossings, the initial costs and changes that firms must incur to avoid obstacles to trade remain.

In addition to C-TPAT, Customs and Border Protection has employed technology and strategies to more effectively target loads requiring extensive inspections. According to Customs and Border Protection, an Automated Targeting System is used in combination with information obtained by the National Targeting Center to provide "tactical targeting" of cargo that may pose a threat to security (Customs and Border Protection 2006). Through the use of intelligence Customs and Border Protection is better able to identify people, firms, and types of goods traditionally of concern to national security. Risk assessments are provided electronically, and agents are able to limit extensive inspections.

Facilitating the trade process is crucial to the economy of the United States and the southern border, but providing for national security is no less important. Customs and Border Protection has worked to develop a program that accommodates both of these values simultaneously. The costs that importers have incurred in order to make their processes more secure are noteworthy.

Although to date there is no comprehensive study of the costs of compliance with US border initiatives on the US–Mexico border, Transport Canada (a Canadian government department) has released a study undertaken by consultants that estimated that similar compliance programs have cost the Canadian trucking business upward of CA$ 290 million (DAMF Consultants 2005). However, Christopher B. Lofgren, president and chief executive of Schneider, Inc., a trucking corporation, said that "immediately afterward [September 11], crossing borders in Canada was much more inefficient. Now, with pre-clearing the loads electronically, that has improved" (*BusinessWeek* 2005). High costs resulted from US–Mexico border waiting and processing times; compliance time; resources for drivers' participation in C-TPAT and other clearance programs; physical security measures adopted to comply with C-TPAT and other program requirements; training and border-crossing bonuses for drivers; administrative costs required for advance reporting requirements; and so on. In that regard, Lofgren said,

> We're more challenged on the time crossing borders in Mexico. It could be an hour, but it could be a day ... Clearly, there are issues around security and immigration law ... one of the things we've got to figure out is how to make that border crossing much more efficient.

The impact of the new security measures on the US–Mexico border is different, however, because Mexican trucking companies have not been allowed to join in the long-haul trucking industry in the United States. Mexican trucking companies can travel only within 32 kilometres (20 miles) of the border, making their trucks essentially drayage trucks (hauling loaded boxes across the border). Thus the greatest impact on the cross-border trucking business on the US–Mexico border is on the drayage system. The added man-hour costs and additional fuel costs related to longer waiting times at ports of entry are mostly concentrated on these drayage companies. In contrast, the long-haul trucking business has not been affected.

The additional costs to the transportation industry, concentrated in the drayage system, represent a hidden tax on the cost of doing business across the US–Mexico border. In turn this represents a cost to the users of shipping services. Down the economic chain these costs are passed to the consumer, generally in the form of higher prices. However, according to the economist Roberto Coronado at the Federal Reserve Bank of El Paso (interviewed on October 20, 2005), these costs were quickly absorbed and, even if they became permanent, did not have an impact on the cross-border trucking statistics or the volume of trade, at least not a cost that can be easily disentangled from the economic slowdown during the second half of 2001. A look at the statistics of incoming truck crossings on the US–Mexico border in all four states shows no clear pattern other than steady growth since 1994. The effect of the months following 9/11 and the lasting effect of the new security measures are negligible. In El Paso, for example, according to figures provided by Mr. Coronado, truck crossings went from 54,381 in August 2001 to 52,597 in September 2001, but they were back up to 57,790 in November 2001, and by May 2005 they had grown to 61,854. Trucking traffic across the border seemed affected much more by the economic conditions of the two countries than by 9/11 and its aftermath. Trade did not diminish considerably after September 11, 2001, and has continued to grow, obeying larger economic forces rather than security concerns or measures on the border.

Despite a significant initial increase in the waiting period for truckers to obtain clearance at ports of entry immediately following 9/11, the normal waiting periods returned not long after. In fact infrastructure investments by the US government at the border have made trucking crossings more efficient, while compliance with security measures appears to be lessening the waiting times for trucks at ports of entry. According to Mr. Coronado, the costs associated with compliance with new border-security measures do not seem to have resulted in either increased costs to the consumer (inflation) or considerably higher costs to the cross-border trade. In fact cross-border surface trade reached a record level in August 2005, when it rose 8.2 percent over August 2004 to reach a total of US$ 21 billion for the month (Bureau of Transportation Statistics 2005).

Returning briefly to the topic of the agent–structure debate, it is clear that the changing structure of the border has stringently confined the behaviours of the agents. One must question whether these agents have been able to react in a manner that reciprocally changes the border's structure. Such a reaction may not yet be observable within the import/export sector: that is, most agents continue to conform to the limitations of the border rather than acting in a manner that changes the border. This particular sector supports the structure-based argument and does not support our hypothesis. However, it is simply one of a number of sectors examined.

Changes in Immigration Costs

Perceptions of the US–Mexico borderland range from a third-world ghetto to barbed wire keeping immigrants at bay. Very few include images of efficient ports of entry that monitor hundreds of thousands of exchanges each day; daily exchanges of students and professors committed to creating curricula that intimately study border relations at the sites of interaction; or intergovernmental cooperation arising from a binational commitment to improving health and the environment. In short, few perceptions include the positive and complex tapestry that is the US–Mexico border. Each year citizens living far from the border, often inspired by misleading perceptions and overwhelmed by fears of uncontrolled immigration, dangers to national security, and economic downturn, propose radical actions, including the installation of electric fencing (Bear 2003) or the use of the military (Smitherman 1997), to ensure that Mexican immigrants are not allowed to enter the country.

Not all immigration along the southern border is illegal, and most crossings at the US–Mexico border are for personal reasons and are harmless to national security. Indeed, each year, of the more than one million undocumented crossers who are detained, perhaps as many as 500,000 make it across the border successfully, in contrast to the 300 million documented, legal border crossers who cross at the thirty-plus ports of entry along the US–Mexico border.

Two new measures related to human mobility are important to note among the new and permanent costs of homeland security. The first is the US VISIT program, mentioned earlier. It requires that everyone crossing US borders be fingerprinted and photographed. The information gathered is then matched with all databases to detect if the border crosser poses a "threat" to national security. The process is already operating at international airports across the nation, but it will be implemented at land ports of entry as well. This is likely to mean longer waiting times at inspection points, unless the program operates efficiently and more inspection stations are opened for both pedestrians and vehicles. The program will eventually require considerable expenditure and will represent an enormous inconvenience to border residents because their exit will be checked with nearly as much care as their entrance or return to the United States. The infrastructure and personnel investment will be considerable.

The second measure related to human mobility is a government initiative, still not implemented but being phased in, that will require US citizens crossing the border by land to carry a passport. Scheduled to come into effect on December 31, 2007, this measure will require millions of Americans who currently visit Mexico without a passport or a visa to pay for and carry a passport, even if they are crossing a land border to visit a relative or friend, to shop, to be a tourist, or to do business, study, research or work. This will represent a personal cost to each American wanting to cross the border, even casually, and to every American border citizen and resident who wants to enter Mexico, no matter the reason.

Both the US VISIT program and the new passport requirement for border crossers, while not yet fully implemented at the US–Mexico border, will clearly affect both the pockets of US citizens and legal residents, and the ease with which they cross the border. As the DHS phases in these requirements over time, the greatest impact will be on families whose members live on both sides of the border and want to maintain contact with their relatives. Many of these daily and weekly border crossers can least afford the costs of obtaining passports for their entire families, or the inconvenience to their lives.

The two new immigration measures that are to be phased in on the border will have an important consequence for life in all US–Mexico border sister towns. The cities on either side of the border share a unique and intimate historical connection that has extended into the contemporary traditions of the region. Because the region was once part of a single country, Mexico, its residents share intimate cultural and familial connections that extend across the international boundary. Families on both sides of the border share daily activities in a manner that turns the border into more of a blur than a line. This connection between sister cities along the southern border is evident simply in the composition of their populations. In most cities along the US side of the border the population is at least 50 percent Hispanic, rising as high as 70–80 percent in some, and 10–20 per cent of the population comprises Mexican-born residents (Migration Policy Institute 2004). Some estimates suggest that more than one-third of the population of El Paso were born in Mexico.

Within this context border communities are in a unique position because many post-DHS policies have failed to improve security practices along the border. Instead they have interfered detrimentally with daily exchanges. A recent publication of the Immigration Policy Center asserted, "We must accept the reality that harsher immigration laws would not have stopped the terrorists, [for] as immigration laws change, terrorists simply adapt" (Johnson and Stock 2003). However, stricter immigration policies have been exactly the result of the homeland security phenomenon. According to the Department of State, "Visa applications take a longer process," and it further noted that "the consular officer must evaluate the security risk presented by the applicant … This affects both tourist and business non-immigrant visas" (Department of State 2003). Since September 11, 2001, processing applications for residency in the United States have averaged more than one year, forcing some families to live separately for at least a year. Lengthy background checks, supplemental forms, and new policies have caused a slowdown in the adjudication of immigration applications. Border cities that once felt like thriving sister communities now feel more like strictly separated and somewhat disintegrated cities. The effects on all areas of life have been innumerable.

However, some accommodations have been made to try to distinguish between daily commuters and individuals intending to enter the United States. In August 2004 the DHS (67 Fed. Reg. 18,065) announced that all Mexican nationals holding "laser-visa cards," cards issued to individuals who make routine visits to the United States for confirmed purposes including business and education, would be allowed to visit border cities for up to thirty days, an increase from the previous limit of seventy-two hours (Migration Policy Institute 2003). Senator Kay Bailey Hutchison of Texas noted (UPI 2004) that

> Today's actions—expanding use of expedited expulsion while easing visa restrictions for legitimate visitors—move us towards a more realistic border policy. Our ultimate goal should be safeguarding our country, and facilitating the cross-border travel and commerce that is so important to our economy.

Life along the southern border depends on interaction, and it includes families, students, businesspeople, and officials who work together daily. It is imperative that the daily interaction of residents and family members across the southern border is allowed as steps are taken to preserve the national security.

Interestingly, although immigration policy was part of the bureaucratic reorganization that followed 9/11, the principles that underlie the policy remain the same. Family reunification remains the main goal of current US immigration policy. The added security measures have increased costs to individual clients of US immigration services, but 9/11 has not substantially changed the policy or the targets of the policy. Moreover, when the new measures are matched against the ultimate objective of stemming the flow of undocumented border crossers, it does not appear to have reduced either the total numbers or the rates of undocumented immigration numbers. Immigration reform, involving a fundamental shift in immigration policy, remains an elusive goal.

Impact on Local Autonomy and Borderland Culture

Not only were flows of investment and market forces affected—however temporarily, albeit with longer-term systemic effects—but a considerable loss of autonomy also occurred. Previously, particularly in the earlier border regimes, local authorities had considerable discretion to deal with their counterparts across the border, but this autonomy was gradually lost and became non-existent after September 11, 2001. Almost all border policy is now made in Washington, DC, with little or no regard for borderland agents. The structure is changed from above and the agents below can only adapt to it. Given this loss of autonomy, and the fact that the border was not a matter of national security, the political clout of the borderland communities has decreased considerably. In fact, if local political communities, through their economic elites, had ever had any power to lobby and affect border policy in any way, the transformation of all border matters into an issue of national security has severely affected their ability to do so.

A word must also be said about the culture of the borderlands and its interaction with the new regime. Whether the new regime was intended to affect the borderlands culturally, it is clear that the border counties of the southern United States have an increasingly Hispanic cultural makeup, a trend that has remained unaffected by the new border regime. Culture does not flow the way market forces flow. Culture is a gradual, more resilient process, which is not necessarily subject to governmental regulation. In this regard culture will likely remain unaffected for a much longer period, even if the new security-based border system remains for a very long time.

THE RETURN ON INVESTMENT

September 11, 2001, meant not only a new era in the pursuit of US security but also new investment in the pursuit of that security. The expected benefits of that investment are found explicitly in the mission of the DHS: (1) fewer drugs crossing the US–Mexico border; (2) fewer illegal aliens crossing the border; (3) the capture of potential terrorists trying to cross the border. All three benefits can be measured by looking at the statistics available from the period 2001–06 and using them to determine whether the goals of homeland security have been achieved.

The Business of Drugs

One of the most important law-enforcement concerns on the US–Mexico border is illegal drugs. Law enforcement in this area has not experienced the same level of "securitization" that immigration underwent after 9/11. Although the Drug Enforcement Administration

(DEA) remains within the Department of Justice, rather than being transferred to the DHS, the rhetoric around illegal drugs is increasingly enveloped in the language of security. In fact the DHS's highlights for the year 2005 expressly stated that the DHS had "thwarted terrorism and protected citizens by breaking up drug smuggling networks and their assets," a sign that there is a level of conflation of the issues of drugs and terrorism at the border (Department of Homeland Security 2005c). Moreover, in designating Roger Mackin as counternarcotics officer and US interdiction coordinator for the DHS, Tom Ridge said on March 25, 2005, that he was "pleased that Roger Mackin will be joining our team at the Department of Homeland Security to help us combat this serious threat posed by drug traffickers who are violating our laws and may be helping terrorism flourish across our borders" (Department of Homeland Security 2005b). Thus, because controlling illegal drugs is a hypothetical component of "securing" the border, it is important to look at the effect of the new border-security strategy on the policy against illegal drugs. Two particular items must be analyzed: the increased efforts of the federal government to stop the flow of illegal drugs on the border; and whether the new homeland security strategy and tactics have indeed stemmed the flow. In other words, has the investment paid off?

To answer this question requires looking first at the additional investment in combating illegal drugs. Table 8.3 shows the annual federal expenditures on drug control according to the US government's *National Drug Control Strategy* (White House 2005).

Table 8.3: US Federal Government Funding for Control of Illegal Drugs, Fiscal Years 2000–2006 (US$ Millions)

FY2000	FY2001	FY2002	FY2003	FY2004	FY2005	FY2006
9,900.0	9,418.6	10,573.9	11,019.1	11,867.4	12,162.7	12,431.1

Source: White House, *The National Drug Control Strategy* (2005).

The DHS Office of Field Operations has over 2,500 Customs and Border Protection officers specifically identified with drug enforcement, in addition to the drug enforcement–related activities of the DEA (11,000), the Border Patrol (11,000), the Office of Information

Technology, the Office of Air and Marine Operations, and other agencies. The federal government has also created a host of new border programs to deal with the issue. For example, many Customs and Border Protection programs have drug law enforcement as part of their mandate, including the Consolidated National Inspectional Anti-Terrorism Contraband Enforcement Team, the Passenger Enforcement Rover Team, the Manifest Review Unit, and the Passenger Analytical Unit (White House 2005).

In general the US government has sought to conflate the issue of illegal drugs with national security, and to invest greater resources and dedicate a large part of its workforce to enforcing drug laws on the border. This level of investment has to be contrasted with the return. The return can be measured in terms of the availability of illegal drugs in the United States, their prices, and their purity. According to a report by the Office of Drug Control Policy, the availability of the five major drugs (cocaine, crack cocaine, heroin, methamphetamines, and marijuana) has generally experienced an upward trend. Moreover, although in certain years there are increases in the price of these drugs, the generally tendency is toward lower prices, signalling increased availability, with the exception of the street price of marijuana, which seems to vary more wildly than that of the other major drugs (White House 2004). The purity of the illegal drugs available is difficult to measure because purity obeys many factors, including availability and "cutting" (diluting the quantity with additives), but in general the trend is toward greater purity.

The general lesson is that the enormous additional investment in anti-drug border security has not paid off. Almost all indicators show that illegal drugs continue to make their way across the border nearly unhindered by the new homeland security measures.

Illegal Immigration

Statistics show that the number of undocumented border crossers detained in 2004 jumped higher even as the US government heightened its security measures along the border. Although Customs and Border Protection argued that the rise in detentions is due to better border security, some border-patrol agents believe that an increase in detentions more often reflects an increased number of undocumented crossers trying to enter the United States than a more effective interception and detention policy. Specifically, both the president of the National Border

Patrol Council, T. J. Bonner, and Wayne Cornelius, of the Center for Comparative Immigration Studies of the University of California at San Diego, have argued that after President Bush announced his support for a national guest-worker program the number of Mexicans who rushed to the border to take advantage of this opportunity went up, resulting in more arrests by the Border Patrol (Berestein 2006). Moreover, between 2000 and 2004 the number of arrests each year along the US–Mexico border remained at over one million (see table 8.4), a pattern that was likely maintained in 2005 and 2006. Every sector of the Border Patrol along the US–Mexico border has experienced an increase in the number of detentions of undocumented border crossers.

Table 8.4: Number of Arrests of Undocumented Border Crossers by the Border Patrol, 2000–04

2000	2001	2002	2003	2004
1,814,729	1,387,486	1,062,279	1,046,422	1,241,089

Note: Final, reliable figures for the years 2005 and 2006 are not yet available.

Sources: Immigration and Naturalization Service. "Enforcement, Fiscal Year 2000." *2000 Statistical Yearbook of the Immigration and Naturalization Service* (2001), and "Enforcement, Fiscal Year 2001." *2001 Statistical Yearbook of the Immigration and Naturalization Service* (2002); Office of Immigration Statistics, Department of Homeland Security. *2002 Yearbook of Immigration Statistics* (2003), *2003 Yearbook of Immigration Statistics* (2004), and *2004 Yearbook of Immigration Statistics* (2005).

Overall, the statistical evidence shows that the number of undocumented border crossers has not diminished since new homeland security measures went into effect, and perhaps as many as 500,000 of those who try in any given year are able to enter US cities throughout the country illegally. Instead, these measures have had three major effects on the border. First, they have increased the risks of slipping across the border for all undocumented workers. Beefed-up security on the US side of the border has not stopped undocumented border crossers from coming to the border. They have simply shifted their crossing locations to places that are less likely to be watched by the Border Patrol. This shift has led to an increase in the number of those crossing in the more dangerous parts of New Mexico and Arizona, and the consequent deaths of perhaps as many as 2,500 undocumented border crossers since 1994, hundreds of them in the Arizona desert every year (Eschbach, Hagan, and Rodríguez 2003).

Table 8.5: Number of Deaths of Undocumented Border Crossers, Fiscal Years 2000–05

FY2000	FY2001	FY2002	FY2003	FY2004	FY2005
383	336	320	346	330	464

Source: Congressional Research Service. *Border Security: The Role of the US Border Patrol* (2005).

The second effect of the new measures is the concentration of the human-smuggling business in the hands of organized criminals. Because it is increasingly more difficult to cross the border alone with no previous knowledge of the terrain, criminal groups have taken advantage of the increased risk to monopolize human smuggling and turn it into an exceedingly profitable business, with potential earnings of up to several billion US dollars a year. Multiplying any of the arrest numbers from table 8.4 by the average price of US$ 2,000 paid by illegal migrants to a coyote (human smuggler) immediately reveals the billions of US dollars that can be made smuggling undocumented crossers toward the United States. Thus border crossers adjust by using the services of human smugglers as much as human smugglers adapt by charging higher fees, given the higher risks of getting caught.

Terrorism and the Border

Part of the success of the new security measures, including increased patrolling of the border between the ports of entry, is the detention of an increased number of unauthorized immigrants, some of whom are presumed to have the intention of harming the United States. Since illegal immigration is now enmeshed with the rhetoric of border security, it is pertinent to ask whether the added efforts and costs of patrolling the border to control illegal immigration have resulted in a number of alleged terrorists being captured. A quick look through various Internet news sites shows hundreds of pieces claiming the capture of terrorists, or of "Arab-looking" men, trying to cross the border illegally into the United States. A good example is a piece from a right-wing British newspaper entitled "Arab Terrorists 'Are Getting into the US over Mexican Border'" (Coleman 2004). Most of the websites that disseminate such claims tend to be vigilante, conservative or anti-immigrant, and very often tend to cite each other or the words of government law-enforcement officials complaining about homeland security and giving anecdotal or undocumented evidence. The reality is that not a single credible, apprehended unauthorized immigrant has been successfully labelled a terrorist. Since 9/11 there have been no credible claims that a terrorist has entered the United States across the Mexican border, even though nearly 50 percent of all apprehended unauthorized crossers are now "other than Mexicans" (also known as OTMs). Overall, the added security measures have not resulted in the detection of terrorist activity occurring on the US–Mexico border.

CONCLUSIONS

Two important conclusions are drawn to answer the questions set out at the beginning of this chapter. First, border concerns have not gone away, despite the enormous investment that the US government has made to secure the border. Illegal drugs are still being brought across the border in sufficient amounts to satisfy the enormous market in the United States, illegal immigration continues unabated, and, although several hundred individuals have been detained as terrorist suspects, the definition of "terrorist" is, arguably, so broad that it may be doubted that most of these individuals truly intended to "hurt America." The investment, therefore, has not necessarily paid off.

The second, and perhaps more interesting, conclusion is that, although there was a slowdown in cross-border business during the weeks immediately following 9/11, business has returned to normal and, in fact, is experiencing a renewed era of growth. Although there were some new costs to complying with new US border-security requirements, these costs have been almost fully absorbed. In some ways the new measures have made it easier to cross the border. A quick glance at how long it takes to cross at the busiest southern ports of entry shows that the current times may be slightly lower than those that were standard before 9/11. More gates have been built, more designated commuter lanes have been created, and, as trucks and drivers begin to function within the C-TPAT system, their waiting times are coming down.

All in all, agents along the border—legitimate and illegitimate, legal and criminal—have adjusted to the new structures. Businesses have complied with the new rules and absorbed the new costs, which in turn has helped a large number to take their merchandise across more efficiently under a new inspections regime. Shoppers and tourists have returned, putting pressure on the authorities to be even more efficient in checking border crossers. The government has responded by adding new designated commuter lanes, opening new crossing lanes, and hiring new inspection agents to expedite border crossings. Students have gone back to school under more stringent rules governing their student visas. Drug dealers have become more efficient smugglers by stepping up their efforts to corrupt agents and preparing better vehicles for smuggling. Human-smuggling chains have adjusted their prices and undocumented border crossers rely increasingly on them. The number of deaths has continued to increase under the new border-patrolling establishment. Terrorists have not found the border any more attractive than they found US airports of entry for entering the country.

Thus the new normalcy of the border implies a new distribution of costs and of benefits, and a new order that requires all border crossers to adjust to the new structure and to place new demands on it. In this interplay the only result has been that costs are now higher for all players; that benefits have flowed both to the bureaucracy and to criminal agents; and that the border has a new normalcy.

More work is needed to understand how the theoretical model of the border advanced in this chapter applies to the US–Mexico border. However, preliminarily, we see that the centralized decision-making of a government can severely affect the way in which border agents interact, although some areas are more deeply affected than others. Market flows have a staying power that allows a strong adaptation to a new system. Local political clout and autonomy, however, are more deeply affected, while culture is resilient for different reasons and is less affected by systemic changes, at least in the short term. Overall, change is gradual and any theoretical effort to understand what is happening on the US–Mexico border is welcome in a place where it is easy to lose sight of the historical trends when under the influence of short-sighted policies.

LITERATURE CITED

Bear, Dan. 2003. "Securing Our Borders" [online]. (November 6) www.usbc.org/profiles/profiles2003/1103secureborders.htm [consulted December 1, 2005].

Berestein, Leslie. 2006. "Border Arrests Surge in S.D. Region." *San Diego Union-Tribune* [online]. (April 15) www.polisci.ucsd.edu/cornelius/news/SDUT-4-16-06.pdf#search=%22amnesty%20border%20arrests%20higher%22.

Bureau of Transportation Statistics, Department of Transportation [US]. 2005. "Surface Trade with Canada and Mexico Rose 12.3 Percent from August 2004 to a Record High in August 2005" [online]. www.bts.gov/press_releases/2005/bts050_05/html/bts050_05.html [consulted November 1, 2005].

BusinessWeek. 2005. "A Truck-Full of Troubles" [online]. (June 20) www.businessweek.com/magazine/content/05_25/b3938116_mz009.htm [consulted October 25, 2005].

City of El Paso Department of Economic Development. 2001–02. *El Paso Profile and Economic Summary* [online]. www.elpasotexas.gov/econdev [consulted December 1, 2005].

City of Laredo. 2004. *Economic Activity, 1999–2004* [online]. www.cityoflaredo.com [consulted December 1, 2005].

Coleman, Julian. 2004. "Arab Terrorists 'Are Getting into the US over Mexican Border.'" *Sunday Telegraph* [London, UK]. (August 15).

Congressional Research Service [US]. 2005. *Border Security: The Role of the US Border Patrol* [online]. (May 10) www.fas.org/sgp/crs/homesec/RL32562.pdf#search=%22CRS%20Report%20for%20Congress%20%E2%80%9CBorder%20Security%3A%20The%20Role%20of%20the%20US%20Border%20Patrol%E2%80%9D%22.

Customs and Border Protection [US]. 2005a. "C-TPAT Importer Security Criteria" [online]. www.cbp.gov/xp/cgov/import/commercial_enforcement/ctpat/security_guideline/ [consulted December 1, 2005].

Customs and Border Protection [US]. 2005b. "Protecting Our Borders Against Terrorism" [online]. www.cbp.gov/xp/cgov/toolbox/about/mission/cbp.xml [consulted December 1, 2005].

DAMF Consultants Inc. 2005. *The Cumulative Impact of US Import Compliance Programs at the Canada/U.S. Land Border on the Canadian Trucking Industry: Final Report*. DAMF Consultants Inc. in association with L.-P. Tardif & Associates.

Department of Commerce, Foreign and Commercial Service, and Department of State [US]. 2005. "Baja California's Border After September 11" [online]. strategis.ic.gc.ca/epic/internet/inimr-ri.nsf/en/gr-79344e.html

Department of Homeland Security [US]. 2004. "2004 Budget in Brief" [online]. www.dhs.gov/interweb/assetlibrary/FY_2004_BUDGET_IN_BRIEF.pdf.
———. 2005. *DHS Organization* [online]. (February 25) www.dhs.gov/dhspublic/display?theme=10&content=3240 [consulted October 20, 2005].
———. 2005b. Press release [on-line]. (March 25) www.dhs.gov/dhspublic/display?content=535 [consulted October 20, 2005].
———. 2005c. *Homeland Security Budget* [online]. www.dhs.gov/dhspublic/interapp/press_release/press_release_0541.xml [consulted October 19, 2005].
Department of State [US]. 2003. *Destination USA: New Procedures* [online]. www.unitedstatesvisas.gov/visapolicy/procedures.html [consulted December 1, 2005].
Emerson, Robert. 2004. "Working with 'Key Incidents.'" *Qualitative Research Practice*, ed. Clive Seale et al. London: Sage Publications, 457–72.
Eschbach, Karl, Jacquelin Hagan, and Néstor Rodríguez. 2003. "Deaths During Undocumented Migration: Trends and Policy Implication in the New Era of Homeland Security." Paper presented at the 26th Annual National Legal Conference on Immigration and Refugee Policy, Washington, DC, April; also published in *In Defense of the Alien* 26, 37–52.
Ghaddar, Suad, and Cynthia Brown. 2005. "The Cross-Border Mexican Shopper: A Profile." *Research Review* 12:2, 46–50.
Government Accounting Office [US]. 2005. *Homeland Security: Overview of Homeland Security Management Challenges*. Washington, DC: General Accounting Office, 2–4.
Immigration and Naturalization Service [US]. 2001. "Enforcement, Fiscal Year 2000." *2000 Statistical Yearbook of the Immigration and Naturalization Service* [online]. uscis.gov/graphics/shared/aboutus/statistics/ENF00yrbk/ENF2000text.pdf.
———. 2002. "Enforcement, Fiscal Year 2001." *2001 Statistical Yearbook of the Immigration and Naturalization Service* [online]. uscis.gov/graphics/shared/aboutus/statistics/ENF2001text.pdf
Johnson, Benjamin, and Margaret D. Stock. 2003. "The Lessons of 9/11: A Failure of Intelligence, Not Immigration Law." *Immigration Policy Focus* 2:3, 1–14.
Migration Policy Institute. 2002. "Chronology of Events Since September 11, 2001, Relating to Immigration and National Security" [online]. www.migrationinformation.org/chronology.pdf [consulted December 1, 2005].
———. 2004. "The Foreign Born from Mexico in the United States As Percentage of Total County Population, 2000" [online]. www.migrationinformation.org/FB_maps/Mexico.pdf [consulted December 1, 2005].
Office of Immigration Statistics, Department of Homeland Security [US]. 2003. *2002 Yearbook of Immigration Statistics* [online]. uscis.gov/graphics/shared/statistics/yearbook/2002/Yearbook2002.pdf.

Office of Immigration Statistics, Department of Homeland Security [US]. 2004. *2003 Yearbook of Immigration Statistics* [online]. uscis.gov/graphics/shared/statistics/yearbook/2003/2003Yearbook.pdf.

———. 2005a. *2004 Yearbook of Immigration Statistics* [online]. uscis.gov/graphics/shared/statistics/yearbook/YrBk04En.htm.

———. 2005b. "Southwest Border Apprehensions." *Immigration Monthly Statistical Report Fiscal Year 2005*, July 2005 [online]. uscis.gov/graphics/shared/aboutus/statistics/msraug05/SWBORD.htm.

Office of Management and Budget [US]. 2006. "Department of Homeland Security" [online]. www.whitehouse.gov/omb/budget/fy2005/homeland.html.

Smitherman, Laura. 1997. "Opposition to Military on Border Grows." *El Paso Times* [online]. (July 13) www.lulac.org/Issues/Immigran/Military.html [consulted December 1, 2005].

State of California. 2004. "Foreign Trade Through California Ports, 1979 to 2003." *California Statistical Abstract 2004* [online]. www.dof.ca.gov/html/fs_data/STAT-ABS/tables/k10.xls [consulted December 1, 2005].

UPI. 2004. "Bush Border Move May Win Votes" [online]. (August 10) www.hispaniconline.com/pol&opi/article.html?SMCContentInd [consulted December 1, 2005].

University of Arizona Economic and Business Research Center. 2005. *Current Indicators* [online]. (March 30) ebr.bpa.arizona.edu/indicators/curindic.aspx?series=az_ret [consulted November 30, 2005].

White House, The. 2004. *The Price and Purity of Illicit Drugs: 1981 Through the Second Quarter of 2003*. Washington, DC: The White House.

———. 2005. *National Drug Control Strategy* [online]. www.whitehousedrugpolicy.gov/publications/policy/06budget/06budget.pdf [consulted October 20, 2005].

Wright, Bruce, Gail Lewis Howard, and Scott Davis. 2002. *Economic Impact of Increased Border Security*. Office of Economic Development, University of Arizona, and Office of Economic Development and Constituent Outreach, Arizona State University [online]. oed.arizona.edu/pubs/regional-development/pubs/EconomicImpactofIncreasedBorderSecurity.ppt#1 [consulted December 1, 2005].

CHAPTER 9

MANAGING US–MEXICO TRANSBORDER COOPERATION ON LOCAL SECURITY ISSUES AND THE CANADIAN RELATIONSHIP

José M. Ramos

This chapter analyzes some concerns and challenges for US–Mexico cross-border cooperation on security issues, with particular emphasis on the experience of the San Diego–Tijuana region. The following three questions are discussed. Why is the Mexico–US border, particularly the Tijuana–San Diego region, important in relation to security issues? What main challenges to transborder management of security issues will occur in the coming years? Can the experience of US–Canada transborder cooperation on security issues be used to improve transborder cooperation on local security issues between Mexico and the United States?

The main argument presented here is that the different perspectives on transborder security cooperation of Mexico and the United States may reduce the level of cooperation between them in the long term. For Mexico it is more important to protect the regular flow of Mexican labour into the United States, in order to promote economic growth. For the United States, in contrast, these migrants are one of the main bilateral security concerns. In this context Canada–US border cooperation on security issues may provide a lesson that would promote a better long-term relationship between Mexico and the United States. Such an improved relationship would depend on US acknowledgment of the strategic importance of the US–Mexico border to Mexico's economic growth and development. Both security and development are necessary to stimulate Mexico's regional and national economies.

The North American Free Trade Agreement (NAFTA) has brought Mexico, the United States, and Canada significantly closer. However, bilateral dealings with the United States continue to be the preferred option of both the other countries.

OVERVIEW OF THE MEXICO–CANADA RELATIONSHIP

Relations among the three countries of North America are, in general, reasonably good. Neither Canada nor Mexico supported the United States in the Iraq war and Canada recently declined to participate in US plans for missile defence, decisions that have caused some strains in US relations with both Canada and Mexico. However, the interdependence of the countries of North America makes it imperative for differences to be put aside and for the countries to work together on many issues.

Table 9.1 outlines the different priorities of Mexico, Canada, and the United States. The main difference between Mexico, on the one hand, and the United States and Canada on the other is that Mexico is a developing country. For Mexico the main priority must be to strive for social and economic development within the economic integration framework of NAFTA.

Clearly, security is important in Mexico's bilateral relationship with the United States, but it has other social and economic priorities that emphasize the importance of North American integration. If the standard of living in Mexico fails to improve under NAFTA, the integration process will be questioned. In this context the experience of the European Union (EU) in embedding a social charter in public policy may be important for Mexico. This leads to a central question: if Mexico negotiated a social charter with the United States and Canada, would this reduce Mexican immigration into the United States? The EU's experience offers two key policy lessons. First, structural changes begin at home. Second, targeted investments of external resources can reinforce good domestic-development strategies. Ultimately a combination of these two strategies has proved beneficial for all the EU's member states. Two approaches based on the experience of EU integration have been proposed for North America: the creation of a North American Development Fund that would involve all three countries in NAFTA; and either an expansion of the substantive and geographic mandate of the North American Development Bank or the creation of targeted funds for infrastructure development through other multilateral institutions (Woodrow Wilson Center 2005).

Table 9.1: Main Concerns of Mexico, Canada, and the United States

	Mexico	Canada	USA
Security		✓	✓
development	✓		
Environment	✓		
Social concerns	✓	✓	✓
Border issues	✓	✓	✓
Local development	✓		
Political stability	✓		
Public security	✓	✓	✓
Terrorism		✓	✓

Figure 9.1: Mexican Challenges under Trilateral Cooperation

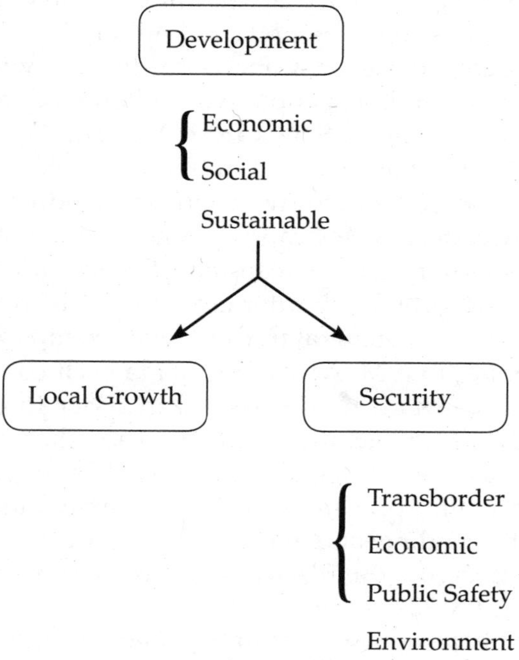

Although security is the priority of the US government, a common agenda for improving the linkage between security and development for the three countries is possible. To this end it is important to discuss what would constitute the main political and economic conditions for such a common agenda, given each country's different conditions.

The concept of a more integrated North America can be difficult to fully comprehend. With the Canada–Mexico bilateral relationship still relatively underdeveloped, North America is generally seen merely as the sum of two separate relationships: Canada–United States and United States–Mexico (Abizaid Bucio 2004). Certainly, Canada is highly dependent on access to the US market: about 70 percent of Canadian GDP crosses the border and 50 percent of Canadian manufactured exports are intercompany trade with the United States. Yet it is in Canada's interest to invest more time and resources in the North American relationship. At present, however, problems that clearly affect all three countries are dealt with bilaterally rather than collectively, and all three countries demonstrate little interest in establishing operational or institutional connections with one another. NAFTA has brought Mexico, the United States, and Canada significantly closer, but bilateral dealings with the United States continue to be the preferred option.

The US–Mexico and the US–Canada borders are vitally important. Each year some 300 million people, 90 million cars, and 4.3 million trucks cross into the United States from Mexico. At the US–Canada frontier the yearly totals are 110 million people and 15 million commercial shipments, and the two countries conduct US$ 1.3 billion in trade each day (Consejo Mexicano de Asuntos Internacionales 2003). Under this transborder scenario, can the US government both control border security and promote border crossings? Given the importance of Canada and Mexico's bilateral trading relationships with the United States, it is essential that Mexico and Canada each collaborate closely with the United States on border issues, in order to ensure the safe and efficient flow of people and goods between them. In this context the three countries share three broad goals: (1) strengthening border security to counter and prevent terrorism; (2) maintaining trade flows that benefit both sending and receiving countries; and (3) ensuring orderly migration across their borders (Consejo Mexicano de Asuntos Internacionales 2003, 32).

The current bilateral relationship between Canada and the United States is larger and more complex than ever, with the two countries sharing fundamental beliefs and values, along with the world's largest trading relationship. Canada, however, demonstrates only minimal interest in Mexico's agenda vis-à-vis the United States, and although the potential for the Canada–Mexico relationship is growing, it is still largely unrealized (Canadian Foundation for the Americas 2002).

Nonetheless, the Canada–US border-security experience may be of interest to Mexicans in seeking answers to questions about promoting economic border development, as well as maintaining and strengthening border security. Clearly, transborder cooperation and planning is the best alternative for long-term economic development. Canada can contribute to Mexico's development through knowledge-sharing, specifically, enhanced cooperation on science and technology, the development of economic clusters, the promotion of small- and medium-sized enterprises as business incubators, and linking public and academic centres for research and development with productive entities, as in the case of the National Research Council's Industrial Research Assistance Program (Abizaid Bucio 2004).

From a Canadian perspective, Mexico, despite its poverty levels and disparities in income and regional development, is a large, vibrant market with a highly educated and capable workforce. Mexico is gradually overtaking Canada's North American market share not only in low-end (assembly-plant) manufacturing but also in heavy manufacturing and high-technology industries. Competition aside, Mexico also presents a huge and timely opportunity for Canadian trade and investment. Canadian prospects are especially opportune in the areas of agro-foods, other food-related products and services, engineering, consulting, and education (Canadian Foundation for the Americas 2002).

In general, enthusiasm in Mexico, the United States, and Canada for bilateral and trilateral cooperative security efforts depends on public perceptions that the particular national security concerns in each country are being addressed. Only an ongoing and informed public debate will create the level of support necessary for sustained cooperation (Consejo Mexicano de Asuntos Internacionales 2003, 32).

OVERVIEW OF THE TIJUANA–SAN DIEGO REGION

The US–Mexico border region is integrated in certain geographic areas. For example, much of the Texas–Mexico border region is essentially a single economic, cultural, and, to an extent, political entity, while in other geographic areas, particularly the California–Mexico region, two distinctly separate entities remain. The border relationship is extremely complex and multilayered. US–Mexico cooperation is often limited by the long and tumultuous history of relations between the two countries, by negative US perceptions of the Mexican migration phenomenon, and by security concerns around drug trafficking, crime, and corruption. In contrast, the US–Canada border can be described as politically closed but economically open. It is also culturally and socially open, in that the region is characterized by strong interpersonal relationships and family ties that straddle the border. Consequently, Mexico must overcome history and negative perceptions to increase its economic integration with the United States and Canada. Improving capacity at the local level is essential for increased economic integration (Canadian Foundation for the Americas 2002). In particular, the main conditions for improving Mexican capacity under trilateral cooperation may be summarized as (1) acquiring better knowledge of regional globalization; (2) achieving a political consensus on economic development; (3) designing projects, strategies, and mechanisms for international cooperation; and (4) promoting a better understanding of local, regional, national, and international issues.

The San Diego–Tijuana region is one of the major gateways for imports and exports between Mexico and the United States. It is also a major area of drug trafficking. Since 1998 Mexico has supplied approximately 60 percent of the cocaine and 20 percent of the heroin sold in the United States. Almost 60 percent of the narcotics and chemical drugs destined for the United States cross the border between Baja California and California (General Accounting Office 2003). Thus the region is important because the transnational nature of its border issues has resulted in a confluence of objectives at the border that have important implications for the United States. Many of the major border issues (drug trafficking and terrorism, for example) are essentially not "domestic" but rather transnational issues that transcend political boundaries. Addressing these complex issues requires knowledge coordination and cooperation both among US agencies and between them and their Mexican counterparts. The role of Mexican local governments is also important in managing the transnational nature of these border issues. Local governance is understood as a set of public and private mechanisms for monitoring and influencing national-security concerns.

North American economic development also begins with regional and local empowerment, since the states, provinces, and other local authorities know their areas best. One of the most significant obstacles to economic development, particularly in Mexico, is poor governance at the local level, which suffers from problems with corruption, unusually high turnover of employees, non-collection of property taxes, and the like. Without better governance, particularly improved public safety and the restoration of the rule of law, the region cannot hope to become more economically competitive either within North America or globally (Consejo Mexicano de Asuntos Internacionales 2003).

To summarize, the major concerns at the US–Mexico border are illegal activities and economic development. Therefore it is crucial to achieve a balance between security and development, despite the different priorities of Mexico, the United States, and Canada.

NEW CONCERNS FOR US–MEXICO BORDER CO-OPERATION: A SECURITY PERIMETER

The recasting of the bilateral agenda on migration between Mexico and the United States, which was well under way even before the terrorist attacks of September 11, 2001, must be reconciled with the new concept of "homeland security" in the United States. Some observers argue that the fight against terrorism is the natural enemy of controlled migration, while others argue that, now more than ever, North America needs to address this issue trilaterally. Migration, security, energy, and labour are among the issues that have the greatest impact on local border cities. Issues such as combating organized crime, drug and human trafficking, and cross-border flows of contraband have already been subjected to intensive cooperative efforts. Currently, however, identifying the problems and opportunities for cooperation under the different political and social systems of Mexico and the United States is the major concern.

In the case of border policy one major concern and challenge is how to achieve equilibrium between improved border security and economic and social integration in border regions. In other words border security should not disrupt trade and commerce along the border. Of particular concern are waiting times at ports of entry that delay the flow of trade and commerce by as much as two hours at the busiest times of day. Security and trade are linked. Increased security will facilitate trade if there is confidence and trust in the measures taken on both sides of the border. Any steps that are taken must be in the context of a risk-assessment model that is aimed at moving low-risk goods and people while focusing resources on threat mitigation. Management of the border on the basis of risk implies new approaches and techniques that allow clearance procedures for goods and people before they arrive at the physical border (Coalition for Secure and Trade-Efficient Borders 2004).

Clearly, addressing security and commerce along the borders requires coordination and cooperation between US and Mexican agencies. The question, however, is whether the governments of the United States and Mexico have the same priorities on border-security issues. Over the past fifty years US and Mexican border authorities have been concerned with managing legitimate cross-border commerce and travel while deterring illegal immigration and the smuggling of drugs and other contraband. Before September 11, 2001, waiting times at the San Ysidro and Otay Mesa ports of entry in the San Diego District were already much longer on average than was deemed reasonable by the community and local authorities alike. The security measures taken since September 11, 2001, have altered the normal rhythm and procedures at all border crossings, which has been particularly disruptive to the San Diego–Tijuana economy, the largest and perhaps most dynamic binational region in North America (San Diego Dialogue 2001). However, those involved believe that better law enforcement and flows at the border can be accomplished based on a comprehensive partnership between the federal agencies responsible for port-of-entry operations and the regional community.

One of the binational management challenges is to identify the knowledge that has been gained about the cross-border phenomenon in recent years and apply it to the current crisis. Identifying very low risk crossers at the San Diego–Tijuana border ports is cited as being particularly important, given that the threat of terrorist penetration is especially acute along the southern border. For example, although in 2004 fewer than 10,000 individuals were apprehended entering the United States illegally from Canada, more than 1.1 million were stopped while trying to cross into the United States from Mexico. According to the US Department of Homeland Security, the vast majority of these individuals were Mexicans crossing the border for economic or family reasons. Only 3,000 to 4,000 of the approximately 100,000 OTMs ("other than Mexicans") who were apprehended were from "countries of interest" such as Somalia, Pakistan or Saudi Arabia, which have produced or been associated with terrorist cells (US Senate 2005).

In addition, research has confirmed that it is important to develop the security aspects of border crossings and that the dedicated commuter lane program (SENTRI) has shown that transparency provides a better basis for law enforcement (San Diego Dialogue 2001). Efforts to create a border that provides greater security depend on better intelligence, coordinated national efforts, and international cooperation against terrorists and other international threats. The US strategy to improve border security implies an interrelationship between federal, state, and local issues, because border security involves public security (local and state enforcement) and the prevention of terrorism and drug trafficking (federal enforcement). According to Commissioner Robert Bonner (2003), in order to safeguard the US and North American economies it is important to "reinvent the border."

The US *National Strategy for Homeland Security* involves six major initiatives on border and transportation security. The most important of these is the creation of "smart borders." The goal of this strategy is to create a "border of the future," the main elements of which are more personnel, new detection equipment, getting advanced information in automated form to manage risk, and working cooperatively with Mexico and Canada (Office of Homeland Security 2002). Accordingly, since 2002 there has been an increase in the number of personnel and the amount of equipment available for detecting potential terrorists along the borders. However, there are some questions about whether the new personnel and the bureaucracy in general understand the new border-security context. Although they may be aware that the new security approach is aimed at ensuring secure and trade-efficient borders, risk management and assessment must be at the heart of border-management systems. To deal effectively with unknown and high-risk movements of people and goods, the border must be understood in terms of control and efficiency. This does not mean the disappearance of the border. Rather, border-management systems must effectively identify and facilitate known low-risk people and goods by using pre-clearance and other procedures before they arrive at the border (Coalition for Secure and Trade-Efficient Borders 2004). To reach this goal there must be a balance between security and economic concerns, that is, individual border delays that harm productivity and increase the cost of doing business in North America. If the border is a barrier to the efficient flow of people and goods, it will directly affect not only the three countries' economic potential and quality of life but also issues such as collective rights, collaboration between the three countries, and sovereignty.

In the case of the security relationship between Mexico and Canada, there are some concerns, the answers to which must be bilateral in nature. Although Mexico shares the same economic space within NAFTA, the border issues between Mexico and the United States are significantly different from those between Canada and the United States. In addition, the dialogue on border issues between Canada and the United States is much more advanced. Indeed, this more advanced Canada–US border cooperation could serve as a model for a US–Mexico accord. However, for now the two borders are so far apart, physically and figuratively, that they require significantly different treatment (Coalition for Secure and Trade-Efficient Borders 2004). Consequently, discussing a strategy for a US–Mexico partnership is important but largely rhetorical (Woodrow Wilson Center 2005) as long as both governments have different approaches and strategies for border security and border economic development.

NEW TRILATERAL INITIATIVES TO PROMOTE SECURITY AND DEVELOPMENT

On April 20, 2005, US Senator Richard Lugar introduced the North American Cooperative Security Act (NACSA) to the Committee on Foreign Relations of the US Senate. The purpose of the bill was to enhance the mutual security and safety of the United States, Canada, and Mexico through better management, communication, and coordination. To achieve these goals, the bill advocated improved procedures for exchanging relevant security information with Mexico and Canada, improved military-to-military relations with Mexico, improved security at the US–Mexico border, establishing a database to track movements of Central American gang members between the United States, Mexico, and Central America, and requiring US government agencies to develop a strategy with their Mexican counterparts to hinder the ability of third-country nationals from using Mexico to gain illegal entry into the United States. The bill recognized that US land borders also serve as channels for illegal immigration, drugs, and other illicit items, and that, given the threat of international terrorism, they may be used by international terrorists, as suggested by reports that al-Qaeda might attempt to have its agents enter the United States illegally through Mexico.

There is, of course, tension between the economic need for the border to run quickly and smoothly ("time is money") and the concern for security, which emphasizes careful inspection of each person and vehicle to ensure that drugs, weapons, or terrorists do not get through. The major challenge is to create a border that is both secure and conducive to the rapid passage of commerce that is vital to both economies.

The United States, Mexico, and Canada released a report entitled *The Security and Prosperity Partnership of North America* on March 23, 2005. The concept of a security and prosperity partnership (SPP) was created by the leaders of the three countries when they met earlier in March. Since September 11, 2001, progress had already been made in deterring cross-border threats while maintaining the efficient movement of people and cargo across North America. The United States signed "smart border'" agreements with Canada and Mexico in December 2001 and March 2002, respectively, in which both parties agreed to improve the pre-screening of immigrants, refugees, and cargo. These agreements also included new documentation requirements and provisions for adding inspectors and updating border-security technologies. Before the United States and Canada formed a united front against terrorists crossing their mutual border they had already signed the "Smart Border/30 Point Action Plan" in 2001 concerning immigration-related issues. The action plan was designed to ensure the secure flow of people and goods, safeguard infrastructure, and provide information-sharing and coordination in the enforcement of these objectives.

By agreeing to be part of the SPP, the United States, Mexico, and Canada pledged to enhance their common security goals and improve border security. The key element of the SPP was the establishment of a common security perimeter by 2010. Members of the Independent Task Force on the Future of North America, which was coordinated by the Council on Foreign Relations, discussed a detailed set of proposals that would build on the recommendations adopted by Canadian Prime Minister Paul Martin, Mexican President Vicente Fox, and US President George W. Bush at their trilateral summit in Texas in March 2005.

The economies of both Canada and Mexico depend on increased cooperation with the United States on the issue of security. As Americans feel more and more unsafe, they will likely demand actions to increase border security. Yet, although security is an increasingly complex issue, and despite tremendous public expectations, the United States does not seem to know how to proceed or what effect its security policies will have on the Canadian and Mexican economies (Canadian Foundation for the Americas 2002).

The concerns that make border issues so difficult to address include the differing levels of development and the dissimilar governmental structures between the United States and Mexico and the United States and Canada. In effect Mexico and Canada have different levels of administrative capacity for implementing US standards of border security and trade flows, and these differing levels have affected the efficacy of the trilateral proposals that have been formulated by local and regional actors since September 11, 2001. Thus, given the new regional agenda of protecting North America and securing its borders in the fight against international terrorism, the question arises whether it is even possible for the United States and Mexico to maintain a common border-security response. The position taken by Mexican President Vicente Fox after September 11, 2001, reflects a close relationship with US President George W. Bush on matters of border security.

Some recommendations to deal with the consequences of Mexico and Canada's differing levels of administrative capacity for implementing border security and regulating flows of people and goods are included here. Among the most urgent of these is to establish procedures for managing crises at the borders, procedures that will prevent a "system crash" in the event of another major terrorist incident. In addition, in order to ensure that the new imperative to secure borders does not obstruct legitimate flows of goods, services, and people, Mexico, the United States, and Canada must put in place a NAFTA-wide security perimeter. Such a perimeter could transform internal borders, in much the same way as the Schengen Agreement has transformed borders within much of continental Europe (Rozental 2002).

The old paradigms for managing common borders in North America are becoming increasingly outmoded. The sheer volume of traffic, both people and goods, dictates that, even without the new pressures created by the threat of terrorism, new technologies, strategies, and ways of working together must be developed to manage this new reality (Consejo Mexicano de Asuntos Internacionales 2003, 27). However, because the US government and, particularly, the Department of Homeland Security continue to emphasize security over the traditional economic interaction along the US–Mexico border, it is difficult to create a new paradigm.

The EU's approach to risk management is at the heart of the "smart border" accords signed by the United States with Canada and Mexico in the wake of 9/11. If properly understood and implemented, the "smart border" concept can both enhance regional security and increase the flow of people and goods across shared frontiers. If properly managed, there would be no contradiction between enhanced security and increased integration. On the contrary, economic development would be part and parcel of security (Consejo Mexicano de Asuntos Internacionales 2003, 28–29). The proposal for an integral security approach put forth in this chapter includes balancing security and development; achieving a thorough understanding of the economic, security, social, and cultural contexts involved; reducing structural concerns regarding border management; and improving coordination and cooperation between US and Mexican agencies involved in border management, in order to decrease the current fragmentation of authority and responsibility, overlapping jurisdictions, duplication of effort, interagency rivalries and "turf battles," and the inconsistent, conflicting, or overburdened missions within single agencies.

Ultimately the success of US border security depends on several factors: human intelligence; redesigning strategic programs; a more thorough understanding of the social, economic, and cultural contexts in developing countries; a clearer analysis of the different faces of terrorism; and improving the capacity of different players to anticipate attacks (a strategic and proactive approach)—in other words, anticipating the future and improving the capacity of local intelligence. This approach to security is crucial for US border-security policy. Its new policy paradigm has, to some extent, failed to reduce border violence and, particularly, transborder vulnerability. Thus it is not without some challenges, which make the human intelligence and development approaches important elements of transborder security.

Another concern is the capacity of Mexican authorities to cope with security issues. There are concerns in a number of areas, including insufficient understanding of the challenges of border security; a limited approach to security (enforcement only); stereotypes (violation of sovereignty) to promote cooperation with US officials; lack of effective governance at the local level (corruption, high turnover of employees); the centralized government structure in which the authority for policy design and for needed resources is in Mexico City; and a shortage of intergovernmental relationships among local, state, and federal governments on Mexican border issues. Thus improved transborder cooperation in security issues is dependent to a large degree on government capacity at the local level, and on improved understanding of the issues at the local and regional levels.

CONCLUSION

The main argument of this chapter is that the different perspectives of Mexico and the United States on border security, and on the flows of people and goods at the Mexico–US border, may reduce the level of transborder cooperation on security concerns in the long term. In this context Canada-US border cooperation on security issues provides a valuable lesson. One of the most important challenges to transborder cooperation is achieving equilibrium at the US–Canada border, which revolves mainly around the movement of transport trucks, and at the US–Mexico border, which is driven mainly by the movement of people. For this to occur the United States must understand and accept that the US–Mexico border is of the utmost strategic importance to Mexico, as it is the major facilitator of economic growth and development in the region.

This chapter contributes to two of the four analytical lenses of the border model developed by Emmanuel Brunet-Jailly (2005): market forces and trade flows; and the policy activities of multiple levels of government on adjacent borders. The US–Mexico border is characterized by a close economic and commercial relationship that has undergone forced cooperation and, in some cases, transborder planning due to the effects of globalization. This has occurred despite the fact that the policy activities of multiple levels of government, both in Mexico and the United States, have different objectives and goals in relation to promoting economic growth in the face of global insecurity. This was particularly clear in the analysis of the overall border-security policy goals of the US Department of Homeland Security presented earlier.

The US government's emphasis on the priority of security along its borders has caused tremendous tensions with US border state and local governments. In this context the strategic role of local or binational local governments or key players in the private sector is essential if a balance between security and development is to be achieved along the US–Mexico border. Border-crossing delays have already had negative impacts on economic growth in the three main binational border regions of Tijuana–San Diego, Ciudad Juarez–El Paso, and Nuevo Laredo–Laredo. The long-term goal should be effective transnational, intergovernmental cooperation between Mexico and the United States that takes into account the differences on economic and border-security issues.

The Mexican government must promote development and border-security cooperation and planning. The strategic relationship between security and development is crucial for stimulating solid economic growth in times of global insecurity. It is also necessary to involve the private sector in the development and implementation of border security and cooperation. Yet, although these measures are vital to the security and prosperity of the country, there are some concerns about this development agenda. Illegal immigration, drug trafficking, the smuggling of small arms and people, organized crime, money-laundering, corruption, and environmental degradation are transnational in nature and affect the possibility of a closer security relationship.

The new security context since September 11, 2001, has necessitated a re-examination of existing practices and mechanisms for cross-border collaboration in law enforcement and security. For example, as noted earlier, measures must be taken to facilitate the passage of low-risk goods and people across borders. This will not only strengthen Canadian, Mexican, and US security and intelligence, immigration and refugee determination and border processing but also improve governance performance at the local level and strengthen institutional capacity to train local government officials, particularly on the Mexican side of the border. The key word is "balancing," whether in relation to border security, trade facilitation, or border crossings, because an emphasis on security does not reduce border insecurity. This is the challenge for Mexico.

The concept of a security perimeter for North America would not mean the elimination of the US–Mexico border or the Canada–US border, nor would it mean Canadian or Mexican adoption of US policies. Rather, it is a collaborative and integrated approach that would improve the coordination and management of existing practices and establish new measures to ensure the protection of all North American citizens by focusing security resources on higher risk areas through three integrated lines of security.

LITERATURE CITED

Abizaid Bucio, Olga. 2004. "The Canada–Mexico Relationship: The Unfinished Highway." FOCAL policy paper. Ottawa: Canadian Foundation for the Americas [online]. www.focal.ca/pdf/canada_mexico04.pdf [consulted January 13, 2007.]

Bonner, Robert C. 2003. "Remarks: Safety and Security in North American Trade." Washington, DC: Center for Strategic and International Studies.

Brunet-Jailly, Emmanuel. 2005. "Understanding Borders: A Model of Border Studies." Paper submitted to Border Regions in Transition Conference VII, Crossing Cultures, Crossing Disciplines, Crossing Scales, Jerusalem, Israel, January 9.

Canadian Foundation for the Americas. 2002. *The New Dynamics of North America: US–Mexico Relations and the Border Economy*. Public Policy Forum Executive Study Tour, Ottawa, Southern United States, and Northern Mexico, May 10–17. Ottawa: Canadian Foundation for the Americas.

Coalition for Secure and Trade-Efficient Borders. 2004. *Rethinking Our Borders: Statement of Principles* [online]. www.cmemec.ca/national/documents/bordercoalition.pdf [consulted July 21, 2005].

Consejo Mexicano de Asuntos Internacionales. 2003. *North America: Secure and Efficient Borders*. Monterrey, Mexico: Consejo Mexicano de Asuntos Internacionales.

General Accounting Office [US]. 2003. *Challenges Facing the Department of Homeland Security in Balancing its Border Security and Trade Facilitation Missions*. Statements by Richard M. Stana, director, Homeland Security and Justice Issues, before the Subcommittee on Infrastructure and Border Security, Select Committee on Homeland Security, House of Representatives, June 16.

Office of Homeland Security. 2002. *The National Strategy for Homeland Security*. Washington, DC: Office of Homeland Security.

Ramos, Jose M. 2004a. "Challenges on Border Security along the US–México Border." Paper presented at conference on Mexico Border Security, Office of External Research, Bureau of Intelligence and Research, Department of State, Washington, DC, September 17.

———. 2004b. *La Gestión y Cooperación Transfronteriza en la Frontera México–Estados Unidos en un Marco de Inseguridad Global: Problemas y Desafíos*. Mexico City: CONACYT, Editorial Porrua, Consejo Mexicano de Asuntos Internacionales, AC y H. Cámara de Diputados.

———, and Ofelia Woo. 2004. *Seguridad Nacional y Fronteriza en la Relación México–Estados Unidos-Canadá*. Guadalajara, Mexico: Universidad de Guadalajara.

Rozental, Andres. 2002. "It's Time to Expand NAFTA." *San Diego Union-Tribune* (March 21).

San Diego Dialogue. 2001. "Tijuana Trabaja: Who Crosses the Border, 2001." Project overview, preliminary information, October.

———. 2002. "Identifying Low Risk Crossers in order to Enhance Security at Ports of Entry into the United States." Forum Fronterizo Briefing Paper, South County Economic Development Council, January.

Senate Standing Committee on Foreign Affairs [Canada]. 2004. *Mexico: Canada's Other Partner in North America: Third Report*. Ottawa: Senate Standing Committee on Foreign Affairs.

US Senate. 2005. Statements by Senator Richard Lugar, *Congressional Record*, Statements on Introduced Bills and Joint Resolutions (p. s4024) (April 20).

Woodrow Wilson Center. 2005. *The United States and Mexico: Forging a Strategic Partnership, Mexico.* Report of the Study Group on US–Mexico Relations. Washington, DC: Mexico Institute, Woodrow Wilson International Center for Scholars.

CHAPTER 10

ANTI-TERRORISM IN NORTH AMERICA: IS THERE CONVERGENCE OR DIVERGENCE IN CANADIAN AND US LEGISLATIVE RESPONSES TO 9/11 AND THE US–CANADA BORDER?

Patrick J. Smith

In early October 2005 members of the Minutemen Civil Defense [*sic*] Corps began patrolling the Canada–US border in Whatcom County, Washington State. Mirroring similar efforts on the borders of Arizona and California with Mexico in April 2005, they said that their mission was to ensure that illegal immigrants, drug smugglers, and terrorists did not enter the United States "because the government . . . [were] not doing their job" (Turnbull and Tu 2005). The group's initiative had begun in mid-July 2005, following the discovery of a major drug-running tunnel between Langley, British Columbia, and Whatcom County, and the subsequent arrest of drug dealers (Lewis 2005; see also Gallagher 2005; Millage 2005; Ritter 2005).

At the same time the Fifteenth Annual Summit of the Pacific Northwest Economic Region (PNWER) was being held in Seattle. Its participants included Christine Gregoire, governor of Washington State, and Anne McLellan, then deputy prime minister and security and emergency preparedness minister of Canada (Pacific Northwest Economic Region 2005). The PNWER Summit involved three policy tours, one of which was at Blaine, Washington, at the British Columbia–Washington State border crossing, part of the PNWER Border Issues Working Group's mandate "to get people and goods across the US–Canadian border faster and with less hassle, without jeopardizing homeland security" (Virgin 2005).

The juxtaposition of these efforts alternatively to squeeze and to ease cross-border flows in "Cascadia," the cross-border region encompassing British Columbia, Washington State, and several of their neighbours (Smith 2002), highlighted some of the policy challenges facing cross-border enthusiasts and governmental agencies in the fifth year after the terrorist attacks against the United States on September 11, 2001. Central to a resolution of the issues of security and open access was the question of converging or diverging security responses to the matter of the US–Canada border, as when, for example, proposals to fence and guard the border resurfaced in late 2006, albeit their timing was too close to the US mid-term elections to be able to weigh their short-term significance (Alberts 2006).

This chapter underlines arguments for increasing the legislative and policy convergence that exists between Canada and the United States in the area of security, particularly border security, a stance enhanced since the election in 2006 of the Conservative government in Canada under Prime Minister Stephen Harper. A focus on two primary analytical lenses—market forces and trade flows; and the policy activities of multiple levels of government—leads to the suggestion that increased security results from growing government interactions across the border in matters of governance and security.

Several questions currently dominate debates about national security legislation in Canada and the United States after September 11, 2001. However, two questions on how such legislation has affected their common border stand out. Has there been policy divergence or convergence in Canadian and US legislative responses to 9/11 and its aftermath? Have security concerns led to the potential for greater cross-border integration? The basic premise of this chapter is that there are three current outcomes of debates around the still relatively new anti-terrorism legislation in Canada and the United States: (1) an increased degree of collective security, with considerably more tools for security intelligence agencies in both countries; (2) an increased convergence on security policy, at least in comparative legislative language; and (3) an ongoing question about whether such conclusions represent greater potential for increased "continentalist" responses to security across the Canada–US border in the name of anti-terrorism, public safety, homeland security, and patriotism, or whether there remains an identifiable divergence on matters of defence and security.

CANADIAN GOVERNMENTS AND RELATIONS WITH THE UNITED STATES, 1984–2006

For many observers the foreign and domestic policies of the Conservative governments of Brian Mulroney, prime minister from 1984 to 1993, gave impetus to the view that Canada was becoming increasingly subordinate to US imperialism (Nossal 1997, 62). The policy record of the Mulroney years—the Canada–US Free Trade Agreement (FTA), the pursuit of deregulation, the elimination of some elements of the welfare state, and the embrace of a more hawkish foreign policy—illustrated, according, for example, to Martin (1993, 272–73), that Mulroney had "closed down the Canadian dream" of autonomy and independence.

Following four months in which Kim Campbell was Conservative prime minister, the Liberal governments of Jean Chrétien, prime minister from 1993 to 2003, were also characterized by the concerted pursuit of neoliberal trade policy that was considerably in step with that of the United States, particularly with respect to hemispheric free trade in the Americas. However, clashes over such issues as softwood lumber and energy came to plague the cross-border relationships between US President George W. Bush and Chrétien, and between Bush and Chrétien's fellow-Liberal successor, Paul Martin. This found expression at the Asia–Pacific Economic Cooperation (APEC) summit in Busan, South Korea, in mid-November 2005, where Prime Minister Martin complained to Bush, President Vicente Fox of Mexico, and President Alejandro Toledo of Peru that "you cannot have free trade where one partner—when a decision goes against it—simply says, we're going to ignore it" (Laghi 2005, A7).

In contrast, when Prime Minister Stephen Harper's Conservative government, which took office in February 2006, announced its policies in the Throne Speech in April, it envisioned swift resolution of the softwood lumber issue (achieved in September) and stated its commitment to being part of the war on terrorism, indicating a shift in the Canada–US working relationship toward more convergent goals. Harper's speech to the UN General Assembly in September 2006 also clearly emphasized a shared Canada–US vision on the war on terrorism (Edwards 2006).

Nevertheless, under Conservative and Liberal governments alike, some aspects of Canadian foreign policy in the early years of the twenty-first century deviated from the "US-friendly" version initially articulated by Brian Mulroney. Most notable were Canada's refusal to contribute troops to the US-led war in Iraq, the adoption of a "human security agenda" that espoused the virtues of multilateralism and the use of "soft power," the decision in 2005 not to join the US Missile Defense Initiative, and continuing Canadian objections to the US "mandatory passport," or PASS card system, which is to take effect in 2008 (see, for example, Bissett 2006 and Kane 2006).

For some the lack of balance in the Canada–US economic relationship in the early twenty-first century created vulnerability for Canada, especially with US security concerns appearing to trump trade concerns (see Smith and McBride 2004). Exports to the United States account for approximately 85 percent of Canada's total exports, while exports from the United States to Canada represent only 25 percent of US exports (Cohn 2002, 38). A report issued by the Standing Committee on Foreign Affairs and International Trade (House of Commons 2002, 14) noted that Gordon Mace, director of Inter-American Studies at the Institut québécois des hautes études internationales, had told the committee that

> the FTA and NAFTA trade deals have fundamentally and inescapably altered the foreign policy landscape. Canada's increased economic vulnerability within the "new economic management framework" . . . has "greatly decreased" Canada's leeway in bilateral relations with the United States.

This has been due, to some extent, to the unilateralism of US foreign policy, as exemplified by the Bush Administration's doctrine set out in *The National Security Strategy of the United States of America* (White House 2002). Its four main components are (1) to follow a policy of pre-emptive war if the United States is threatened by terrorists or states; (2) to pursue pre-emptive unilateral military action where a multilateral agreement is not apparent; (3) to keep military predominance beyond challenge and allow no rival to emerge; and (4) to promote democracy and freedom around the world. Teeple (2004, 183–91) has traced the deep roots of this strategy, which had been in preparation for at least ten years and for which, he argues, the events of September 11, 2001, provided a launchpad into official US policy.

Immediately after September 11 there was widespread sympathy for the United States, but President Bush's foreign policy clearly contributed to a waning of this sympathy, both in Canada and elsewhere, and it was replaced by anxiety about, and sometimes hostility to, US security policies.

In this context the assertion of an autonomous role for Canada in relation to the war in Iraq showed an impressive degree of fortitude. In May 2003 Condoleezza Rice, then US national security adviser (and now secretary of state) was reported as saying "I think there was disappointment in the United States that a friend like Canada was unable to support the United States in what we considered to be an extremely important issue for our security." Ms. Rice went on to say that the United States expected Canada, as a friend, to respond to the Iraq situation by saying, "Well, how can we help?" (Appleby 2003). That Canada was also opposed to participating in a nuclear missile defence system or in North American ballistic missile defence suggested some residual Canadian preference for alternatives, although when the missile defence issue came up again, in mid-2006, albeit in respect of Europe, Stephen Harper's Conservative government expressed renewed interest (Blanchfield 2006).

However, some have argued that Canada has more influence in Washington than is commonly believed because of the degree of Canada–US economic integration. Christopher Sands, director of the Canada Project at the Center for Security and International Studies in Washington, DC (2003, 71–74), considers that, "thanks to deepening interdependence through economic integration, Canada is not a fading power in the United States. It is instead a rising power, more important to Americans and their prosperity today than ever before in US history." However, Sands maintains, in order to be a "rising power" Canada must adopt a "strong state strategy" that includes "improving Canadian domestic security and implementing a creative counter-terrorism effort," since a "weak state strategy" would treat "the threat of international terrorism largely [as] a US concern, and [seek] to placate US pressure with minimum efforts while husbanding Canadian sovereignty and avoiding commitments to undertake new responsibilities with regard to the defence of North America." Canada's adoption of either strategy, Sands claims, would have a "decisive impact on its relationship with the United States," but the United States will view a weak state strategy as "an obstacle to progress towards greater security."

Thus, while Canada may stand to gain some leverage due to its significant trade relationship, this leverage is contingent upon greater cross-border cooperation, if not integration, with the United States on security policy. At a minimum, Canada must be seen to be mirroring US security policy in language and intent, which leaves the question of whether it has the capacity to do so and still maintain enough divergence to be identifiably Canadian.

According to the former Liberal deputy prime minister Anne McLellan, "a government's most important duty is to ensure the safety and security of its citizens." Her government's statement on national security policy, issued in April 2004 (Prime Minister's Office 2004a) identified three core national security interests: (1) protecting Canada and Canadians at home and abroad; (2) ensuring that Canada is not a base for threats to its allies; and (3) contributing to international security. It also provided a blueprint for action in six key areas: intelligence, emergency management, public health, transportation, border security, and international security. Canada's financial investment in national security under Paul Martin's Liberal government was CA$ 690 million, comprising CA$ 308 million for marine security, CA$ 137 million for "enhancing intelligence capabilities," CA$ 100 million for fingerprinting systems to be used by the Royal Canadian Mounted Police (RCMP), CA$ 85 million for governmental information systems, CA$ 30 million for an "Integrated Threat Assessment Centre," CA$ 10.31 million for face-recognition biometric passport technology, and smaller amounts (under CA$ 19.69 million in total) for a government operations centre, cybersecurity, health emergency response teams, and a critical infrastructure protection strategy (Prime Minister's Office 2004a and 2004b). The national security policy contained several other measures that expanded the policy tent and reflected some important Canadian differences: the establishment of a permanent federal–provincial/territorial forum on emergencies, to allow for regular strategic discussion of emergency management among key national players; the establishment of a National Security Advisory Council, made up of security experts external to government; and the creation of a Cross-Cultural Roundtable, comprising members of Canada's ethnocultural and religious communities (Department of National Defence 2004).

This divergent perspective appears to have continued under Harper's Conservative government. In May 2006, for example, when Public Safety and Emergency Preparedness Minister Stockwell Day announced a new set of federal emergency preparedness initiatives, he was joined by senior officials of the Canadian Red Cross, the St. John Ambulance, and the Salvation Army, not the police or security agency representatives (Department of Public Safety and Emergency Preparedness 2006).

In 2004 some media coverage assumed that "more spying" and "more secrecy" would be the likely by-products of federal elections in both Canada and the United States (MacCharles 2004). In November 2005 the Liberal government introduced Bill C-74 (the Modernization of Investigative Techniques Act), an initiative to standardize Canadian security practice on broadened access to cellphone and Internet use and users to reflect existing law in the United States (and also in the United Kingdom, Australia, and New Zealand). This too was seen by some commentators as simply the latest example of Canada–US policy convergence (Clark 2005). The official "Overview" of Bill C-74 noted the need for global cooperation to ensure security (Department of Public Safety and Emergency Preparedness 2005). Indeed, many have argued that the events of September 11, 2001, necessitate greater integration with the United States and that Canadian foreign policy must be articulated more within a North American context.

Questions surrounding how far this integration should go, within what areas it should be implemented, what its consequences might be, whether further integration is necessary, and if it is happening at all are all the subject of some debate within the current landscape of Canadian politics. A report on national security by a group of parliamentarians (Privy Council Office 2004, 14) suggested that Canada must conduct a cost-benefit analysis in order to determine in which areas "more integrated policies make sense, as well as where Canadian policies—on foreign, defence, security, and trade issues, and in affected domestic fields—ought to be different from, or even at odds with, those of its North American partners." However, the report went on to say that "this analysis must take into account cross-border effects, given how costly disruptions to established continental connections could be, potentially, raising the 'price of difference' to unacceptable levels." A seemingly key question for Canada is whether the government can walk a line that acknowledges US security concerns but also reflects the clear differences of opinion that underlie security policy-making in domestic terms. The latter part of the report's recommendation was very much in keeping with various Canadian governments' trade-focused and pro-liberalization foreign policy trajectory, which either views the trade-off of some degree of sovereignty as an acceptable cost for securing open markets and unrestricted borders, or insists, as this report does, that these trade-offs are an "expression of sovereignty."

TRADING SECURITY FOR MARKET ACCESS

In a report for the C. D. Howe Institute, Wendy Dobson (2002) advanced the proposition that, as a result of the events of September 11, 2001, the

United States was open to its friends and allies, and that Canada should take advantage of this by securing better access to the US market. Dobson argued that this was essential to Canadian economic performance but was less assured than formerly because of the US preoccupation with border security and defence. She argued that only a "big idea" would capture the attention of US decision-makers and make it possible to address US objectives while creating better economic opportunities for Canada. Having noted that "we are now deeply integrated with our large neighbour to the south through market forces and through policies of openness, such as those reflected in the Canada–US Free Trade Agreement (FTA) and the North American Free Trade Agreement (NAFTA)," she went on to argue that 9/11 illustrated that openness can create vulnerability and that US reactions to those events could damage Canada economically. She concluded that "today, even more than in the past, removing barriers to deeper bilateral integration should be high on Canada's list of interests," but achieving this would require generating US interest in a North American economic security pact, that is, in "cooperation between neighbours to produce the public goods of homeland security and economic stability that neither country can produce on its own." This must be achieved on Canadian terms, "without sacrificing political independence or distinctive institutions," and "Canada's goal should be to achieve customs-union and common-market-like integration without full-scale harmonization and the resulting erosion of political independence."

In another report for the C. D. Howe Institute, J. L. Granatstein (2002) noted that because Canada is inextricably linked to the United States economically, refusing support for US ventures such as the war on terrorism would have major costs, not all of them economic. Granatstein proposed that Canadian sovereignty would be seriously diminished if the United States acted to protect itself from attack without working with the Canadian government and the Canadian armed forces. However, since the United States will defend itself whether or not Canada cooperates fully, supports a nuclear missile defence scheme, and/or backs an expanded war on terrorism, the only question is how best to protect Canadian sovereignty: by joining in or by hanging back. Granatstein argued that there is no choice at all: "Canada must cooperate with the United States in its own interest." He went on to reinforce the notion that Canadian sovereignty consists of recognizing the inevitable by observing that "Canada's links with the United States are key to our survival as an independent and sovereign state . . . Washington's capacity to inflict pain and enforce compliance on Canada is boundless. Canadian policy must be devoted to keeping the elephant well-fed and happy." However, in retrospect it seems that the Bush Administration's responses to 9/11 have somewhat cooled the ardour of Canada's business elite, which funds the C. D. Howe Institute, for closer integration with the United States.

Indeed, the push for a grand bargain or a "big idea" approach to Canada–US relations has given way, in the face of US indifference and some Canadian second thoughts, to a more incremental approach. One aspect of this approach was the move to a "smart border," with greater collaboration on security and immigration issues. This was mainly due to the lack of US interest in either a "big deal" with Canada or a common security perimeter. The Canadian Liberal governments of Jean Chrétien and Paul Martin did not evince much enthusiasm for either of these approaches, and thus incrementalism was the more political strategy (Clarkson and Banda 2004, 22–24).

Despite occasional criticisms that Canada was not cooperating enough with the United States, rapid progress was made on certain border issues. On December 12, 2001, a Smart Border Declaration was signed by Deputy Prime Minister John Manley and US Homeland Security Director Tom Ridge (Department of Foreign Affairs and International Trade 2001). The Action Plan for Creating a Secure and Smart Border, more commonly referred to as the 30-Point Action Plan, was also signed by Manley and Ridge. The plan has four pillars: (1) the secure flow of people; (2) the secure flow of goods; (3) secure infrastructure and coordination; and (4) information-sharing in the enforcement of these objectives. The plan's progress was indicated by the expansion of FAST, a program for pre-approved, low-risk commercial traffic, and NEXUS, a program for pre-approved low-risk travellers (Customs and Revenue Agency 2003b). Another sign of its progress was Canadian participation in TOPOFF 2, an operation of the US Department of Homeland Security (DHS) and the US Department of State, in cooperation with federal, state, local, and Canadian partners, comprising a full-scale exercise and simulation, lasting five days, of how the United States (and Canada) would respond in the event of an attack on Seattle and Chicago involving weapons of mass destruction. This fulfilled Canada's commitment to conduct joint exercises (point 30 of the plan) (Department of Public Safety and Emergency Preparedness 2003). In addition, CANPASS-Air was launched at the Vancouver International Airport, making it the first airport in North America to implement iris-recognition technology (Customs and Revenue Agency 2003a; Blain 2003).

The new border system was tested when the United States went to its orange security level at the beginning of the war in Iraq in 2003. Both the FAST and NEXUS programs remained in place throughout the security alert. Strengthening anti-terrorism legislation can be viewed through the same lens. During the security alert Canada identified American priorities and sought to provide northern-border responses that were similar, at least in tone.

In the United States the USA PATRIOT Act (an acronym for its official title, Uniting and Strengthening America by Providing Appropriate Tools Required to Intercept and Obstruct Terrorism) contained, according to some commentators, "all the fundamentals of a police state" (Teeple 2004, 203). It was also passed with considerable dispatch. As described by the American Civil Liberties Union (2004)

> The Senate version of the Patriot [*sic*] Act . . . was sent straight to the floor with no discussion, debate or hearings. Many Senators complained that they had little chance to read it, much less analyze it, before having to vote. In the House hearings were held, and a carefully constructed compromise Bill emerged from the Judiciary Committee. But then, with no debate or consultation with rank-and-file members, the House leadership threw out the compromise Bill and replaced it with legislation that mirrored the Senate version. Neither discussion nor amendments were permitted, and once again members barely had time to read the thick Bill before they were forced to cast an up-or-down vote on it. The Bush Administration implied that members who voted against it would be blamed for any further attacks—a powerful threat at a time when the nation was expecting a second set of attacks to come any moment and when reports of new anthrax letters were appearing daily.

Canada moved swiftly to change its legislation to reflect the new US priorities (see Roach 2003). Two pieces of legislation were central: the Anti-Terrorism Act and the Public Safety Act. Like its US counterpart, the Anti-Terrorism Act was passed with impressive speed. It adopted a broad definition of terrorism, although, importantly, it was subsequently amended to respond to concerns that illegal political or industrial protests or expressions of political or religious belief could be defined as terrorism. It enabled the cabinet to designate groups as "terrorist" with only a limited possibility of judicial review of its decision (Roach 2003, 37), created a range of new offences (Roach 2003, 38– 46), expanded police powers, and provided for preventative arrest. A range of opposition from civil society groups and from critics inside the government produced some important changes to the legislation, suggesting more nuanced differences in the Canadian response while mirroring US concerns and its expeditious response (Roach 2003, 37).

Initial reaction to the Public Safety Act focused on the power it gave to the minister of national defence to designate certain areas as "military security zones," thus preventing demonstrations or protests from occurring. This provision was withdrawn after considerable negative response from Canadians, and an amended version of the act concentrated on airline security measures and the manufacture and transport of biological, chemical, and hazardous materials. Although some concerns over civil liberties remained, many were addressed as the legislation was progressively modified (Roach 2003, 174).

This difference between Canadian and US approaches is not insignificant. The pattern of the Canadian government's approach was for legislative proposals to mirror, to a large extent, the legislative language prevailing in the United States. When this produced considerable negative response from Canadians, amendments were made within the original legislation to take into account their opposition (a topic to which this discussion returns later).

Thus the state of Canada–US relations has partially shaped Canadian security policy. Although the issues of prioritizing security, asserting the primacy of individual rights, and achieving a satisfactory balance between these positions have long been part of the Canadian political discourse, the immediate priority had certainly shifted to dealing with international terrorism. When it became apparent that the Bush Administration was committed to the invasion of Iraq, efforts that had formerly gone into the struggle against neoliberal globalization focused instead on preventing Canadian involvement in the war. Canadian participation with the United Nations in Afghanistan preserved Canada's multilateral inclinations and, for potential critics in the United States, softened its decision not to become involved in Iraq.

Despite the apparent policy convergence on anti-terrorism, a decipherable policy divergence between Canada and the United States remains, a divergence that speaks to the continuing significance of borders and what separates each country as much as what holds them together. The legislative responses of various western democracies in the aftermath of 9/11 have included numerous similarities and some differences.

Historically Canada has tended to mirror various US security statutes and actions, including the work of the House Un-American Activities Committee in the 1950s, culminating in the USA PATRIOT Act and the Homeland Security Act. It has also mirrored British security statutes. The War Measures Act, passed in 1914, replicated the United Kingdom's Defence of the Realm Act passed the same year (De Brou and Waiser 1992, 237–39). Following the use of powers under the War Measures Act in 1970, in the "October crisis" over the Front de Libération du Québec, the Canadian Parliament subsequently amended, then repealed, the act, replacing it with the Emergencies Act, 1988, which, interestingly, takes a much broader view of the concept of "emergency" to include, for example, natural disasters (De Brou and Waiser 1992, 644–56).

The war on terrorism has now spawned a whole new set of security legislation. The remaining sections of this chapter examine the legislative responses of the United States and compare them with key components of recent Canadian anti-terrorism and security laws. They are both strikingly similar and profoundly different.

SEPTEMBER 11, 2001, AS A POLICY WINDOW: RESETTING THE CANADA–US SECURITY AGENDAS

John Kingdon (1984) suggested that the confluence of particular events (policy streams) provides opportunities (windows) where dramatic policy change may occur. Few events in recent years have been more dramatic than the events of September 11, 2001. The policy determinants afforded by these events have significantly affected the political agendas of many countries, but nowhere more obviously than in liberal democracies such as the United States and Canada.

There is an ongoing tension in liberal democracies across the policy spectrum between those who, at one extreme, might be termed strict "constructionists" with regard to the constitutional and legislative protection of human rights, and those who, at the other extreme, often see such rights as impediments to collective security and public order and who might be termed strict "securitivists." The events of 9/11 provided a significant policy window for resetting national policy agendas more in the direction favoured by the strict securitivists. The resultant rebalancing of security versus rights in countries such as the United States and Canada has not only illustrated how certain interests and values can be marginalized in the process of agenda-setting but also demonstrated the implications of problem redefinition for subsequent stages of the policy process. As Orwell (1946) noted, whoever determines the language of policy discourse appropriates a significant advantage in any subsequent decision-making.

The responses of the United States and Canada have also revealed a great deal about their convergence and divergence. Certainly their legislative responses to the 9/11 tragedies have been dominated by language that eschews much consideration of the long-term human-rights implications of action to bolster national security. On that issue there has been cross-border convergence. However, this is not to downplay the significance of the threat represented by perpetrators of international terrorist acts. Rather, it is to seek to answer the concerns of those who argue for constitutionally and legislatively established rights in such liberal democracies. Each society must find and maintain its own balance, but all nations must also consider the longer term implications of allowing short-term exigencies to determine answers to the question of security versus rights. Truncating the debate by trying to exclude dissonant voices does not serve the interests of any democracy. Indeed, ensuring, even encouraging, such voices is the very expression of a rights culture in a true democracy. In a full examination of US and Canadian legislative responses to the new war on terrorism there is room for identifying important differences across the border.

Krane and Blair (1999, 13–14) have suggested that when scholars are describing the capabilities of political actors (in their study, local governments) to influence policy agendas and policy formulation, excessive reliance on legal documents may lead to the mistaken assumption "that the legal language of constitutions and statutes accurately reflects actual practice." They describe this phenomenon, which creates several important problems in trying to unravel the scope of governmental powers and intergovernmental relations, as the "LexisNexis Fallacy." Avoiding the LexisNexis fallacy and focusing on what might actually be occurring on the ground is one place to start.

ANTI-TERRORISM LEGISLATION: US LESSONS AND QUESTIONS

The experience of the United States in finding the delicate balance between human rights and security needs has not differed much from that of Canada. Although the issue of constitutionally protected rights is of great significance in the United States, imbalances between rights and considerations of security and public order have existed. For example, notwithstanding its original powerful Bill of Rights, it took the passage of the thirteenth, fourteenth, and fifteenth Amendments after the Civil War, as well as Supreme Court decisions under the leadership of Chief Justice Earl Warren almost one hundred years later, to achieve effective "equal protection" rights. It also took some time for Americans to rebalance their rights after the excesses of the McCarthy era, when the House Un-American Activities Committee and other anti-Communist institutions secured the domination of perceived security needs in policy-making during the early years of the Cold War, although some balance was achieved.

The USA PATRIOT Act 2001

On October 24, 2001, just five weeks after the terrorist attacks on the United States, the US Congress passed the USA PATRIOT Act. The act involved changes, some small, some large, to fifteen previous acts and ran 342 pages. According to the Electronic Frontier Foundation (2001), a non-profit organization concerned with citizens' "digital" rights, the new act

> gave sweeping new powers to both domestic law enforcement and international intelligence agencies and . . . eliminated the checks and balances that previously gave courts the opportunity to ensure that these powers were not abused. Most of these checks and balances were put into place after previous misuse of surveillance powers by these agencies, including the revelation in 1974 that the FBI and foreign intelligence agencies had spied on over 10,000 US citizens, including Martin Luther King [Jr].

Furthermore, the PATRIOT Act was a "rush job" and

> even just considering the surveillance and online provisions ... it is a large and complex law that had over four different names and several versions in the five weeks between the introduction of its first predecessor and its final passage into law. While containing some sections that seem appropriate—providing for victims of the September 11 attacks, increasing translation facilities, and increasing forensic cybercrime capabilities—it seems clear that the vast majority

> of the sections included have not been carefully studied by Congress, nor was sufficient time taken to debate it or to hear testimony from experts outside of law enforcement in the fields where it makes major changes. This concern is amplified because several of the key procedural processes applicable to any other proposed laws, including inter-agency review, the normal committee and hearing processes and thorough voting, were suspended for this Bill.

The response of Americans to the PATRIOT Act was more mixed than this critique might suggest. For those who were traumatized by the events of 9/11, the act contained measures that were prudent and deliberate. However, the question for members of the Electronic Frontier Foundation, and others, was, "Were our freedoms the problem?" Their answer was that the provisions of the PATRIOT Act (abbreviated as "USAPA" in their text) represented a victory for those who would alter the American way of life:

> The civil liberties of ordinary Americans have taken a tremendous blow with this law, especially the right to privacy in our online communications and activities. Yet there is no evidence that our previous civil liberties posed a barrier to the effective tracking or prosecution of terrorists. In fact, in asking for these broad new powers, the government made no showing that the previous powers of law enforcement and intelligence agencies to spy on US citizens were insufficient to allow them to investigate and prosecute acts of terrorism. The process leading to the passage of the Bill did little to ease these concerns. To the contrary, they are amplified by the inclusion of so many provisions that, instead of [being] aimed at terrorism, are aimed at non-violent, domestic computer crime. In addition, although many of the provisions facially appear aimed at terrorism, the Government made no showing that the reasons they failed to detect the planning of the recent attacks or any other terrorist attacks were the civil liberties compromised with the passage of USAPA.

The foundation's chief concerns about the act included the following:

> 1. Expanded Surveillance With Reduced Checks and Balances. USAPA expands all four traditional tools of surveillance—wiretaps, search warrants, pen/trap orders, and subpoenas. Their counterparts under the Foreign Intelligence Surveillance Act (FISA) that allow

spying in the US by foreign intelligence agencies have similarly been expanded. This means:

a. Be careful what you put in that Google search. The government may now spy on web surfing of innocent Americans, including terms entered into search engines, by merely telling a judge anywhere in the US that the spying could lead to information that is "relevant" to an ongoing criminal investigation. The person spied on does not have to be the target of the investigation. This application must be granted and the government is not obligated to report to the court or tell the person spied upon what it has done.

b. Nationwide roving wiretaps. [The] FBI and [the] CIA can now go from phone to phone, computer to computer, without demonstrating that each is even being used by a suspect or target of an order. The government may now serve a single wiretap, FISA wiretap or pen/trap order on any person or entity nationwide, regardless of whether that person or entity is named in the order. The government need not make any showing to a court that the particular information or communication to be acquired is relevant to a criminal investigation.

c. ISPs hand over more user information.

d. New definitions of terrorism expand scope of surveillance. One new definition of terrorism and three expansions of previous terms also expand the scope of surveillance. They are § 802 definition of "domestic terrorism" (amending 18 USC §2331), which raises concerns about legitimate protest activity resulting in conviction on terrorism charges, especially if violence erupts, [and] adds to three existing definitions of terrorism (international terrorism per 18 USC §2331, terrorism transcending national borders per 18 USC §2332b, and federal terrorism per amended 18 USC §2332b(g)(5)(B)). These new definitions also expose more people to surveillance (and potential "harboring" and "material support" liability, §§ 803, 805).

2. Overbreadth with a lack of focus on terrorism. Several provisions of the USAPA have no apparent connection to preventing terrorism. These include:

a. Government spying on suspected computer trespassers with no need for court order. Sec. 217.

b. Adding samples to DNA database for those convicted of "any crime of violence." Sec. 503. The provision adds collection of DNA for terrorists, but then inexplicably also adds collection for the broad, non-terrorist category of "any crime of violence."

c. Wiretaps now allowed for suspected violations of the Computer Fraud and Abuse Act. This includes anyone suspected of "exceeding the authority" of a computer used in interstate commerce, causing over $5000 worth of combined damage.

d. Dramatic increases to the scope and penalties of the Computer Fraud and Abuse Act.

3. Allows Americans to be More Easily Spied Upon by US Foreign Intelligence Agencies. Just as the domestic law enforcement surveillance powers have expanded, the corollary powers under the Foreign Intelligence Surveillance Act have also been greatly expanded, including:

a. General Expansion of FISA Authority. FISA authority to spy on Americans or foreign persons in the US (and those who communicate with them) increased from situations where the suspicion that the person is the agent of a foreign government is "the" purpose of the surveillance to anytime that this is "a significant purpose" of the surveillance.

b. Increased information-sharing between domestic law enforcement and intelligence. This is a partial repeal of the wall put up in the 1970s after the discovery that the FBI and [the] CIA had been conducting investigations on over half a million Americans during the McCarthy era and afterwards, including the pervasive surveillance of Martin Luther King[, Jr.,] in the 1960s. It allows wiretap results and grand jury information and other information collected in a criminal case to be disclosed to the intelligence agencies when the information constitutes foreign intelligence or foreign intelligence information, the latter being a broad new category created by this law.

c. FISA detour around federal domestic surveillance limitations; domestic detour around FISA limitations. Domestic surveillance limits can be skirted by the Attorney General, for instance, by obtaining a FISA wiretap against a US person where "probable cause" does not exist, but when the person is suspected to be an agent of a foreign government. The information can then be shared with the FBI. The reverse is also true.

This analysis supported the conclusion that the PATRIOT Act, like anti-terrorism legislation in Canada, the United Kingdom, and elsewhere, was cut from the same "security over rights" cloth, representing a loss or curtailment of basic human rights, and that many of the new measures had little to do with making borders more secure or fighting terrorism.

The Homeland Security Act 2002

Little in the subsequent Homeland Security Act of 2002 altered the views of "constructionist" and other critics of US anti-terrorism policy (see Herman 2002). The Homeland Security Bill was introduced in the US Congress in January 2002, only to be immediately bogged down in partisan fighting between Republicans and Democrats, largely over the powers it afforded the president. The Democrats had considerable support from a range of civil liberty, professional, and media entities, but after the Democrats lost seats in the mid-term elections in November 2002, Republican control of both houses of Congress convinced Democrats to support the legislation. Its passage in late November 2002 included a favourable vote in the Senate of ninety senators to nine. The new act (Herman 2002, 7) defined terrorism as

> any activity that involves an act that is dangerous to human life or potentially destructive of critical infrastructure or key resources; and is a violation of the criminal code of the US or any state . . .; and appears to be intended to intimidate or coerce a civilian population; or to influence the policy of a government by intimidation or coercion; or to affect the conduct of a government by mass destruction, assassination or kidnapping.

The act also created the DHS, which took over several existing agencies, such as the Immigration and Naturalization Service (INS), the Coast Guard, Customs and Border Patrol, the Federal Emergency Management Agency, the Secret Service, the Transportation Security Administration, and the border inspection authority of the Animal and Plant Health Inspection Service. In addition, homeland security intelligence analyses from such sources as the Central Intelligence Agency (CIA), the National Security Agency (NSA), the Federal Bureau of Investigation (FBI), the Drug Enforcement Administration, the Department of Energy, the Customs Service, and the Department of Transportation have come under the control of the DHS.

Critics of this second piece of US anti-terrorism legislation mirrored complaints made in many other liberal democracies about the scope of such laws. Chaddock (2002) summarized these concerns:

> The Homeland Security Act . . . is sweeping in scope and will have big consequences, intended and unintended, on everything from civil liberties of Americans to due process for immigrants. Some have little to do with homeland security, but emerged out of the intensive, last-minute bargaining that shaped this effort to refocus the nation's resources to defeat terrorism.

According to the DHS itself (Department of Homeland Security 2006b) the implications of the act go considerably beyond specific anti-terrorism threats to include

- new authority for agencies to collect and mine data on individuals and groups, including databases that combine personal, governmental, and corporate records, including e-mails and websites viewed;
- limits on the information citizens can request under the Freedom of Information Act, and criminal penalties for government employees who leak information;
- more latitude for government advisory committees to meet in secret, not subject to the requirements of the open meeting laws;
- limits on liability for those who manufacture "antiterrorism technologies," including vaccines, gas masks, and baggage-screening equipment; and
- new powers to government officials to declare national health emergencies, including quarantines and forced vaccination.

As a successful strategy for gathering legislative approval and co-opting opposition, the introduction and passage of the Homeland Security Act were instructive. Many US civil liberties groups, for example, welcomed the withdrawal of a proposal by US Attorney General John Ashcroft for a "Terrorism Information and Prevention System" or "TIPS" to centralize all the surveillance activities allowed under the PATRIOT Act. Nevertheless, Lisa Dean, Director of the Free Congress Foundation, declared that Americans eventually "may find that their conversations have been monitored or [that they have been] caught walking past a surveillance camera and be outraged, but find they have no legal recourse" (Chaddock 2002). The fact that centralized information-gathering and analysis would initially fall under the aegis of retired admiral John Poindexter, who had been convicted of wrongdoing in the Iran–Contra Affair (Liman 1998), offered more fuel to critics wondering whether abuses might occur beyond the task of fighting terrorist threats to the United States.

The Domestic Security Enhancement Act 2003

A third piece of anti-terrorist legislation, the Domestic Security Enhancement Act, quickly came to be known as "USA PATRIOT Act II" (or "USAPA II" for short). The Electronic Frontier Foundation (2003) asserted that the new law was,

> like its predecessor, ... a grab bag of provisions spread throughout the legal landscape. One clear difference exists, however. Unlike USAPA, USAPA II had no provisions that "sunset" after a certain time. All of its changes were to be permanent.

The foundation noted that the Domestic Security Enhancement Act includes

> Privacy Invasions. USAPA II dramatically widens the powers of government to invade the privacy of Americans and others living here.
>
> More "End Runs" Around Limitations on Surveillance and Information Sharing. Federal, state and local officials can now freely share information, regardless of the original reason for gathering it.
>
> Gag Orders and Increased Governmental Secrecy. The "sunshine of public review" is a key check on abuses of governmental power. But USAPA II makes it even harder for the public to evaluate what the government is doing with its broad new powers.
>
> Expanded Reach of Powers under the Control of Secret Courts.
>
> Not Targeted to Terrorism. As with its predecessor, USAPA II contains many provisions that appear to be nothing more than an opportunistic attempt to increase governmental powers in areas unrelated to terrorism.

Prevalence of the "Securitivist" Approach

In the years since the passage of the PATRIOT Act, the Homeland Security Act, and the Domestic Security Enhancement Act, the "securitivist" approach to anti-terrorism has continued to influence public debate and government action in the United States. For the fiscal year 2006 Congress allocated US$ 41.1 billion to the DHS (Department of Homeland Security 2006a), an amount that was due to increase by 6 percent to US$ 42.7 billion for fiscal 2007 (Department of Homeland Security 2006b). These funds were to be divided among four major areas: border and transportation security; emergency preparedness and response;

chemical, biological, radiological, and nuclear countermeasures; and information analysis and infrastructure protection.

However, the "constructionists" have maintained their opposition to these measures. In 2006, for example, the disclosure of centralized monitoring produced some headaches for President Bush in his relations with Congress (Freeze 2006; Koring 2006). The revelation that a database of all US telephone calls had been assembled at the NSA under General Michael Hayden, prior to his nomination as director of the CIA, also added credence to earlier criticisms (see, for example, Associated Press 2006).

Finally, issues such as the use of torture in the war on terrorism have come to represent a major human rights and public relations fiasco. According to former US President Jimmy Carter, for example, the US use of torture, in settings unavailable to bodies such as the (former) UN Human Rights Commission, is, simply, "an abomination" (Carter 2005). However, US Vice President Dick Cheney's reluctance in late 2005 to accept efforts in Congress to ban torture, and to bring US practice into line with international agreements on human rights and treatment of enemy combatants, only underscored the continuing influence of the "securitivist" approach.

OFF BALANCE? MAINTAINING DIFFERENCE? SECURITY, ANTI-TERRORISM, AND PUBLIC SAFETY IN CANADA AFTER 9/11

Within a few weeks of the events of September 11, 2001, and before the Canadian government had introduced any anti-terrorism legislation, civil libertarians were already anticipating a "trampling of civil rights" in the war on terrorism. Sixteen days after the attacks, for example, John Dixon, president of the British Columbia Civil Liberties Association, reminded Canadians of the McCarthy-era attack on "civil rights—presumptions of innocence, privacy, and freedoms of conscience, association and speech." According to Dixon, overriding privacy rights in order to gather intelligence was likely to alter "the balance to be struck between principle and need . . . that depends both upon the importance of the principle and the likelihood that some sacrifice of it will yield significant results." He concluded that "trampling on civil rights will not lead to a genuine victory against terrorism" (Dixon 2001).

Some journalists came to the same conclusion. Less than four weeks after the attacks David Beers (2001), for example, writing, like Dixon, in the *Vancouver Sun*, bemoaned what he saw as attacks on free speech and declared that assertions that "you're either with us or you're against us" made him wonder "whether any of it served to bring us closer to defeating the enemy out there, or whether it really was about manufacturing an enemy within."

The Anti-Terrorism Act, 2001

On October 15, 2001, the government introduced Bill C-36 (An Act to Amend the Criminal Code, the Official Secrets Act, the Canada Evidence Act, the Proceeds of Crime [Money Laundering] Act and other Acts, and to enact measures respecting the registration of charities, in order to combat terrorism), better known as the Anti-Terrorism Act. Bill C-36 had four central objectives: (1) to stop terrorists from getting into Canada and to protect citizens from terrorist acts; (2) to design and implement tools to identify, prosecute, convict, and punish terrorists; (3) to prevent terrorists taking control of the Canada–US border and affecting the Canadian economy; and (4) to work with the international community to bring terrorists to justice and to address the root causes of their hatred (Department of Justice 2001a).

Safety and security, rather than the concern for a balance between security and rights that was evident in the early 1980s, was the order of the day. As noted by some government ministers, the bill would "give law enforcement and national security agencies new investigative tools to gather knowledge about and prosecute terrorists and terrorist groups, as well as protect Canadians from terrorist attacks." To counter anticipated criticisms, "the scope of the Criminal Code provisions [were] clearly defined to ensure they only apply to terrorists and terrorist groups," and a "three-year parliamentary review" of the legislation was added, producing further extensions of security powers (Canada. Department of Justice 2001a).

Within days there were widespread calls for amendments to this speedily drafted legislation. The definition of terrorism in Bill C-36 was one of the biggest issues, as it seemed to include both illegal strikes and acts of civil disobedience within its terms: "an act or omission . . . intended to endanger a person's life . . . [and] to cause serious interference with or serious disruption of an essential service," or an unlawful act committed for an "ideological purpose" that causes "serious disruption of an essential service, facility or system." Moreover, the inclusion of "premeditated, politically motivated violence perpetrated against non-combatant targets by subnational groups or clandestine agents" gave it a far wider compass than the US definition of terrorism. Beyond this, critics objected to other powers and controls outlined in Bill C-36, specifically: the power to detain a suspect without charge, with judicial approval, for seventy-two hours; the power to detain a suspect without charge, with judicial approval, for up to one year if the person did not agree to reasonable restrictions on his or her behaviour as a condition of release; the possibility of up to ten years' imprisonment for "legally participating or contributing" to the activities of a known terrorist group; the requirement to testify at "investigative hearings"; and the new power given to the solicitor general to create a list of terrorists on "reasonable grounds" without any requirement to notify individuals or groups that they were on the list

A positive governmental response to some of these concerns was largely predicated on the recommendation of the Canadian Senate that a five-year "sunset clause" be included in the legislation. In a unanimous report a bipartisan Senate committee noted that "Bill C-36 gives powers that, if abused by the executive or security establishments of this country, could have severe implications for democracy in Canada," and recommended that "new police powers of detention, investigation, and surveillance be rescinded in five years unless specifically extended by Parliament" (LeBlanc 2001). This view was supported by civil libertarians and groups such as the Canadian Bar Association, while the *Globe and Mail* (2001) editorialized

> There are provisions in this Bill that should be accepted only in the context of an emergency. . . Those who value the liberties enshrined in the [Canadian] Charter [of Rights and Freedoms], and championed in earlier laws, are unwilling to see their curtailment become the status quo, an accepted part of the legislative scenery.

In the context of weighing convergence or divergence in security and anti-terrorism legislation across the border, Bill C-36 was amended due to the extensive opposition to it. The key amendments introduced on November 20, 2001, included the following responses to criticisms. (1) In addition to the three-year parliamentary review, the government agreed to add a "sunset" provision to the provisions on preventive arrest and investigative hearings, which would expire after five years unless renewed by Parliament. (2) A new provision required the federal attorney general and solicitor general, and their provincial equivalents, to report annually to Parliament on any use of either preventive arrest or investigative hearings. (3) A separate interpretative clause was added for greater clarity regarding the protection of political, religious, or ideological beliefs/expression, "to ensure that protest activity, whether lawful or unlawful, would not be considered a terrorist activity unless it was intended to cause death, serious bodily harm, endangerment of life or serious risk to public health or safety." (4) Rather than being issued "at any time," attorney general's certificates could be issued only after an order by the Federal Court in a proceeding, they were to be published in the *Canadian Gazette*, and they could last for no more than fifteen years. Freedom of information provisions were to be the rule rather than the exception. (5) Offences related to "facilitating" terrorism were to be clarified by an interpretative section on such activity. (Canada, Department of Justice 2001b). Bill C-36 was passed by the House of Commons in November 2001 (Canadian Press 2001) and, as the Anti-Terrorism Act, received Royal Assent on December 18, 2001.

Bill C-42

Overlapping this initial Canadian anti-terrorism legislation was another important piece of the anti-terrorism plans of Jean Chrétien's Liberal government: Bill C-42, the Public Security Act. This second anti-terrorism statute was introduced in November 2001, before final approval had been given to Bill C-36. From the government's perspective the Public Security Act was "an appropriate continuation of the legislative amendments tabled in Bill C-36 and introduce[d] new amendments to the National Defence Act (NDA), etc." (see Smith 2003).

Bill C-36 had garnered criticism for the range of its provisions, but Bill C-42 was seen as unsupportable on narrower grounds. Criticisms from Liberal backbenchers, opposition politicians, and of rights-centred entities all suggested that one of its central purposes was to allow the minister of national defence to declare the site of the G-8 Summit of June 2002, at Kananaskis, Alberta, "a military zone" in order to prevent protests. Substantial internal dissent and extensive external criticism led the government to withdraw Bill C-42 on April 24, 2002.

Bills C-55 and C-17

On April 29, 2002, five days after the withdrawal of Bill C-42, the Chrétien government introduced Bill C-55, titled the Public Safety Act, which it termed "an improved package of public safety initiatives in support of its Anti-Terrorism Plan." This single integrated bill, amending twenty-one Acts of the Canadian Parliament, retained key elements of the tarnished Bill C-42 and was seen by the government as the next step in its plan, addressing what it called "gaps in the federal legislative framework for public safety and protection." It was bolstered by a provision of CA$ 7.7 billion in the federal budget of December 2001. According to David Collenette (2002), minister of transport at the time, "This legislation . . . respond[ed] to the need for enhanced security while respecting the rights of Canadians." Not everyone agreed and the bill garnered mostly negative responses.

One of the measures that caused concern was the set of powers given to the new Canadian Air Transport Security Authority, which had been allocated CA$ 2.2 billion in the federal budget and been given responsibility for aviation security services in Canada. Bill C-55 made changes to the Aeronautics Act to allow security or police agents access to passenger data if it was required in the interest of transportation security. George Radwanski, privacy commissioner of Canada at the time, considered this an unnecessary intrusion on the privacy rights of Canadians. In a letter to Collenette Radwanski expressed "serious concerns" about Bill C-55, noting that it "raised very, very serious privacy issues" (Bronskill 2002a), a view supported by the privacy commissioners of several provinces. These concerns were also expressed within the Liberal caucus, and Irwin Cotler, Liberal Member of Parliament for Mount Royal, publicly criticized the bill (Bronskill 2002a). The Canadian branch of Amnesty International raised concerns about the capacity of cabinet ministers to designate "controlled access military zones" in ways that, it said, might "effectively restrict the peaceful exercise of the rights to free expression and free assembly" (Amnesty International Canada 2002).

Bill C-55 died on the Order Paper when the parliamentary session ended. A successor, Bill C-17, also titled the Public Safety Act, was somewhat different. The changes accepted by the government and tabled on October 31, 2002, prevented the RCMP from combing airline passenger manifests, as Bill C-55 had proposed, but RCMP officers would be able to screen passenger lists on grounds of transportation security and the Canadian Security Intelligence Service (CSIS) would be able to do likewise on grounds of either transportation security or national security. The revised bill would also provide some limits on designating security zones, now limited to established military areas or "on a case-by-case" basis (Bronskill 2002a). Despite these small concessions, many commentators repeated their criticism that the thrust of Canada's most recent anti-terrorism response appeared to be significantly dictated by its closest neighbour in North America (Bronskill 2002b).

The Modernization of Investigative Techniques Initiative

The Modernization of Investigative Techniques Act (Bill C-74) was given its first reading in the House of Commons on November 15, 2005. This bill was almost entirely premised on cross-border pressures to ensure policy convergence on governmental access to newer electronic services (cellphone and Internet) for Canada's security services. Several of its provisions, which would have expanded surveillance while reducing checks and balances, were copied from the USA PATRIOT Act, although Deputy Prime Minister Anne McLellan described it as "simply an update of Canada's 30-year-old telephone wiretap bill" (CBC News 2005, November 16).

Critics argued at the time the bill was introduced that, in effect, the government was acknowledging the need to conform to the new "western standard" on such matters. However, the bill died on the order paper when Parliament was dissolved pending the general election of January 2006 and the Conservative government of Stephen Harper has not attempted to reintroduce it.

"Racial Profiling" and Security Intelligence

In October 2002 the introduction by the US government of "racial profiling" led the Canadian government to issue a travel advisory for Canadians of Arab origin, suggesting that they should avoid visiting the United States (Canadian Press 2002). Although Canadian pressure and the prospect of domestic constitutional challenges produced an alteration to the US policy, so that photographing and fingerprinting would "no longer be automatic by place of birth," the policy continued where it was deemed useful by INS officials (Trickey 2002).

Four years later the report of the inquiry into the treatment of Maher Arar, a dual Canadian-Syrian citizen who was deported to Syria based on incorrect information provided to the United States by RCMP security officials, identified a range of related issues where security has trumped rights, not the least of which is the relative unaccountability of virtually all of Canada's security-intelligence agencies, especially the RCMP (O'Connor 2006). Warren Allmand, counsel for the International Civil Liberties Monitoring Group, had made this point in front of the inquiry (Allmand 2005).

CONCLUSION

The vernacular of the policy discourse of 200–02 around anti-terrorism (Bill C-36) and public safety (Bills C-42, C-55, C-17, and C-74) was not dramatically different from that of the debates in the early 1980s over Bills C-157 and C-9, and the creation of the CSIS. The government of the day tended to exaggerate threats and overemphasize security needs, and, in both cases, critics were able either to force the withdrawal of legislation (C-157 and C-42) or to wring concessions from the government, as with the Public Safety Act. However, despite those successes, ground was lost in terms of the balance between rights and security, which represented a significant divergence from the US experience with its PATRIOT, Homeland Security, and Domestic Security Enhancement acts. More importantly, the content of the criticisms in Canada was remarkably similar, emphasizing the need to move toward a closer balance between security needs and protection of rights. Again, this was much less the case in the United States.

In 2002, as mentioned above, Privacy Commissioner George Radwanski criticized Bill C-55, saying that it "raise[d] the spectre of a 'police state'" (Bronskill 2002c). Radwanski (2002) also issued a statement about the bill in which he said,

> In Canada it is well-established that we are not required to identify ourselves to police unless we are being arrested or we are carrying out a licensed activity such as driving. The right to anonymity with regard to the state is a crucial privacy right. Since we are required to identify ourselves to airlines as a condition of air travel and since section 4.82 [of the Bill] would give the RCMP unrestricted access to the passenger information obtained by airlines, this would set the extraordinarily privacy-invasive precedent of effectively requiring compulsory self-identification to the police . . . If the police were able to carry out their regular Criminal Code law enforcement duties without this new power before September 11, they should likewise be able to do so now. The events of September 11 were a great tragedy and a great crime;

> they should not be manipulated into becoming an opportunity—an opportunity to expand privacy-invasive police powers for purposes that have nothing to do with anti-terrorism.

The following year, speaking at a conference in Victoria, British Columbia, on privacy and security issues, Radwanski (2003) asserted, "We must guard against falling prey to the illusion that wholesale erosion of privacy is a reasonable, necessary or effective way to enhance security." This once again reflects an important divergence from the US experience. On the matter of a possible national identity card as one way to ensure greater security, Radwanski noted that "the creation of a national identity card is . . . an idea totally without merit. [It] would radically change Canadian society by drastically infringing on the right to anonymity that is part of our fundamental right of privacy. [It] is unthinkably invasive." He went on to argue that "one of the clearest lessons of history is that the greatest threats to liberty come not when times are tranquil and all is well, but in times of turmoil, when fidelity to values and principle seems an extravagance we cannot afford."

In 1999 Canada's Security Intelligence Review Committee recognized that "in any democratic society security intelligence activities are among the most serious a government can undertake. They warrant the constant and meticulous attention of all who cherish democratic values and civil discourse in a turbulent and dangerous world" (Security Intelligence Review Committee 1999). However, George Radwanski offered the most telling test: "If we react to terrorism by excessively and unreasonably depriving ourselves of privacy and the freedoms that flow from it, then terrorism will have won a great and terrible victory" (Office of the Privacy Commissioner 2001, 4). The deletion of significant data-gathering and analysis from the Public Safety Act allowed Radwanski to conclude that "a precedent-setting and extraordinarily grave intrusion on privacy rights has been averted in Canada" (Bronskill 2003).

Thus US and Canadian security responses continue both to converge and to diverge. On the one hand, there is evidence that successive Canadian governments have recognized that US security concerns need legislative reflection, even though the significant rebalancing of security versus rights in the name of anti-terrorism in the United States, and elsewhere, is, as the International Helsinki Federation for Human Rights concluded, "severely curtailing human rights and civil liberties in much of the world," and new measures "often threaten freedoms because they are too broad, too vague, and applied too arbitrarily" (News Services 2003). On the other hand, there is clear evidence that, beyond the broad legislative language in such "equivalent" legislative responses, the Canadian response to matters of security since September 11, 2001, has been significantly different. This continuing cross-border divergence is a product of the legislative and non-governmental responses and opposition to initial Canadian legislative drafting, which initially more closely mirrored US security concerns. The ongoing Canadian responses on required travel documents for North American travel throughout early 2007continues to reflect such an approach." The Canadian balancing act has come to consist not only of legislative language that reflects such US concerns but also of security policy that reflects Canadian differences. This negotiated convergence points to new forms of continental governance that straddle the Canada–US border and strengthen border security in North America.

ACKNOWLEDGEMENT

The author is grateful to Reg Whittaker of the University of Victoria for an early commentary on this chapter.

LITERATURE CITED

Alberts, Sheldon. 2006. "Virtual Fence to Line BC Border: Provincial Crossings Vulnerable to Smugglers and Terrorists." *Vancouver Sun*, (September 22) A1–A2.

Allmand, Warren. 2005. *Brief to the O'Connor Inquiry into the Arar Affair*. Ottawa: International Civil Liberties Monitoring Group

American Civil Liberties Union. 2003. *Surveillance Under the USA PATRIOT Act* [online]. www.aclu.org/Safeandfree.cfm?ID=12263&c=206 [consulted January 12, 2007].

Amnesty International Canada. 2002. *Real Security: A Human Rights Agenda for Canada* [online]. www.amnesty.ca/resource_centre/HRagenda.pdf [consulted January 12, 2007].

Appleby, Timothy. 2003. "US Still Upset with Canada: Rice, Bush Adviser, Says Time Needed to Heal Rift." *Globe and Mail* [Toronto], (May 31) A1.

Associated Press. 2006. "Civil Liberties Protected, Bush Claims: US Security / President Reacts to Published Story that Spy Agency Has Collected Phone Records on Millions." *Vancouver Sun*, (May 12) A13.

Beers, David. 2001. "Commentary: 'The New McCarthyism.'" *Vancouver Sun*, (October 6) A6.

Bissett, Kevin. 2006. "Our Man Wilson Turns to Passport Issue: Canadian Ambassador Asked to Deal with Thorny Questions, Including Border Security." *Vancouver Sun*, (May 12) A16.

Blain, Joan. 2003. "The Biometrics Boom." *Vancouver Sun*, (July 12) C1, C4, C5.

Blanchfield, Mike. 2006. "Canada Backs NATO Decision on Missile Shield for Europe: Defence / 15 Months After Spurning US Plan for North America, New Discussion to Begin." *Vancouver Sun*, (May 12) A8.

Bronskill, Jim. 2002a. "New Anti-terrorism Bill Worries Privacy Chief: Provisions Would Allow Police to Check Air Travellers." *Vancouver Sun*, (May 8) A8.

———. 2002b. "Security Bill Watered Down: RCMP Would Have Had Increased Powers." *Vancouver Sun*, (November 1) A6.

———. 2002c. "Privacy Watchdog Still Opposes Anti-terror Bill: George Radwanski Says the Latest Changes Don't Allay His Fears of a 'Police State'." *Vancouver Sun*, (November 2) A6.

———. 2003. "Database Changes Fair, Says Privacy Czar." *The Province* [Vancouver], (April 10) A26.

Canadian Press. 2001. "Festive Mood at Anti-terrorism-Bill Sit-in." *The Province* [Vancouver], (December 9) A25.

———. 2002. "Canadians of Arab Origin Advised Not to Visit the US." *Vancouver Sun*, (October 31) A9.

Carter, Jimmy. 2005. *Our Endangered Values: America's Moral Crisis*. New York: Simon & Schuster.

CBC News. 2005. "New Surveillance Bill Introduced." *The National*. [online]. (November 15) www.cbc/ca/story/canada/national/2005/11/15/surveillance051114.html [consulted November 16, 2005].

Chaddock, Gail. 2002. "Security Act to Pervade Daily Lives." *Christian Science Monitor* [online]. (November 21) www.csmonitor.com/2002/1121/p01s03-usju.html [consulted January 12, 2007].

Clark, Campbell. 2005. "Privacy Advocates Blast Web Surveillance Bill." *Globe and Mail* [Toronto], (November 16) A6.

Clarkson, Stephen, and Maria Banda. 2004. "Foreign Policy in Focus: Paradigm Shift or Paradigm Twist: The Impact of the Bush Doctrine on Canada" [online]. www.fpif.org/papers/2004/Canada_htm [consulted September 20, 2006].

Cohn, Theodore H. 2002. *Governing Global Trade: International Institutions in Conflict and Convergence*. Aldershot, UK: Ashgate.

Collenette, David. 2002. Ministerial Statement on Bill C-55. House of Commons, 37th Parliament of Canada, 1st session (April 29).

Customs and Revenue Agency [Canada]. 2003a. "News Release: 'CANPASS-Air Launched at Vancouver International Airport'" [online]. www.ccra-adrc.gc.ca/newsroom/releases/2003/july/0717vancouver-e.html [consulted July 15, 2003].

Customs and Revenue Agency [Canada]. 2003b. "Canada and US Announce Expansion of FAST and NEXUS Programs" [online]. www.ccra-adrc.gc.ca/newsroom/releases/2003/may/fast-nexus-e.html [consulted July 15, 2003].

De Brou, Dave, and Bill Waiser, eds. 1992. *Documenting Canada: A History of Modern Canada in Documents*. Saskatoon, SK: Fifth House.

Department of Foreign Affairs and International Trade [Canada]. 2001, December 12. *Smart Border Declaration*. [online]. geo.international.gc.ca/can-am/main/border/smart_border_declaration-en.asp [consulted January 12, 2007].

Department of Homeland Security [US]. 2006a. *Fact Sheet: US Department of Homeland Security FY 2006 Budget Request Includes 7% Increase* [online]. www.dhs.gov/dhspublic/display?theme+43&content [consulted May 13, 2006].

———. 2006b. *Fact Sheet: US Department of Homeland Security Announces 6% Increase in FY 2006 Budget Request* [online]. www.dhs.gov/dhspublic/interapp/press_release_0849.xml [consulted May 13, 2006].

Department of Justice [Canada]. 2001a. "News Release: 'Government of Canada Introduces Anti-Terrorism Act,' October 15, 2001." [online]. canada.justice.gc.ca/en/news/nr/2001/doc_27785.htm [consulted September 19, 2006].

———. 2001b. "News Release: 'Royal Assent To Bill C-36,' December 18, 2001" [online]. canada.justice.gc.ca/en/news/nr2001/doc_28217.htm [consulted January 7, 2002].

Department of National Defence [Canada]. 2004. "News Release: 'Securing an Open Society: Canada's National Security Policy: Backgrounder,' April 27, 2004." Ottawa: Department of National Defence.

Department of Public Safety and Emergency Preparedness [Canada]. 2003. "News Release: 'TOPOFF 2—Week-long National Combating Terrorism Exercise Begins May 12,' May 5, 2003." [online]. www.ocipep-bpiepc.gc.ca/info_pro/NewsReleases/NR03-0502topoff_e.asp [consulted July 20, 2003].

———. 2005. *International Approaches to Interception of Communications Capabilities* [online]. www.psepc-sppcc.gc.ca/world/site/includes/print.asp?lang=en [consulted November 18, 2005].

———. 2006. "News Release: 'Public Safety Minister Stockwell Day Announces Initiatives to Help Canadians Prepare for Emergencies,' May 8, 2006." [online]. news.gc.ca/cfmx/view/en/index.jsp?articleid=211719 [consulted May 14, 2006].

Dixon, John. 2001. "Repeat of McCarthy Era Would Imperil Democracy." *Vancouver Sun*, (September 27) A15.

Dobson, Wendy. 2002. "Shaping the Future of the North American Economic Space: A Framework for Action." C. D. Howe Institute Border Papers series [online]. (April) www.cdhowe.org/pdf/commentary_162.pdf [consulted January 12, 2007].

Edwards, Steven. 2006. "PM Defends Afghan Mission: Restoring Peace Despite 'Difficulties' Is Vital to Defeating Terrorism, Harper Says in First Speech to UN Summit." *Vancouver Sun*, (September 22) A11.

Electronic Frontier Foundation. 2001. *EFF Analysis of the Provisions of the USA PATRIOT Act that Relate to Online Activities* [online]. www.eff.org/Privacy/Surveillance/Terrorism/20011031_eff_usa_patriot_analysis.php [consulted January 12, 2007].

Electronic Frontier Foundation 2003. *EFF Analysis of "Patriot II": Provisions of the Domestic Security Enhancement Act of 2003 that Impact the Internet and Surveillance* [online]. www.eff.org/Censorship/Terrorism_militias/patriot-act-II-analysis.php [consulted January 12, 2007].

Freeze, Colin. 2006. "Huge Database of Phone Calls a Hidden Trove of Behaviours." *Globe and Mail* [Toronto], (May 12) A11.

Gallagher, Mary. 2005. "Minutemen Seek Help Guarding Border." *Bellingham* [Washington State] *Herald* (September 26).

Globe and Mail. 2001. Editorial, "Sunset's Good Sense." *Globe and Mail* [Toronto], (November 2) A14.

Granatstein, J. L. 2002. "A Friendly Agreement in Advance: Canada–US Defence Relations Past, Present, and Future" [online]. www.cdhowe.org/pdf/commentary_166.pdf [consulted January 12, 2007].

Herman, Susan. 2002. "The USA PATRIOT Act and the US Department of Justice: Losing Our Balances?" *The JURIST* [online]. jurist.law.pitt.edu/forum/forumnew40.htm [consulted January 12, 2007].

House of Commons [Canada]. 2002. *Report of the Standing Committee on Foreign Affairs and International Trade*. Ottawa: House of Commons (February 26).

Kane, Michael 2006. "No Turning Back on New US Border Rules: Ambassador–Security: A Passport or a Pass Card Will Be Needed, David Wilkins Says." *Vancouver Sun*, (September 22) H6.

Kingdon, John W. 1984. *Agendas, Alternatives and Public Policies*. Boston: Little, Brown.

Koring, Paul. 2006. "Tracking of Calls Sparks Furor in US: Phone Companies Gave Data to NSA—Democrats Warn of Constitutional Challenge." *Globe and Mail* [Toronto], (May 12) A1, A11.

Krane, Dale, and Robert Blair. 1999. *The Practice of Home Rule: Report for the Nebraska Commission on Local Government Innovation and Restructuring*. Lincoln: Nebraska Commission on Local Government Innovation and Restructuring.

Laghi, Brian. 2005. "Disrespect for NAFTA Strains US Credibility, PM Warns." *Globe and Mail* [Toronto], (November 18) A7.

LeBlanc, Daniel. 2001. "Senators Unite Against Anti-terror Bill." *Globe and Mail* [Toronto], (November 2) A10.

Lewis, Peter. 2005. "Feds Move to Take Whatcom County Tunnel House." *Seattle Times* [online]. (July 27) archives.seattletimes.nwsource.com/cgi-bin/texis.cgi/web/vortex/display?slug=tunnel27m&date=20050727 [consulted January 12, 2007.]

Liman, Andrew. 1998. "Hostile Witness." *Washington Post Magazine* (August 16).

MacCharles, Tonda. 2004. "More Spying to Come in Canada's National Security Plan." *Toronto Star* (April 28).

Martin, Laurence. 1993. *Pledge of Allegiance: The Americanization of Canada in the Mulroney Years*. Toronto: McClelland & Stewart.

Millage, Kira. 2005. "Minutemen to Start Patrols." *Bellingham* [Washington State] *Herald*, (October 2) 1.

News Services. 2003. "Anti-Terror Laws 'Curb Freedoms'." *The Province* [Vancouver], (April 17) A4.

Nossal, Kim. 1997. *The Politics of Canadian Foreign Policy*. Scarborough, ON: Prentice–Hall.

O'Connor, Denis. 2006. *Report of an Inquiry into the Activities of Canadian Officials in Relation to Maher Arar*. Ottawa: Government of Canada.

Office of the Privacy Commissioner [Canada]. 2001. *Annual Report, 2000–2001*. Ottawa: Privacy Commission.

Orwell, George. 1946. "Politics and the English Language." *Horizon* [and online]. (April) www.netcharles.com/orwell/essays/politics-english-language1.htm [consulted January 12, 2007].

Pacific Northwest Economic Region. 2005. "Final Resolutions and Action Items" [online]. www.pnwer.org/meetings/summer2005/announcement.htm [consulted October 31, 2005].

Prime Minister's Office [Canada]. 2004a. "News Release: 'Government of Canada Releases Comprehensive National Security Policy,' April 27, 2004." Ottawa: Prime Minister's Office.

Prime Minister's Office {Canada]. 2004b. "Backgrounder, April 27, 2004." Ottawa: Prime Minister's Office.

Privy Council Office [Canada]. 2004. *Securing an Open Society: Canada's National Security Policy*. Ottawa: Privy Council Office [online]. www.pco-bcp.gc.ca/docs/Publications/NatSecurnat/natsecurnat_e.pdf [consulted January 12, 2007].

Radwanski, George. 2002. "Statement Regarding the Public Safety Act, Bill C-17." News Release by the Media Centre of the Office of the Privacy Commissioner of Canada [online]. (November 1) www.privcom.gc.ca/media/nr-c/02_05_b_021101_e.asp [consulted January 13, 2007].

Radwanski, George. 2003. "Privacy at the Crossroads." Paper presented at the conference The Frontiers of Privacy and Security: New Challenges for a New Century, Victoria, BC.

Ritter, John. 2005. "'Minuteman' Effort Moves Northwest." *USA Today* (October 24).

Roach, Ken. 2003. *September 11: Consequences for Canada*. Montreal and Kingston, ON: McGill–Queen's University Press.

Sands, Christopher. 2003. "Partners in North America: Advancing Canada's Relations with the United States" [online]. www.parl.gc.ca/infoComDoc/37/2/FAIT/Studies/Reports/FAIT/003-e.pdf [consulted September 22, 2006].

Security Intelligence Review Committee [Canada]. 1999. *Annual Report, 1998–1999*. Ottawa: Security Intelligence Review Committee.

Smith, Patrick J. 2002. "Cascading Concepts of Cascadia: A Territory or a Notion?" *International Journal of Canadian Studies* 25, 113–48.

Smith, Patrick J. 2003. "Anti-Terrorism and Rights in Canada: Policy Discourse on the 'Delicate Balance.'" *Arab Studies Quarterly* 25:1–2, 137–58.

Smith, Patrick J. and Stephen K. McBride. 2004. "The Global and Domestic Politics of Anti-Terrorism in North America: Canadian–American Responses to 9/11." Paper presented at the conference Convergence and Divergence in North America: Canada and the United States, fifth Interdisciplinary Association for Canadian Studies in the US-in-Canada Colloquium, Simon Fraser University, Vancouver, British Columbia (October).

Teeple, Gary. 2004. *The Riddle of Human Rights*. Aurora, ON: Garamond.

Trickey, Mike. 2002. "US to Ease Entry Rules for Us: Place of Birth No Longer an Automatic Trigger for Rigour, Cellucci Tells Graham." *Vancouver Sun*, (November 1) A6.

Turnbull, Lornet, and Janet Tu. 2005. "Minutemen Watch US-Canada Border." *Seattle Times* [online]. (October 4) www.seattletimes.newsource.com/html/localnews/200538/96-borderpatrol04m.htm [consulted September 21, 2006].

Virgin, Bill. 2005. "Cross-border Group Has Bold Agenda." *Seattle Post Intelligencer* [online]. (July 9) www.pnwer.org/news/cross-border%20group%20has%20bold%20agenda.htm [consulted September 22, 2006].

White House. 2002. *The National Security Strategy of the United States of America* [online]. (September 17) www.whitehouse.gov/nsc/nss.html [consulted January 12, 2007].

CHAPTER 11

THE SOUTHERN BORDER OF MEXICO IN THE AGE OF GLOBALIZATION

Daniel Villafuerte Solís

translated into English by Bruno Dupeyron

> "Mexico, from Chiapas to the Río Bravo and Tijuana, has become a broad vertical border that forms a cross of thorns and shame with the US one. Our passage to the North is a path that runs between the uniform Mexican minefield and the tenderness of the Mexican 'tortilla.'" —Honduran migrant quoted in *Cuarto Poder* (2005c).

At the beginning of the twenty-first century a renewed interest in the southern Mexican border can be observed. This interest is due, on one hand, to the rise of the Ejército Zapatista de Liberación Nacional (Zapatista Army of National Liberation, or EZLN) and, on the other hand, to US President George W. Bush's concern for the security of his country. Another aspect is the importance of the Mexico-Guatemala-Belize borderland as the link between northern Mexico and Central America, an area with huge potential in strategic resources, the use of which could revitalize the integration process in the Americas and improve US economic competitiveness in the context of globalization. Although the concept of globalization is not discussed in this chapter, its premise is that there is a dialectic of inclusion and exclusion in backward regions, as in southern Mexico and Central America (see Villafuerte 2002).

In this regard, the US government's desire to make progress on the proposed Free Trade Area of the Americas (FTAA) was indicated by its haste to reach agreements with countries in Central America and its intense efforts to have the Central American Free Trade Agreement (CAFTA) ratified by Congress. Negotiations on the North American

Free Trade Agreement (NAFTA) took almost three years, but those on CAFTA were concluded within one year. The ratification of CAFTA reinforced the FTAA project to the extent that US influence now extends from Canada to Nicaragua, and, with the bilateral negotiation of a free trade agreement with Panama, will soon extend beyond Central America, possibly to include Columbia, Peru, Ecuador, and Bolivia. Since 2003 the United States has negotiated free trade agreements with the latter three countries. This negotiation process began a cycle in which the northern border of Mexico was stretched into the South, and the South, with all its unresolved economic and sociopolitical problems, became integrated with the North.

The interests of the US administration in having CAFTA ratified quickly were twofold: to increase control over a key space for US national security purposes; and to advance the FTAA project, which includes, among other priorities, energy integration, in which southern Mexico would have a significant role.

The first step in this direction was taken by Mexican President Vicente Fox the day before the Fourth Summit of the Americas, in Mar del Plata, Argentina, on November 4–5, 2005, when he announced an energy-integration process between Mexico and Central America within the framework of the Plan Puebla Panamá. Subsequently, given that the Sistema de Interconexión Eléctrica para América Central (Electric Networking System for Latin America) was then under development, the idea of building a gas pipeline between Mexico and Panama received renewed interest, as did the proposal to build a refinery, in a still unspecified Central American country, that could process between 250,000 and 300,000 barrels of crude oil per day, both of which were important elements in the creation of a pipeline network. Indeed, this strengthened the energy integration proposal, which was scheduled to begin, following technical and financial approval, in early 2006. According to the Mexican government's proposal, it was a matter of integrating three markets: the electricity market, the oil market, and the natural gas market. The estimated global cost of the project was between US$ 7 billion and 9 billion, with the largest investment expected to be in the construction of the refinery. Its original cost was calculated at $US 3.125 billion, but the Panamanian deputy minister of commerce, Manuel José Paredes, indicated that costs could reach $US 4 billion (*El Financiero* 2005c). As a result the southern Mexican border was transformed into a point of interest for the Mexican and US governments, international organizations such as the World Bank, and non-governmental organizations (NGOs) from around the world.

The development of so-called biological corridors, free trade agreements, financial flows, and telecommunication networks has tended to produce a more complex southern Mexico. Moreover, it should be emphasized that, after the terrorist attacks on the United States on September 11, 2001, the southern border has come to play a significant role in restraining the trafficking of drugs and the flow of Central American migrants to the United States, both of which are considered national security threats by the White House.

Although experts on migration (for example, Massey et al. 1991/1987) have identified a variety of influences on migratory dynamics and processes, they have emphasized structural changes affecting both communities of origin and communities of destination. The adjustment and productivity requirements of the current economic restructuring process have resulted in modified labour markets, increased unemployment rates, and lower wages (Mármora 2002). From this perspective contemporary international migration is modified by economic articulations in the context of a growing globalization of production (Canales 2002). Recent studies (Maier 2003; Burke 2004) have provided data on the increase in migration of nuclear indigenous families from southern Mexico, including Chiapas, to the northern regions of the country, the United States, and Canada. Elizabeth Maier (2003, 121) concludes that

> the Mexican indigenous diaspora at present extends from Alaska across Canada, New York State, Oregon, Washington State, Texas, Wyoming, Arizona, Georgia, Nevada, and California to Florida, diversifying the cultural and geographic landscapes of urban centres and agricultural labour markets across the country.

As a result migratory activities in the South, including Central America, have become part of the new relationship between the North and the South and increasingly relevant in the context of international security.

Within this framework, the most important new law, signed by President Bush during the third week of October 2005, was undoubtedly the Homeland Security Appropriations Act 2006 (White House 2005). Basically, this law was aimed at increasing US control over illegal migrants and creating more secure US borders. The act comprised two strategies, one aimed at non-Mexican migrants and the other at Mexican migrants. In general it was about strengthening internal security and border control. As President Bush stated in a radio address about the act (Bush 2005),

> The Bill I signed includes [US]$ 7.5 billion that will help us address the problem of illegal immigration in two important ways. First, it provides more than [US]$ 2.3 billion for the Border Patrol so we can keep more illegal immigrants from getting into the country in the first place. These funds will help us hire a thousand new border patrol agents, improve our technology and intelligence, expand and improve Border Patrol stations, and install and improve fencing, lighting, vehicle barriers, and roads along our border areas.
>
> Second, this Bill also provides [US]$ 3.7 billion for Immigration and Customs Enforcement, so we can find and return the illegal immigrants who are entering our country. With these funds, we can expand the holding capacity of our detention facilities by ten percent. This will allow us to hold more non-Mexican illegal immigrants while we process them through a program we call "expedited removal." This will make the process faster and more efficient. Putting more non-Mexican illegal immigrants through expedited removal is crucial to sending back people who have come here illegally.

In addition, on December 16, 2005, the US House of Representatives approved Bill HR4437, also then known as the Border Protection, Antiterrorism, and Illegal Immigration Control Act. This bill was intended to authorize the construction of more than 1,000 kilometres of fence along the southern borders of California, Arizona, Texas, and New Mexico. In the event, after considerable debate and amendment, and in the face of large-scale protests, the bill was enacted as the Secure Fence Act in October 2006 (White House 2006). Because no appropriation has been made for it in the US budget, it is unlikely that the fence will ever be built.

This chapter analyzes the importance of Mexico's southern border as an area involved both in the energy-integration process between Mexico–Central America and in the making of US national security policy. Three topics are raised, all of which contribute to explanations for, and empirical evidence about, the geoeconomic and geopolitical significance of this cross-border space, as well as issues of concern to the United States.

The first concerns the remodelling of the southern border, emphasizing recent changes in border crossings and the presence of multinational corporations. The key relationship with Central America, without which it would be impossible to understand the importance of the border, is also examined.

The second topic is the southern border as observed from the US perspective. Here the emphasis is on the nature of the Third Border Initiative, which, although it appears to be an economic support and cooperation program with Central American and Caribbean countries, is actually a strategy to watch over and control the territories of those countries in the interest of US national security.

The third topic is an analysis of three issues that are key points on the US agenda and that, while they are not necessarily linked to each other, are nonetheless closely tied to poverty and social exclusion: migrants, youth gangs, and guerrillas. Poverty and social exclusion are indicated by the fact that from 1990 to 2001 the proportion of the population whose income was equivalent to two US dollars a day reached 37.4 percent in Guatemala, 45 percent in El Salvador, 44.4 percent in Honduras, and 94.4 percent in Nicaragua, figures that are comparable to those registered for African countries such as Namibia, Botswana, Sierra Leone, and Nigeria (Programa de las Naciones Unidas para el Desarrollo 2004).

A reflection on the complexity of the southern Mexican cross-border space, and the contradictions between US interests and Mexican government policies to solve the problems emerging in the region, concludes the chapter. With reference to Emmanuel Brunet-Jailly's model of border studies and security, it is suggested that market forces, local culture, and local political clout are the defining features of the Mexico–Guatemala border, and that they clearly undermine the policy activities of governments.

THE REMODELLING OF MEXICO'S SOUTHERN BORDER

In the current era of globalization the rationale for borders has evolved quickly, although they remain substantial features of nation-states. Drawing on Heilbroner (1990/1985), who considers both the social environment and the institutions configuring our behaviour and relationships, as well as the logic of a model of configurational change generated by its own structure, one can conclude that borders are moving due to the need to accumulate capital but at the same time maintain their essence as barriers in limiting processes. In some cases borders have evolved from being internal to being external; in others they have become more flexible; in still others they have become more rigid, as in the case of the United States. On November 28, 2005, President Bush declared at the Davis–Monthan Air Force Base,

> [Homeland Security] Secretary [Michael] Chertoff recently used the authority granted by the Congress to order the completion of a fourteen-mile barrier near San Diego . . . Our actions to integrate manpower, technology and infrastructure are getting results. And one of the best examples of success is the Arizona Border Control Initiative, which the government launched in 2004. In the first year of this initiative agents in Arizona apprehended nearly 500,000 illegal immigrants, a 42-percent increase over the previous year.

Although the Berlin Wall collapsed, a fence is currently being built between Israel and the Palestinian territories. Thus we are far from thinking that borders tend to be diluted in the global age.

In contrast, Monteforte (1997, 14) alludes to the "mobile frontier" in the relationship between Mexico and Guatemala when he discusses the problem of setting limits: "Throughout the history of treaties and conventions with Mexico, there are various criteria defining what is considered the border zone or border region. It has never been firmly established, and we are inclined to think that it is not necessary to do so." The porosity and the mobility of such borders depend on policies and agreements between states, as in the European Union (Cairo 2003, 32):

> The state borders of the world, which arose from [the Peace of] Westphalia [in 1648], were basically conceived as "walls" that separated the territories under the sovereignty of states. The obstacles to the movement of people and goods were part of the logic of clearly establishing the interior and the exterior of the state. Today, not only are we seeing a spectacular increase in cross-border trade, but also borderlands are perceived more as potential areas of exchange than as peripheral zones or spaces of fortification and state defence . . .

> although the dividing line remains, or may even be reinforced in the external parts of the integrated region, as the case of the European Union attests.

Mexico's southern borderland, like any geographic region, does not exist independently from human beings. It is a social building block that acquires its meaning in a broader historical context. In the era of globalization such spatial constructions basically follow a market perspective, so that there is no direct correlation between the southern border and its corresponding identity. In this context it is possible to say that the reactions to such megaprojects as the Plan Puebla Panamá (PPP) are responses to the logic "in which the official representations of space and its contents are called into question" (Cairo 2003, 43).

The PPP was announced by Mexican President Vicente Fox during a ceremony at his official residence, Los Pinos, on February 21, 2001. Present at the ceremony, apart from some advisers to Fox's cabinet, were the foreign ministers of Costa Rica, Panama, and Belize, and the presidents of the Inter-American Development Bank, the Secretario de Integración Centroamericana (Central American Integration Secretariat), and the Central American Bank for Economic Integration. The PPP is a megaproject promoted by President Fox as a significant contribution to the Central American integration process. It covers a territory of 1,026,117 square kilometres and a total population of approximately sixty-five million in the Mexican states of Chiapas, Campeche, Tabasco, Quintana Roo, Yucatán, Veracruz, Guerrero, Oaxaca, and Puebla, as well as the Central American countries of Belize, Costa Rica, El Salvador, Guatemala, Honduras, Nicaragua, and Panama.

During the final moments of the PPP presentation Florencio Salazar, coordinator of the plan, stated (Villafuerte 2004, 153),

> The presidential initiative expresses a profound vision in proposing to connect the South-South-East [of Mexico] with Central America; it is an essential measure pursued by the eight governments in this broad Meso-American region in order to take joint advantage of our potentialities, and to optimize the South-South-East and Central American strategic spaces within the process of globalization.

"Counterhegemonic" forces could not stop the process of globalization, still less advance the construction of an alternative. On

August 9, 2003, during a ceremony to celebrate the creation of the *caracoles*, the EZLN's organs of local political coordination, the EZLN announced its Plan La Realidad–Tijuana, also called Plan Reali–Ti. This plan, formulated in opposition to the PPP, proclaimed seven goals, including respect for the autonomy and independence of social organizations, the promotion of self-governance and self-management across the whole national territory, and the use of rebellion and of civil and peaceful resistance against "bad" government measures and "bad" political parties (Ramírez 2003). However, neither Plan Reali–Ti nor the Plebeian Alternatives to the Plan Puebla Panamá (Bartra et al. 2001), proposed by a group of intellectuals, has had any impact on broad sectors of Mexican society.

To date studies of the southern Mexican border have not focused on the processes that tend to restructure the cross-border space. As a result there is currently neither a specific definition nor an exact demarcation of the southern border. Rather, the cross-border element in most studies is attributed to the conventional legal borderline between Mexico and the Central American countries of Belize and Guatemala. That borderline, which extends for 1,138 kilometres, is characterized by Mexican municipalities in close contact with similar towns in the two Central American countries (Ciudad Hidalgo, Cacahoatán, and Tapachula in Chiapas; Tenosique in Tabasco; and Othón P. Blanco in Quintana Roo). Each of these towns is the site of an intense exchange of legal and illegal goods and of persons, culture, family relations, and so on. The majority of these flows occur from Central America to Mexico, and only to a lesser extent from Mexico to Central America. This is the most visible, measurable, and verifiable part of the process: an intense but tolerable trade flow that happens every day on the banks of the Río Suchiate, which divides Mexico and Guatemala, and involves the crossing of day-labourers to the coffee plantations in the Soconusco and Sierra Madre regions of Chiapas, and to the banana and sugar-cane plantations in the towns of Suchiate and Huixtla.

It is not possible to understand the dynamics of Mexico's southern border without considering Central America and reopening the Mexico–Central America debate. Moreover, the debate must be linked to the broader context of global integration initiatives, such as NAFTA. Nieman (2000) was correct when he argued that the regional aspect cannot be analyzed in isolation, even if he had to separate it out to meet the needs of his study (which is precisely the goal of this chapter).

In this chapter, then, the southern border refers to a vast territory that integrates five Mexican states—Campeche, Chiapas, Quintana Roo, Tabasco, and Yucatán—that share not only common features but also significant differences in various fields. These five states shape the immense region of the southern borderland, which covers 238,904 square kilometres, or 12.2 percent of Mexican territory, and is thus comparable in size to the entire land surface of the United Kingdom, or the land areas of Belgium, Austria, and Greece together. In the context of globalization this territory is being redefined according to its relationship with the global market, as demonstrated by the fact that the whole of the region is being promoted by TELCEL, the most important mobile phone company in Mexico, as "TELCEL territory." TELCEL uses the advertising slogan "All Mexico is TELCEL territory" as a metaphor for its globalization strategy. Various multinational companies, such as Chiquita Banana, Halliburton, and Flour Daniel, also have a presence in the region, the latter two having contracts for oil wells in Campeche, Chiapas, and Tabasco, while textile *maquiladoras*, such as the Calkiní Short Company or Transtextil International, are present in Campeche and Chiapas.

THE SOUTHERN BORDER'S MOST VISIBLE SPACE

Spaces become visible to the wider world insofar as they are sites of newsworthy phenomena: wars, natural disasters, important discoveries of strategic resources, the construction of tourist attraction centres, and so on. In this sense the southern border of Mexico is no exception. During the past few years this cross-border space has not been visible to the rest of Mexico since no major events have occurred there, its population density compared to that of the centre of the country is relatively low, and there is no dispute over its natural resources.

Chiapas is the most visible of the states in the southern border region. Its proximity to regions of important demographic mobility in Guatemala has made it a key state and a link with the rest of Mexico and Central America. The state of Chiapas is immensely complex, economically, socially, and politically, and its complexity is compounded by the presence of the EZLN. At the same time it is one of the most rural and marginalized states in Mexico.

Quintana Roo is also a visible entity, but that is not particularly due to border crossings, even though they are significant. Its visibility is due to its natural attractions, its international centre for mass tourism, Cancún, and, until recently, its drug trafficking.

In order to provide some insight into the number of documented crossings of the Mexico–Guatemala border, table 11.1 illustrates the dynamics of the four major border crossings. It is interesting to note that for each Guatemalan who enters Guatemala three others leave, indicating the importance of Mexico as a space of landing, entry, and crossing for Guatemalan migrants. In a later section of this chapter there is a discussion of the Central American transmigrants who cross the border to work in the agricultural plantations of Soconusco. Their status as legal migrants is valid for one year and is regulated by the use of the Forma Migratoria para Visitantes Agrícolas (Migratory Form for Agricultural Visitors).

Table 11.1: Arrivals and Departures at Major Guatemalan Border Crossings with Mexico, June to December 2004

	Arrivals		Departures	
Border crossings	Guatemalans	Aliens	Guatemalans	Aliens
El Carmen	7,418	18,448	41,601	9,894
Tecún Umán	13,181	12,100	17,335	9,053
La Mesilla	2,074	15,175	14,184	5,243
Gracias a Dios	248	1,887	6,083	1,713
Total	22,921	47,610	79,203	25,903

Source: Dirección General de Migración. Oficina de Estadística, Estudios y Políticas Migratorias [Directorate General of Migration, Office of Migratory Statistics, Studies, and Policies], Guatemala.

About thirty-six border crossings have been identified along the dividing line between Mexico and Guatemala, but until 2002 only four were officially recognized. Since May 2003 another four have become part of the regulated border-crossing system, so that there are now eight in all: (1) Ciudad Hidalgo, México–Tecún Umán, Guatemala, across the Puente Dr. Rodolfo Robles; (2) Ciudad Hidalgo–Tecún Umán across the Puente Ing. Luis Cabrera; (3) Talismán, México–El Carmen, Guatemala, across the Puente Talismán; (4) Ciudad Cuauhtémoc, México–La Mesilla, Guatemala; (5) Carmen Xhan, México–Gracias a Dios, Guatemala;

(6) Nuevo Orizaba, México–Ingenieros, Guatemala; 7) Frontera Corozal, México–Bethel, Guatemala; and (8) El Ceibo, México–El Ceibo, Guatemala (Campuzano 2004, 185). Of the four new crossings the one at El Ceibo has the greatest potential to become more important in the immediate future, as "it is the point of entry into the state of Tabasco and the Department of Petén" (Campuzano 2004, 185), a strategic area for tourists visiting Palenque, Chiapas–Tikal, and Petén, and travelling on to the Yucatán Peninsula. Currently underpopulated, the area became a crossing space for Central American migrants travelling to the United States due to the presence of immigration officers and, more recently, youth gangs, at the traditional border crossings at El Carmen and Tecún Umán.

THE THIRD US BORDER: A VITAL SPACE FOR US SECURITY AND GEOECONOMICS?

In the context of globalization, spaces acquire new meanings. Cross-border territories in particular have reached new dimensions with hegemonic projects such as the US Initiative for the Americas, launched in 1990. Beginning with this initiative, the United States has engaged in a process of building a "new spirit of the border," throughout which institutions oriented toward globalization have been notoriously evident—in particular, the World Bank, the Organization of American States, and the Inter-American Development Bank. The initial attempt to integrate Latin America ended in crisis, but new attempts at integration have arisen, with a focus on a renewed interest in free trade and the goal of protecting the sovereignty of consumers. The newest feature of these attempts is the relationship between small and big economies—between South and North—and the most recent and most significant illustration of this approach was the approval of a free trade agreement between the United States, the member states of CAFTA, and the Dominican Republic.

The Initiative for the Americas project was converted by former US president Bill Clinton into the project for the FTAA (as mentioned earlier), an umbrella agreement that covers US strategic issues. It not only addresses the question of free trade but also includes important social, political, cultural, and military aspects. The current draft of the FTAA (the third) illustrates the dimension of the project and the broad scope of topics that is involved.

In this context the security of Mexico's southern border remains a topic of the utmost concern for the US government, largely due to the border's high level of porosity and weak institutions, and the lack of coordination among them, as demonstrated by the proliferation of illegal groups in the region. The terrorist attacks of September 11, 2001, significantly increased US interest in the security of this border and (as noted earlier) President Bush subsequently authorized the accelerated negotiation of CAFTA in order to achieve greater US hegemony in Central America. Likewise, according to Benítez (2005, 2),

> a complete reform of the national security system occurred in the United States in order to react to the terrorist threat. There are two axes in this doctrinal revolution: "homeland security" and "pre-emptive action." Both are intimately linked, but the priority of the first is the defence of the territory and the US population, and implies a whole bureaucratic reorganization, while the second is oriented toward external political actions: diplomatic, military, economic cooperation, intelligence actions, and so on.

The events of September 11, 2001, represented a point of inflexion in the conception of borders, a circumstance that involved the forgotten southern border. One goal of US border-security policy was the control of illegal migrants. According to Ramos (2004, 157),

> Among recent antecedents the Security Initiative on the Border that started in June 1998 should be emphasized as a contribution to better securing the border with Mexico. The Initiative had four components: prevention, search and rescue, identification and follow-up, as well as registration of illegal migrants. Subsequently, in June 2001, both administrations signed the Action Plan for Cooperation on Border Security, which included, among other measures, a policy of deterrent migration in areas considered as high risk, such as the border of Tijuana-San Diego. However, since September 2001, the core of US policy has consisted of associating illegal migrants with terrorism and national security.

One consequence of the events, according to Tirado (2005, 12) was

> the *de facto* slippage of the US southern border [to run], not at the Río Bravo but at the Río Suchiate. The Mexican government has

> implemented effective policies in order to fulfill the US requirements, with the premise that they share the same national security interests for their borders, in particular for the southern one.

In the context of the events of 9/11 new initiatives that represent continuity have emerged as two faces of the same coin: geoeconomics and geopolitics. An example of this is the Third Border Initiative. While he was US secretary of state, Colin Powell (2002) explained why this initiative was so important:

> While world attention has focused intensely on Central and South Asia in recent months, neither President Bush nor his administration has lost sight of our commitment to America's "Third Border," which connects us to our neighbors in the Caribbean. In fact, the events of September 11, with their devastating economic effect in the region and the loss of Caribbean nationals, have increased our concern for the countries of the Caribbean.

Powell went on to discuss this issue in more detail:

> As I made clear to my Caribbean colleagues, US government programs address the full range of problems in the region, but our pre-eminent goals are the expansion of free trade as the most effective way to bring about economic recovery, development and stability, and the promotion of democracy and the rule of law. The Bush administration's Third Border Initiative (TBI) seeks to broaden our engagement with the Caribbean based on recommendations by the region's leaders on the areas most critical to their economic and social development. The initiative is centered on economic capacity-building and on leveraging public/private partnerships to help meet the pressing needs of the region.

The Third Border Initiative appeared in Powell's speech as a basic economic initiative and was presented as an extension of the Caribbean Basin (or Cuenca del Caribe) Initiative, launched nearly twenty years before. The new programs would "build on the substantial gains made in the region" through that initiative, which the Central American countries had already benefited from and which were institutionalized when CAFTA came into force. Powell also pointed out that the most outstanding component in the new initiative was security, and in particular, "It will help Caribbean authorities enhance the safety and security of their airports, which are vital for maintaining a flourishing tourist industry."

The southern border of Mexico, along with the Caribbean, was transformed into a strategic space for the operation of security programs. In fact, according to Benítez (2005),

> in 2001 the [Mexican] Secretary of the Interior, through the National Migration Institute, designed the Plan Sur (Southern Plan), with the aim of "strengthening vigilance and control of migratory flows between the Isthmus of Tehuantepec and the Southern Border."

However, by far the most complete proposal regarding the southern border was found in the "smart border" agreements signed by Colin Powell and Jorge Castañeda in March 2002. Simultaneously the proposal for creating a North American Command was announced, including the defence of borders and deployment of troops in border zones when considered necessary (see Ramos 2004, 160).

The initiative on smart borders, which, in the opinion of Robert B. Bonner, a member of the US Bureau of Customs and Border Protection, is aimed at reinventing the border in order to preserve the US and North American economy, is composed of twenty-two points and is a major part of the US strategy on homeland security (see Ramos 2004, 161).

NATIONAL SECURITY IN MEXICO AND ON THE SOUTHERN BORDER

In the 1980s the phenomenon of displaced persons, arising from the civil war in Guatemala, took the Mexican state by surprise. In the early twenty-first century, once again, the Mexican government has had to face uncertainty about security issues because of the increasing flow of migrants from Central America, the enduring presence of the EZLN, and the tightening of US security measures following the events of 9/11. Indeed, US pressure on Mexico to control borders and criminal activities has led to questions about the Mexican government's capacity to deal with these possible "national security threats." Salazar (2002, 85) has pointed out that "when an issue is included in the national security strategies of a country it means that the state has failed and that previous attempts to solve problems have not worked."

Table 11.2: Components of the Mexico–US Smart Border Agreement, March 2002

Secure Infrastructure	Secure Flow of People	Secure Flow of Goods
Long-term planning	Pre-cleared travellers	Public/private-sector cooperation
Relief of bottlenecks	Advanced passenger information	Electronic exchange of information
Infrastructure protection	NAFTA travel	Secure in-transit shipments
Harmonization of port-of-entry operations	Safe borders and deterrence of alien smuggling	Technology-sharing
Demonstration projects	Visa policy consultations	Secure railways
Cross-border cooperation	Joint training	Combating fraud
Financing projects at the border	Compatible databases	Interdiction of contraband
	Screening of third-country nationals	

Note: Further details are available in the White House fact sheet "Smart Border: 22-Point Agreement/ US–Mexico Border Partnership Action Plan" (2002).

Source: adapted from Urubiel Tirado. *Frontera Sur y Seguridad Nacional. El olvido intermitente* (2005).

There are two basic reasons why this has occurred. The first arose from the international context. The old concept of national security, sustained by Cold War assumptions and the consequential preservation of vital spaces, changed substantially. The new scenario was based on the global dilemma of security and insecurity. National security appeared to be linked to global conditions and, as a result, new threats to national security have arisen. The second reason relates to the substantial difference between developed and underdeveloped countries. The former, such as the United States, suffer from their intervention in Third World countries, whereas the latter must deal with challenges that are inseparable from their backward conditions. Villagra (2003, 138) has depicted this situation well:

> In the past few years it has been considered more and more important that the security threats faced by Latin American and Caribbean countries no longer stem from external military threats, but from new and complex phenomena that have been generally designated as "new threats" or "new challenges" to security. In this category have been included very different issues, such as drug trafficking, organized crime, gun traffic, terrorism, illegal migration, extreme poverty, damage to the environment, economic instability, corruption, democratic ungovernability, and so on.

A consideration of this list of "new threats" may lead to the conclusion that, except for terrorism, all of these threats are present on Mexico's southern border. In the face of the poor demarcation of the Mexican border, weak institutions, and the lack of financial resources, the threats have intensified. On both the Central American and Mexican sides of the border, flows of illegal migrants to the United States, drug trafficking, and the proliferation of youth gangs have increased significantly due to the lack of border-security policies. The management of security issues by the military and the police has also not helped to solve the problems. For example, recent measures taken by Honduras and El Salvador to put an end to youth gangs at the border merely caused the gangs to spread to other countries such as Mexico, especially along its southern border.

Mexico's New National Security Policy

On December 9, 2004, the Mexican House of Representatives adopted the Ley de Seguridad Nacional (National Security Act) by a majority. The new law had been presented to the Senate on October 30, 2003, where it was approved (sixty-eight votes for, twelve against, and two abstentions) on April 15, 2004, and then referred to the House of Representatives for the purpose of study and reporting. This process produced several amendments, with an emphasis on two areas in particular: the transformation of the National Security Cabinet into the National Security Council and details of the concept of "national security." These modifications were accepted by the Senate because they enriched and clarified the original proposal, and, in response to some critical comments, they centred on regulating the Centro de Investigación y Seguridad Nacional (Investigation and National Security Centre, or CISEN). As reported in the Senate on December 14 (Ley de Seguridad Nacional 2004),

> Although this law entered into force eight months ago, the Bicameral Commission on Matters of National Security ignores the actions of the federal executive power, so as to avoid the presence and crossing of groups or persons related to terrorism. Article 56 stipulates that "policies and actions related to National Security will be subject to control and assessment by the Federal Legislative Power, through a Bicameral Commission including three Senators and three Congressmen." Among the powers of the Bicameral Commission (Article 58) the following should be emphasized: (1) approval of the report mentioned in Article 58: "in the month during which the ordinary session of the Congress begins the Technical Secretariat of the Council shall deliver a general report on the activities implemented during the previous six months"; (2) approval of general reports on the implementation of directives, given in writing by the Executive Secretary to the General Director of CISEN; (3) approval of cooperation agreements initiated by the CISEN and actions that are implemented on the basis of such Agreements.

Moreover, there were serious limitations in the original conception of the act, such as the lack of any definition of basic concepts such as "national security" or "the national interest," or of any detailed distinction between national security issues and public security issues.

The first three articles of the National Security Act are central, as they define the objective and the concept of, and the responsibility for, the national security policy. Article 1 specifies that the aim of the act is "to provide the basis for integration and action coordinated with the institutions and authorities in charge of the preservation of national security, within their usual range of powers." Article 2 outlines the responsibility of the head of the Federal Executive in determining this policy. Article 3 defines the national security concept as "actions intended in an immediate and direct way to maintain the integrity, stability, and permanence of the Mexican state."

Articles 4 and 5 are also important, as they complement the first three. Article 4 provides that "national security is governed by the principles of legality, responsibility, the protection of fundamental human, individual, and social rights, confidentiality, loyalty, transparency, efficiency, coordination, and cooperation." Article 5 defines twelve threats to national security. For example, the first refers to "acts of espionage, sabotage, terrorism, rebellion, genocide, and treason against the United States of Mexico within its national territory," while the tenth concerns "any form of financing of terrorist actions and organizations."

The general concept of national security used within this act frequently does not adequately define matters of public security such as organized crime, which does not automatically result in a threat to national security, nor does it specify how to define "terrorist organizations" or "acts of rebellion." In addition, there is no consideration of the effects of issues such as poverty, economic development, or the use of natural resources, all of which present potential threats to national stability. In this sense Salazar (2002, 81) stresses that

> in Mexico the concept of national security is an unclear, controversial and politicized term. Controversy results from its use during the Cold War in order to weaken democratic processes, to support military governments, and to facilitate foreign interference in internal affairs.

Moreover, Salazar argues, national security was not a topic of debate in Mexico and, apart from the security and intelligence institutions, it was a mystery to the rest of society.

The lack of clear and detailed definitions allows the Federal Executive and the National Security Council to interpret issues such as gun trafficking, drug trafficking, transnational youth gangs, trafficking of people, and the presence of armed groups such as the EZLN in such a way that declarations from high-level officials and members of the legislature are often to the effect that youth gangs, for example, are a national security issue. These views also extend to a number of debates on science and technology, which, according to some scholars, should be considered as national security issues as well.

Recently the CISEN confirmed the existence of five armed groups in Mexico that "could affect social peace and national security," although it did not include the EZLN among them. The five groups are the Ejército Popular Revolucionario (Popular Revolutionary Army) and its four splinter groups: the Partido Democrático Popular Revolucionario (Democratic Popular Revolutionary Party); the Ejército Revolucionario del Pueblo Insurgente (Insurgent People's Revolutionary Army); the Ejército Villista Revolucionario del Pueblo (People's Villistan

Revolutionary Army); and the Fuerzas Armadas Revolucionarias del Pueblo (People's Revolutionary Armed Forces). This list differs from that presented in a report by the Secretaría de la Defensa Nacional (National Defence Secretariat, or SEDENA) on the existence of armed groups and their features, which concluded that there are eight such groups, this time including the EZLN, "with at least four of them having a probable presence in Chiapas and Guerrero, although there is evidence of some presence in the Mexico Valley" (*El Universal* 2005).

Timing, however, is very important in the typology of threats to national security. For example, the emergence of the Zapatista guerrillas was initially depicted as a national security issue, but twelve years later public authorities do not have the same perspective. The issue is no longer considered to be related to the structural state of the country, although the actions of the Zapatistas may lead to a destabilization process that could challenge the strength of Mexican state institutions.

Security Cooperation Between Mexico and Central American States

Significantly, a bilateral Grupo de Alto Nivel sobre Seguridad Fronteriza (High-Level Group on Border Security, or GANSEF) began to operate as early as October 2002. According to Campuzano (2004, 186),

> The group operates at the level of the ministries of the interior in both countries, Mexico and Guatemala, but also includes technical meetings and working groups on (a) migration, human rights and border issues; (b) international terrorism; (c) organized crime and legal cooperation; (d) public security; and (e) customs.

To date GANSEF has had a number of achievements based on recommendations from the Inter-American Committee against Terrorism, which was established in Guatemala City in 1999 by the General Assembly of the Organization of American States. For example, in January 2004 the Working Group on International Terrorism "studied the creation of a general 'protocol for coordinated security operations at formal and informal border crossings between Mexico and Guatemala,' which would include a bilateral framework for early response to terrorism" (Ministerio de Relaciones Exteriores de Guatemala 2004, 2). Likewise, progress has also been made by the Working Group on Public Security:

> The Guatemalan Ministry of the Interior has worked on a plan named Fuerza de Tarea (Task Force), which is intended to eradicate illegal activity on the Guatemala–Mexico border, including the smuggling of guns, people and other goods, organized crime, drug trafficking, terrorism and crimes related to the environment and tourism, so as to "establish a mechanism for reinforcing the relationship between GANSEF, drug control groups and public security activities by federal entities along the border."

Then, on June 28, 2005, the governments of Mexico and Belize signed an agreement on border and security cooperation as a basis for collaboration on border vigilance and supervision. Vicente Fox, then President of Mexico, declared that with this agreement Mexico had sealed and shielded its three borders with the United States, Guatemala, and Belize against organized crime, drug trafficking, terrorism, and the smuggling of guns and people. The agreement covered five areas: migration, customs, public security, the power of attorney, and international terrorism. According to President Fox, "All of these have the same purpose: secure borders, and the flexible and rapid transition of goods and persons across them" (*El Financiero* 2005a).

The southern border of Mexico has received little attention from local, state or federal institutions. In Guatemala, Belize, and beyond there is a significant lack of financial and material resources for responding to basic social problems and to those derived from organized crime. Thus, the border space is a fertile ground for the operation of illegal groups. Recently a local newspaper (*Cuarto Poder* 2005a) noted that

> military intelligence reports reveal that the southern border region, especially the state of Chiapas, is becoming more relevant to the operations and expansion plans of drug barons, since it is propitious for the transport and storage of drugs. These reports refer to the proven existence of competition within the Cartel del Golfo ["Golf Cartel"] between Joaquin "El Chapo" Guzmán and Osiel Cárdenas, with his "Zetas," [a group of "hitmen"] for the control of this strategic Central American cocaine crossing point.

In 2005 a report from the Mexican Procuraduría General de la República (Office of the Attorney General, or PGR) on the drug-trafficking situation asserted (Sánchez 2005, 20) that

> the Zetas have a presence in 13 states of the country, in which small cells have been created. Today the Cartel del Golfo and its armed wing of *sicarios* [contract killers] are present in Tamaulipas, Quintana Roo, Yucatán, Michoacán, San Luis Potosí, Campeche, Sinaloa, Jalisco, Veracruz, Chiapas, Querétaro, and Tabasco.

The PGR's officials have not yet agreed on what to do about the presence of the Zetas. When Attorney General Daniel Cabeza de Vaca was asked whether it was possible for the Zetas to come to some agreement with the Agencia Federal de Investigaciones (Federal Agency of Investigations, or AFI) or the army, his answer was unambiguous: "First, I want to make it clear that we do not have any indication of more Zetas. We know that there are *sicarios* in the organized crime scene, that some people, unfortunately, are hired to kill, and that these people are trained, but the Zetas are dead or in jail" (Rios 2005, 8). However, Santiago Vasconcelos, an assistant prosecutor in the PGR, noted (Sanchez 2005, 21) that

> this group of *sicarios* will keep on operating for Osiel [Cárdenas]. They continue, but the trend is that little by little they are getting out of Osiel's cartel, because there is no strong leadership. The leader is incarcerated and, because of that, we have witnessed an attempt to free him.

Because of concern that the Cartel del Golfo might be looking for new locations along the southern border, Antonio Cadena Méndez, the regional head of the AFI in Tamaulipas, was transferred to Chiapas on July 22, 2005. The Office of the Public Prosecutor in Chiapas pointed out that there was no evidence to confirm the presence of any drug cartel or of hired assassins from the Zetas, and police authorities confirmed that they had not been overwhelmed by any increase in crime. However, the launch of the México Seguro (Secure Mexico) program, which was created originally for the states of northern Mexico, went ahead in Chiapas as well. Between January and August 2005 a significant number of homicides occurred in the Soconusco, the most dynamic region on the southern border, although the public prosecutor's office accepted only nineteen of those as violent homicides. In the last week of August three people were killed on one day alone: two of them were travelling with their family in a van with a licence plate from Frontera Tamaulipas but originating from Frontera Hidalgo, a border town close to Guatemala, and the third was found beheaded in the town of Mapastepec, very close to the border.

Various human rights organizations have pointed to the rising levels of violence in Chiapas, in particular in the areas closest to the border with Guatemala. Some estimates suggest that about 400 women were murdered violently in 2004, ten times more than in Ciudad Juárez. Jaime Javier Aguirre Martínez, president of the organization Masculinity and Politics, reported that "the levels of violence in Chiapas are similar to those in Jalisco, Guerrero, the State of Mexico, and the Federal District [of Mexico City]" (*Cuarto Poder* 2005b).

Previously, the US ambassador to Mexico, Tony Garcia, had accused the Mexican government of failing in the war against violence and drug trafficking along Mexico's northern border, which had caused Janet Napolitano, governor of Arizona, and Bill Richardson, governor of New Mexico, to declare a state of emergency. The situation on the southern border was addressed at the forty-fourth Inter-Parliamentary Meeting between Mexico and the United States in Newport, Rhode Island, where US legislators reportedly told the Mexican representatives that Mexico had lost control of its southern border. Indeed, US concerns about security on Mexico's southern border were raised at every forum or meeting that addressed bilateral issues. On September 8, 2005, during the annual conference of attorneys from the ten states that border Mexico, held in Phoenix, Arizona, Governor Napolitano urged the Mexican government to contain the flow of illegal migrants and reinforce the fight against the smuggling of human beings on its border with Guatemala: "I would like to see them restrain the flow of illegal immigration, the origin of which is located in the south of Mexico. I think they could do more on that border" (*El Financiero* 2005b).

The situation in Guatemala is of equal concern. The border regions of Guatemala are points of departure and arrival not only for Mexico but also for the rest of Central America. The high porosity of Guatemala's shared borders with Mexico, Belize, El Salvador, and Honduras has created an ideal area for the transit of people, weapons, and drugs. Many migrants from the South and beyond believe that arriving in Guatemala means that they have reached the "Guatemalan Dream," as it is then possible to cross Mexican territory into the United States.

As a border country with a high level of institutional weakness, Guatemala is open to the proliferation of organized crime, in particular drug trafficking. Manuel de Jesús Xitumul Ismalej, head of intelligence with Guatemala's anti-drug squad, recently pointed out the existence of vast marijuana and poppy plantations in the municipalities of El Petén and San Marcos, which are adjacent to the states of Chiapas and Tabasco. At the same time the Guatemalan Servicio de Análisis e Información Antinarcóticos (Anti-drug Analysis and Information Service, or SAIA) proclaimed the existence of Quitacargas groups, composed of police agents, judges, and public prosecutors and devoted to halting the arrival of drugs and money by air, land, or sea from Colombia, Panama, and Mexico. The SAIA noted a case in June 2005 when members of a Columbian drug gang transporting 2,000 kilograms of cocaine were detained by authorities in the Pacific Ocean, had their load confiscated, and were then killed (*Prensa Libre* 2005). According to the SAIA, drug dealers pay peasants to sow poppy and marijuana seeds in the municipalities of Sololá, Quetzaltenango, San Marcos, and Huehuetenango (the latter two bordering the Mexican state of Chiapas). This is a very profitable business for the peasants, since they can earn US$ 1,800 for one hectare of poppies compared to only about US$ 150 for a hectare of tomatoes.

As of September 15, 2003, Guatemala was no longer on the list of countries not complying with US-imposed goals for drug trafficking. However, in September 2005 the US government decided that Guatemala was once again to be regarded as non-compliant, because it believed that Guatemala had failed to meet its goals: no major drug dealers had been detained, and no new laws against organized crime and for the improvement of civilian intelligence had been approved. The US government went ahead with this despite the fact that in 2005 the Guatemalan government had confiscated 2,500 kilograms of cocaine, 8,747 grams of crack cocaine, 102 vehicles, and 123 guns (*Prensa Libre* 2005).

MIGRANTS, TRANSNATIONAL GANGS, AND GUERRILLAS

On January 11, 1991, a new cycle started for Central America when a summit of the Mexican and Central American presidents took place in Tuxtla Gutierrez, the capital of the state of Chiapas. This meeting was key to defining a strategy for relations between Mexico and the countries of Central America. After its substantial participation in the Nicaraguan peace process, Mexico looked on Central America with renewed interest, taking into account the Initiative for the Americas announced by US President George H. W. Bush in 1996. The Tuxtla summit resulted in, among other decisions, the formation of a high-level Mexican–Central American commission to conduct a feasibility analysis for the creation of a free trade area by December 31, 1996.

By January 1991 the end of the civil wars in both El Salvador and Guatemala was very close. After twelve years of armed conflict that had caused more than 75,000 deaths, El Salvador was about to finalize an agreement with the Farabundo Marti Front, which subsequently resulted in the signing of the Chapultepec Agreements in January 1992. In Guatemala the Framework Agreement on Democratization in the Search for Peace by Political Means was signed in July 1991 in the municipality of Querétaro, Mexico, and in December 1991, the Framework Agreement for the Reactivation of the Negotiation Process between the government of Guatemala and the Unidad Revolucionaria Nacional Guatemalteca (Guatemalan National Revolutionary Unity) was signed in Mexico City. Five years later, on December 4, 1996, an agreement on a definitive ceasefire was signed. These and other agreements signed between 1991 and 1996 culminated on December 29, 1996, in the signing of the Acuerdo de Paz Firme y Duradera (Firm and Durable Peace Agreement), ending thirty years of armed conflict in Guatemala.

Parallel to the peace process, negotiations for free trade, according to neoliberal and US logic, were implemented to fight against poverty and tyranny. The first issue faced by the Central American countries was their inability, due to their lack of political cooperation, to negotiate, as a bloc, a free trade agreement with Mexico. Ten years later, in the CAFTA negotiations, they still could not achieve this, despite the United States having imposed it as a condition of the negotiation process. This weakness of the Central American countries has been useful to both Mexico and the United States. The preconditions imposed by the United States on Mexico during the NAFTA negotiations were imposed by Mexico on the Central American countries, and the United States used the same approach with Central America in the recent negotiations. This asymmetry reoccurs whenever governments of small economies are forced to accept that they have a great deal at stake, but it also allows them to keep the few concessions they currently enjoy.

Since the signing of the peace agreements in El Salvador and Guatemala, emigration from Central America has evolved from forced displacement, caused by conditions of conflict and labour-related issues beyond Mexico's southern border, to predominantly transnational migration. This shift has been a matter of concern because trade integration policies that seek to guarantee the free flow of goods and services are in direct contrast with the stricter physical and legal barriers that have been imposed on the free movement of people. Yet, despite the fact that the various free trade agreements that have been signed do not include sections on migration and, moreover, that borders have become more rigid in restraining migratory flows, migration has rapidly increased. Although the designers of the free trade agreements, viewing matters from the neoliberal theoretical perspective, have claimed that these agreements would result in local and regional economic growth, and, consequently, enhanced opportunities for work, a greatly accelerated migratory flow to the United States has been observed. Just as Mexico has experienced during twelve years of NAFTA, the Central American free trade agreements will lead, sooner rather than later, to national industries being replaced by transnational industries, which, in turn, will result in the elimination of thousands of local jobs.

Migrants and Agricultural Day-labourers

A steady flow of Central American migrants into the Mexican border states, in particular Chiapas, began during the 1960s and 1970s. The growth of coffee plantations, an economic activity demanding a large workforce especially at harvest time, generated an extended labour market. The influx of workers from regions in Mexico other than Chiapas, such as Los Altos, which is located on the edge of the southern border's coffee zone, was not enough to stop the hiring of Guatemalan workers. There are two main reasons why, little by little, temporary workers from the Guatemalan Altiplano have replaced Mexican day-labourers: first, the opening up of new development opportunities and thus new job opportunities in other states along the southern border, especially the Cancún tourist region; and, second, the conditions of poverty and conflict in Guatemala.

In effect the plantation economy in the zone closest to the Guatemalan border generated interdependence, in that a significant part of the accumulation of capital could not be realized without the presence of Guatemalan temporary workers. In more recent years the influx of labour in the form of a migratory population has spread to banana, sugar cane, and mango plantations, while in urban zones, primarily in the town of Tapachula, a growing demand for domestic workers has been reported, although there has also been a decrease in the influx of

Table 11.3: Inflows of Legal Temporary Farm Workers into Chiapas, 1990–2003

1990	71,353	1997	60,783
1991	92,687	1998	49,655
1992	74,165	1999	64,691
1993	78,895	2000	69,036
1994	76,822	2001	42,471
1995	67,737	2002	39,321
1996	66,728	2003	46,318

Source: Gobierno del Estado de Chiapas. *Propuesta de Política Migratoria para el Estado de Chiapas 2004.*

legal farm workers in Chiapas over the past thirteen years.

This trend can also be explained by reference to two recent developments. The first is linked to the crisis in international coffee prices, which started in 1989: plantation owners were sometimes unable to cover even their production costs, which in turn affected the pay and conditions of their workforce. The second relates to the deepening global crisis in agriculture, which affects Mexico's southern border region as much as other parts of Central America and has resulted in many migrants heading to the United States in the hope of achieving better working conditions. It is also possible that a significant part of the labour arrangements related to agricultural activities in the coffee zone and elsewhere on the southern border takes place on the black market, without the mediation of contractors and without the necessary immigration processes.

Migratory Flows

Mexico's southern border has thus experienced a significant increase in migratory flows following the ending of the armed conflicts in Central America, against the background of structural-adjustment policies and free trade agreements, as well as natural disasters, such as Hurricane Mitch in 1998 and the crisis in international coffee prices. The economic vulnerability of the region, which is due to the fact that its export base composed solely of agricultural products, has generated a constant growth in the numbers of migrants from Central America passing through to enter the United States.

Mexico's Instituto Nacional de Migración (National Migration Institute, or INM) has estimated that approximately two million illegal migrants cross the southern border annually, which must be a conservative estimate considering that the number of arrests exceeds 200,000 a year. In addition, there are numerous agricultural day-labourers who cross the border either legally or illegally, as well as visitors who cross daily and at weekends in order to shop in the city of Tapachula and in towns closer to the border. According to the Mexican Centro de Estudios Migratorios (2005),

> Illegal or irregular crossings are essentially composed of Guatemalans who cross the border in order to work temporarily in the state of Chiapas and, to a smaller extent, in the state of Quintana Roo, as well as those who stay in Mexican territory in order to go to the United States, the large majority being Guatemalans, Hondurans, and Salvadorans. The majority of these, if detected, are taken into custody by migration authorities, detained, and sent back home.

According to the INM, the majority of the migrants who cross the Mexico–Guatemala border come from the Triangulo del Norte (Guatemala, Honduras, and El Salvador). This region has also had a problem with youth gangs, known in Central American slang as *maras*. The governments of El Salvador and Honduras have implemented laws to eliminate these gangs, but to little effect. The laws were not severe enough and the governments failed to create structural policies that would address the origins of this phenomenon. Indeed, none of the Central American countries has yet to develop a program that attends to or offers alternatives to young people excluded from the labour market and the education sector.

In 2000 the Consejo Nacional de Población (National Population Council) (2000, 2) reported that

> in 1980 the number of displaced persons exceeded 10,000 and in 1990 it increased to over 100,000 a year, with a similar figure until 1999, compared to a total record of 123,680 persons sent back, according to data from the INM. Almost all deportations made in these past years related to migrants from Guatemala, Honduras, and El Salvador, who

Table 11.4: Detentions of Central Americans in Mexico, 2001–04 (Numbers and %)

	2001		2002		2003		2004	
Detentions by selected countries of origin	144,346	95.9	131,546	95.3	179,374	95.6	204,113	94.6
Guatemala	67,522	44.9	67,336	48.8	86,023	45.8	94,404	43.8
Honduras	40,105	26.6	41,801	30.3	61,900	32.9	72,684	33.7
El Salvador	35,007	23.3	20,800	15.1	29,301	15.6	34,572	16.0
Nicaragua	1,712	1.1	1,609	1.2	2,150	1.1	2,453	1.1
Detentions in Chiapas	80,022	53.2	60,695	44.0	73,136	39.0	91,194	45.6
Total numbers detained	150,530		138,061		187,614		215,695	

Source: Instituto Nacional de Migración 2005.

represented 97 percent of deported persons in 1999.

As table 11.4 shows, the number of arrests of Central Americans in Mexican territory increased by 43.3 percent between 2001 and 2004, while the fact that a large proportion of the detentions took place in the state of Chiapas is a further indication of its importance as an entry point to the United States for illegal migrants. Another interesting phenomenon revealed by the official figures is the increase in the number of Hondurans who were arrested, by 81.2 percent. In contrast, the number of Guatemalans who were arrested increased by only 39.8 percent.

The substantial increase in the migratory flow from Honduras in recent years reflects the poor economic and social conditions in the country, conditions that do not guarantee a promising future to its population. According to the United Nations Development Program (see Programa de las Naciones Unidas para el Desarrollo 2004),

Honduras has one of the highest levels of poverty in Central America. Poverty affects almost 72 percent of Hondurans and 53 percent live in extreme poverty. The situation is even more critical in rural areas, where the poverty rate is slightly below 78 percent and the extreme poverty rate is 70.4 percent. As of 2003 Honduras also had one of the lowest average incomes per capita in the region, US$ 909 a year, surpassed only by Nicaragua's, at less than $US 500 a year. As for the distribution of wealth in Honduras, the 53 percent of the population who live in extreme poverty receive less than 12 percent of the national income, whereas the 10 percent of the population who are the richest control more than 36 percent of the income generated in the country.

A significant increase in the *maquiladora* industry in Honduras since the early 1990s has not been sufficient to reverse the economic and social situation. In 1993 more than 33,000 workers were employed in the *maquiladora* industry. Preliminary figures showed that ten years later the industry employed 114,237 people, an increase of 243 percent, and generated 6.5 percent of Honduras's gross domestic product, constituted 35.5 percent of its manufacturing industry, produced 15 percent of all government revenues, and represented 30 percent of the industrial workforce.

Youth Gangs

In the context of national security in Mexico and its southern border region in particular, a significant and disturbing trend is undoubtedly the recent emergence of the transnational youth gangs (*maras*), in particular, the Mara Salvatrucha (MS) and the Mara 18 (M-18). The activities of the MS have caused particular concern in Central America, Mexico, and the United States. These gangs are an outgrowth of the political and military conflicts in Central American. In the 1970s groups such as the Mao Mao, the Piojo, the Gallo, and the Chancleta were formed in El Salvador, and the subsequent Salvadoran migration to the United States generated a proliferation of cells that were influenced by similar US gangs, such as the Pachucos and the Chulos.

There are no detailed statistics on the number of gang members, but in an interview with this author in 2005, Oscar E. Bonilla, El Salvador's public security adviser, estimated that there were then 4,000 active members of Maras in Canada, 20,000 in the United States, 3,000 in Mexicali and Mexico City, 15,000 in Guatemala, 30,000 in Honduras, 22,000 in El Salvador, and 4,000 in Nicaragua. As noted earlier, anti-

mara legislation in El Salvador and Honduras has failed to reduce the gangs' activities and growth, since they are extremely adaptable to new circumstances.

A report on gang activity in El Salvador, presented by the Salvadoran Police Intelligence Unit at an international anti-gang conference held in San Salvador from February 21 to 23, 2005, revealed that 219 members of the MS and 137 *mara* members in general carried at least one weapon each in 2004. The authors of this report, which was shared with US security agencies including the Federal Bureau of Investigation (FBI), maintained that 48.9 percent of all homicides in El Salvador were committed by gang members, and it noted the seizure of 356 weapons, 303 of which were short calibre and the rest AK-47 rifles, shotguns, and submachine guns (*Diario El Mundo* 2005). An increase in gang assassinations was also revealed in this report. During January 2005 alone the Salvadoran police reported 138 gang-related homicides: seventy-nine people were killed by the MS and eleven of its members were assassinated, while the M-18 killed thirty-seven people and three of its members were assassinated.

One of the most significant findings of this conference was that El Salvador was the Latin American headquarters for the fight against the *maras*. Consequently the Salvadoran police and US officials agreed to set up a cooperative relationship in order to exchange information on *maras* operating in both countries. The first example of this cooperative effort occurred when US police officers and FBI agents participated as observers in an anti-*maras* operation in the San Salvador area, which includes the towns of Apopa, San Marcos, Soyopango, Ciudad Delgado, and San Salvador (*Prensa Gráfica* 2005a). Two attacks occurred in Apopa, for example, between August 7 and 13, 2004: a group of businessmen travelling in a truck were attacked and then four young people in a video arcade in Santa Teresa las Flores were assassinated. In March 2005 the US government donated $US 52,000 worth of bullet-proof vests and $US 25,000 worth of other equipment to the Salvadoran police force (*Prensa Gráfica* 2005a).

The presence of youth gangs in Mexican territory is an obvious reality. Tirado (2005) reports that

> According to data from the CISEN . . ., *maras* groups were detected in 21 entities of the country . . . Chiapas is the natural and original centre of their operations in Mexico. According to statistics from the Chiapas

> Secretary of Public Security, as of last February [2005] their presence had been detected in 21 towns both along the border and in urban areas (mainly in Tuxtla, Tapachula, and Suchiate). These numbers provoked a permanent emergency situation for the federal and local authorities, as well as the implementation of a very severe policy in order to contain *maras* operations: between 2002 and January 2004 831 *pandilleros* [gang members] were arrested.

In the Soconusco region, the most dynamic on the southern border, these gangs operate in a more visible way. The recent rise of the *mara* phenomenon in the Soconusco region is intimately linked to the social exclusion of significant parts of the population, particularly young people, in Guatemala, Honduras, and El Salvador. The activities of the MS and the M-18 are centred in the border cities close to Guatemala, especially in the town of Tapachula.

Political actors and civil society have expressed concern about the presence of youth gangs in the state of Chiapas, but an incident in the city of Tapachula raised the alarm about the increasing presence of *maras* in the region. On November 20, 2004, only two days after Santiago Creel, minister of the interior, announced at a press conference that Mexico's southern border would be reinforced in strategic areas, including migration control and the presence of the military (*Cuarto Poder* 2004a, B22), a fight took place between the MS and the M-18. For at least six years just such an event had been anticipated by the border region's population, particularly those living in Tapachula. The news quickly spread at the national level, and both print and electronic media widely disseminated news about the conflict, which had occurred during the annual celebrations of the anniversary of the Mexican Revolution. The day after Creel's declaration Chiapas Senator Arely Madrid Tovilla declared that national security measures must be doubled in the region (*Cuarto Poder* 2004a, B19):

> It would be very serious to deny what is happening on the southern border, since appropriate measures would not be taken to strengthen national security. One does not need to be an expert to know that Chiapas has a border with another nation. It is very important, and that is why appropriate measures must be taken.

On November 26, a large demonstration of up to 7,000 people, according to the local press, marched through the streets of Tapachula to protest against the *maras*. Banners carried by the demonstrators read, "Death Penalty for the *Maras*," "Security in Schools," "We Demand an End to Insecurity in the Region of Tapachula," "We Want Peace in the Schools," and "Burn All the Maras Salvatruchas, as they are Killed and Burned in Honduras, El Salvador, and Guatemala" (*Cuarto Poder* 2004b, B8).

The federal government's response to the *mara* violence that erupted on November 20 was to mount a police operation Acero II (Steel II), in which 1,200 federal, state, and municipal agents were sent to safeguard the border region from Suchiate to Mapastepec, with the assistance of 670 patrols and three helicopters. According to the attorney general of Chiapas, Steel II was a permanent operation that had been in effect since 2003 and the measures implemented after the conflict represented the biggest orchestrated operation so far in the fight against the *maras* on the southern border. In addition to these efforts, Attorney General Mariano Herrán Salvati disclosed that Operation Costa would be implemented in twenty-six towns in the Costa, Soconusco, Fronteriza, and Sierra regions, in coordination with the Federal Preventative Police, the AFI, the INM, Chiapas's own investigation agency, and the municipal police (*Cuarto Poder* 2004b, B12).

International cooperation to deal with the *maras* has since moved forward. On September 7–8, 2005, an international plan for simultaneous operations, the first and to date the biggest operation of its kind, was implemented simultaneously in El Salvador, Honduras, Guatemala, Mexico, and the United States. Some 6,400 police officers participated in the operation and arrested 660 members of *maras*: 237 in El Salvador, 162 in Honduras, 98 in Guatemala, 90 in Mexico, and 73 in the United States. The operations in El Salvador were part of a project known as Mano Dura (Hard Hand), which has been started by the government in mid-2003 that had already resulted in more than 20,000 arrests (*Prensa Gráfica* 2005b). In Mexico the operation was called Escudo Comunitario (Community Shield). Over 1,500 state and municipal police officers participated in the operation, which was conducted in the towns of Tuzantán, Villa Comaltitlán, Tapachula, Huixtla, Cacahuatán, Suchiate, Unión Juárez, and Tuxtla Chico, all of which are situated in the Soconusco region of Chiapas, a border space that clearly suffers from the effects of the economic and social problems in Guatemala, El Salvador, and Honduras. In recent years the Soconusco region and its urban centre, Tapachula, the economic centre of Chiapas, have been transformed into a place of arrival for hundreds of migrants hoping to reach the United States.

Guerrillas and Militarization

The year 1994 represented a turning point in security policy along the southern border of Mexico. On January 1 that year, the Mexican people awoke to hear news of the armed uprising of the EZLN (the "Zapatistas"), news that spread around the world in a matter of hours. As Villafuerte and Montero (2005, 14) explain,

> The uprising of the [EZLN] consisted of simultaneously taking control of the administrative centres in San Cristóbal de las Casas, Ocosingo, Altamirano, and Las Margaritas, towns where the Declaration of the Lacandon Jungle was widely disseminated. It asked "international organizations, including the Red Cross, to monitor and regulate our fight, so that our efforts are carried out while still protecting our civilian population. We declare that now and always we are subject to the Geneva Conventions in forming the EZLN as the fighting arm of our liberation struggle." The EZLN also took control of a radio station, EXOCH, in Ocosingo and broadcast messages to the population of Chiapas all day long.
>
> The federal government, through the Ministry of the Interior, issued a statement asking the rebels to lay down their arms, while recognizing the serious historical backwardness of the region. The bishops of the three Chiapas dioceses condemned the rising but said that it should be interpreted as a warning about the danger of abandoning marginalized groups.
>
> On January 2, there was still a lot of confusion and little news. The EZLN had left the central square of San Cristóbal in order to go to Rancho Nuevo, general headquarters of Military Zone 31, where heavy fighting with the Mexican Army took place. Clashes were restricted to the town of Ocosingo and the Army announced that the central square had been reconquered. The official casualties on the second day of clashes [were] up to 50.

The first response of the Mexican government to the armed uprising of the EZLN was to deploy military force. The deployment of troops from various parts of the country to Chiapas was obvious in the first twelve days of the armed conflict, and during the remainder of 1994 there was an impressive movement of military forces, mainly to the border zone with Guatemala.

Today (early 2007) the presence of the Mexican army in Chiapas is still very evident, not only in sheer numbers but also in the constant patrolling of roads and rural paths in Chiapas. As the Centro de Análisis Político e Investigaciones Sociales y Económicas (2004, 3–4) reported:

> The official arguments for the operations of the Mexican Army in the zone are mixed: the flow of illegal migrants, drug trafficking, traffic in weapons and high-value timber, the social attention paid to poverty and natural disasters, organized crime, and so on, all justified by the Act Establishing the Basis of Coordination for the National Public Security System [approved November 21, 1995], which includes the Army and the Navy in these actions.

No exact figures are available on the number of military personnel deployed to Chiapas during the years of increased tensions and disputes, but some human rights organizations have estimated that the numbers have fluctuated between 40,000 and 70,000 (*Contralinea Chiapas* 2006, 16–18). In 2003 the Oficina del Alto Comisionado de las Naciones Unidas para los Derechos Humanos en México (Office of the United Nations High Commissioner for Human Rights in Mexico 2003, 156) estimated smaller numbers, but expressed concern about their activities:

> There is speculation about the number of soldiers in the zone, and the SEDENA [reports] that there are at present 15,000 soldiers in Military Region 7. The presence of camps and military bases close to the indigenous communities, as well as military patrols and blockades on the roads, contributes to a climate favourable to provocations and friction with the civilian population.

What is certain is that the Zapatista uprising has compelled the federal government to substantially increase the number of military zones in Chiapas. In this regard José Luis Sierra (2003, 139) observed,

> The Chiapas conflict also had a major impact on military arrangements

> in the territory [of Chiapas]. With the objective of improving the coordination and movement of troops, the Mexican Army and Air Force changed their territorial structures through the creation of military zones and air bases around the region of conflict in Chiapas. These changes consisted of creating two military zones, the 38th in Tenosique, Tabasco, and the 39th in Ocosingo, Chiapas, as well as two Air Force bases in Copalar and Altamirano. Five years after the uprising Military Region 7 still consists of five military zones: the 30th in Villahermosa, Tabasco; the 31st in Rancho Nuevo, Chiapas; the 36th in Tapachula; and the zones of Tenosique and Ocosingo.

With the increase in the number of military zones the main section of the border strip between Mexico and Guatemala has remained under military control. This includes the most frequented points, such as in the zone of Tapachula, as well as points in zones such as Tenosique, which had previously seen few people and goods cross the border but which has undoubtedly been quickly transformed into a very important crossing zone due to its location adjacent to the Petén region of Guatemala.

Thus it is possible to assert that the armed uprising of the EZLN has been a factor in the redefinition of the southern border in geopolitical terms. The vulnerability of this territory has been revealed, as well as the role it can play in terms of national security. The continued presence of Mexican armed forces in the borderland fulfills several functions, including control not only of the movements of the EZLN but also of drug trafficking and of flows of illegal migrants from Central America. The likely resurgence of armed groups in Guatemala, and the possibility of renewed guerrilla activity in Chiapas and other Mexican states along the southern border, the strengthening of drug cartels in the region, and the US government's demands that Mexico increase security on its southern border all indicate that the Mexican army will remain in this region.

CONCLUSION

Mexico's southern border is the most complex and the weakest link in its relations with the countries of Central America. Its problems are particularly associated with the movement toward globalization in the Americas. To date the Mexican state has been unable to respond to the region's most critical issues, such as poverty and the lack of employment, especially for young people. Consequently since 1994 the demands of the EZLN have taken a heavy toll on every government in the region. The lack of solutions has produced other problems that were previously perceived as less significant, such as international migration from Central America and from the region itself, drug trafficking, transnational youth gangs, and the smuggling of human beings. Parts of the borderlands of Guatemala and Mexico are now in the hands of revolutionary groups and criminal networks that the Mexican state has been unable to undermine.

This chapter has emphasized that market forces, local culture, and local political clout are clearly challenging the policy activities of the Mexican government. This is also an important contribution to the application of Brunet-Jailly's model of border security.

As Sepúlveda (2002, 12) has noted, "The first duty of any state is to protect its citizens and to defend its national territory, since they are essential elements of its national security." However, there are indications that the security measures implemented by Mexico on its southern border respond more to US than to Mexican interests. Although the concept of "security" has a military connotation that must be complemented by a political agenda, security policies have so far been aimed neither at the most vulnerable groups in Mexican society nor at increasing the strength of institutions. The lack of economic policies for people living in the border region is also evident, which is why there are no opportunities for stable and well-paid jobs.

In this context migrants who cross Mexico's southern border from Central America are viewed in the same way as Mexicans trying to cross the Mexico–US border: as a security threat. However, as González (2002, 229) has pointed out, "The migrants are not the cause of the threat, but the effect of a global process that has convulsed economic stability, the concept of traditional identity, and the asymmetric distribution of development opportunities." Clearly, it is important to consider the spheres of security and development as related issues without subordinating the development agenda to security goals.

ACKNOWLEDGEMENTS

The author would like to thank Bruno Dupeyron for his extensive comments on, and his translations of, my talks and previous drafts of this paper, including this final version.

The author and the translator would like to thank Jessica Worsley, research support assistant in the School of Public Administration, University of Victoria, for her initial editing of the English version.

The translator acknowledges that, instead of being retranslated from Spanish, the following excerpts have been taken direct from English-language texts available on the Internet, as cited in the bibliography below: from President Bush's radio address; from the EZLN's First Declaration of the Lacandon Jungle; and from Colin Powell's speech.

LITERATURE CITED

Bartra, Armando, et al. 2001. *Mesoamérica. Los ríos profundos. Alternativas plebeyas al Plan Puebla-Panamá.* Mexico City: Instituto Maya, et al.

Benítez Manuat, Raúl. 2005. *Seguridad y nuevos desafíos de las fronteras de México* [mimeo]. Paper presented to the international workshop The Southern Border of Mexico—An Analysis, Tapachula Chiapas, Mexico.

Burke, Garance. 2003. "Yucatecos y chiapanecos en San Francisco: la formación de comunidades de inmigrantes indígenas y su incorporación a un mercado laboral menguante." *Indígenas mexicanos migrantes en los Estados Unidos,* eds. Jonathan Fox and Gaspar Rivera-Salgado. Mexico City: Cámara de Diputados, Universidad Autónoma de Zacatecas, and Grupo Editorial Miguel Ángel Porrúa, 375–86.

Bush, George W. 2005. "President's Radio Address. In Focus: Homeland Security" [online]. (October 22) www.whitehouse.gov/news/releases/2005/10/20051022.html [consulted January 12, 2007].

Cairo Carou, Heriberto. 2003. "Panregiones: viejas y nuevas ideas geopolíticas." *La integración regional de América Latina en una encrucijada histórica,* ed. Alberto Rocha. Guadalajara: Universidad de Guadalajara, 31–48.

Campuzano López, Juan José. 2004. "México y Guatemala: de la vecindad a la asociación." *Revista Mexicana de Política Exterior* 72, 171–94.

Canales, Alejandro. 2002. "Migración internacional y flexibilidad laboral en el contexto del TLCAN." *Revista Mexicana de Sociología* 2:62, México, 3–28.

Centro de Análisis Político e Investigaciones Sociales y Económicas [Centre for Political Analysis and Social and Economic Investigations] 2004. *La ocupación Militar en Chiapas: El dilema del Prisionero* [online]. www.capise.org.mx/informes/espanol/dilemaprisionero.php [consulted October 8, 2005].

Centro de Estudios Migratorios [Centre for Migratory Studies]. 2005. *Flujo de entradas de extranjeros por la frontera sur terrestre de México registradas por el Instituto Nacional de Migración* [online]. archivos.diputados.gob.

mx/Centros_Estudio/Cesop/Eje_tematico/2_poblacion.htm [consulted October 10, 2005].
Consejo Nacional de Población [National Population Council]. 2002. "Migración internacional en la frontera sur de México, Migración Internacional." *Boletín editado por el Consejo Nacional de Población* 4:12, 1–16.
Contralínea Chiapas [Mexico City; 1:18]. 2006, May.
Cuarto Poder [Tuxtla Gutiérrez, Chiapas]. 2004a, November 20.
———. 2004b. (November 27).
———. 2005a. (August 18).
———. 2005b. (August 24).
———. 2005c. (August 26).
———. 2005d. (December 17).
Diario El Mundo. 2005. El Salvador (February 22).
El Financiero [Mexico City]. 2005a. (June 29).
———. 2005b. (September 9).
———. 2005c. (December 13).
El Universal [Mexico City]. 2005. (August 29).
Ejército Zapatista de Liberación Nacional [EZLN]. 1993. *The First Declaration of the Lacandon Jungle* [online]. www.ezln.org/documentos/1994/199312xx.en.htm [consulted November 18, 2005].
Gobierno del Estado de Chiapas. 2004. *Propuesta de Política Migratoria para el Estado de Chiapas 2004* [mimeo]. Tuxtla Gutiérrez, Chiapas, México: Gobierno del Estado de Chiapas.
González, Patricia. 2004. "Migración, seguridad y derechos humanos." *Después de Nuestro Señor, Estados Unidos,* ed. Silvia Irene Palma. Guatemala City: FLACSO, 227–48.
Heilbroner, Robert L. 1990. *Naturaleza y lógica del capitalismo*. Barcelona, Spain: Ediciones Península. Internacional de Medios de Comunicación. [Spanish-language version of Robert L. Heilbroner. 1985. *The Nature and Logic of Capitalism*. New York: W. W. Norton.]
Ley de Seguridad Nacional, Cámara de Senadores. 2004. *Gaceta Parlamentaria No. 85*. Mexico: DF.
Maier, Elizabeth. 2003. "Migración y ciudadanía femenina indígena: cuerpos desplazados y la renegociación diaria del sujeto femenino." *Diagnóstico dela discriminación hacia las mujeres indígenas,* eds. Paloma Bonfil and Elvia Rosa Martínez. Colección mujeres indígenas. Mexico City: Comisión Nacional para el Desarrollo de los Pueblos Indígenas, 115–48.
Mármora, Lelio. 2002. *Las políticas de migraciones internacionales*. Buenos Aires: Paidós and Organización Internacional para las migraciones.
Massey, Douglas S., et al. 1991. *Los ausentes. El proceso social de la migración internacional en México Occidental*. Colección Los Noventa no. 61. Mexico City: Alianza Editorial Mexicana and Consejo Nacional para la Cultura

y las Artes. [Spanish-language version of Douglas S. Massey, et al. 1987. *Return to Aztlan: The Social Process of International Migration from Western Mexico*. Berkeley and Los Angeles: University of California Press.]

Ministerio de Relaciones Exteriores de Guatemala [Ministry of External Relations of Guatemala] 2004. *Informe de Guatemala al Comité Interamericano contra terrorismo* [mimeo]. Cuarto período de sesiones, 28 al 30 de enero, Montevideo, Uruguay.

Monteforte Toledo, Mario. 1997. *La Frontera Móvil*. Guatemala City: Universidad Nacional Autónoma de México, Naciones Unidas, and Ministerio de Cultura y Deportes de Guatemala.

Nieman, Michael. 2000. *A Spatial Approach to Regionalism in the Global Economy*. Basingstoke, UK: Macmillan Press.

Oficina del Alto Comisionado de las Naciones Unidas para los Derechos Humanos en México [Office of the United Nations High Commissioner for Human Rights in Mexico]. 2003. *Diagnóstico sobre la situación de los derechos humanos en México*. Mexico City: Mundi-prensa.

Powell, Colin. 2002. "Estados Unidos y el Caribe: Comercio, democracia y desarrollo." Agencia de los Estados Unidos para el Desarrollo Internacional, Diario de Las Américas. (February 20) [Spanish-language version of Colin Powell. "The United States and the Caribbean: Trade, Democracy, and Development" (text of speech, available online). www.revistainterforum.com/english/articles/022502artprin_en.html (consulted January 12, 2007)].

Prensa Gráfica. 2005a. El Salvador (February 24).

———. 2005b. El Salvador (September 9).

Prensa Libre [Guatemala City]. 2005. (August 23).

Programa de las Naciones Unidas para el Desarrollo. 2004. *Segundo Informe sobre Desarrollo Humano en Centroamérica y Panamá 2003* [Spanish-language version of United Nations Development Program. *Second Report on Human Development in Central America and the Caribbean*. Costa Rica: Programa de las Naciones Unidas para el Desarrollo.

Ramírez, Jesús. 2003. "Anuncia el EZLN el Plan La Realidad-Tijuana." *La Jornada* [Mexico City] (August 10).

Ramos, José María. 2004. *La gestión de la cooperación transfronteriza México–Estados Unidos en un marco de inseguridad global: problemas y desafíos*. Mexico City: Grupo Editorial Miguel Ángel Porrúa, Cámara de Diputados, and Consejo Mexicano de Asuntos Internacionales.

Ríos, Humberto. 2005. "Los dolores de cabeza de vaca." *Milenio Semanal* 413, 8–11.

Salazar, Ana María. 2002. *La seguridad nacional hoy. El reto de las democracies*. Mexico City: Editorial Aguilar.

Sánchez, Omar. 2005. "La guerra sin fin. Crece su influencia en 13 estados." *Milenio Semanal* 413, 20–23.

Sepúlveda, Bernardo. 2002. "Terrorismo transnacional y seguridad colectiva." *Este País* 140, 2–14.

Sierra, José Luis. 2003. *El enemigo interno. Contra insurgencia y fuerzas armadas en México*. Mexico City: Centro de Estudios Estratégicos de América del Norte, Universidad Iberoamericana, and Plaza y Valdés Editores.

Tirado, Urubiel. 2005. *Frontera Sur y Seguridad Nacional. El olvido intermitente.* [mimeo]. Paper presented to the international workshop The Southern Border of Mexico—An Analysis, Tapachula Chiapas, Mexico.

Villafuerte, Daniel. 2002. *Bases teóricas y consecuencias prácticas de la globalización en la periferia*. Chiapas, Mexico: Universidad de Ciencias y Artes de Chiapas.

———. 2004. *La Frontera Sur de México*. Chiapas, Mexico: Del TLC México–Centroamérica al Plan Puebla Panamá, Universidad Nacional Autónoma de México, Plaza y Valdés, and Consejo de Ciencia y Tecnología del estado de Chiapas.

———, and José Montero. 2005. *Chiapas en la coyuntura actual desde la visión de los actors*. Guatemala: WSP Internacional, Oficina para América Latina.

Villagra, Pedro. 2003. "Un nuevo paradigma de seguridad hemisférica." *Foreign Affairs en Español* 3:4, 130–43.

White House 2002. "Smart Border: 22-Point Agreement/ US–Mexico Border Partnership Action Plan" [fact sheet available online]. www.whitehouse.gov/infocus/usmxborder/22points.html [consulted January 12, 2007].

———. 2005. "President Signs Homeland Security Appropriations Act for 2006" [online]. (October 18) www.whitehouse.gov/news/releases/2005/10/20051018-2.html [consulted January 12, 2007].

———. 2006. "President Bush Signs Secure Fence Act" [online]. (October 26) www.whitehouse.gov/news/releases/2006/10/20061026.html [consulted January 12, 2007].

CHAPTER 12

CONCLUSION: BORDERS, BORDERLANDS, AND SECURITY: EUROPEAN AND NORTH AMERICAN LESSONS AND PUBLIC POLICY SUGGESTIONS

Emmanuel Brunet-Jailly

Originally the editor and the authors of this book had three themes in mind: first, to discuss the relative importance of human agency on borders; second, to examine the porosity of borders; and third, to suggest new policy guidelines to governments and security agencies that might strengthen border security objectives. The overall finding presented collectively by the contributors to this book is that the human agency exercised in borderlands establishes the complex environment with which border security policies must struggle.

Borders are porous due to such critical factors as market forces, flows of trade, and the movements of people, as shaped by the local culture and the local political clout of borderland communities. Contrary to some well-known views (see Biger 1995), no border or borderland in Europe or North America is unique. Borders and borderlands display different features, but these result from the common dynamics of the interplay between collective decisions to establish border policies and individual decisions to comply, or not to comply, with the intent of those policies. While governments pursue institutional arrangements to establish and recognize formal borders, and then regulate flows and other activities across them, individuals consider their own interests in determining whether or not to act in accordance with the intent of such regulations. Their decisions reflect the strength of the incentives leading to market transactions and trade flows, as well as to movements of people, capital, and currencies. Moreover, their decisions reflect the political clout of borderland communities affected by such flows and the social ties that bind individuals within the many cultures of those communities. In turn these myriad individual decisions generate, in aggregate, forces that restructure border policies and institutions. It is the interaction of these forces, rather than the particularities of geography, that makes the comparative study of borders—or, more accurately, borderlands—worthwhile, not just from an academic perspective but also from a public-policy perspective.

Thus border policies and borderland security are highly dependent on the clear identification of the specific traits of agent power exercised within each borderland in question. The first and central policy implication is that border security cannot be achieved by pursuing uniform and inflexible policies that are established centrally.

Border security policies are generally unsuccessful because the very nature of borders, as artificial barriers to the achievement of the goals of individual human beings, is to be porous (Andreas 2000; Andreas and Biersteker 2003; Andreas and Snyder 2000). Typically, security agencies and central government departments underestimate the influence of specific borderland characteristics because they have only partial or limited understanding of borderlands. For instance, they may substantially misread or misinterpret the relative influence of market flows or the cross-border pulls of the local culture and the political clout of local borderland organizations pursuing objectives particular to the region. Finally, and most important, these centralized organizations may have a unilateral view of the borderland that leads them to overlook government activities on the other side. A mismatch between security policies on either side of the border also contributes to greater unregulated flows and increased porosity.

This governmental top-down approach to developing and implementing border policies thus leads to ineffective border security policies. Designing and implementing effective border security policies necessitate factoring in local economic, cultural, and political elements. In their attempts to filter out dangerous individuals and substances, policy-makers must recognize that their activities are competing not only with increasingly strong market forces, which lead to growing market-driven flows of goods and people across borders, but also with the evolving ties of people that are shaped by the local culture of each borderland region and the political clout of local organizations within it. They also need a deeper understanding of the multiple policies and activities of other government levels and agencies that are implemented locally on both sides of the border.

This book's concrete public policy contribution is to illustrate these general findings by providing a critical and comparative perspective for the implementation of security policies in several borderland regions. The contributors to this book found that market forces, local culture, and the local political clout of urban cross-border regions were empirically important in the cases they examined. These factors offered powerful analytical dimensions for understanding how individual agency may be exercised in the presence of borders, to differentiate such agency from formal structure and to identify the real and multiple challenges faced by border security policy-makers.

As for the structuring effect of the multiple activities of governments, Clochard, Smith, Ramos, and Patrick each suggest that cooperation across borders is central. They also suggest that, without such cooperation, governments' border and borderland security policies will struggle to make an impact, and indeed may be ineffective in the face of strong human forces militating against compliance with restrictive regulations that may limit their potential opportunities across the boundary line. Ferrer suggests that the relative structuring effect of a security policy may be amended by specific local needs, while Patrick argues that the structuring effect of the US border security policy depends not only on the strength of individuals' interest in cross-border interactions but also on cross-border government cooperation. Finally, Daniel Villafuerte Solís notes that the Mexican state has been unable to effectively resist the local political clout and cross-continental market forces that structure the Guatemalan borderland.

As for the impact of local culture and local political clout, Murphy Erfani argues that these two factors have blocked the realization of a "smart border" security policy, despite strong integrating local market forces and important government investments. Melissa Gauthier demonstrates how the illicit trade in used clothing that is grounded in the local economic fabric of the border regions of El Paso (Texas, United States) and Ciudad Juarez (Chihuahua, Mexico) seems to have remained undisturbed by increased border security. In the same vein van der Velde and Marcińczak find that, despite the implementation of the Schengen Agreement, local economic agents have adapted successfully in the Łódź region. Payan and Vasquez point out how local culture, local political clout, and market forces have been engaged in a structuring tug of war with the policy activities of the central state, while Heininen and Nicol suggest that borderland cultures and political clout are increasingly central to understanding Arctic borderlands, as well as becoming increasingly entrenched in more extensive circumpolar structures and institutions.

In effect the contributors to this book have argued that four kinds of local conditions influence the security of borders and borderlands: market forces, the diverse and multiple activities of governments, local political clout, and local culture. Each provides an important analytical lens for security policy and each has significant theoretical implications for security policy.

The first and primary characteristic of borders and borderlands noted in this book is that they cannot be reduced to any one specific structure or feature of human agency. Borders and borderlands are defined by the historically and geographically variable expression of agent power exercised within institutional structures of varying force and influence. It is the interplay and interdependence between individual incentives to action and the surrounding structures, understood as those processes constructed socially to contain and constrain individual action, that determine the effectiveness of formal borders within a borderland region. It is the human agency behind the multiple activities of governments, market forces, the culture of borderlands, and the political clout of borderland communities that is critical to understanding and characterizing the porosity of any one border or borderland region. In turn this agency is fundamental to border and borderland security.

Each chapter in this book is a powerful vignette of the individual human determinants of the nature of life in individual borderlands. It is apparent from the review of the literature and the findings discussed in this book that borders and borderlands are human creations, and that their formal manifestations result from life as it is lived through market activities, flows of trade, and the local and regional cultures and political clout of borderlands.

In most cases borders result from complex processes of state formation, which have emerged from the complex interaction of multiple governments. Yet Ramos, Smith, Murphy Erfani, and Ferrer remind us that border policies also struggle with the integrative force of human ties in borderland communities, which, it seems, limits the impact of government policies in forming and imposing formal borders on living borderlands. Evidently, central government policy-makers have so far failed to sufficiently factor in an adequate assessment of the relative level of integration of the borderlands examined in this volume.

As underscored by nearly all the contributors, the second primary characteristic of borders and borderlands is that they are highly permeable. Although borders and borderlands are lines of demarcation, they are also highly porous, due to local culture, local political clout, market forces and trade flows. As early as the beginning of the twentieth century scholars had identified borders as permeable, some even arguing that when natural borders were poorly settled they were "good," while more urbanized borderland regions were "bad" (Holdich 1916; Lyde 1915).

In the end what emerge are two analytical dimensions of local culture: local political clout, market forces and trade flows; and their polar opposite, multiple government activities taking place across the borderlands. When culture, political clout, and market forces and trade flows straddle the border they integrate the borderland. Similarly,

Figure 12.1: MODEL OF BORDERLAND SECURITY

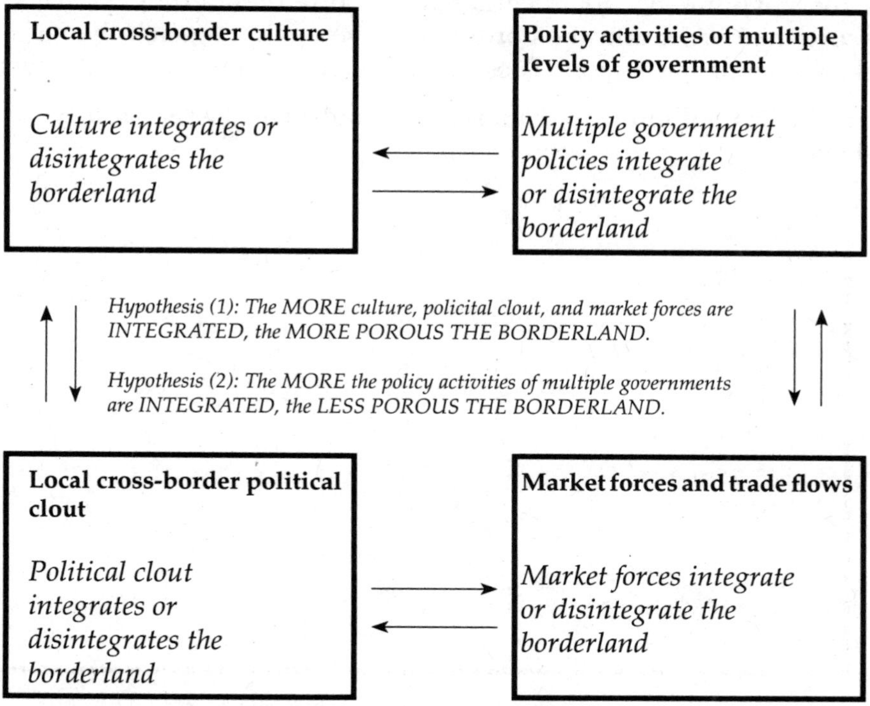

when multiple government policies straddle the border they integrate borderland security. However, as the authors of this book have explained in detail, in most cases these four factors are not generally understood as polar opposites that compete with each other to either integrate or disintegrate the borderland.

As Payan and Vásquez or Villafuerte have demonstrated, the more culture, political clout, and market forces integrate the borderland, the more porous the border. In contrast, as both Ramos and Smith have suggested, the more integrated the policy activities of multiple governments, the more secure and the less porous the borderland.

The result of these two opposing dimensions is a policy challenge and a border security dilemma. On the one hand, the less integrated the borderland, due to weak culture, political clout, and market forces, the less need there is for governments to integrate policies in order to implement border-straddling security. On the other hand, the more integrated the borderland, due to similar culture, strong local cross-border political clout, and strong market forces, the more need there is for governments to integrate their border-straddling policies to secure the border and the borderland, even going against the natural tendencies of the region. These points can be summed up this way:

Figure 12.2: Controlling for Porous Borderlands: The Border Security Dilemma

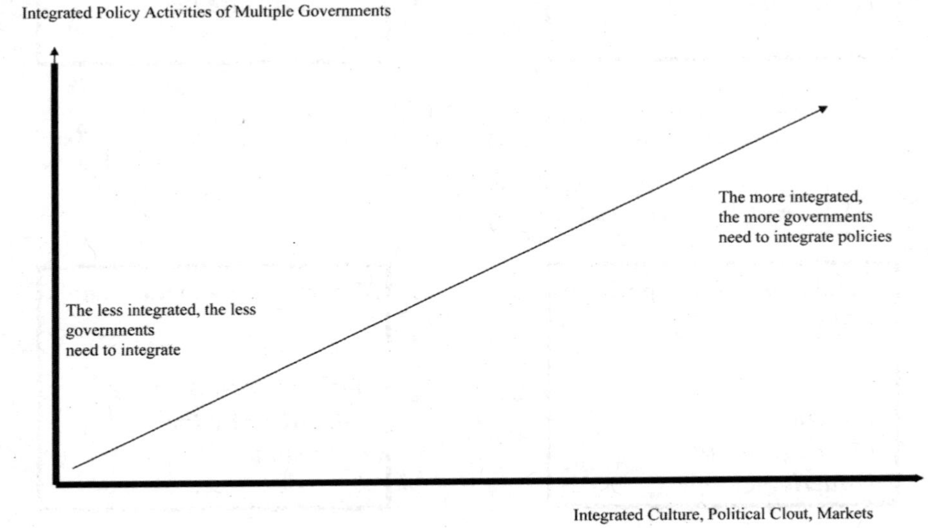

(1) the more culture, political clout, and market forces are integrated with any given scale of government intervention, the more porous the border; and (2) in any given region the more integrated the security policy activities of multiple governments, the less porous the border in matters of security.

The implications of this policy statement are important and profound. The less integrated the borderland, the less government activities straddling the border need to be integrated. Conversely, the more integrated the borderland, the more governments need to integrate border-straddling security policies. From this model it may be concluded that an integrating borderland region has an integrating culture, integrating local political clout, and an integrating regional economy, and thus governments must work at integrating a multitude of government activities to enforce security.

In the introduction to this book it was noted that the study of borders and borderlands needs more than the partial explanations currently available to explain the porosity of borders. All those who have contributed to this book have helped to close this gap in the literature and have provided government policy-makers with critically important information on the porosity of borders and borderlands.

LITERATURE CITED

Andreas, Peter. 2000. *Border Games: Policing the US-Mexico Divide*. Ithaca, NY: Cornell University Press.

Andreas, Peter, and Thomas Biersteker. 2003. *The Rebordering of North America*. New York: Routledge.

Andreas, Peter, and Timothy Snyder. 2000. *The Wall Around the West*. Boulder, CO: Rowman & Littlefield.

Biger, Gideon. 1995. *The Encyclopedia of International Boundaries*. Jerusalem, Israel: Jerusalem Publishing House.

Holdich, Thomas H. 1916. *Political Frontiers and Boundary-Making*. London, UK: Macmillan.

Lyde, Lionel William. 1915. *Some Frontiers of Tomorrow: An Aspiration for Europe*. London, UK: A. & C. Black.

LIST OF CONTRIBUTORS

Emmanuel Brunet-Jailly, Local Government Institute, School of Public Administration, University of Victoria, Victoria, British Columbia, Canada

Olivier Clochard, PhD candidate, Maison des Sciences de L'Homme, Paris, France

Rodney Dobell, School of Public Administration, University of Victoria, Victoria, British Columbia, Canada

Bruno Dupeyron, Post-Doctoral researcher at the Local Government Institute, School of Public Administration, and lecturer, Department of Sociology, University of Victoria, British Columbia, Canada

Julie A. Murphy Erfani, Department of Politics, Arizona State University, Tempe, Arizona, United States

Xavier Ferrer Gallardo, PhD candidate, Human Geography, Autonomous University of Barcelona, Barcelona, Spain

Mélissa Gauthier, PhD candidate, Humanities,Concordia University, Montreal, Quebec, Canada

Lassi Heininen, Arctic Centre, University of Lapland, Rovaniemi, Finland

Szymon Marcińczak, Department of Geography, University of Łódź, Poland

Heather N. Nicol, Canadian Studies Center, University of West Georgia, Carrollton, Georgia, United States

J. Michael Patrick, College of Business Administration and Graduate School of International Trade and Business, Texas A&M International University, College Station, Texas, United States

Tony Payan, Department of Political Science, University of Texas, El Paso, Texas, United States

José M. Ramos, Department of Public Administration Studies, El Colegio de la Frontera Norte, Tijuana, Mexico
Gordon Smith, Centre for Global Studies, University of Victoria, Victoria, British Columbia, Canada
Patrick J. Smith, Department of Political Science and Institute of Governance Studies, Simon Fraser University, Vancouver, British Columbia, Canada
Martin van der Velde, Department of Human Geography and Nijmegen Centre for Border Research, Radboud University, Nijmegen, the Netherlands
Amanda Vásquez, University of Texas, El Paso, Texas, United States
Daniel Villafuerte Solís, Metropolitan Autonomous University, Mexico City, Mexico, and Centre for Mexican and Central American Studies, University of Chiapas, Tuxtla Gutierrez, Mexico

INDEX

A

ABC Initiative. *See* Arizona Border Control (ABC) Initiative
ABS. *See* Association of Borderland Studies (ABS)
ACTE. *See* Association of European Textile Collectivities (ACTE)
Action Plan for Cooperation on Border Security, 322
Acuerdo de Paz Firme y Duradera (Firm and Durable Peace Agreement), 334
AEPS. *See* Arctic Environmental Protection Strategy (AEPS); Task Force on Sustainable Development (AEPS)
Afghanistan, 30
Agencia Federal de Investigaciones (Federal Agency of Investigations (AFI)), 331
Agreement on Military Environmental Cooperation (AMEC), 127
Agua Prieta (town), 51–52
Alaska, 148, 151–52
Albania, 29, 30, 33
Albanian exiles, 29, 30, 33
Aliens Law (Poland), 177
AMAP. *See* Arctic Monitoring and Assessment Program (AMAP)
Ambos Nogales–Tucson (faith-based NGO), 47
AMEC. *See* Agreement on Military Environmental Cooperation (AMEC)
American Civil Liberties Union, 286
American Patrol, 50
Amsterdam Treaty, 176
Andalusian coast, 35
ant trade (fayuca hormiga), 98
Anti-drug Analysis and Information Service. *See* Guatemalan Servicio de Análisis e Información Antinarcóticos (Anti-drug Analysis and Information Service (SAIA))
Anti-Terrorism Act, 286, 297–300
ANWR. *See* Arctic National Wildlife Refuge (ANWR)
APEC. *See* Asia-Pacific Economic Cooperation (APEC) summit

Arab-looking men (terrorists), 253–54
Arar, Maher, 302–303
Arctic borders
  Agreement on Military Environmental Cooperation (AMEC), 127
  Alaska, 148, 151–52
  Arctic Council, 125, 128, 132, 134, 138, 145, 152
  Arctic Eight, 129
  Arctic Environmental Protection Strategy (AEPS), 128, 129, 129 f5.2
  Arctic Monitoring and Assessment Program (AMAP), 128, 130
  Arctic National Wildlife Refuge (ANWR), 131
  Barents Euro-Arctic Region (BEAR), 127, 129, 134
  Barents Sea region, nuclear waste in, 122, 123, 124 f5.1, 126
  borderlands, 135, 137, 142
  Brandt Commission, 117
  CAFF agreement, 146
  Canada and the Circumpolar World: The Northern Dimension of Canada's Foreign Policy, 119
  Canada-US bilateral relationship, 153
  Canada-US military alliance, 146
  Canadian foreign policy on, 146–48
  caribou herds, Central Arctic and Porcupine, 131
  Chelyabinsk nuclear reprocessing plant, 126
  climate change, 122, 127, 154
  Cold War legacy, 117, 122, 138, 154
  Conservation of Arctic Fauna and Flora (CAFF), 128
  cultural crossroads, 136
  cultural survival, 121
  decision-making, local, 133
  DEW line, 146, 148
  Emergency Preparedness and Response (EPPR), 128
  Enhanced Partnership in Northern Europe (e-PINE), 149–50, 152
  environmental catastrophe, 125, 126, 127
  environmental threats, 126, 134, 146–47
  Estonian–Russian border, 141
  EUND's trans-Atlantic agenda, 147–48
  Euregio Karelia, 143
  EU–Russia dialogue, 140–41
  EU–Russian border, 142
  EU–Russian Summit (2005), 141
  EU's Northern Dimension (EUND) strategy, 119, 139–44, 147, 152
  Finland's concerns, 128, 145
  Finnish–Russian border, 141, 144
  Gorbachev, Mikhail, 122, 124, 128, 138, 146, 154
  governance, internationalized, 133
  Greenland, 147
  Gwich'in people, 131
  Haparanda-Tornio borderland, 142–43, 144

High Arctic, 146
indigenous peoples, 118, 132
Inuit Circumpolar Conference, 151, 152
Inuit Tapisariat, 151, 152
Karjalat katsovat toisiaan, 144
Komi Republic (Russia), 143
Kuhmo Summer Academy, 144
Lakselv, reindeer herding area, 125
Land Claims and Self-government Agreement, 133
Lapland province (Finland), 143
maritime boundaries, 136
military training and missile testing, 125
Murmansk, city of, 122
North America, 144–53
north as frontier, 137–38
North as geographical frontier, 136
North Europe Initiative (NEI), 131–32
Northern Dimension Action Plans, 147
northern Europe, regionalism, 137–39
Northern Forum, 143
Norway's concerns, 123, 128, 139
nuclear material and weapons, smuggling of, 126
nuclear waste, 123–25, 124 f5.1, 154
Nunavut, Canadian Territory of, 134
oil reserves, 130–31, 150
På Gränsen/Rajalla (At the Boundary), 142
Palme Commission, 117
persistent organic pollutants (POPs), 133
pollution, transboundary, 118, 119, 122, 128, 154, 158
pollution from DEW line radar stations, 122
Protection of the Arctic Marine Environment (PAME), 128
Putin, Vladimir, 138
resource reserve, geostrategically, 138
Russia-Finland border, 142
security, circumpolar boundries, 135
security, civil, 121
security, environmental, 119, 120, 122, 127–32
security, human, 119, 121, 130, 139, 154, 157
security, military, 120–21, 123–27
security, regionally-based, 134–35
security and governance, 132–35
Sellafield, nuclear reprocessing plants, 126
Soviet Union, regionalism, 137–39
Stockholm Convention, 133
sustainable development, 130, 154
Sustainable Development Working Group, 125
Sweden's concerns, 145
Task Force on Sustainable Development (AEPS), 128
Tli Cho people, 133
traditional, redrawing, 156

United Nations Commission on Human Security, 121
US National Missile Defense (NMD) system, 126
US northern policy, 148–53
Working Group on Sustainable Development (SDWG), 128
Arctic Council, 125, 128, 132, 134, 138, 145, 152
Arctic Eight, 129
Arctic Environmental Protection Strategy (AEPS), 128, 129, 129 f5.2
Arctic Monitoring and Assessment Program (AMAP), 128, 130
Arctic National Wildlife Refuge (ANWR), 131
ARGO program, 33–34
Arizona Border Control (ABC) Initiative, 41, 52, 54, 316
Arizona Coalition for Migrant Rights, 65
Arizona Contractors Association, 48–49
Arizona Department of Commerce, 238
Arizona Homeland Defense, 50
Arizona–Sonora borderlands
Agua Prieta (town), 51–52
Ambos Nogales–Tucson (faith-based NGO), 47
American Patrol, 50
anti-migrant activists and vigilantes, 46, 47, 49–54, 65
Arizona Border Control (ABC) Initiative, 41, 52, 54
Arizona Coalition for Migrant Rights, 65
Arizona Contractors Association, 48–49
Arizona Homeland Defense, 50
Arizona voters, polls of, 59–60
automobile theft, 59
Bill 1157, 64
Bill HR4437, 48, 64
Border Action Network, 50
border patrols, DHS, 45
border security and human rights, 47–48
border-security policy, self-defeating, 44
border surveillance, self-defeating, 42
border towns, 41, 99f2.1, 99 f2.1
BorderLinks, 44, 47
Buenos Aires National Wildlife Refuge, 54, 55
car theft, 44
casas de huéspedes (guest houses), 52
Center for Recuperation and Rehabilitation from Drug and Alcohol Addictions (CRREDA), 53
Christian Peacemaker Teams, 53
clout, local culture and political, 11
Cochise County, vigilantes in, 49–54
Cochise County Concerned Citizens (CCCC), 50
Coronado National Memorial, 56
coyote law to prosecute migrants, 61–62
crackdowns, ineffective border, 41–45
crime, accelerate, 41–45

criminal traffickers, humans and narcotics, 52
cross-border flows, 11, 45
cross-border Mexican shoppers, 51, 63
Derechos Humanos (human rights NGO), 47
Dever, County Sheriff Larry, 64
Douglas (town), 51, 52–53
Douglas–Agua Prieta (faith-based NGO), 47
drug trafficking, 42
false arrests of legal Latino residents, 62
Federal lands and Indian reservations, 67 f2.2
Frontera de Cristo (Healing Our Borders), 47, 53
gang violence, 44
guest-worker policy, 43, 44, 49
human trafficking, organized, 42, 43–44, 59, 60–61
Humane Borders, 47, 53, 54
humanitarian networks, 53
Hungry Bear Café, 51
ID production, fake, 59
informal networks, legal and criminal, 41
jails, tent city, 62
Maricopa County Attorney's office, 46
migrant assistance camp, 53
migrant assistance organizations, 42, 43, 47
migrant deaths by walking distance, 70 f2.5
migrant deaths in California, 71 f2.6
migrant deaths in Tuscon sector, 68 f2.3, 69 f2.4
migrant deaths in West Desert (Arizona), 71 f2.6
migrants, criminals, terrorists *vs.* guest-worker, 42–43
migrants, criminals if undocumented, 46
migrants as illegal aliens, 43
migrants as inexpensive labour, 43
militia volunteers, US civilian, 42, 43
militias, organized civilian, 46
Minutemen, 46, 50, 51, 63
money-laundering by smugglers, 52
Napolitano, Governor Janet, 60, 65, 332
narcotics trafficking, 41, 56, 57
national park, militarization of, 58
national park, security costs, 58
National Park Service, 56–57
National Park Service ranger killed, 56, 57
Native American tribal reservation, 55
No More Deaths (No Más Muertes) NGO, 47
Operation Gatekeeper (California), 41
Operation Hawk, 50
OrganPipeMonument,56,57,58
park rangers' national security duties, 57
Pearce, Russell, 65
personal security, diminished, 42, 44
Phoenix, undocumented immigrants, 59–64
porous borderlands, transnational, 46–47

Proposition 200, 46, 63
racial profiling, 42, 52, 62
Ranch Rescue, 50
sensors on migrant paths, 55
smart-border, advocates of, 48
smart-border, undermining, 64–65
smugglers, small-scale, 43
social activists, 45
social struggles of rival groups, 45–49
Sonoran wilderness, insecurity in, 54–58
Thomas, Attorney Andrew, 61–62, 63
Tohono O'odham Nation Reservation, 54
US Air Force and Marine Corps gunnery range, 55
US Border Patrol's Operation Safeguard 99, 49–50
US Bureau of Land Management, 55
vehicle barrier along border, 57
waterstations,networkof,54–55
wildlife habitat destruction, 55–56, 58

armpit smugglers, 98
Ashcroft, Attorney General John, 295
Asia-Pacific Economic Cooperation (APEC) summit, 279
Association of Borderland Studies (ABS), 9
Association of European Textile Collectivities (ACTE), 189
asylum applicants, 19, 34, 36–39
At the Boundary. *See* På Gränsen/ Rajalla (At the Boundary)
Automated Entry-Exit Control System, 198
Automated Targeting System, 243
Autonomous Cities, 85

B

Barcelona process, 84, 89
Barents Euro-Arctic Region (BEAR), 127, 129, 134
Barents Sea region, 122, 123, 124 f5.1, 126
Barnett, Roger, 50
bazaar. *See* Lódz, Poland
BEAR. *See* Barents Euro-Arctic Region (BEAR)
Berlin Wall, 316
Bicameral Commission, 327
Bill 1157, 64
Bill C-74 (Modernization of Investigative Techniques), 302
Bill C-74 (Modernization of Investigative Techniques Act), 283
Bill C-17 (Public Safety Act), 300–302
Bill C-55 (Public Safety Act), 300–301
Bill C-42 (Public Security Act), 300
Bill HR4437, 48, 64
biological identification method, 38
biometric identifiers, 197, 198, 210
biometric passport technology, 282
Bonner, T.J., 209, 252, 267, 324
Borane, Mayor Ray, 52
border
agents, changing behaviours, 232
assaults, 86–87
crossing, 240, 273–74
crossing, arrests of undocumented, 252, 252 t8.4
crossing, deaths of undocumented, 253, 253 t8.5
expenditures on personnel, 235, 236 t8.2

patrols, DHS, 45
police force (EU), 11, 32
residents, 233, 236
security and human rights, 47–48
security expenditures, 236 t8.1
security factors, 271
security policy, self-defeating, 44
surveillance, self-defeating, 42
towns, 41, 99f2.1, 99 f2.1
towns, fortification of, 11
border, militarized, 345
Border Action Network, 50
Border Crossing Card. *See* laser-visa cards
border crossings points, 320–21
Border Patrol, 231, 251, 314
Border Protection, Antiterrorism, and Illegal Immigration Control Act, 314
Border Region in Transition (BRIT), 9
Border Security Conference, 237
Border Trade Alliance (BTA), 102–103
borderland
Arctic borders, 135, 137, 142
communities, 6, 7
culture, 248–49
culture of, 3, 6
defined, 135
environments, complex, 351
global market forces, 5
political clout, 8, 9, 353
power, geographic balance of, 2
BorderLinks, 44, 47
borders
agenda of states, national, 3
barriers to trade, 5
buffer zones, 3
cities, 7–8
communities, role of, 6
community interests, 351
cooperation across, 353
cross-border regions, 5
culture, 6, 7, 9, 353
economic regions, 5
geographic frontiers, natural, 2
globalization, 5, 6, 8
human activities, 1
as human creations, 2
human ties, 1, 354
individual interests, 351, 353, 354
institutional constructs, 3
institutions spanning, 8
international, 6, 7, 8
irrelevance of, vii
market forces, 5, 6, 7, 9, 353
policies, criminalization, 8
policing, 8
political difficulties, lessen, 2
porous, 2, 8, 9, 351–52, 355, 356 f12.2
security challenges, 8
security policies, 6–9, 352, 356
smart, 353
social processes, 1, 2, 3
sovereign, 2, 7
state, 7
structural nature of, 4
tensions, balanced economic, 2
Brandt Commission, 117
BRIT. *See* Border Region in Transition (BRIT)
British Royal Air Force *(Nimrod)*, 32–33
Brunet-Jailly, E.
Arctic borders, 156–58
border model, 9, 10 f1, 355 f12.1

EU's eastern border, 169
Mexico-US border, 113, 272
Mexico's southern border, 346
southern Mexican borderland, 315
Texas-Mexico borderland, 226–27
Van Schendel-Abraham model *vs.*, 98
Buenos Aires National Wildlife Refuge, 54, 55

C

C. D. Howe Institute, 283–84
C-BEST. *See* Center for Border Economic Studies (C-BEST)
C-TPAT. *See* Customs Trade Partnership against Terrorism (C-TPAT)
CAFF (Conservation of Arctic Flora and Fauna)Agreement, 146
CAFTA. *See* Central America Free Trade Agreement (CAFTA)
Campbell, Prime Minister Kim, 279
Canada
Anti-Terrorism Act, 297–300
Arctic, foreign policy on, 146–48
Arctic Council, 145
Bill C-74 (Modernization of Investigative Techniques), 302
Bill C-17 (Public Safety Act), 300–302
Bill C-55 (Public Safety Act), 300–301
Bill C-42 (Public Security Act), 300
CAFF agreement, 146
Canadian Security Intelligence Service (CSIS), 301, 304
core security interests, 282
economic policy frames, 4
Emergencies Act, 288
environmental threats, 146–47
foreign policy on Arctic borders, 146–48
military alliance with United States in Arctic, 146
northern habitants, 146–47
privacy rights, 301
racial profiling, 302–303
Radwanski, George, 301, 303–304
Royal Commission on Aboriginal Peoples, 145
US relations, 278–83
War Measures Act, 288
Canada and the Circumpolar World: The Northern Dimension of Canada's Foreign Policy, 119
Canada Project at the Center for Security and International Studies, 281
Canada-US border
Arctic borders, 146, 153
Bill C-74, 283
biometric passport technology, 282
border cooperation, 272
border security, 13
C. D. Howe Institute, 283–84
Canadian core security interests, 282
Canadian relations with US, 278–83
CANPASS-Air, 285–86
Cross-CulturalRoundtable,282
FAST (low risk traffic), 285, 286

human rights *vs.* security, 288–90
Integrated Threat Assessment Centre, 282
iris-recognition technology, 286
legislative and policy convergence, 13
linking, 8
Minutemen Civil Defense, 277
National Security Advisory Council, 282
NEXUS (low risk travellers), 285, 286
PASS card system, 280
PNWER Border Issues Working Group, 277
security priorities, 261 t9.1–9.2
Smart Border/30 Point Action Plan, 285
Smart Border Agreement, 13, 269, 285
smuggling, drug, 277
Summit of the Pacific Northwest Economic Region (PNWER), 277
TOPOFF 2, 285
transborder cooperation, 263
US foreign policy, unilateralism of, 280
vehicle crossings, 262
Canada–Mexico relationship, 262–63
Canadian Security Intelligence Service (CSIS), 301, 304
Canaintex. *See* Mexican National Chamber of the Textile Industry (Canaintex)
Canary Islands, 32, 35
CANPASS-Air, 285–86
CAP. *See* Common Agricultural Policy (CAP)
Caribbean Basin (Cuenca del Caribe) Initiative, 323
caribou herds, Central Arctic and Porcupine, 131
Cartel del Golfo (Golf Cartel), 330, 331
Carter, President Jimmy, 301
casas de huéspedes (guest houses), 52
CCCC. *See* Cochise County Concerned Citizens (CCCC)
CDP. *See* Comité de Defensa Popular (Popular Defense Commiittee (CDP))
Center for Border Economic Studies (C-BEST), 215
Center for Comparative Immigration Studies, 252
Center for Recuperation and Rehabilitation from Drug and Alcohol Addictions (CRREDA), 53
Central America Free Trade Agreement (CAFTA), 321, 322
Central American
day-labourers, 335–36, 336 t11.3
detentions in Mexico, 337–38, 338 t11.4
migrants to Mexico, 335–39, 336 t11.3, 346
migrants to US, 313, 324, 346
Central American Bank for Economic Integration, 318
Central American Free Trade Agreement (CAFTA), 311–12
Central Arctic caribou herd, 131
Centro de Investigación y Seguridad Nacional (Investigation and National Security Centre (CISEN)), 326, 328–29
Ceuta, 11, 34
CFDA. *See* French Coordination for the Right of Asylum (CFDA)

Channel of Otranto, 33
Chapultepec Agreements, 334
Charter of the United Nations, 22
Chelyabinsk, nuclear reprocessing plants, 126
Cheney, Vice President Dick, 301
Chiapas state, 319, 330, 331–32, 335–36, 336 t11.3, 338
Chinese Market. *See* Józsefvárosi V Market (Chinese Market)
Chrétien, Prime Minister Jean, 279, 285
Christian Peacemaker Teams, 53
CISEN. *See* Centro de Investigación y Seguridad Nacional (Investigation and National Security Centre (CISEN))
CIVIPOL, 26
Clinton, President Bill, 321
CMEA. *See* Council for Mutual Economic Assistance (CMEA)
Coalition for Secure and Trade-Efficient Borders, 266, 267
Cochise County Concerned Citizens (CCCC), 50
Cochise County vigalantes, 49–54
coffee prices, 336
Cold War legacy, 117, 122, 138, 154
Comité de Defensa Popular (Popular Defense Committee (CDP)), 108
Common Agricultural Policy (CAP), 80
Common Consular Instruction, 22
Community Shield. *See* Escudo Comunitario (Community Shield)
Conservation of Arctic Fauna and Flora (CAFF), 128
Consolidated National Inspectional Anti-Terrorism Contraband Enforcement Team, 251
Control of Secret Courts, 296
conveyance companies, 11, 19, 26–27
Cornelius, Wayne, 252
Coronado National Memorial, 56
Council for Mutual Economic Assistance (CMEA), 179
Council on Foreign Relations, 269
coyote law, 61–62
criminal networks, 96, 346
Cross-Cultural Roundtable, 282
CRREDA. *See* Center for Recuperation and Rehabilitation from Drug and Alcohol Addictions (CRREDA)
CSIS. *See* Canadian Security Intelligence Service (CSIS)
Cuenca del Caribe. *See* Caribbean Basin (Cuenca del Caribe) Initiative
Customs and Border Protection, 235, 243, 251
Customs Trade Partnership against Terrorism (C-TPAT), 234, 241–43
Cyprus, 33

D

DEA. *See* Drug Enforcement Administration (DEA)
Dean, Lisa, 295
Debt Restructuring Department, 180
Declaration of Barcelona, 21–22, 30
Declaration of the Lacandon Jungle, 343
Defence of the Realm Act (UK), 288
Democratic Popular Revolutionary Party. *See* Partido Democrático Popular Revolucionario (Democratic Popular Revolutionary Party)

Department of Homeland Security (DHS)
agencies, consolidation of existing, 294–95
American Civil Liberties Union, 286
annual funding, 296
anti-drug border security, 251
Anti-Terrorism Act, 286
Arab-looking men, 253–54
Arizona Department of Commerce, 238
Automated Targeting System, 243
border agents, changing behaviours, 232
border crossing, 240, 273–74
border-crossing, arrests of undocumented, 252, 252 t8.4
border-crossing, deaths of undocumented, 253, 253 t8.5
Border Patrol, 231, 251
Border Security Conference, 237
border security factors, 271
borderland culture, 248–49
Center for Comparative Immigration Studies, 252
Consolidated National Inspectional Anti-Terrorism Contraband Enforcement Team, 251
consumer price increases, 244, 245
container security, 242
Control of Secret Courts, 296
cost and cost-effectiveness of, 13
cost burden on trucking firms, 242–43
Customs and Border Protection, 235, 243, 251
Customs Trade Partnership against Terrorism (C-TPAT), 234, 241–43
decision-making, centralized, 255
Domestic Security Enhancement Act, 296
drayage system, 244
drug cartels, 241
Drug Enforcement Administration (DEA), 249–50
drugs, illegal, 254, 255
El Paso, Texas, 237–38
employee identification, 242
expenditures on border security, 236 t8.1
expenditures on personnel, 235, 236 t8.2
family reunification, 248
Field Operations, 250–51
guest-worker program, national, 252
Homeland Security Act, 234, 294–95
House Un-American Activities Committee, 288, 290
human rights *vs.* security, 289–90
illegal drugs, 249–51, 250 t8.3
immigrants, illegal Mexican, 266
immigration, illegal, 251–53, 254
immigration costs, changes in, 245–48
initiatives of, 267–68
inspection policies, 241
Laredo port, 239
laser-visa cards, 248
Manifest Review Unit, 251
maquiladora industry, 237

Mexican-born residents, 247
Mexican exports, 239
Mexican imports, 239
Mexican maquiladoras, securing supply chain, 234
NAFTA-wide security perimeter, 270
National Border Patrol Council, 252
national security, redefining, 232
National Targeting Center, 234–35, 243
Nogales, San Diego, 238–39
North American Free Trade Agreement (NAFTA), 237
Office of Air and Marine Operations, 251
Office of Drug Control Policy, 251
Office of Information Technology, 250–51
Office of the Undersecretary for Border and Transportation Security, 234
PASS card system, 280
Passenger Analytical Unit, 251
Passenger Enforcement Rover Team, 251
passports for Americans, 246–47
photo identification, 242
physical access controls, 242
Public Safety Act, 286–87
residents, border, 236
residents, burden on border, 233
risk assessments, electronic, 243
Schneider, Inc., 243–44
Smart Border/30 Point Action Plan, 269, 271, 285
smuggling, human, 253, 255
state and local governments, 272
telephone calls, database of, 297
Terrorism Information and Prevention System (TIPS), 295
Texas Workforce Commission, 237
Texas–Mexico borderland, 211
torture, use of, 297
Transport Canada, 243
trilateral initiatives, 268–71
trucking business, 240–45
United States Visitor and Immigrant Status Indicator Technology (US VISIT) program., 235
University of Arizona and Arizona State University study, 238
University of Arizona Economic and Business Research Center, 238
University of Texas-Pan American Study, 237
US and Foreign Commerce Service, 238–39
US Border Patrol, 235
US civil liberties groups, 295
US Department of State, 239, 240
US Patriot Act, 234, 286, 288, 290–94, 296
US–Mexico border, 231, 237
visitor monitoring, 242
Derechos Humanos (human rights NGO), 47
detection technologies, 34–35, 36, 39
Dever, County Sheriff Larry, 64

DEW line, 146, 148
DHS. *See* Department of Homeland Security (DHS)
Dobson, Wendy, 283–84
Domestic Security Enhancement Act, 296
Douglas (town), 51, 52–53
Douglas–Agua Prieta (faith-based NGO), 47
drayage system, 244
Drug Enforcement Administration (DEA), 249–50
drug trafficking
  Arizona–Sonora borderlands, 42
  Canada-US border, 277
  Central America, 313
  Columbian gangs, 333
  drug cartels, 241, 345
  EU external border, 31, 36
  Homeland Security, 254, 255
  Mexico–Guatemala-Belize border, 326, 330–31, 332, 333, 346
  Mexico–US border, 264

E

e-PINE. *See* Enhanced Partnership in Northern Europe (e-PINE)
East Sea (Syrian ship), 28
Ejército Popular Revolucionario (Popular Revolutionary Army), 328
Ejército Revolucionario del Pueblo Insurgente (Insurgent People's Revolutionary Army), 328
Ejército Villista Revolucionario del Pueblo (People's Villistan Revolutionary Army), 328–29
Ejército Zapatista de Liberación Nacional (Zapatista Army of National Liberation (EZLN)), 311, 324, 343–45
El Paso, Texas, 101–102, 109–110, 237–38
El Paso–Juarez border, 44
El Salvador, 326, 334, 340
Electric Networking System for Latin America. *See* Sistema de Interconexión Eléctrica para América Central (Electric Networking System for Latin America)
Electronic Frontier Foundation, 290–91, 296
ELISE Declaration, 24–25
Emergencies Act, 288
Emergency Preparedness and Response (EPPR), 128
Emerson, Robert, 232
Enhanced Partnership in Northern Europe (e-PINE), 149–50, 152
Enterprise Monitoring Department, 180
environmental threats, 146–47
EPPR. *See* Emergency Preparedness and Response (EPPR)
Escudo Comunitario (Community Shield), 342
Estonian–Russian border, 141
EU-Ceuta and Melilla borders, 86
  Autonomous Cities, 85
  Barcelona process, 84, 89
  border assaults, 86–87
  borders, Morocco doesn't recognize, 83, 86
  Common Agricultural Policy (CAP), 80
  cross-border flow, illicit, 83

economic gap, Spain and Morocco, 83
enclaves' perimeters, militarization of, 80
Euro-Mediterranean Free Trade Area, 80, 89
free-port status, 83
Gated Community model, 88
geopolitical background, 75–76
geopolitical controversy, 81
Granada, Kingdom of, 76
high-tech control mechanisms, 85–86
historical evolution of, 76–80
illegal migration, strict control over, 88
Integrated System of External Surveillance (SIVE), 86
Isla Perejil dispute, 86
Ley de Extranjería (immigration law), 81
Maghrebian territories, 76
map, 77 f3.1
migrant riots, 85
migrants, desirable *vs.* undesirable, 82, 87, 88
migrants, illegal entry of, 85, 87
militarized fencing of enclaves, 85, 87
military garrsions (presidios), 78
Morocco, underdevelopment of, 83
Muslim issue, 81
region of Nador, 82
region of Tétouan, 82
Schengenization, 80, 81–82
smuggling, 83, 84
sociospatial bordering, 89
Spanish–French Protectorate of Morocco, 79
Statute of Autonomy, 80
Straits of Gibraltar, migrant route, 82
tax regime, special, 83
trade, liberalization of, 80
Treaty of Tétouan (1860), 78–79
visa for Moroccan citizens, 82
xenophobic protests, 85

EU (European Union)
Inter-Region (INTERREG), 140
Northern Dimension (EUND) strategy, 119, 139–44, 147, 152
Poland and Hungary: Assistance for Restructuring their Economies (PHARE), 140
Technical Aid to the Commonwealth of Independent States (TACIS), 140

EU external border. *See also* Schengen visa
Albanian exiles, 29, 30, 33
Andalusian coast, 35
ARGO program, 33–34
asylum applicants, control of, 19, 34, 37–39
asylum procedures, 36
border-police force, 11, 32
border towns, fortification of, 11
camps for foreigners, 36–39
Canary Islands, 32, 35
Ceuta, foreign nationals from, 11, 34
Channel of Otranto, 33
collaboration of neighbouring states, 19

conveyance companies, 11, 19, 26–27
Cyprus, 33
detection technologies, 34–35, 36, 39
drug trafficking, 31, 36
Euro-Mediterranean Partnership (MEDA) Program, 30–31
European Maritime Force (Euromarfor), 33
French Coordination for the Right of Asylum (CFDA), 31
High Level Asylum and Immigration Group, 30
human trafficking, 28, 29, 30
identification, biological methods of, 38
illegal immigrants, desperate strategies, 36
illegal transit through third countries, 29
immigration as criminal offence, 38
immigration flow, control of, 11, 19, 27
information networks, interstate, 19
joint operations of member states, 33–34
Kurds, illegal immigrants, 28
Libya given control technology, 37
Malta, 33
maritime control, 26, 28–29, 32
maritime police, French, 29
MEDA-CEPOL (European College of Police) program, 30–31
Mediterranean, illegal migrant flow, 31
Melilla, foreign nationals from, 34
money laundering, 31
Moroccan foreign nationals, 35
Moroccan Royal Gendarmerie, 34
multinationals, use of externalization, 38
operations by member-states, joint, 32–33
police activity in countries of departure, 27–29
regional protecion areas, 36
Regulation (EC) 377/2004, 27
Schengen Agreement, 12
security policies, illegal aliens, 11
Senegal, foreign nationals of, 25
Spanish Guardia Civil, 34–36
Strait of Gibraltar, 32, 34, 35
Strategic Committee on Immigration, Frontiers and Asylum (SCIFA), 31
transit centres in Libya, 37
Tunisian foreign nationals, 25
visa policy, 11, 19
EUND. *See* Northern Dimension (EUND) strategy
EUND's trans-Atlantic agenda, 147–48
Euregio Karelia, 143
Euro-Mediterranean Free Trade Area, 80, 89
Euro-Mediterranean Partnership (MEDA) Program, 30–31
Euromarfor. *See* European Maritime Force (Euromarfor)
European College of Police (MEDA-CEPOL), 30–31

European Council of Seville (2002), 27
European Maritime Force (Euromarfor), 33
EU–Russian
border, 142
dialogue, 140–41
Summit (2005), 141
EZLN. *See* Ejército Zapatista de Liberación Nacional (Zapatista Army of National Liberation (EZLN))

F

faith-based NGO
Ambos Nogales-Tucson, 47
Douglas–Agua Prieta, 47
Humane Borders, 47
Farabundo Marti Front, 334
FAST (low risk traffic), 285, 286
Federal lands and Indian reservations, 67 f2.2
Federal Preventative Police. *See* Policia Federal Preventiva (Federal Preventative Police)
Finland, 37, 128, 145
Finnish–Russian border, 141, 144
Foote, Jack, 50
Forma Migratoria para Visitantes Agrícolas (Migratory Form for Agricultural Visitors), 320
Fox, President Vicente, 269, 270, 279, 312, 317, 330
Framework Agreement for the Reactivation of the Negotiation Process, 334
Framework Agreement on Democratization in the Search for Peace by Political Means, 334
France, 29
Free Trade Area of the Americas (FTAA), 311–12, 321
French Coordination for the Right of Asylum (CFDA), 31
French Marine Nationale *(Atlantic)*, 32
Frontera de Cristo (Healing Our Borders), 47, 53
FTAA. *See* Free Trade Area of the Americas (FTAA)
Fuerza de Tarea (Task Force), 330
Fuerzas Armadas Revolucionarias del Pueblo (People's Revolutionary Armed Forces), 329

G

gang violence, 44. *See also* youth gangs
GANSEF. *See* Grupo de Alto Nivel sobre Seguridad Fronteriza (High-Level Group on Border Security (GANSEF))
Gated Community model, 88
Geneva Convention on Refugees, 37
Giddensian structuration theory, 188
Golf Cartel. *See* Cartel del Golfo (Golf Cartel)
Goodwill Industries, 101, 109
Gorbachev, Mikhail, 122, 124, 128, 138, 146, 154
governance, internationalized, 133
Granada, Kingdom of, 76
Granatstein, J. L., 284–85
Greece, 32
Greenland, 147
Gregoire, Governor Christine 277
Grupo Beta (migrant assistance), 54
Grupo de Alto Nivel sobre Seguridad Fronteriza (High-Level Group on Border Security (GANSEF)), 329

Guatemala, 320, 320 t11.1, 332, 334
Guatemalan National Revolutionary Unity. *See* Unidad Revolucionaria Nacional Guatemalteca (Guatemalan National Revolutionary Unity)
Guatemalan Servicio de Análisis e Información Antinarcóticos (Anti-drug Analysis and Information Service (SAIA)), 333
guest houses. *See* casas de huéspedes (guest houses)
guest-worker program, 43, 44, 49, 252
Gwich'in people, 131

H

Hall, Governor Jane, 50
Haparanda-Tornio borderland, 142–43, 144
Harper, Prime Minister Stephen, 278, 279
Healing Our Borders. *See* Frontera de Cristo (Healing Our Borders)
High Arctic, 146
High Level Asylum and Immigration Group, 30
High-Level Group on Border Security. *See* Grupo de Alto Nivel sobre Seguridad Fronteriza (High-Level Group on Border Security (GANSEF))
Homeland Security Act, 234, 294–95
Homeland Security Appropriations Act, 313–14
Homeland Security (DHS). *See* Department of Homeland Security (DHS)
Honduras, 326, 338–39
House Un-American Activities Committee, 288, 290
human rights. *See also* International Helsinki Federation for Human Rights; torture; United Nations High Commissioner for Human Rights in Mexico; Universal Declaration of Human Rights
    border security and, 47–48
    NGO, Derechos Humanos, 47
    security *vs.*, 47–48, 288–90, 289–90
human trafficking, 28–30, 42–44, 59–61
Humane Borders (faith-based NGO), 47, 53, 54
Hungarian open-air bazaars, 174–75
Hungry Bear Café, 51

I

I-94 Visa, 210, 223 t7.21, 224 t7.24
illegal drugs, 249–51, 250 t8.3
IMM. *See* Instituto Nacional de Migración (National Migration Institute (INM))
immigration
    costs, 245–48
    as criminal offence, 38
    illegal, 25, 28, 251–53, 254, 266–67
    illegal, controlling, 11, 19, 24–25, 27, 313–14, 322
    illegal transit through third countries, 29
    migrants, desperate strategies of, 36
    migrants, expedited removal, 314
    migrants, undocumented, 59–64
    officers at airports, 20

Independent Task Force on the Future of North America, 269
indigenous peoples, 12, 118, 132
Initiative for the Americas, 334
Instituto Nacional de Migración (National Migration Institute (INM)), 324, 337
Insurgent People's Revolutionary Army. *See* Ejército Revolucionario del Pueblo Insurgente (Insurgent People's Revolutionary Army)
Integrated System of Exterior Vigilance. *See* Sistema Integrado de Vigilancia Exterior (Integrated System of Exterior Vigilance (SIVE))
Integrated System of External Surveillance (SIVE), 86
Integrated Threat Assessment Centre, 282
Inter-American Committee against Terrorism, 329
Inter-American Development Bank, 318, 321
Inter-Region (INTERREG), 140
International Civil Liberties Monitoring Group, 303
International Helsinki Federation for Human Rights, 304–305
INTERREG. *See* Inter-Region (INTERREG)
Inuit Circumpolar Conference, 151, 152
Inuit Tapisariat, 151, 152
Iraq, 30
iris-recognition technology, 286
Isla Perejil dispute, 86
Ismalej, Manuel de Jesús Xitumul, 332
Italy, 32, 33

J

Józsefvárosi V Market (Chinese Market), 175
Juarez traders, 102, 109

K

Karjalat katsovat toisiaan, 144
Komi Republic (Russia), 143
Kuhmo Summer Academy, 144
Kurds, 28

L

Lakselv, reindeer herding area, 125
Land Claims and Self-government Agreement, 133
Lapland province (Finland), 143
Laredo (port), 201, 207, 216, 222–24, 223 t7.21, 224 t7.24, 239
laser-visa cards, 102, 103, 109, 210, 248
Law 2005–371 (France), 29
Lebanon, 28
Ley de Extranjería (immigration law), 81
Ley de Seguridad Nacional (National Security Act), 326–33, 326–333
Libya, 37
Lódz, Poland
  Aliens Law, 177
  Asian traders, 175
  Association of European Textile Collectivities (ACTE), 189
  bazaar, definition, 170–71
  bazaar (open-air market), 165, 169–76

bazaar taxes, 183 f6.5, 192
bazaarundercapitalism,171–75
bazaar under socialist regimes, 171
bazaars, business volume, 174
bazaars, customers at, 184–87
bazaars, illegality of, 172
bazaars, structural changes, 172–73
border traders, 173
coalition-building capacity, 168
Council for Mutual Economic Assistance (CMEA), 179
cross-border interactions, 173
cross-border sellers and buyers, 192
Debt Restructuring Department, 180
eastern markets, dependence on, 183
Enterprise Monitoring Department, 180
enterprises, industry and service, 183, 184 f6.6
EU integration, 190–91
expenditures, expected, 186
Giddensian structuration theory, 188
map of main roads, 166 f6.1
meso level with spatial dimension, 168
micro–macro dialectics, 168
PTAK bazaar, 189
regime theory, 168
regional history, 178–81
Rzgow and Tuszyn, map of, 166f 6.2
Rzgów bazaar, 167, 170 f6.3, 181–87, 191–92
scalar approach, 188
Schengen Agreement, 12, 174, 175, 176–78, 191
Schengenization of Polish border, 169
socialism, legacy of, 190
stalls, number of, 182 f6.4
structuration, societal and geographical, 188
structuration theory, 167
suitcase traders, 173, 193
Tenth Anniversary Stadium, 165
textile product outlets, 167
tourist vouchers, 182
Tuszyn bazaar, 167, 170 f6.3, 181–87, 189–90, 191–92
visa, before and after, 187
visa, local response to, 188–90
visiting frequencies, 186 f6.8
voivodship, 188, 189, 190
Lugar, Senator Richard, 268–69

M

Mace, Gordon, 280
Maghrebian territories, 76
Mali, 25
Malta, 33
Manifest Review Unit, 251
Manley, Deputy Prime Minister John, 285
maquiladora industry
Honduras, 339
Mexico–Guatemala-Belize border, 319
Mexico's, 201
Mexico–US border, 99
NAFTA, 237
Maricopa County Attorney's office, 46

marijuana plantations, 333
maritime
boundaries, 136
boundaries, Arctic, 136
control, 26, 28–29, 32
police, French, 29
Martin, Prime Minister Paul, 269, 279, 282, 285
Masculinity and Politics, 332
McLellan, Deputy Prime Minister Anne, 277, 282, 302
MEDA. *See* Euro-Mediterranean Partnership (MEDA)
MEDA-CEPOL. *See* European College of Police (MEDA-CEPOL)
Melilla, 34
Méndez, Antonio Cadena, 331
Mexican Centro de Estudios Migratorios, 337
Mexican National Chamber of the Textile Industry (Canaintex), 103–104
Mexico
cross-border shoppers, 201, 208 t7.8, 215, 216, 219–20, 220, 220 t7.18, 221 t7.19
exports, 201, 206 t7.6, 239
imports, 201, 239
maquiladoras, 234
US exports to, 201, 207 t7.7, 219
México Seguro (Secure Mexico) program, 331
Mexico-US border
borderland clout, cultural and political, 12
clothing, illegal flow of used, 11–12
Mexico–Guatemala-Belize border
Action Plan for Cooperation on Border Security, 322
Acuerdo de Paz Firme y Duradera (Firm and Durable Peace Agreement), 334
Agencia Federal de Investigaciones (Federal Agency of Investigations (AFI)), 331
Arizona Border Control Initiative, 316
armed groups, 328–29
Bicameral Commission, 327
border, militarized, 345
border crossings points, 320–21
Border patrol, 314
Border Protection, Antiterrorism, and Illegal Immigration Control Act, 314
buffer zone, uncontrollable, 14
CAFTA, 321, 322
Cartel del Golfo (Golf Cartel), 330, 331
Central America day-labourers, 335–36, 336 t11.3
Central America migrants, 335–36
Central American detentions in Mexico, 337–38, 338 t11.4
Central American Free Trade Agreement (CAFTA), 311–12
Central American migrants to Mexico, 335–39, 336 t11.3, 346
Central American migrants to US, 313, 324, 346
Centro de Investigación y Seguridad Nacional

(Investigation and National Security Centre (CISEN)), 326, 328–29
Chapultepec Agreements, 334
Chiapas state, 319, 330, 331–32, 335–36, 336 t11.3, 338
coffee prices, crisis in international, 336
Columbian drug gangs, 333
criminal networks, 346
cross-border movement, illegal and legal, 318
Declaration of the Lacandon Jungle, 343
drug cartels, 345
drug gangs, Columbian, 333
drug trafficking, 313, 326, 330–31, 332, 333, 346
Ejército Popular Revolucionario (Popular Revolutionary Army), 328
Ejército Revolucionario del Pueblo Insurgente (Insurgent People's Revolutionary Army), 328
Ejército Villista Revolucionario del Pueblo (People's Villistan Revolutionary Army), 328–29
Ejército Zapatista de Liberación Nacional (Zapatista Army of National Liberation (EZLN)), 311, 324, 343–45
Escudo Comunitario (Community Shield), 342
Farabundo Marti Front, 334
Federal Preventative Police, 342
Forma Migratoria para Visitantes Agrícolas (Migratory Form for Agricultural Visitors), 320
Fourth Summit of the Americas, 312
Framework Agreement for the Reactivation of the Negotiation Process, 334
Framework Agreement on Democratization in the Search for Peace by Political Means, 334
Free Trade Area of the Americas (FTAA), 311–12, 321
Fuerza de Tarea (Task Force), 330
Fuerzas Armadas Revolucionarias del Pueblo (People's Revolutionary Armed Forces), 329
Grupo de Alto Nivel sobre Seguridad Fronteriza (High-Level Group on Border Security (GANSEF)), 329
Guatemalan border crossings, 320, 320 t11.1
Guatemalan Servicio de Análisis e Información Antinarcóticos (Anti-drug Analysis and Information Service (SAIA)), 333
Guatemala's borders, 332
guerrillas and militarization, 343–45
Homeland Security Appropriations Act, 313–14
Honduras migrants, 338–39
immigrants, controlling illegal, 313–14, 322

immigrants, expedited removal of, 314
Initiative for the Americas, 334
Instituto Nacional de Migración (National Migration Institute (INM)), 324, 337
Inter-American Committee against Terrorism, 329
Ley de Seguridad Nacional (National Security Act), 326–33
maquiladora industry in Honduras, 339
maquiladoras, textile, 319
marijuana and poppy plantations, 333
Masculinity and Politics, 332
Mexican Centro de Estudios Migratorios, 337
Mexican states, 319
México Seguro (Secure Mexico) program, 331
Mexico's south border, remodelling, 315–19
multinational companies, 319
NAFTA and elimination of jobs, 335
National Security Act (Mexico), 326–33
National Security Council (Mexico), 326
North American Command, 324
Oficina del Alto Comisionado de las Naciones Unidas para los Derechos Humanos en México (Office of the UN High Commissioner for Human Rights in Mexico), 344
Operation Costa, 342
Organization of American States, 329
organized crime, 330, 332
Partido Democrático Popular Revolucionario (Democratic Popular Revolutionary Party), 328
Plan Puebla Panamá (energy integration), 312, 317
political cooperation, lack of, 334
poverty and social exclusion, 315, 346
Quintana Roo state, 319–20
Quitacargas groups, 333
Secretaría de la Defensa Nacional (National Defence Secretariat (SEDENA)), 329
Secure Fence Act, 314
Sistema de Interconexión Eléctrica para América Central (Electric Networking System for Latin America), 312–13
smart border agreements, 324, 325 t11.2
smuggling of guns and people, 330, 332, 346
southern border, loss of control, 332
southern Mexico migrants to US, 313
Third Border Initiative (TBI), 315, 323
Unidad Revolucionaria Nacional Guatemalteca (Guatemalan National Revolutionary Unity), 334
US Initiative for the Americas, 321

youth gangs in Mexico, 339–43
youth gangs (maras), 321, 326, 328–29, 337, 339–43
Zapatista guerrillas, 329
Zetas, 330–31
Mexico–US border
ant trade (fayuca hormiga), 98
armpit smugglers, 98
border region, economic integration, 113
border security, mismatched, 13
Border Trade Alliance (BTA), 102–103
branded clothing copies, Chinese, 112
Comité de Defensa Popular (Popular Defense Commiittee (CDP)), 108
corruption, Mexican governance, 265
corruption of Mexican customs authorities, 104, 110, 111, 112
drug trafficking, 264
duty-free zone, 99
economy of discards, 99–100
El Paso wholesale dealers, 101–102, 109–110
Goodwill Industries, 101, 109
Grupo Beta (migrant assistance), 54
Homeland Security, cost effectiveness of, 13
immigrants, illegal, 266–67
import license (permiso previo), 105
import trade policies, 113
imported used clothing, illegally, 105–109
Juarez traders, 102, 109
laser visa, 102, 103, 109
law enforcement, municipal government, 107
Ley de Seguridad Nacional (National Security Act), 326–333
maquiladoras (foreign-owned assembly plants), 99
Mexican labour, 259
Mexican National Chamber of the Textile Industry (Canaintex), 103–104
Mid-West Textile Company, 109
NAFTA and used clothing, 96, 104–105
Noamex, Inc, 109
Nogales–Tucson corridor, 103
Otay Mesa port, 266
penalties for illegal importing, 107
Policia Federal Preventiva (Federal Preventative Police), 111, 342
Procuraduría General de la República (Office of the Federal Attorney General), 107
protectionist policies against used clothing, 101
Salvation Army, 101
San Diego–Tijuana region, 263–65, 263–68
San Ysidro port, 266
Secretaria de Comercio y Fomento Industrial (Secretariat of Commerce and Industrial Development (Secofi)), 104
Secretaría de Economía (Ministry of the Economy), 105, 106

security challenges, 271–72
security priorities, 260, 261 t9.1–9.2
SENTRI (dedicated commuter lane program), 267
Smart Border Agreement, 269, 325 t11.2
social charter, negotiated, 260
surtidoras (sorters), 110
textile and garment industry, domestic, 103
transborder cooperation, 263
transborder flow, consumer demand for, 112
transnational criminal activities, 96
trash, recycled, 100
trilateral cooperation, 261 t9.1
United States Visitor and Immigrant Status Indicator Technology (US VISIT) program, 103
used clothing, illegal *vs.* social legitimacy, 96, 98, 108, 113
used clothing (fayuca), smuggling, 95, 98, 100–101, 111
used clothing from charity, 101
used clothing import volumes, 106–107
Van Schendel-Abraham model, 96–98
vehicle crossings, 262
vending permits, used-clothing, 107–108

Mid-West Textile Company, 109
migrant assistance. *See* Grupo Beta (migrant assistance)
Migratory Form for Agricultural Visitors. *See* Forma Migratoria para Visitantes Agrícolas (Migratory Form for Agricultural Visitors)
The Militant, 50
Ministry of the Economy. *See* Secretaría de Economía (Ministry of the Economy)
Minutemen Civil Defense, 46, 50, 51, 63, 277
Modernization of Investigative Techniques Act (Bill C-74), 283, 302
money-laundering, 31, 52
Le Monica (ship), 28
Moroccan Royal Gendarmerie, 34
Morocco, 27, 30, 34, 35, 79, 82, 83
Mulroney, Prime Minister Brian, 278–79
multinational companies, 38, 319
Murmansk, 122
Muslim issue, 81

N

NAFTA. *See* North American Free Trade Agreement (NAFTA)
Napolitano, Governor Janet, 60, 65, 332
narcotics trafficking, 41, 56, 57
National Border Patrol Council, 209, 252
National Migration Institute. *See* Instituto Nacional de Migración (National Migration Institute (INM))
National Park Service, 56–57, 57
National Security Act. *See* Ley de Seguridad Nacional (National Security Act)
National Security Act (Mexico), 326–33

National Security Advisory Council, 282
National Security Council (Mexico), 326
The National Security Strategy of the United States of America, 280
National Targeting Center, 234–35, 243
NEI. *See* North Europe Initiative (NEI)
NEXUS (low risk travellers), 285, 286
No More Deaths (No Más Muertes) NGO, 47
Noamex, Inc, 109
Nogales, San Diego, 238–39
Nogales–Tucson corridor, 103
Nordic Passport Union, 176
North America, 144–53
North American Command, 324
North American Development Bank, 260
North American Development Fund, 260
North American Free Trade Agreement (NAFTA)
    Arizona-Sonora borderlands, 45
    job elimination, 335
    maquiladora industry, 237
    security perimeter, 270
    Texas–Mexico borderland, 199
    used clothing, 96, 104–105
North Calotte Council, 14
North Europe Initiative (NEI), 131–32
northern borders. *See* Arctic borders
Northern Dimension (EUND) strategy, 119, 147
northern Europe, 137–39
Northern Forum, 143
northern habitants, 146–47
Norway's concerns, 123, 128, 139
nuclear material smuggling, 126
nuclear waste, 123–25, 124 f5.1, 154
Nunavut (Canadian Territory), 134

O

OAS. *See* Organization of American States (OAS)
Office of Air and Marine Operations, 251
Office of Drug Control Policy, 251
Office of Information Technology, 250–51
Office of the Federal Attorney General. *See* Procuraduría General de la República (Office of the Federal Attorney General)
Office of the Undersecretary for Border and Transportation Security, 234
Official Journal of the European Communities (C313), 22
Oficina del Alto Comisionado de las Naciones Unidas para los Derechos Humanos en México, 344
oil reserves, 130–31, 150
Operation Costa, 342
Operation Gatekeeper (California), 41
Operation Hawk, 50
Organ Pipe Monument, 56, 57, 58
Organization of American States (OAS), 321, 329
organized crime, 330, 332
Otay Mesa port, 266

P

På Gränsen/Rajalla (At the Boundary), 142

Palme Commission, 117
PAME. *See* Protection of the Arctic Marine Environment (PAME)
Partido Democrático Popular Revolucionario (Democratic Popular Revolutionary Party), 328
PASS card system, 280
Passenger Analytical Unit, 251
Passenger Enforcement Rover Team, 251
Pearce, Russell, 65
People's Revolutionary Armed Forces. *See* Fuerzas Armadas Revolucionarias del Pueblo (People's Revolutionary Armed Forces)
People's Villistan Revolutionary Army. *See* Ejército Villista Revolucionario del Pueblo (People's Villistan Revolutionary Army)
Perryman Group study, 212–15, 213 t7.9, 213 t7.10–7.11, 214 t7.12–7.14
persistent organic pollutants (POPs), 133
PHARE. *See* Poland and Hungary: Assistance for Restructuring their Economies (PHARE)
Phoenix, 59–64
Plan Puebla Panamá (energy integration), 312, 317
PNWER Border Issues Working Group, 277
Poindexter, John, 295
Poland, 32
Poland and Hungary: Assistance for Restructuring their Economies (PHARE), 140
police activity in countries of departure, 27–29
Police International Technical Cooperation Service (SCTIP), 28
Policia Federal Preventiva (Federal Preventative Police), 111, 342
pollution, transboundary, 118, 119, 122, 128, 154, 158
poppy plantations, 333
POPs. *See* persistent organic pollutants (POPs)
Popular Revolutionary Army. *See* Ejército Popular Revolucionario (Popular Revolutionary Army)
Porcupine caribou herd, 131
Portuguese navy, 32
Powell, Secretary of State Colin, 323, 324
privacy rights, 301
Procuraduría General de la República (Office of the Federal Attorney General), 107
Proposition 200, 46, 63
Protection of the Arctic Marine Environment (PAME), 128
PTAK bazaar, 189
Public Safety Act, 286–87
Public Safety Act (Bill C-17), 300–302
Public Safety Act (Bill C-55), 300–301
Public Security Act (Bill C-42), 300
Putin, Vladimir, 138

Q

Quintana Roo state, 319–20
Quitacargas groups, 333

R

racial profiling, 42, 52, 62, 302–303
Radwanski, George, 301, 303–304
Ranch Rescue, 50

regime theory, 168
regional protecion areas, 36
Regulation (EC) 377/2004, 27
resource reserve, geostrategically, 138
Rice, Condoleezza, 280
Richardson, Governor Bill, 332
Royal Commission on Aboriginal Peoples, 145
Russia-Finland border, 142
Rzgów bazaar, 167, 170 f6.3, 181–87, 191–92

S

SAIA. *See* Guatemalan Servicio de Análisis e Información Antinarcóticos (Anti-drug Analysis and Information Service (SAIA))
Salazar, Florencio, 317
Salvation Army, 101
San Diego Association of Governments (SANDAG), 212
San Diego–Tijuana border, 44
San Diego–Tijuana region, 263–65, 263–68
San Ysidro port, 266
SANDAG. *See* San Diego Association of Governments (SANDAG)
Sands, Christopher, 281
Schengen Agreement, 12, 174–78, 191
Schengen visa
- border police, 20
- Charter of the United Nations, 22
- Common Consular Instruction, 22
- consular agents, restrictive practices of, 20, 22
- consular network, 25
- consular passes, 25
- customs agents, 20
- Declaration of Barcelona, 21–22
- ELISE Declaration meeting, 24–25
- EU, protection *vs.* travel to, 21
- EU-Ceuta and Melilla borders, 80, 81–82
- fide, bona *vs.* mala, 25
- illegal immigrants, alternatives for, 25
- illegal immigration, control of, 24–25
- immigration officers at airports, 20
- liaison officers, network of, 25, 26, 27, 28, 39
- policy harmonization, 21
- Polish border, 169
- practices, secret arbitrary, 23–24
- regulations are contradictory, 21
- rules for third-country nationals, 20
- tool for migratory control, 20, 21
- Universal Declaration of Human Rights, 22, 24
- visa, criteria for granting, 22–24

Schneider, Inc., 243–44
SCIFA. *See* Strategic Committee on Immigration, Frontiers and Asylum (SCIFA)
SCTIP. *See* Police International Technical Cooperation Service (SCTIP)
SDWG. *See* Sustainable Development Working Group (SDWG); Working Group on Sustainable Development (SDWG)

Secretaria de Comercio y Fomento Industrial (Secretariat of Commerce and Industrial Development (Secofi)), 104
Secretaría de Economía (Ministry of the Economy), 105, 106
Secretaría de la Defensa Nacional (National Defence Secretariat (SEDENA)), 329
Secure Fence Act, 314
Secure Mexico. *See* México Seguro (Secure Mexico) program
security
- anti-drug, 251
- border policy, self-defeating, 44
- challenges, 8
- circumpolar boundaries, 135
- civil, 121
- costs, in national park, 58
- duties of park rangers, 57
- environmental, 12, 119, 120, 122, 127–32
- expenditures, 236 t8.1
- factors, 271
- governance and, 132–35
- human, 12, 119, 121, 130, 139, 154, 157
- human rights *vs.*, 47–48, 288–90
- military, 12, 120–21, 123–27
- personal, diminished, 42, 44
- policies, 6, 7–9, 352
- priorities, 261 t9.1–9.2
- regionally-based, 134–35

The Security and Prosperity Partnership of North America (SPP), 269
security policies, illegal aliens, 11
SEDENA. *See* Secretaría de la Defensa Nacional (National Defence Secretariat (SEDENA))
Sellafield, nuclear reprocessing plants, 126
Senegal, 25
SENTRI (dedicated commuter lane program), 267
Seville summit (2002), 31
Simcox, Chris, 50, 51
Sistema de Interconexión Eléctrica para América Central (Electric Networking System for Latin America), 312–13
Sistema Integrado de Vigilancia Exterior (Integrated System of Exterior Vigilance (SIVE)), 34
Slown, John, 56
Smart Border/30 Point Action Plan, 269, 271, 285
Smart Border Agreement
- Canada-US border, 13, 269, 285
- Mexico–Guatemala-Belize border, 324, 325 t11.2
- Mexico–US border, 269, 325 t11.2
- Texas–Mexico borderland, 197–98, 226

smuggling
- drugs, 277
- EU-Ceuta and Melilla borders, 83, 84
- guns and people, 330, 332, 346
- human, 253, 255
- nuclear material and weapons, 126
- used clothing (fayuca), 95, 98, 100–101, 111

Somalia, 30
Sonoran wilderness, 54–58
Soviet Union, 137–39
Spain, 32
Spanish Guardia Civil, 34–36

Sri Lanka, 30
Statute of Autonomy, 80
Stockholm Convention, 133
Strait of Gibraltar, 32, 34, 35
Strait of Sicily, 25
Straits of Gibraltar, 82
Strategic Committee on Immigration, Frontiers and Asylum (SCIFA), 31
structuration theory, 167
suitcase traders, 173, 193
Summit of the Americas, 312
Summit of the Pacific Northwest Economic Region (PNWER), 277
surtidoras (sorters), 110
sustainable development, 130, 154
Sustainable Development Working Group (SDWG), 125
Sweden, 145
Syria, 28

T

TACIS. *See* Technical Aid to the Commonwealth of Independent States (TACIS)
Task Force. *See* Fuerza de Tarea (Task Force)
Task Force on Sustainable Development, 128
Technical Aid to the Commonwealth of Independent States (TACIS), 140
Tenth Anniversary Stadium (Poland), 165
Terrorism Information and Prevention System (TIPS), 295
terrorists, 253–54
Texas A&M International University Studies, 215–221, 217 t7.1, 218 t7.15b, 219 t7.16–7.17, 220 t7.18, 221 t7.19
Texas Center for Border Economic and Enterprise Development, 215
Texas Workforce Commission, 237
Texas–Mexico borderland
- Automated Entry-Exit Control System, 198
- biometric identifiers, 197, 198, 210
- Bonner, T.J., 209, 252, 267
- border-crossing delays, impact of, 221–24, 222t 7.20
- border crossings, decline in, 217 t7.15, 218 t7.15b
- border pedestrian crossings, 202 t7.1
- border rail crossings, 204 t7.4
- border retail/wholesale trade and sales, 208 t7.8
- border security, economic impact, 227–28
- border truck crossings, 204 t7.3
- border vehicle crossings, 203 t7.2
- border waiting times, 198, 212, 228
- bridge revenues, 216
- Center for Border Economic Studies (C-BEST), 215
- cross-border commerces and trade, 216
- cross-border shoppers, 216, 219 t7.17
- Department of Homeland Security (DHS), 198, 211
- exports of Mexico, value of, 201, 206 t7.6
- exports to Mexico, 201, 207 t7.7, 219

I-94 Visa, 210, 223 t7.21, 224 t7.24
infrastructure of southern border, 224–25
International Bank of Commerce, 210–11
International Bank of Commerce of Laredo, 212
Laredo (port), 201, 207, 216, 222–24, 223 t7.21, 224 t7.24
laser-visa (Border Crossing Card), 210
maquiladora industry, Mexico's, 201
Mexican cross-border shoppers, 201, 208 t7.8, 215, 216, 219–20, 220, 220 t7.18, 221 t7.19
Mexican imports, leading, 201
National Border Patrol Council, 209
North American Free Trade Agreement (NAFTA), 199
Perryman Group study, 212–15, 213 t7.9, 213 t7.10–7.11, 214 t7.12–7.14
policy-making, multi-level government, 225
pre-screening of people and cargo, 197–98
sales tax rebates, 216
sales tax revenue, 211, 216
San Diego (California) Association of Governments (SANDAG), 212
smart borders, 197–98, 226
southern border, porous, 207–209
Texas A&M International University Studies, 215–221, 217 t7.1, 218 t7.15b, 219 t7.16–7.17, 220 t7.18, 221 t7.19
Texas Center for Border Economic and Enterprise Development, 215
Texas gross domestic product and exports, 201, 206 t7.5
Texas ports of entry, 201
trade and commerce, importance of, 199–207
unemployment level, 216
University of Texas–Pan American Study, 215, 237
US Border Patrol, 197
US Customs Services, 197
US VISIT exit program, 210, 224
US VISIT Program, 12–13, 209–11, 222–26
US Visitor and Immigrant Status Indicators Technology (US VISIT), 198
US–Mexico Border Governors' Conference., 211
US–Mexico trade, 199, 200 f7.1
Third Border Initiative (TBI), 315, 323
30 Point Action Plan. *See* Smart Border/30 Point Action Plan
Thomas, Attorney Andrew, 61–62, 63
TIPS. *See* Terrorism Information and Prevention System (TIPS)
Tli Cho people, 133
Tohono O'odham Nation Reservation, 54
Toledo, President Alejandro, 279
TOPOFF 2, 285
torture, 297
Towards an Integrated Management of the Member States External Borders of the European Union, 31

Transport Canada, 243
Treaty of Tétouan (1860), 78–79
Tunisia, 25
Tuszyn bazaar, 167, 170 f6.3, 181–87, 189–90, 191–92

U

Ulysses I and II (operations), 32
Unidad Revolucionaria Nacional Guatemalteca (Guatemalan National Revolutionary Unity), 334
United Kingdom, 288
United Nations
  Commission on Human Security, 121
  Convention on the Law of the Sea, 29
  Development Program, 338–39
  High Commissioner for Human Rights in Mexico, 344
  Human Rights Commission, 297
United States and Foreign Commerce Service, 238–39
United States-Canada border. *See* Canada-US border
United States-Mexico border. *See* Mexico-US border
United States-Mexico Border Governors' Conference, 211
United States (US). *See also* Department of Homeland Security (DHS)
  Air Force and Marine Corps gunnery range, 55
  Border Patrol, 197, 235
  Border Patrol's Operation Safeguard 99, 49–50
  border security frames, 4
  Bureau of Land Management, 55
  civil liberties groups, 295
  Customs Services, 197
  Department of State, 239, 240
  foreign policy, unilateralism of, 280
  imperialism, 279
  Initiative for the Americas, 321
  Missile Defense Initiative, 279, 281
  National Missile Defense (NMD) system, 126
  National Strategy for Homeland Security, 267
  northern policy, 148–53
  Patriot Act, 234, 286, 288, 290–94, 296
  VISIT exit program, 210, 224
  VISIT Program, 12–13, 209–11, 222–26
  Visitor and Immigrant Status Indicators Technology (US VISIT), 103, 198, 235
Universal Declaration of Human Rights, 22, 24
University of Arizona and Arizona State University study, 238
University of Arizona Economic and Business Research Center, 238
University of Texas-Pan American Study, 215, 237
used clothing
  from charity, 101
  illegal *vs.* social legitimacy, 96, 98, 108, 113
  import volumes, 106–107

V

Vaca, Attorney General Daniel Cabeza de, 331
Van Schendel-Abraham model, 96–98
Vance, Larry, 50
voivodship, 188, 189, 190

W

War Measures Act, 288
Weigand, Thane, 57
Working Group on Sustainable Development (SDWG), 128
World Bank, 321

Y

youth gangs (maras), 321, 326, 328–29, 337, 339–43

Z

Zapatista Army of National Liberation. *See* Ejército Zapatista de Liberación Nacional (Zapatista Army of National Liberation (EZLN))
Zetas, 330–31

Printed and bound in May 2007
by L'IMPRIMERIE GAUVIN, Gatineau, Quebec,
for THE UNIVERSITY OF OTTAWA PRESS

Typeset in 10 on 12 Palatino Linotype by Brad Horning

Edited by Patrick Heenan
Proofread by David Bernardi
Cover designed by Cathy Maclean, CATHYMACLEANDESIGN
Indexed by Clive Pyne

Printed on Enviro 100 White